PIRATE NATION

For George and Samuel
Hoping pirates provide you with pleasure

PIRATE NATION

Elizabeth I and her Royal Sea Rovers

David Childs

Seaforth

PUBLISHING

First published in Great Britain in 2014 by
Seaforth Publishing,
Pen & Sword Books Ltd,
47 Church Street,
Barnsley S70 2AS

www.seaforthpublishing.com

British Library Cataloguing in Publication Data
A catalogue record for this book is available from the British Library

ISBN 978 1 84832 190 8

Typeset by MATS Typesetting, Leigh-on-Sea, Essex SS9 5EB
Printed and bound in Great Britain by CPI Group (UK) Ltd, Croydon, CR0 4YY

Contents

Exchange Rates

£1 in 1600 would be worth about £130 in 2014.

***

There were 20 shillings to the pound and twelve pennies to the shilling.
One crown was worth five shillings.

***

(approximate for the period)
One gold ducat was worth seven shillings.
One silver ducat was worth 5s 6d.
One pesos de oro was worth 8s 3d.
One real was worth six pennies.

***

34 maravedis = one real.
8 reals = one peso.
One pound weight (lb) = 0.45 kilograms.
One hundredweight (cwt) = 50.8 kilograms.
One foot = 30 centimetres.

CHAPTER 1

Protestants in Pursuit of Profit

I write not this in favour of piracies, for I hate all pirates mortally.[1]
Lord Burghley, Lord Treasurer, November 1590

For two hundred years, the least safe track along which an Englishman could travel upon his lawful occasion was the sea lane that lay between Ushant and London Bridge, along which, as if in sea-thickets, pirates waited to snag in their barbs all whom appeared weaker than themselves.

This barbed infestation arose because exploitable gaps existed in the surveillance of the sea by the forces of law and order. Such piracy took root because it was nurtured by sections of society ashore, including many in the magistracy who, charged with its eradication, dealt in maritime malfeasance and took an active role in its ordering and establishment while protecting those engaged in the trade. It grew stoutly during the last two decades of the sixteenth century because Queen Elizabeth I, her Lord Admiral and most of her Privy Council, with the honourable exception of William Cecil, Lord Burghley, profited from supporting the leading practitioners of this illegal trade.

Each level of growth had a geographical locus. Thus a local rogue turned rover might land and dispose of his piratical gains under cover of darkness near the harbour which was his home. At county level, a crooked but influential member of the gentry, such as the local vice admiral, could make it known that he was prepared to turn a blind eye to such activities at a price, or even sponsor a few ships and seamen of his own. At this stage of growth the Crown, when so minded, attempted to cauterise the activity, although there were always those in authority, such as the Lord Admiral, who controlled both the navy and the Admiralty Court, who could covertly condone that which they were charged to condemn.[2] The result was that the pruning hooks of legality were handled with such discretion that those dispatched by both sea and land to root out piracy wielded their secateurs in a lackadaisical manner – only snipping with full force on those least able to offer rich rewards in their defence. No effort was ever made to constrain those who returned with the most golden fruits from further afield, regardless from whose orchard they had been snatched.

By the mid sixteenth century England had earned her epithet of a nation of pirates, but in the quarter century that closed with Elizabeth's death in 1603, the country turned from being a nation of pirates into a pirate nation; a state whose own ruler was identified as a pirate queen who (along with most her advisers, favourites and legal practioners) was a beneficiary of piracy.

In this environment, piracy – meaning robbery at sea – came to refer to several different ways in which merchandise could be removed from ships by force. At the Jolly Roger, skull-and-crossbones end, it included the swashbuckling exploits of many an opportunist, as well as the activities of half-starved men struggling to survive by robbing little of value from their fellow seagoers.[3] Hundreds of lowly pirates plied this trade in comparative obscurity, unless they were captured, tried and, lacking influential friends, hanged at the Execution Dock at Wapping between the high and low water marks, a muddy strand that came within the jurisdiction of the Lord High Admiral. Their activities indicated a lack of law enforcement, but not the financial and moral vacuum at the very top which was essential for the careers of a few of the most successful pirates to flourish.

For such men to thrive they needed both the challenge of cargoes worth capturing and security from prosecution. One of the problems with the persecution of piracy arose because many of these crimes took place beyond the jurisdiction of the nations whose citizens were involved, ie on the high seas. Pirates were in this respect natural outlaws, roving as satellites beyond the gravitational pull of the Admiralty and its officials, whose response to pirates returning to land depended much more on the political and financial fallout from their activities rather than the legality of their actions – making many of them outlaws, but not outcasts.

To manage this lawlessness one league out from land, states recognised a system of compensation whereby a merchant could reclaim the value of plundered goods from the nation of the pirate. This was achieved through the issue, by a state or convenient pretender, of letters of reprisal (or 'marque' in French), often valid for just six months, which granted to the wronged party the right to board vessels linked to the perpetrator by port of origin, nation or even religion, and seize goods up to the assessed value of that which had been taken. When well-ordered the system worked: in 1546 the owners of *Kathryn of Bristol* fell in with a Breton ship whose owner owed them £100. Coming alongside, they persuaded the master to be escorted to St David's where 'without compulsion, the Breton delivered him 11 tun of wine, priced £22, and 9 ton of salt, price £6, as parcel of that £100.'[4] The cargo claimed by *Kathryn of Bristol* represented the typical, everyday, boring bulk freight that was so frequently seized piratically in the first half of the sixteenth century. The fact that many considered it worthwhile risking their necks to seize a barrel of salted herring and some wax candles says more about the social deprivation that existed in many a coastal town and village than it does about a natural streak of thievery running through the veins of English seamen. Besides which, the latter quarter of the sixteenth century was a period of dearth, when food taken at sea became a form of famine relief. Yet far offshore, a new type of cargo was now being carried across the oceans creating new opportunities and fresh temptations.

This sea-change into something rich, if not strange, had made itself apparent the year before the successful conclusion of *Kathryn*'s claim. On 1 March 1545, Robert Reneger, acting with the invalid authority of a letter of reprisal issued two years earlier, seized the carrack *San Salvador*, near Seville, whence she was returning from a voyage to New Spain laden with gold and other goods to the value of £4,300 (£560,000 today). However exaggerated Reneger's original claim for compensation had been, there is no chance that it could have amounted to more than a single digit percentage of what he saw stowed in the hold of *San Salvador*. He brought it home where, whatever his desire, it was so valuable that he had to involve the Crown in its disposal. The treasure was taken to the Tower, but not so Reneger who, to the intense annoyance of the imperial ambassador, 'instead of being punished like a pirate, was treated like a hero'.[5]

It was to be many years before the successors to Reneger would emerge to serve a new sovereign, but the circumstances that would lead to Elizabeth sponsoring such lawlessness existed throughout the long Tudor century, from 1485 to 1603. This was an age of avarice in which the Crown led by example. The dynasty was always short of money and found the raising of revenue through parliament both unsatisfactory and embarrassing. Funds were needed both to establish the Crown's legitimacy and engender awe at home, and its recognition by foreigners of its position as a major European power. Henry VII succeeded in doing just this through taxing the peerage and wealthy (and not so wealthy) merchants, extracting money from them to pay for wars which he then had his enemies pay to prevent.

Not so his son Henry VIII who, desperate to be acclaimed a renaissance warrior prince, spent his father's fortune several times over in wasteful and unsuccessful wars against the French, and only replenished his coffers by assuming the role of rogue landlord to the country's vast monastic estates, turfing out the sitting tenants, minus their possessions, and selling the freehold to his cronies. Even this rapacious behaviour did not restore the nation's fortunes and, after two short reigns and two even shorter but costly wars, Elizabeth came to the throne in 1559, not only with debts of £200,000, but to find that the coffers were bare. The expulsion of the French from Scotland and the financing of an expedition to Rouen cost her a further £650,000. She also loaned money to both France and the Netherlands for them to repulse the Spanish. By 1596 the former owed her £445,125 and the latter almost £800,000, so she had a very small war-chest available to fund her own fight against Spain, as well as sustain an army bogged down in Ireland.

The money that the queen had available to maintain her court, her armed forces, her government and her lifestyle came from income generated by the Crown lands, customs and a variety of additional sources. This was referred to as her 'ordinary revenue' and amounted in the early years of her reign to about £120,000 a year, rising to £300,000 after 1593. To meet the occasional, the unforeseen, or emergencies such as wars or additional defence, the queen relied upon her 'extraordinary expenditure', to raise which she was entitled to call on parliament for support by way of taxation that on average through her reign amounted to just £80,000 a year. This meant that by 1588, the year of the nation's greatest peril, Elizabeth had a little over £250,000 annual income with which to fight her foes and fund those European Protestants whose rebellions she chose to underwrite.[6]

Today she could have managed her finances by raising taxes on the wealthy or reducing welfare benefits to the poor, but neither of these options was available to her. The rich avoided taxation, while the poor drew no state benefit: indeed, Elizabeth, by nature parsimonious, found it difficult enough to pay her employees, such as her soldiers and sailors, what they were due, although their officers seldom went short. Borrowing was one option open to her and for this she relied upon the Flemish money market where much funding could be obtained if the (normally high) interest rate could be agreed. As collateral, the goods of London merchants made a juicy bond, meaning that the whole of the City became anxious whenever the queen asked Antwerp to fill her empty coffers.

In such circumstances it is no wonder that the maritime initiatives proposed by the Plymouth merchant pirate turned administrator, John Hawkins, found favour. In 1564 Elizabeth had reduced the 'ordinary' budget of the navy from £13,000 to £6,000, and later to £5,714. In 1579, Hawkins's offer to maintain twenty-five vessels for £1,200 a year, with a further £1,000 being paid to the naval shipwrights was accepted. Bargain struck, Hawkins managed through creative accountancy, and a robust defence when challenged, to keep his side of the deal.[7] At the same time, prudent, peaceful men like Lord Treasurer Burghley were losing the argument over peace with Spain with belligerent advocates of spending, such as Secretary of State Walsingham and the queen's favourite the earl of Leicester, and avaricious and dishonest servants, such as Lord Admiral Howard. So when, in 1580, Hawkins proposed to take some of these, now well-maintained, ships to the Azores to capture a treasure fleet worth 'two myllyons of pounds', it was no wonder that the idea enthused the queen, who saw her fleet as being the only part of her business that could make a profit.

Help was thus on its way from those who were most unwilling to give it. Henry VIII, through his myopic francophobia, and Mary, with her papal Holy Father and Spanish husband, had not thought much about the potential threat or the opportunities for their tiny state that were developing in Iberia, where Spain and Portugal were shipping wealth beyond the dreams of avarice into their ports, or perhaps not English avarice. The challenge for the emerging piratocracy was how to get hold of the gold, silver, ivory, silks, cloves, nutmeg, pepper and other spices which were being transported across the oceans in slow-moving, poorly manoeuvrable, badly defended bulk carriers. From the moment Protestant Elizabeth came to the throne, religious rivalry begat a righteous covetousness that would lead English pirates to feel they lacked neither morals nor honour in inviting Spanish and

4

Portuguese merchants to discharge these cargoes at sea into English hulls, rather than waiting to purchase the goods from warehouses in Lisbon or Seville.

The problem for the pirates was that if they were caught by foreign nationals they could be imprisoned or executed, and if they avoided that, they could still have their loot confiscated. This was a European-wide practice: in July 1588 the Dutch captured a well-armed Scottish pirate ship and executed the crew of ninety-four.[8] The problem for the Privy Council was to create a loophole in the law which would provide, literally, some sort of life insurance for its privileged pirates, while avoiding the reparation and restoration of valuable illegal seizures which the nation would rather retain. The solution lay with the issuing of letters of reprisal (each one of which earned the Lord Admiral a fee), not for specific incidents but by way of a general free-for-all.

This innovation was experimented with during the undeclared war with France of 1560–64 when the earl of Warwick, besieged in Le Havre, and the Huguenot champion, the prince of Condé, issued letters of reprisal without any reference to any loss claimed. Shortly afterwards, Elizabeth herself issued a supportive proclamation licensing attacks on 'enemy' merchant ships. This was, in Rodger's phrase, 'a flimsy legal cover' which strengthened the 'established connections between Protestantism and piracy.'[9]

The French war was just a rehearsal for the longer, more serious Spanish war to come. So, in 1585 when hostilities could neither be avoided nor ignored, although the requirement to prove loss for non-Iberian incidents was continued (Appendix 1A), any rover could purchase a letter of reprisal to seize as much in the way of Spanish goods as he could lay his hands on (Appendix 1B), as long as he also purchased a bond guaranteeing his good behaviour (Appendix 1C).

Letters of reprisal issued by allied would-be heads of state, such as Dom Antonio of Portugal or the Prince of Orange, were also considered to be valid. This safeguard increased the number of seamen willing to take a risk on plunder, while it was not long before the limits imposed by bonds were being ignored without consequence.

The potential advantage for the queen was obvious and in June 1585, just two months after the Spanish had impounded a number of English vessels, their cargo and crews, leading to a clamour for letters of reprisal, Sir George Carey wrote: 'her Majesty shall not need to espy the faults of those that venture their own to do her service.'[10] Very soon the queen would turn this blind-eyed tacit approval into eyes wide-open active participation, as she sought to maximise her own take from the plunder.

In the twenty years between the French war and the Spanish one, Elizabeth had learned much, including the fact that the imposition of legal due process when examining any doubtfully legitimate prize could lose her a share of many a valuable cargo. So with her famed pragmatism, Elizabeth turned herself into a pirate queen, protesting her innocence or impotence to foreign ambassadors, while accepting her share from her wayward, and always disownable, pirates. Every relevant facet of her state was involved in the plundering, including the Privy Council, of which the Lord Admiral was a member; the High Court of Admiralty, to which the Lord Admiral appointed the judges; the vice admirals of the coastal counties, who were often related to the Lord Admiral, as were many of the naval commanders who seized the goods. At a local level, sheriffs and magistrates soon learned the peculiarities of administering justice to pecuniary advantage, while merchants found out how to make gains by obtaining 'letters of reprisal' which enabled them to thieve at sea with legal authority. And as this great organic growth took hold, so it attracted its symbiotic partners; corruption and theft twined around every aspect of naval life, achieving such a stranglehold over truth that the results of inquiries against corruption, even when they managed to expose the filching that they had found, were ignored. Many of those holding high office had either their own private pirate fleets and lairs, or invested heavily in the piratical activities of others; at the turn of the century, even the queen's new secretary, Robert Cecil, lacking his old father William's sensitivity, partnered the Lord Admiral in such endeavours, although not for great reward. Thus England, whose sophisticated legal system developed over centuries to pronounce on every aspect of national life, far from being immune, or incompetent to manage piracy, chose to apply its adequate laws in an arbitrary way for personal gain, not public good.

Such state sponsorship, amounting to a private/public piratical partnership, was, whatever it lacked in legitimacy, logical. England's mariners were, until Hawkins's voyages to Africa and the West Indies showed the way, mostly coast-hugging sailors, engaged in either the wool trade to the Low Countries or the wine trade to Gascony. Her fishermen had reached the Newfoundland Banks, had even stepped ashore on that island's beaches, but they could not claim to be blue-water venturers. Whereas Columbus's voyages of the 1490s to the Americas and da Gama's passage to the East Indies were soon followed up with trading and exploiting enterprises, in England Cabot's landing in Newfoundland in 1497 had led to almost a century of explorative inactivity by the English, save for the banging of their heads against the impenetrable walls of ice which blocked their way east or west to Cathay.

Even had they so wanted, international law in the form of the papally inspired and approved Treaty of Tordisillas of 1494 precluded nations other than Spain and Portugal from venturing to trade or settle in unknown lands to the east or west of a line drawn 370 leagues beyond the Cape Verde Islands. Any venture into these closed waters, albeit with legitimate trade in mind, was viewed as trespass. Thus the Portuguese ambassador complained to Elizabeth that John Hawkins's 1567 voyage to Guinea and Sierra Leone had involved trespass and piracy, the latter to the value of 70,000 ducats. He also told her that:

> If she would prohibit her subjects from all trade on the coasts of Guinea under pain of death and confiscation of goods. His subjects can never endure that

foreigners should reap the advantage of that commerce which his ancestors acquired by a great expense of blood and treasure. The King is pricked to the heart that she refused immediate recompense to his subjects for piracies committed by the English, and again demands that she will do so. The King promises justice to two of her subjects. The King forbears to answer the other points contained in her reply, as they have nothing to do with the subject in question.[11]

With such a drastic response for foraying thus far, if English merchants wanted to trade for the wealth of the west or the spices of the east without risking their lives, they were expected so to do at considerable disadvantage in the markets of Seville or Lisbon. It was thus not surprising that some saw more advantage in investing in powder and shot discharged from reusable canisters, than in wool and cloth which those in warmer climes did not wish to wear. High-seas piracy thus became stay-at-home England's answer to the well-rewarded global expansion of the Iberian states. Realistically, it was the only way that the nation could keep pace with their economic rise, and it offered Elizabeth a swifter and surer return on investment than did any equivalent support for the creation of her own new world common-wealth. Indeed, Frobisher's failure to return from his voyages to the northwest without either discovering a sea-route to Cathay or gold-enriched ores, and the disappearance of Ralegh's ill-supported settlers on Roanoke, must have contrasted forcefully in the queen's mind with the wealth which Drake, 'the master thief of the unknown world', laid before her in 1580 following his successful piratical circumnavigation.

The blanket issue of letters of reprisal did not make the queen rich. After the costs of a voyage had been deducted, the Lord Admiral received 10 per cent of the value of the prize, and the Crown just 5 per cent in customs dues, with the residue being split three ways between the victuallers, the owners and the crew. As the rewards for pillage became greater (Andrews estimates that between 1585 and 1603 the value of prize goods ranged from about £100,000 to £200,000 a year[12]), so the queen's desire to be included in the distribution grew. This she achieved by issuing her own letters of commission to her favourite pirates, meaning that she could also dispatch her own ships to strengthen their forces. Ironically, the first and most famous of these commissions, the one which Drake referred to in his prosecution of Thomas Doughty during his circumnavigation, may not even have existed. If it did it would have been written on the same lines as those she gave to her most persistent pirate, George Clifford, earl of Cumberland, in 1595 (Appendix 2). Elizabeth also recorded in advance the return that she expected from her contribution which was '£10,000 for every carrack bound from Portugal for the Indies, or £20,000 on any from the Indies to Portugal.'[13]

Experience had already taught Cumberland that the queen could demand more than was ever suggested by pre-sailing agreements. In the taking of the richest prize of all, *Madre de Dios* in 1592, his reward had been minimal. Under the rules that were accepted as standard, Elizabeth would have been entitled in this instance to a share of £20,000 of that ship's £141,000 invoiced worth, with the earl receiving at the least £66,000, and Walter Ralegh, the London merchants and Hawkins sharing the remainder. Instead, the queen was constrained from keeping it all only by the argument that to do so would discourage further similar sorties. In the end she kept £80,000, and with ill grace handed over £36,000 to Cumberland and £24,000 to Ralegh, with the merchants sharing the remainder.[14] Ralegh had invested over £34,000 in the voyage, Cumberland some £19,000, while Her Majesty had provided two ships and £1,800. This was not untypical of Elizabeth who, faced with the opportunity of being leanly right or richly wrong, never hesitated to select the road to wealth.

By sponsoring her pirates Elizabeth took a step beyond that which her great rival was prepared to take. Richard Hawkins, himself captured by the Spanish while on a piratical voyage, noted that if a Spanish ship operating as a pirate:

> . . . should fall athwart his King's armado or galleys, I make no doubt but they would hang the captain and his company for pirates . . . for by a special law it is enacted that no man in the kingdom of Spain may arm any ship and go in warfare, without the King's special licence and commission, upon pain to be reputed a pirate, and to be so chastised . . . In England the case is different: for the war once proclaimed, every man may arm that will . . . which maketh for our greater exemption from being comprehended within the number of pirates.[15]

For Elizabeth's laxer rules on piracy to be effective, she needed men in the right quantity and with the right qualifications to serve her both offensively and defensively. In July 1545 Reneger had brought four of his pirate fleet and a French prize to the Solent to join Lord Admiral Lisle's force to repulse the French invasion. In 1588 not one but a dozen pirates formed up with Howard's fleet to face the Spanish Armada. Elizabeth, needing more Renegers, had found a cohort prepared to make the transference from nautical outlaw to naval officer and from knave to knight, a progression that made idols of the 'sea dogs' such as Drake, Hawkins, Grenville, Frobisher, Cumberland and Ralegh.[16]

These men formed a new piratocracy whose voyages, covertly or overtly blessed by the state, were to associate them with great wealth, although not all of them were successful in its retention. Most significantly, they were well received at court and it is this symbiotic relationship between government and the cream of the corsairs that showed the state up for what, from 1580, it was – a pariah nation over whose maritime affairs this piratocracy had risen to take command and reap rewards.

Thus there arose two very separate levels of piracy: close inshore this was the equivalent of breaking and entry; on the ocean it was grand larceny and it is this latter offence to which the state gave its blessing. The gulf between the two forms of the same crime can be illustrated by the fact that many who committed the grander crime, such as Richard Grenville, were content to sit as local magistrates in judgement of those who were accused of the lesser.[17] Under Elizabeth's watchful eye the state dealt with petty pirates as the law demanded while Mafia-like godfather figures, such as Lord Admiral Howard, not only ensured that organised crime and corruption was left unhindered, but that the major perpetrators, such as Drake or Frobisher, became acceptable members of society.

There is an argument that the rovers who sailed in search of prizes could not be considered pirates, as they voyaged with letters of reprisal or a queen's commission. Yet both in the excuse and the execution this is palpably not so. First, although such authority exonerated those with a genuine grievance, many endeavoured to capture far more than the losses they claimed when applying for a letter of reprisal. Drake, for example, justified his seizures of a great treasure in the Pacific by saying that he sought only compensation for the (much exaggerated) loss suffered by his cousin, John Hawkins, when his fleet was battered by the Spanish at San Juan de Ulua in 1568, although he did not cease his activities once he reached that mark. Many produced no evidence of loss to justify their receipt of a letter of reprisal; in fact, after 1585 the Admiralty no longer made this a prerequisite. Indeed, with each prize having a potential value in excess of the court's annual income, there was no possibility of an adventurer claiming a loss equivalent to his capture. The very value of these captures made false the virtue of legitimate reprisal claims, thus making their seizure different only from piracy in the perpetrators' possession of a scrap of paper and/or the approval of the Crown.

Secondly, neither the Crown nor the Admiralty took stern action to ensure their pirates took goods only from enemy nationals. Whatever their stated position, they encouraged a free-for-all in which the greater crime became not the illegal seizure of ships and their cargoes, but the failure to surrender them on return to England.

Thirdly, the Elizabethans were swift to condemn the piracy of others, whatever legal justification those rovers claimed. The Barbary states of Tripoli, Tunis and Algiers, along with neighbouring Morocco, all had state-sponsored corsairs' fleets whose captains and crews were considered to be pirates, and were treated as such if captured. Elizabeth's support for her own rovers may have been less open and less evident, but dissembling and cloaking does not absolve her from supporting activities which if committed by any other nation were considered wrongful.

Fourthly, the whole of Europe considered England to be a pirate state. Could they all be mistaken? With a typical xenophobic myopia, Elizabeth's beautiful but brainless favourite, the earl of Essex, saw things only from his nation's point of view. In commenting on the unsatisfactory terms of the treaty of Vervins, by which France had independently agreed peace terms with Spain, the impetuous earl, failing to see the true cause of English isolation, remarked:

> The French King hath broken the league and abandoned us . . . our late good neighbour of Denmark has confiscated English goods upon a pretext, Poland has

9

already braved us and will either arrest or banish our merchants . . . the Emperor has exiled our nation from all trade within the Empire . . . while the Hanse towns were our professed enemies.[18]

Drawing such evident conclusions as to the nation's pariah status creates the problem that it reflects badly on national idols: Drake is the second most revered sailor in English history, while Elizabeth is the country's most admired, and loved, monarch. This status has meant that many have written hagiographies rather than biographies, only for others to endeavour to demolish the pedestals on which these gods have been placed. Thus Julian Corbett, still the greatest biographer of Drake, considered him to have been a naval strategist of genius, a forefather of the Royal Navy and a jolly good sort to boot. Much of that is evidently not so, and a very readable and well-reasoned study far closer to the truth was produced by Andrews, based on the historic, rather than surmised, evidence.[19] However, not content with the hero's return to earth, Kelsey tried to bury him with slander that was as wide of its mark as was Corbett's panegyric. Without any supporting evidence, he claimed that: 'Drake's personal bravery was accompanied by a complete lack of moral scruples. It did not bother him in the least to deprive someone, friend or foe, of life or property', before dismissing him as 'an interesting fellow' without a 'well-developed moral sense.'[20] Yet in the many accounts of Drake's activities, it is his humanity that stands out as rather special in a savage age. Kelsey does not compare Drake's treatment of captives with that meted out by the Spanish, who enslaved, tortured, strangled, burnt and held captive most of those whom they seized at sea, the fortunate survivors of *Revenge* and *Dainty* being very much the exception.

Michael Turner, the most knowledgeable of all Drake scholars, prefers the use of the term corsair or privateer to describe the status of Drake, and by implication that of his fellow rovers who had been issued with letters of reprisal or commissions. However, as the term 'privateer' did not come into common use until the mid seventeenth century, the word 'pirateering' has been coined in this book to describe the major state-sponsored piracy that became widespread after 1585. As for 'corsair', it is really only an alternative term for pirate most applicable to those based in the Barbary States.[21] Although Alexander McKee's excellent study of Drake's circumnavigation is entitled *The Queen's Corsair*, it could equally have been called *The Queen's Pirate*, for it was without her disapproval he sailed and seized ships belonging to both Portugal and Spain, neither of which nations was at war with England.

There were those, like Burghley, Elizabeth's longest serving and most loyal adviser, who held indominantly to his abhorrence of piracy. Sadly for his sensitivities, Elizabeth did not. But before the queen could reap her unjust rewards, those who would form her piratocracy, her pirateers, had a trade to learn, and a very tough one at that.

CHAPTER 2

Apprentice to a Pirate

There is a tide in the affairs of men
Which, taken at the flood, leads on to fortune;
Omitted, all the voyage of their life
Is bound in shallows and in miseries.
On such a full sea are we now afloat,
And we must take the current when it serves
William Shakespeare, *Julius Caesar*, 1599

At the age of fourteen, the fatherless Martin Frobisher was packed off to the London home of his mother's relative, the merchant Sir John Yorke. The poor boy's backwardness won him no preferment as a relative of that aggressive businessman, and Yorke soon decided that he could best fulfil his obligations by sending the young man off to sea. Neither did young Martin's age or relationship earn him an easy passage. By his later testament 'he was on the first and second voyages in the parties of Guinea'[1] which took place in 1553 and 1554 to a stretch of coastal water that was to claim many an English life through illness, famishment and fighting.

These were voyages that flouted internationally understood arrangements which recognised Portugal as holding a monopoly on trade in this region; the Portuguese agents in London objected strongly to the proposal, and even tried to kidnap the two Portuguese pilots whom the merchants had hired for their first voyage. At this obstruction the Admiralty Court weighed in, imprisoning the potential saboteurs until they repented of their acts.

After many delays the adventurers departed on 12 August 1553. Their fleet was commanded by Thomas Wyndham who, having led two trading expeditions to the Barbary Coast, was one of the few Englishmen who had sailed south of Gibraltar. The ships, comprising *Lion of London*, *Primrose* and the pinnace *Moon*, were crewed by 140 seamen and a number of merchants, including the apprentice Martin Frobisher.

Rather than taking the Portuguese objections seriously and acting with circumspection, Wyndham chose to accept them as a challenge, behaving with a cavalier contempt towards all from that nation whom he encountered. Having called at Madeira for victuals, he sailed and seized two Portuguese vessels just outside the harbour. He then crossed to launch a foiled raid on Deserta Island, retreating with several other ships as prizes. Unsatisfied with the completion of his trade on the Mina Coast, Wyndham subsequently ignored the advice of his Portuguese pilots, carried especially for this role, and sailed into the Bight of Benin, thus becoming one of the first Englishmen to justify the saw: 'Beware and take care of the Bay of Benin/ Where few come out although many go in.'

Wyndham, along with many of his crew, was soon fatally stricken with Benin's portfolio of diseases, meaning that *Lion* had to be abandoned, as too few fit men remained to sail her. Then, possibly because the pilots had lost interest, instead of hauling out into the Atlantic to catch the favourable trade-winds, the ignorant navigators made slow passage homeward, close to the coast and feeding the trailing sharks with the bodies of their dead companions.

Forty survivors, some of them dying, worked the two frail vessels up the Thames in May 1554. As those unhappy few represented a major saving in wages, the investors were more than content with the goods that were disembarked. The voyage had been an epic of incompetence, during which the crew had endured most of the perils known to English mariners, along with some new ones. Few teenagers would have survived such a deep baptism into life afloat; few would not have been scarred by what they witnessed – Frobisher throve.[2] When in November 1554 the next Guinea-bound fleet sailed from Dartmouth under the command of John Lok (whose relative, Michael, would sponsor Frobisher's voyages to find a northwest passage), Frobisher was embarked.

This was another three-ship group with *Trinity of London* the admiral, being accompanied by *John Evangelist* and *Bartholomew*. Lok had learned from the earlier errors of Wyndham and his ships sailed directly to what is now the coast of Liberia to purchase pepper and gold. The local traders only insisted on one caveat: that a hostage be landed for the duration of the trading. Whether it was a short straw, a shortage of years, a desire for adventure or, given his emerging character, a wish to be rid of an awkward hand, Frobisher was the one selected to be landed. And thus it was that when a Portuguese warship hove in sight, the English weighed anchor and fled, leaving their young colleague behind them to be locked up in the infamous fort at São Jorge da Minas, where much of the high-value trading goods were stowed for safe-keeping.

For Frobisher the fort was an open prison and he charmed his jailers sufficiently to be allowed out hunting during his nine-month stay. It was probably over a year before he saw England again. For his foster-father, Sir John Yorke, he was no great loss, being expendable while at sea and an extra mouth to feed when ashore. He certainly does not seem to have considered Frobisher to be worth a ransom. Neither did he indulge in fatted calf-killing when the wanderer returned: Frobisher appears to have been denied both his share of the expedition's profit and his back pay. A mutual good-riddance ensued.

A cloud cloaks the activities of the masterless Frobisher for the next few years, although there are some hints that he undertook another two voyages to Guinea, possibly in command. Whether or not he did, he drew the conclusion that piracy paid better and was less dangerous than attempts at semi-legitimate trading. Maybe, following his treatment, he harboured a desire to revenge himself on the merchant class who had considered his life as of so little value, in much the same way as Drake swore to be revenged on the Spanish after their treachery at San Juan de Ulua. Maybe, as a young man who could handle a ship but very little else, he followed a logical career progression. Whatever his reasoning, for the next decade Frobisher was a pirate and, being Frobisher, he made a shambles of it.

The young pirate's initial plan does seem to have been based on a good idea. In company with the notorious pirate Henry Strangways (how did they meet?) it seems he intended to make a raid on the fortress store at São Jorge da Minas, the layout of which he would have known in great detail. Still, it was not the best-laid plan and it was totally upset when in September 1559 Strangways was brought before the Admiralty Court, accused of planning this very endeavour. On this occasion the hardened pirate might have considered himself unlucky, not only because accusations of conspiracy were more frequently linked to treasonable plots than plundering expeditions, but also because the subtle difference between breaking trade embargoes and raiding a friendly nation's warehouses was a distinction based on political expediency, rather than illegal activity. Had the plan remained concealed and a richly rewarding raid taken place, there would have been every possibility that the right size bribe in the right podgy palms would have allowed the miscreants to escape unscathed. In the dock, Strangways laid the blame for the plan on his young friend, a ploy that earned him his pardon. After that one appearance in the court record, Frobisher exits the stage yet again making his next appearance in a farce performed in 1563.

By this time he had returned to Yorkshire, where his brother John had part-ownership with a John Appleyard of the modestly named ship *John Appleyard* aka *Bark Frobisher* (presumably depending whose turn it was to command). Appleyard had obtained letters of marque issued by the French Huguenot leader, the prince of Condé, which probably licensed the holder to seize only French Catholic vessels. Few pirates, many of whom could claim to be illiterate, took notice of the fine print in their authorisations, even when the caveats were backed up with the requirement to post a bond, in this case of about £50, as a guarantee of good behaviour. The Appleyard letters ordered the captains of this three-ship group not to 'robbe, spoyle, infest, trouble, evil intreate, apprehende, ne take any Portingales, Spaniardes, or any other persouns whiche be in league and amitie with her majestie', an undertaking that they felt would be more honoured in the breach than the observance.

There is a good indication of the company that Frobisher brothers had been keeping of late, in that their fellow commander was Peter Killigrew, a member of the piratical princes of Cornwall who dominated seaborne crime in the West

Country from their stronghold of Pendennis Castle, with the added aura of untouchability that came with the appointment of Sir John Killigrew as the commissioner for piracy in Cornwall

The three ships sailed south in March and in May entered Plymouth Sound to dispose of the cargo legally taken from five French Catholic vessels. Immediately things began to unravel, for the goods were seized, the Admiralty Court justifying this action by accusing Martin Frobisher of aiding and abetting another pirate, Thomas Cobham, in a fierce fight against a Spanish ship, *Katherine*. Cobham claimed that he had always suspected his target to have been French and thus was quite at liberty to show his gratitude to Frobisher for *Anne Appleyard*'s assistance by rewarding that skipper with a part of the prize cargo of wines and tapestries, some of which was disposed of at Baltimore in Ireland, before the ship returned to Plymouth to sell the rest.

Unfortunately, the pirates' actions had sparked off a diplomatic row. The tapestries had been sent by the Spanish ambassador in London, Guzmán de Silva, as a gift to Philip of Spain; more unfortunate still was that this was also a period in Elizabeth's roller-coaster relationship with Spain in which she was favouring appeasement. The pirates and their plunder were both seized, with the former being sent to London under escort.

In London the brothers gave a good account of themselves, and they and their French prizes were freed. However, in their absence John Appleyard's agent, the well-connected Thomas Bowes, had travelled to Plymouth and, quoting Privy Council authority, removed *Katherine*'s wine from bondage and disappeared with both the wine and, possibly, the tapestries. All was unravelling for the brothers who, no sooner than they were released, found themselves cited in a lawsuit for the recovery of the wine, instigated by their one-time partner, John Appleyard. Unable to produce the barrels, they were flung into Launceston Jail on 15 July, from where they were sent to London in September to appear before a sympathetic Privy Council, who once more ordered their release.

Not so their casual acquaintance, Cobham. On being apprehended he was taken to the Tower to endure the harshest of punishments. This began with him being stripped and hung upside down so that the soles of his feet could be beaten, a most painful torture. Then he was spreadeagled on the filthy cell floor with a sharp stone under his back and a heavy round of shot placed on his stomach. This excruciating punishment, coupled with starvation rations, would have brought about his certain death, had not friends in high places (the family name gives an indication as to whom they were) pleaded successfully for his release. Yet again it was not the seriousness of a crime that had dictated the severity of the sentence, but to whom the miscreant could turn to for support.

Undeterred by their lucky escape, the now impecunious Frobishers reverted to their chosen career and it was not long before their practice of non-selective prize-taking was again being brought to the attention of the courts. In May 1565 they were named as the plunderers of a cargo of cochineal being carried in the Spanish ship, *Flying Spirit*. Escaping judgement, they amassed sufficient ill-gotten funds to purchase their own craft, the 100-ton *Mary Flower*, a ship in which Frobisher staged one of his several fiascos.

Frobisher joined his new command on Tyneside in September. By then she had been made seaworthy and just needed victualling, a master and crew, and a fair wind to waft her southward into the predatory shipping lanes. The victualling took some time to complete, probably because of a lack of ready cash, and it was not until late December that she slipped down to the sea on the outgoing tide.

Frobisher had prepared a plausible cover-story to mask his intentions, telling the authorities that his destination was Guinea, although a crew of just thirty-six would indicate that he was not making any allowance for the high death-rate that this destination inevitably inflicted.

Not that he was going to experience such mortality. Off the Humber, *Mary Flower* was pounded by a storm so fierce that she lost both her sails and her masts, and only Frobisher's skill in beaching her on the sands near Scarborough saved the crew from drowning. Once beached, the brothers' penury resulted in their being detained, for they had insufficient funds to pay for either the ship's repairs and refloating, or to meet the demands of creditors who had travelled down the coastal road to pay them a visit. The result was that the ship was impounded until some outstanding debts were settled.

Then, with beer, bread, biscuit and beef embarked and paid for, officers from the Court of Admiralty turned up and took Martin Frobisher into custody for questioning. Very sensibly John Frobisher did not wait for him to return, but floated off, only to meet more stormy weather. Records show that he passed into the Thames in May – the voyage from Tyneside having taken four and a half months to accomplish. What happened thereafter is not recorded but the Admiralty judge, Dr Lewes, was not convinced by Martin Frobisher's explanation as to his lawful intentions. An attempt was made to frame him for the seizure of the Flemish ship *White Unicorn*, whose path approximated to that taken by *Mary Flower*, but when this failed to hold water he had to be released.

However fierce the force of the court's warning to Frobisher, it does not seem to have penetrated into his consciousness. Within days, maybe hours, of being released, he had obtained letters of marque from the exiled Huguenot leader, Admiral Coligny, authorising him to seize any French Catholic vessels. Such a letter acted as a passport to a new command, and it was not long before Frobisher was back at sea as captain of *Robert*, which was based at Rye, along with several other pirate ships.

Once again the inability to read the small print on Coligny's commission was the undoing of Frobisher, who was soon taking prizes based on the riches rather than the religion of their owners. Protests were made and noted until, in March 1569, Frobisher was apprehended ashore and charged with the seizing of *Mary of*

Montaigne and the disposal of her cargo of wine. Naturally, Frobisher pleaded innocence and in keeping with tradition blamed his absent partner for the deed. Although his crew turned against him and stated that he had taken a share of 50 tunnes of wine, he was released to return to his established ways. But this time he had made an implacable and industrious foe. Robert Friar, the owner of *Mary*'s stolen wine, turned detective and tracked down most of his missing barrels, also acquiring evidence that Frobisher, far from being innocent, had sold six barrels of the wine to a merchant in Chichester. Yet again, Dr Lewes sent his officers out to invite Frobisher to explain himself.

He was apprehended in Aldeburgh to which he had come in his new ship, the prize *Magdalene*, which he had exchanged for *Robert*. It was a case of foolishness overtopping misfortune. *Magdalene* and her cargo of lead, ivory and wine was owned by a syndicate of merchants of Rouen who had contacts inside the Privy Council, whom they petitioned for restitution and redress. The thinking pirate would have disposed of both ship and cargo privily at Baltimore, as Frobisher had done with his earlier haul of wine, but no one ever accused Frobisher of being too bright. By now he had also to explain his involvement with the capture and ransacking of *Saint John of Bordeaux* and several other vessels not covered by Coligny's letters.

Even if Dr Lewes's patience had not run out, that of the Privy Council, anxious to keep international relations on an even keel, had. In late August the High Court of Admiralty judge was given clear direction:

> We send unto you by this bearer, one of the knight Marshall's men, Martyn Furbusher, against whom you know what grievous complaints have been made of divers and sundry piracies by him committed. We pray you therefore to send him to the Marshalsea where he may remain in sure and safe custody, until you send for him again and may upon such information as he is to be charged withal, proceed against him with severity . . .

Lewes responded by throwing Frobisher into the Marshalsea, his release dependent on the payment of a massive fine of £900, which was well outside his ability to pay. At that time a sailor on a merchant ship might receive £10 a year, a sum which a crew member of a reasonably successful pirate ship might occasionally be paid after the taking of a moderately rich cargo. When Frobisher appeared to turn traitor in 1572, he was rewarded with £20 for offering to bring three hundred English seamen over to the Spanish side. Now, incarcerated, with neither accumulated wealth nor rich relations, Frobisher faced a life sentence: many of his fellow practitioners would have been sentenced to death for lesser crimes. That he was not might be due to the fact that most of his illegally-seized vessels were foreign and not English-owned.

Yet rot inside he did not. Along his erratic and unsuccessful way he had made just the sort of contacts a pirate in distress needed. The Huguenot exiles sprang to his aid, with the Cardinal of Châtillon writing to William Cecil, Elizabeth's principal secretary, that the wife of Captain Frobisher had begged him to write and require Cecil's aid in delivering her husband from the misery and captivity in which he found himself.[3]

More important was the involvement of Lord Admiral Clinton whose wife, Elizabeth Fiennes, made an offer to buy *Robert*, the sale of which would have made a major contribution to the fine. In the end it did not require payment, for on another February note ordering the transfer of Frobisher from the Marshalsea to the Fleet prison, above the words stating that the pirate be kept in jail until 'he shall satisfy and pay the same', Cecil scrawled 'or otherwise be released by us.' That release took place in March.

As a sign of his undeserved fortune, in October 1571 Frobisher was appointed to command *Carrack Lane* and a squadron of three other Portsmouth-based ships entrusted to enforce the more stringent anti-piracy laws that Elizabeth had approved as part of her attempt to clear the Channel of foreign freebooters. Now, rather than pay her professionals to do the job, she contracted out to reformed pirates, believing them to be more knowledgeable of the ways of their late colleagues, besides being the cheaper option. Cheap, but not necessarily efficacious: Frobisher cruised and failed to make contact. His obvious partiality for his past companions failed to become an embarrassment for his new employers when his task was switched to that of transporting the army and its accoutrements to Ireland. Here indeed was gainful employment, but the temptations remained, for Frobisher was now required to sail past eminently seizable, laden merchant ships, giving them a friendly salute rather than a salvo. In the end, he cracked and reverted to his old ways, escorting several French ships into Plymouth – claiming them as legitimate prizes. The arrest warrants were not long awaiting issue.

However, Frobisher had become associated with legitimate maritime tasks and had also shown himself to be most biddable in areas that required a certain derring-do. Over the next few years he entered into the murky world of treachery and double-dealing, claiming clean hands however muddied the waters through which he passed. By 1574 his unsuccessful independent piratical career was over: in future Frobisher was to serve the state, which valued the skills which they thought he must have acquired through his illegal activities. In 1576, '77 and '78 he made three voyages to the far north of America: the first to search for the northwest passage to Cathay; the second two to mine for gold. They were two tasks which he completed with his usual lack of success. However, others sailing astern of him on similar voyages were able to open up new opportunities for those with a lust for wealth and limited scruples. Among these were John Hawkins and the 'master-thief', Francis Drake.

Drake might have been a Devon man, but he spent his apprenticeship on the opposite shore, off Kent, whence his father had fled from Tavistock to avoid either prosecution or persecution or both.[4] Here, on a hulk moored in the Medway, the elder Drake made a sort of living running an early mission to seamen, while apprenticing his son Francis to the master of a small bark, who taught him all the pilotage skills necessary to handle a ship safely in the featureless and mud-bank strewn waters of the Thames. When the ship owner died, he bequeathed his craft to the young man, but Drake dreamed of further horizons and together with a few of his crew sailed for Plymouth to offer his services to his distant relative, John Hawkins.

Like Sir John Yorke, John Hawkins, the son of the Plymouth merchant and convicted pirate, William Hawkins, saw trading opportunities in the steaming and unhealthy shores of Guinea. His interest, however, lay not in gold and ivory, but in a human cargo. He aimed to turn the trading voyage from simple outward and homeward legs into a triangular trade with the West Indies, as he tried to brush aside the Portuguese and Spanish monopolies on the capture and sale of slaves. With him on those voyages sailed the young Francis Drake, keen to learn the science of navigation beyond the sight of land.

In 1562 John Hawkins, after a few exploratory trading voyages as far as the Canaries, sailed on his first slaving voyage. He had planned well, establishing a partnership with a merchant family in the Canaries who would guarantee his fleet a friendly watering and recuperation stop while on passage. Just three small ships, *Salomon* of 140 tons, and *Jonas* and *Swallow* just 40 and 30 tons respectively, departed from Plymouth, but they were precursors of a great armada of infamy – the slave traders. Hawkins, as did those that came after, realised that if a reasonable profit was to be made from the venture, then the slaves would have to be crammed between decks which meant, paradoxically, they would suffer a high death rate. Nevertheless, although the trade might be inglorious it was not piracy. The means employed to assist the voyagers, however, were.

Reaching the coast of Sierra Leone, Hawkins seized his first slaves from several Portuguese vessels which he captured. And along with those four hundred slaves came a by-cargo of cloves and ivory which was sent home in a ship commanded by Hawkins's cousin, the young Francis Drake. Hawkins himself sailed to Hispaniola where he arrived having lost about half of his slaves, but getting a good price for the survivors. With an eye to the even greater profit the sale could make, Hawkins bought all the sugar, hides, pearls and ginger available in the warehouses of Isabella. His eyes were larger than that which his ships' holds could stomach, as a result of which he had to load two Spanish ships with the overflow and dispatch them back to Spain, with instructions to offload them through an English factor in Seville. That this arrangement would work was a naive assumption, for the cargo of both ships was impounded as contraband, one at Lisbon and one at Seville. Hawkins did not receive compensation and thus made merely a good profit rather than an extraordinary one from his voyage. The reduced return was, however, sufficient to interest the avaricious queen, who became a major partner in Hawkins's next voyage through the loan of two of her own ships.

As his flagship Hawkins would now sail in the elderly, but capacious, 700-ton *Jesus of Lubeck*, purchased from Hamburg by Henry VIII in 1545. Aged she might be, but she represented the queen's willingness to approve and invest in a voyage, the purpose of which was very apparent: the capture and illegal trading of slaves. Moreover, both the procurement and the disposal of this human cargo would involve her directly in the breaking of internationally recognised trading embargoes held by Portugal in West Africa and Spain in the West Indies. The vessel thus represented a significant shift in the move from royal indulgence of wayward seamen to royal involvement in illegal trading – the first step to the approval of piracy.

Yet outwardly the queen was still active in her pursuit of pirates, if only to calm down the exasperated and protesting ambassadors from her aggrieved European neighbours. In November 1564 she asked the Admiralty Court judge, David Lewes, to carry out an investigation into the complaints by the Spanish ambassador about piratical depredations committed at sea on the subjects of the king of Spain. As the inquiry was to involve the county commissioners against piracy, many of whom were well-known supporters of the trade, a disinterested report was most unlikely.[5] She had also allayed the fears raised by the Spanish ambassador, Guzmán de Silva, about Hawkins's intentions by telling the incredulous gentleman that Hawkins, far from being a pirate, was just an honest and wealthy trader, to which de Silva retorted that if this were so, he failed to see why the ships were carrying so many armed men.

In company with the creaking *Jesus of Lubeck* were *Solomon* and *Swallow*, as well as a 50-ton vessel, *Tiger*. Francis Drake was included in the crew of just 150 men, but still only as an ordinary seaman. Stopping to call on his friends in the Canaries, the refreshed Hawkins sailed on to the Guinea coast where he committed the first piratical act of the voyage by capturing and de-storing a small Portuguese fishing fleet. His second was the capture of some larger vessels along with their slaves and other valuable cargo, all of which was recorded by their aggrieved owners, who petitioned the Privy Council, more in hope than expectation of restitution. Further slaves, to a total of about four hundred, were captured after some severe skirmishing ashore.

This time the Atlantic crossing proved not so deadly for the slaves, possibly because the larger *Jesus of Lubeck* allowed for less cramped conditions below decks and the freer circulation of air. Even then, about thirty died before landfall. There just remained the problem of disposing of the remainder at a good price. To achieve that profit from communities who were well aware that they were forbidden to trade with the English required the repetitive use of a tactic, the purpose of which was well understood by both sides. First, Hawkins would state his innocence in that he had been forced westward by strong winds and now very much needed a licence to trade to obtain fresh victuals. This the local magnate would refuse to grant. Hawkins would then threaten violence, even landing an armed party to look sternly at the locals who, subdued by such a threat, would reluctantly trade, simply to spare their town and to rid themselves of the pestilent foreigner. Honour satisfied and excuses provided, an amicable exchange ensued. Once that charade was complete, trade was brisk and very, very profitable.

Guzmán de Silva reported home that Hawkins had returned with gold, pearls, hides and sugar to the value of 50,000 ducados, which, if it were so, represented a profit of 60 per cent. With such a profit available, it was worth the queen regarding the source with a merry myopia and the protestations of the Spanish and Portuguese ambassadors with a selective deafness. Hawkins could gain no more obvious approval than from her continuing to loan him her ships. Yet this time strange auguries might have been seen as prophesying doom.

In September 1567 Hawkins's fleet of six ships was anchored in the shelter of the Cattewater below Plymouth town, waiting for a fair wind to waft them southwesterly. But even at this stage in the preparation, Hawkins was aware that the queen might be tempted to prevent his departure or to insist on certain caveats which would impinge on his profits. Chief amongst these was her usual desire to placate the Spanish, in the person of de Silva, by assuring him that Hawkins would observe the embargoes of which he was fully aware. Indeed, in a way her loan of both *Jesus of Lubeck* and the smaller *Minion* was a guarantee of Hawkins's good behaviour, a fact about which the fleet admiral sought to reassure her, writing from the anchorage: 'I do ascertain Your Highness that I have provision sufficient and an able army to defend our charge and to bring home (with God's help) forty thousand marks gain without the offence of the least of any of Your Highness' allies or friends' – which if true would hardly have necessitated the shipping of 'an able army'.

Hawkins's letter-writing was interrupted by an urgent summons to come on deck. A lookout had sighted a squadron of seven Spanish warships heading down Plymouth Sound, making towards their own fleet anchorage. Hawkins took one look and ordered his crew to action stations, secure in the knowledge that the guns he had mounted could do grave damage to any vessels closing with hostile intent. At the time England and Spain were at peace but, as with rival football teams, it was not the management, but the fans that could cause trouble to erupt.

Hawkins gazed at the mast tops of the steadily approaching fleet to see if, as custom dictated, they would dip their ensigns as a token of respect and a signal of peaceful intent. The ensigns remained close up, while there was neither a slackening of speed nor an indication of an intention to anchor in the outer harbour so, once Hawkins was sure that the insolent foreigners were within range of his guns, he fired a warning salvo in their direction. When that failed to stem the oncoming fleet or cause them to dip their ensigns, Hawkins ordered his crews to lower their sights and the second salvo hit the hulls. That was warning enough: the foreign fleet went about, dipping its ensigns as it did so, and anchored out of range of the irritated English. From their admiral an envoy was soon dispatched to voice the protests of the Spanish commander, the aristocratic Alphonse de Borgogne, at their rough reception. Hawkins countered by claiming that the insult to the Crown which the brazen entry of the foreign fleet had caused required a stern response.

Shortly after this incident Hawkins received a letter from the queen, fully endorsing his mission. Unfettered by any of the restraining caveats he had anticipated, his third and final slaving voyage got underway.

Great storms soon scattered the fleet and showed up the crankiness of the leaky and aged *Jesus*, but Hawkins, by dint of his carefully worded sailing orders, managed to reunite his ships in the Canaries before descending to Cabo Blanco, the landfall for all Guinea voyages, and thus the site of a small Portuguese fort. Treating the garrison with disdain, Hawkins surveyed four abandoned Portuguese ships and selected the most seaworthy to sail with him, cheekily accepting a promissory note for the sale of two of the others back to the legal owner.

After one botched slaving raid secured far fewer captives than they wished for, the English sailed on to Cabo Rojo for supplies, much of which were seized from seven Portuguese ships. A few more slave raids were then carried out, with the alerted villages yielding few recruits for Hawkins's hold. One of these raids resulted in a rare cause of a boat capsizing: it was attacked and smashed by a herd of hippopotamus, their herbivore credentials coming into question by the claim that two of the men were eaten by the beasts.

Eventually an alliance, rather than a raid, brought Hawkins his slaves, but only after his men had witnessed a cannibalistic feast from the bodies of the slain. For the loss of some sixty men he had gained a cargo of five hundred wretches, whom he would endeavour to keep alive for the seven-week Atlantic crossing on a diet of dried beans, the very stores that had alerted de Silva to his true intentions so many months earlier in London. Given the number of slaves that he managed to sell in the Indies and the group that were left unsold, it has been estimated that around one hundred of them died on passage, a death rate that scarcely dented his profit.[6]

Having gone through the usual charade of threatening and cajoling the governors, by late August Hawkins had made sufficient profit to satisfy the queen, himself and the other investors so, reducing his fleet to the most seaworthy of his vessels, he led the remaining eight northeast towards the Florida Channel from where they would turn homeward. They never made it. A hurricane, the full violence of which is well-described by Rayner Unwin, fell upon the fleet, leaving in its wake a flagship that was no longer seaworthy and in desperate need of a sheltered anchorage before she foundered.[7] Basing his decision on local knowledge obtained from the pilots of two captured Spanish ships, Hawkins went about and led his fleet limping back south to the island harbour of San Juan de Ulua, the port for Vera Cruz.

Unlike the welcome that had been given to the similar-sized Spanish fleet when it had entered Plymouth Sound at the start of Hawkins's voyage, the inhabitants of San Juan fired a five-gun salute and waved and cheered as the English entered harbour: they had been mistaken for their own *flota* expected at any time soon. By the time the error had been realised it was too late to prevent Hawkins from berthing his ships' bows to the jetty with kedge anchors run out to secure his stern. While this was being done he sent parties ashore to seize the nearby gun emplacements, the crews of which had conveniently fled on realising the 'the Lutherans' were upon them. There followed a stand-off which neither side risked upsetting and if such an armed hostility had continued it is likely that Hawkins would have managed to complete his repairs and continue his voyage unimpeded.

Then a day later, on 17 September, the balance was upset when the anticipated fleet arrived, and the authorities ashore had to inform the admiral, Fransisco de Luxan, and his very important passenger, the new viceroy of New Spain, Martín Enríquez, that their berths were occupied by English ships. No viceroy would have wished to begin his reign by accepting such a snub and when the Spanish finally entered harbour, Hawkins must have known that he faced a swift and unpleasant eviction.

It was delivered by stealth, with the Spanish sneaking soldiers and gunners as close to the alert English as they dared approach under cover. The English opened fire first, but were unable to prevent their shore parties from being overwhelmed and slaughtered. To avoid the soldiers from boarding from the jetty, the English ships cut their mooring lines and drifted into the harbour, all the time firing at close-range on the enemy ships, several of which caught fire. But *Jesus* was too unwieldy to manoeuvre herself out of trouble, and Hawkins ordered his men to transfer both themselves and the readily reached goods to *Minion*, which was lying alongside. Drake in *Judith* was also ordered to close to assist in the evacuation, but how long she stayed to give succour is put into doubt by Hawkins's pithy comment that she 'forsoke us in our great misery.'

But Hawkins was also forced to 'forsoke'. Five ships, and the unlucky remnants of their crews, were abandoned at San Juan de Ulua, the ships to be ransacked for their riches and the men racked for their religion. Out at sea the survivors had exchanged one hell for another. *Judith* made haste homeward, arriving in Plymouth on 22 January 1569. A sympathetic veil has been drawn over her return passage, for it must have been a low point in the career of her captain that he was unlikely to forget.

We know more about the sad voyage of John Hawkins. With scarce enough provisions to feed her normal crew, *Minion* was far too overcrowded for many to survive the journey home. Hawkins was forced therefore to close the coast of Mexico and land ninety men at Campeche near the town of Tampico. Even then, with every scrap of food consumed, including the trapped rodent population, men starved. In an ironic imitation of the westward voyage, the ship left a trail of bodies in her wake, but this time they were the corpses of Englishmen not slaves.

Near Galicia Hawkins captured and emptied three Portuguese vessels of their provisions, although there is no evidence to support the claim that he cut off the limbs of their crews and flung their living torsos overboard. A few days later he anchored off Ponteverda where, deploying the only weapons he had left, charm and bluff, he managed to purchase sufficient supplies to set sail homeward. The weather, however, had more tricks to play and *Minion* was forced back to shelter near Vigo, from where she finally got underway on 20 January to anchor in Mounts Bay four days later.

The casualty list was lengthy. The battle at San Juan de Ulua had claimed 130 English dead with fifty-two more taken prisoner, while to the ninety landed at Tampico had to be added a further forty-five who died during *Minion*'s voyage home. Few survived to totter ashore at Plymouth, ridge-ribbed and ragged. The two leaders applied both for restitution of goods and the repatriation of prisoners. Eventually some of the latter came home with great tales to tell, but of the former there was to be no redress, principally because the queen refused the issue of a letter of reprisal. She had her reasons. For once Elizabeth must have realised that she had allowed her ruffians to sail in her ships far too close to the wind which was by now chilling rapidly in wintry and warlike blasts from Spain

Hawkins's and Drake's reactions to the defeat and humiliation at San Juan de Ulua were very different. The elder man withdrew from an active career at sea to turn his fertile mind to management, including that of his own pirate vessels. In 1575 he proposed that, for an investment of £3,750, he be allowed to take three royal ships, *Dreadnought*, *Foresight* and *Bull*, and five merchant ships to intercept the Spanish treasure fleet, which if successful would produce, he claimed, a profit of £2 million. The plan was not approved but neither, more significantly, did Hawkins endeavour to lead an expedition for this purpose himself. Instead, he chose to employ his busy mind with internal quarrels, deliberately picking a fight with the Wynter brothers on the Navy Board by claiming malfeasance and his own ability to provide a more cost-effective, honest system of management. By 1578, with the support of Cecil, now Lord Burghley, Hawkins was Treasurer of the Navy.

Drake, his eager apprentice, sought a more confrontational role to gain his revenge. He would never more sail on a trading voyage, exchanging culverin for coin as his means of barter. Appropriately for one whose exploits would earn for him the nickname from the Spanish of *El Draque*, the dragon, Drake sailed again for the Indies in 1570 onboard *Dragon* with *Swan* in company. Little is known of this voyage, but when he returned to those waters the following year in *Swan* it was to 'rob divers barks' of goods to the value of at least £66,000, almost £40,000 more than the inflated claim made by John Hawkins for his losses at San Juan de Ulua. Drake had simply committed several acts of piracy, as the Panamanian authorities recognised when they wrote to King Philip informing him that they had:

> Sent out three expeditions on which were expended more than 4,000 pesos; and he has always had the luck to escape. Once the fleet is gone, when the town and the port are deserted, it is plain we are going to suffer from this corsair and others,

unless Your Majesty apply the remedy hoped for, by sending a couple of galleys to protect and defend this coast and the town, which is in the greatest danger.[8]

However, in the early 1570s the expatriate population on the Isthmus feared the violent deprivations of the permanently present *cimaroons*, escaped slaves, more than they did the occasional visit by a rover. Drake's genius was to befriend the black rebels and work with them to attack their common foe for mutual advantage. Oxenham, endeavouring to repeat Drake's success in 1576, failed and was captured and executed, largely because he upset these erstwhile allies. He also failed because Drake's visit a few months earlier had alerted the authorities, who were ready to respond to the next assault on their trading routes. Drake himself was wise enough to avoid returning to the scenes of his earlier successes.

Drake was a great believer in seizing the moment and in the next few years the time was ripe for West-Country adventurers to enrich themselves while the queen, her council and Admiralty Court were focused on events at the other end of the Channel. These were years of moment affecting the whole of Europe as the struggle for control over the Netherlands between the Spanish occupiers and their rebellious subjects became more bloody and more expensive. It was the behaviour of pirates in the waters between Dover and Flanders that was exercising the English councillors, foreign ambassadors and the unfortunate merchants and ship owners who were struggling both to transport their cargoes unmolested and to be compensated for those goods that were being seized on a regular basis. Activities in the West Indies lay far beyond the horizon of these protagonists.

One Sunday in August 1573 the church bells of Plymouth pealed to welcome Drake home from a voyage in which he had ambushed a mule train loaded with silver bars, thrown off his pursuers and re-embarked with another fortune in his hold, but one bought at the cost of the loss of over half his crew, including two of his brothers. They would not be the last of that family to lose their lives or liberty on these ventures until Drake himself was 'slung between the round shot in Nombre Dios Bay.' For the moment, to avoid over-much embarrassment through the lionising of her rover, the queen was content to see Drake dispatched as the naval adviser to the earl of Essex who was trying to pacify Ireland; it also gave the council a chance to see whether he could be entrusted with the less rewarding role of loyal service to the Crown. He succeeded but his Iberian infamy remained: in1575 Philip sent Elizabeth a list of those Englishmen whom he considered to be no more than pirates – it included Sir William Wynter, a member of the Navy Board, the Drakes and the Hawkins brothers. There is no evidence to indicate that Philip was mistaken. A few years later and he might have added another name to the list.

In contrast to Francis Drake, whose family background is always shown to be modest, Walter Ralegh's father was a country gentlemen moving in the sort of society about which Jane Austen would later write. But he was a pirate. A case brought before the Admiralty Court in 1557 is worth some examination for it is an example of the way such gentlemen pirates behaved prior to the targeting of the treasure fleets. The petition was brought by Portuguese merchants whose ship, *Conception of Vienna*, was seized off the Scillies on 26 August while on passage between Ireland and Portugal. Her attackers arrived in two vessels, *Nicholas of Kenton*, commanded by John Ralegh, and *Katheryne Ralegh*, whose captain was his brother George, both sons of Walter Ralegh senior. The Portingale did not surrender easily, struggling to escape all day while receiving 'divers pieces of ordnance'. In the late afternoon she was boarded by fifteen sword-waving sailors, who forced the crew below decks and kept them battened down for nine days until the ship was driven into Cork by a gale. Here the captives were set ashore while *Conception* was sailed back to Cornwall, where the crew were challenged as to her identity, once by the master of another merchant ship and once by the captain of the naval vessel *Anne Gallant*. Unhelpful questions ceased, in the first instance with a bribe of one bale of cloth, in the second instance with a bribe of two bales of cloth. Warned by his men of the interest in the prize, Walter Ralegh told her crew to describe her as French and ordered her to be brought to Exmouth where, it being his home port, questions would not be asked. Once more the wind intervened and *Conception* was blown into Looe, where she was seized by the Admiralty agent and her crew brought in for questioning. Faced with this difficulty, Walter Ralegh wrote to the Lord Admiral, offering him a bribe of £100 to help resolve matters in the Raleghs' favour. This ploy having failed to prevent George's arrest, Walter Ralegh put up 500 marks to get his son released on bail, being quite happy, so it seems, to forfeit this amount when the miscreant failed to keep his appointment in court.

While all this intrigue was afoot, the Portuguese merchants remained without either their ship or their goods. Their plea to the court deserves quoting at length for it sums up the frustrations that so many felt about following the due process to no avail. They wrote:

> And as against the said Walter Ralegh your said orators have no remedy or action by the civil law for the recovery of their ship and goods as they be informed by their learned council . . . and thus . . . piteously spoiled and robbed of their said ship and goods and not able by the ordinary course of law to recover the same being themselves but strangers and poor men without friendship and the said Walter Ralegh being a man of worship of great power and friendship in this country. In consideration whereof may it please your honours that the same Walter Ralegh may be constrained without further suit in law which your orators be not able for lack of money to follow either to bring the said John and George Ralegh his sons to have justice and execution of the law or himself to satisfy and recompense your said orators for their ship and goods.[9]

Summed up in heartfelt plea is the essential element that enabled piracy to thrive during Elizabeth's reign, principally, that rank had more sway than right, so that the poor man, especially if he was foreign, could follow the law to the letter and yet be denied recompense.

With a father and brothers like that, the boyhood of Ralegh was not spent sitting on the sands at Budleigh Salterton listening to tales of the great blue yonder spun by some hairy old salt, but just waiting to join in the looting of passing trade. His first chance so to do came when his eccentric elder half-brother Humphrey Gilbert offered him a command on his ill-planned transatlantic expedition of 1578. And not only any command, but that of the queen's ship, the 100-ton *Falcon*.

Gilbert, after much persistence, written and personal, had finally in June 1578 been issued with letters patent authorising him to seek out new lands in America. To assist him he assembled a bunch of pirates whose primary interest was loot, not lengthy voyages. They achieved neither, for having sailed from Dartmouth on 26 September 1578, the fleet, with the exception of *Falcon*, was back in that harbour, voyage abandoned, by 21 November.

Ralegh remained at sea, not to continue westward, but to attempt the taking of prizes in the Bay of Biscay. In this he was not successful, challenging superior forces and receiving a pasting which killed several of his crew and badly damaged the queen's ship. It was a sobering experience. Thereafter Ralegh was inclined to send others to sea on his behalf. Even when he became heir to Gilbert's charter, he sent others to America rather than sail himself. What he did do was to win sufficient royal favour to invest heavily in creating his own pirate fleet. By the time Gilbert was ready for a second attempt on America in 1583, Ralegh was in the position to lend him the modern equivalent of a quarter of a million pounds and his ship, the modestly named 200-ton *Bark Ralegh*. The ship returned safely, having abandoned the ill-fated voyage while still in European waters, so that it was only Ralegh's investment that went west. A year later Ralegh was organising his own western voyages and appointing a fellow pirate, Richard Grenville, in command of the expedition to land settlers at Roanoke in 1585. Being a pirate, Grenville made the most of his opportunity by seizing a rich prize when homeward-bound.

George Clifford, 3rd earl of Cumberland, was the most senior and least successful of the piratocracy, being the only one who, in his own words, threw his land into the sea. However, it was his primrose path to poverty that led him down to the water's edge and to seek salvation over the horizon. Along the way, a weakness for women, an inability to gamble well, either at cards or on horses, and a desire for finery saw him fling his fortune in all directions other than into his own pockets. His genial character and manly skills made him several times the queen's champion at the joust, and Elizabeth took pleasure in his performance without making him a favourite, thus rewarding without enriching or clipping his wings. Needing to settle his debts, for he was an honourable man, Cumberland saw a fortune awaiting him in the hulls of foreign ships and towards them he, or his ships, set sail on numerous occasions. He had no time for, nor did his exalted position allow, an apprenticeship: he trained on the job and it showed.

Cumberland's first voyage, as Purchas refers to it, sailed without the earl being onboard. Instead, he raised the money to dispatch four ships with plans for them to pass the Straits of Magellan and enter the South Seas. The admiral, commanded by Captain Robert Widrington, was *Red Dragon*, a 260-ton ship with a crew of 130. She left Gravesend on 26 June 1586 in company with the bark *Clifford* of 130 tons, with Captain Christopher Lister as vice admiral. During a wind-dictated lengthy stay at Plymouth they were joined by Captain Haws in *Roe* and a 'fine' small pinnace, *Dorothy*, owned, as might have been *Roe*, by Walter Ralegh. It seemed a fleet ideal to make passage to and cause havoc in the Spanish Pacific. Cumberland had high hopes, telling his admiral not to return home until they had £6,000 of profitable loot to unload.

The fighting, but not the fortune-making, began early. Three days after leaving Plymouth on 17 August, the group engaged sixteen hulks from Hamburg which were sailing home from Lisbon and did not wish to tarry for these pesky Englishmen. Selecting a foe, 'Our admiral lent him a piece of ordnance which they repaid double so that we grew to some quarrel', which the English won by boarding, only to have the time just to 'take out of her some provisions', before rumour of greater reward led to them endeavouring to intercept another convoy of seven ships. In this they were unsuccessful, as strong winds blew them back to Dartmouth for an enforced week's break. After this they made passage to the Canaries, before landing in Sierra Leone where they had a St George and the Dragon like fight with a crocodile and a less noble pillage of a native village. Then across the ocean to Brazil where they irritated a couple of townships and captured several ships loaded with appetising, but not enriching, marmalade. Their best prize 'took fire and perished, ship, men and goods'. During this sojourn on the coast they held a major conference at which it was decided not to push southwards to the Straits of Magellan. By 29 September they were back alongside in England, giving Cumberland no reasonable return on his investment, a template for most of his subsequent efforts.

Cumberland got to sea himself the following year, when he sailed to support the English forces besieged in Sluys, only to find that he had arrived too late. Moving on to Ostend and finding that it too was soon to be besieged, he returned home in time to offer himself and *Red Dragon*, renamed *Sampson*, for service against the Armada, while he sailed in *Elizabeth Bonaventure* as her volunteer commander.[10] In return for his contribution to that campaign, the queen loaned Cumberland *Golden Lion* for a piratical voyage in which he seized the slow *Hare* heading from Dunkirk for Spain, but was then himself driven to take shelter in Freshwater Bay off the Isle of Wight. Here, with the winds threatening to drive the ship aground, the master recommended that the mainmast be cast away but, being the queen's property, 'no sailor durst attempt this until his Lordship had himself stricken the first stroke.' Safe but no longer sailable, *Golden Lion* limped into Portsmouth, bringing another unrewarding voyage to an end. But before that storm Cumberland had been in high spirits, writing to his wife in that spirit of optimism that endeared him not only to his queen and peers, but to subsequent generations.

> Sweet Meg,
> God, I must humbly thank him, hath so mightily bless me, that already I have taken a Dunkirk ship bound for Saint Lucar in Spain. I have sent Lister to see her unladen in Portsmouth, and to send all that is mine to you, which I would have you use according to your discretion, and let it be opened with secrecy. If there be anything fit to give to my Lord Chamberlain, I would have you do it, it will make him the reedier to do for me, if there be a cause. This man I have taken tells me that there are four ships now ready in Dunkirk, going for Spain. I hope within these three days to meet them, if I do, I shall make a good voyage, for all the ordnance of the galleys and rich lading. Commend me to my Lord of Warwick and my lady. Excuse me for not writing to them but I have scanty leisure to write to you.
> Thus with God's blessing to our little ones, and hearty prayers for their well being, I commit you all to God.
> Yours only now and ever,
> George Cumberland

That one prize scarcely earned Cumberland the praise granted to him in a letter to Essex in June 1588, in which the writer refers to Cumberland as 'the English Lord that doth great harm to the Spanish at sea', but it might have been the source of the 'jewel of gold like a sacrifice' and the 'pair of bracelets' which he and his wife presented to the queen on the following New Year's Day. That aside, those voyages, along with his contribution against the Armada, equipped Cumberland, or so he believed, with the necessary experience to expand his horizons and ambitions: in 1589 he was to make his first voyage to the Azores hunting ground.

Nine years earlier, while Gilbert and Ralegh were floundering in the western Atlantic; while John Hawkins was beginning his reforms as the new Treasurer of the Navy; while Frobisher was experiencing failure in the frozen north; while the teenage, newly-married Cumberland was establishing himself in his northern estates, plain Francis Drake was engaged in the voyage that would forever change English aspirations on the rewards for roving. Before he could do this, however, he had to make sure that he had a ship that would suit his purposes, and by this time his career had advanced sufficiently for him to be able to build bespoke.

CHAPTER 3

Pirate Ships of War at Sea

Were I to choose a ship for myself, I would have her sail well, yet
strongly built, her decks flush and flat, and so roomy that men might
pass with ease; her bow and chase so galley like contrived, should bear
as many ordnance as with convenience she could, for that always cometh
most to fight, and so stiff, she should bear a stiff sail, and bear out her
lower tier of guns in any reasonable weather.

Captain John Smith, *A Sea Grammar*

Visit any seaside resort in England and there will be an opportunity for the young,
and the not so young, to dress up and participate in piratical re-enactments or visit
pirate ships and grottos. Supreme amongst these, and host to hundreds of school
parties, are the replicas of *Golden Hind* in both London and Brixham. Across the
Atlantic youthful imaginations can be similarly stimulated by walking the boards
of *Elizabeth* at Roanoke in North Carolina, a replica of a ship that sailed with the
pirate Richard Grenville when he tried to establish a pirate base on that island in
1581. Further up the coast, at Jamestown, Virginia, are tied up replicas of *Susan
Constant*, *Godspeed*, and *Discovery*, the ships which brought the first permanent
English settlers to Virginia and, although these were not pirate vessels, their
commander Christopher Newport was an ex-pirate and a very successful one at
that. The replica Pilgrim Fathers' *Mayflower*, secured at Plymouth, Massachusetts,
represents well the vessels of the English merchant fleet that were subject to piracy
and, although she herself avoided such trouble, the Pilgrims suffered a major
setback when their resupply vessel, *Fortune*, was taken by pirates on her voyage
home, as was another of their ships, *Little James*, while heading for England richly
laden with beaver-pelts.

Back in England the remarkable original timbers and artefacts of *Mary Rose*,
preserved and displayed in Portsmouth Historic Dockyard, give a wonderful feel
for what a medium-sized royal vessel was like and, although she was built in 1509
and sank in 1545, her shape, structure and, most certainly, many of the weapons and
objects recovered, would have been similar to those aboard pirate vessels of
Elizabeth's time. Nothing, no lesson, however well-delivered, no book, however

well-written, no film, however vivid, captures as well what life was like onboard a small ship of the late sixteenth century as these original or reconstructed vessels. This century's generations are indebted to those who built them, for without them we would have a very limited idea of what such ships looked like, because although many travelled by sea in the sixteenth century, few described the ship beneath their feet. This is not so surprising for such ships were commonplace; in centuries to come few will be able to visualise an airliner from reading the works of travel writers. However, as with airline flights, comments were recorded when things went wrong: in the case of Richard Hawkins's voyage to the Pacific in *Dainty*, plenty did, which he duly noted, and for which honesty subsequent generations must be duly grateful.[1]

Elizabethan England possessed four growing seagoing fleets. Smallest in size but not in number were her fishing boats, which were undertaking longer and longer voyages, as far as the kingdom of cod that was the Newfoundland Banks. Her merchant vessels, once the despair of their sovereign because of their unwillingness to venture much beyond Flanders with wool, and Gascony, for wine, gradually felt their way into the Mediterranean, seeking out more exotic cargoes. Merchant enterprise was also responsible for establishing the famous but forlorn English voyages into the northern ice where they fumbled, failing to find an eastward or westward passage to Cathay, until by the very end of the sixteenth century such endeavours were superseded by the establishment of the East India Company, whose vessels plied the longer route to the east via the Cape of Good Hope. The third fleet was the Navy Royal, which had been revived by Henry VII and grown large during the reign of his son, only to shrink thereafter, before the threat from Spain forced Elizabeth to restore its fortunes with her own. The fourth arm was the pirate fleet, which ranged from a single small vessel manned by a few men and their dog to squadrons of well-armed ships capable of taking several hundred men to sea. Their appearance marked the return of the privately-owned warship, which had all but disappeared between 1485 and 1543, and meant that the policy of state piracy could be practised with success.

These fleets were not mutually exclusive and although the fishing boats of all nations offered easy pickings to predators as diverse as Barbary pirates and England's own Peter Easton and Henry Mainwaring, their skippers were not themselves averse to robbing from weaker foreign hulls. Neither, of course, were the merchants who became better armed the further they ventured, for as they traded to more distant ports they became open to attack, not only from the Dunkirkers on their doorstep, but also from the Barbary galleys that lay in wait off the Straits of Gibraltar, and their Turkish cousins who infested the eastern Mediterranean. To counter this they required to be well-armed and once so equipped could yield easily to the temptation to plunder a passing weaker seafarer. The result was a private arms race leading to many a merchant ship becoming as well-armed as most state warships.

The added armament of a letter of reprisal could provide justification for a most lucrative sideline, especially when the arrangements and understanding with the nation's legal authorities almost guaranteed no awkward questions being asked and no restitutions being awarded. As far as her own fleet was concerned, Elizabeth was always looking for ways for reducing the costs of its manning and upkeep, unlike her father, Henry VIII, for whom the waging of war was so glorious an enterprise that it justified any expenditure so long as it bought honour. For Elizabeth, conflict, if it had to be undertaken, needed to be prosecuted at least cost to the Crown. This parsimony created a permeable membrane between the Navy Royal and the merchant and pirate fleet, so that in times of national crisis, most notably the Armada campaign, the sovereign could call on the latter to supplement her own ships, while in times of quiet the queen was content to loan her ships for pirateering operations, such as Drake's West Indies raid, or explorative/settlement ventures such as Frobisher's search for the northwest passage and Grenville's voyage to Roanoke – provided, of course, that she had the promise of a profit from these ventures.

Many ships were thus given over to piracy at some time in their career, but a fair few were built specifically for this purpose. Of these, Drake's *Golden Hind* was the most notorious, illustrious and successful, Richard Hawkins's *Dainty* the least successful and most mismanaged; while Cumberland's *Scourge of Malice* was the one that made the successful transit from the age of piracy to the age of trade. Hakluyt's account of the tribulations endured by a fourth vessel, *Desire*, which having been Cavendish's flagship during his successful circumnavigation also accompanied him on his disastrous second attempt, provided a very clear account of the far horizons of endurance to which both ships and their seamen could be driven when things went wrong.[2]

The *Golden Hind*

In 1573 Drake climbed up a tree at the invitation of a *cimaroon*, or escaped slave, named Pedro, and gazed upon the Pacific. Well-informed navigator that he was, he knew that nothing lay between the blue horizon to his west and the distant, fabulously wealthy Spice Islands or, to the northwest, the equally rich and distant shores of Cathay. Well-practised pirate that he was, he knew that close inshore a third fabulously rich treasure trove beckoned in the form of deep-draughted, poorly armed and unescorted merchant ships trekking towards Panama with cargoes of silver. All he needed to do was to sail a suitable ship on those seas to take prizes that would more than compensate for the losses, in ships, men, cargo and self-esteem, that he and his cousin John Hawkins had suffered in 1568 at San Juan de Ulua.

Drake and his partner John Oxenham returned to Plymouth in August 1573, rich beyond their expectations, but with the knowledge that further wealth lay ready for the taking. Oxenham, too impetuous to seek a suitable vessel for the proposed voyage, sailed to the Caribbean, crossed over the isthmus and seized a small ship on the further shore. He was soon caught, imprisoned and eventually killed. Drake, a better brain, took his time, drawing up plans for the sort of vessel he would need to sail the long route from England to the Pacific hunting ground via the seldom visited, but notorious, dangerous waters of the Straits of Magellan. He also spent time learning about the great ocean on which he planned to rove and built up a library of navigational works to improve his ability to sail out of sight of land on seas upon which no Englishman had ever floated.

For the voyage which would make his name, Drake needed a ship which, requiring few to man her, could nonetheless sail fast enough to overhaul her potential prey. Yet she needed to be deep-draughted and beamy so that she could hold both sufficient stores and a great deal of booty. Weaponry sufficient to awe she needed, but not of such power that they might sink a potential prize. Drake named his ship *Pelican*, which might have been an appropriate name for a ship designed to swallow up a large haul of plunder, yet she proved so capable of managing her incredible task that she fully deserved her name-change to the sleeker *Golden Hind* (*Golden Fleece* might have been even more appropriate!).

No plans of the ship survive, if any ever existed, for this was an age where the shipwright's practised eye was the equal of the draughtsman's sharpened pen. The few drawings that purport to show her are neither detailed nor accurate, but luckily we have a short description of her which was written by a Portuguese pilot, Nuña da Silva, whom Drake captured off the Cape Verde Islands in January 1578 and found so professionally useful that he did not release him until he was departing from Guatulco on the Pacific coast of New Spain in April 1579. *Golden Hind*, da Silva wrote, was:

> in a great measure stout and strong. She has two sheathings, one as perfectly finished as the other. She is fit for warfare and is a ship of the French pattern, well fitted out and finished with a good mast, tackle and double sails. She is a good sailer and the rudder governs her well. She is not new, nor is she coppered nor ballasted. She has seven armed port-holes on each side, and inside she carries eighteen pieces of artillery, thirteen being of bronze and the rest of cast iron*
> . . . This vessel is waterfast when she is navigated with the wind astern and this is not violent, but when the sea is high, as she has to labour, she leaks not a little whether sailing before the wind or with the bowlines hauled out. Taking it all in all, she is a ship which is in a fit condition to make a couple of voyages from Portugal to Brazil.[3]

It might be a brief description – certainly with that information alone it would not be possible to make a drawing, let alone a reconstruction of the vessel, but fortunately sufficient contemporary sketches of sailing ships and shipwrights'

---

* Another Spanish prisoner records fifteen pieces of artillery onboard.

instructions as how to build one complete with the beam:keel:draught:tonnage ratios exist, along with details of the relevant mast size, sail fit, anchors and cables required, for the present generation to visualise these state-of-the art creations.

Her dimensions can be estimated from those of the dry dock that was built to preserve her on public display at Deptford. These suggest that England's first preserved historic ship had a length of 67ft, a beam of 19ft and a draught of around 9ft, making her about a 120-ton ship.[4] She carried three masts and a bowsprit supporting six sails with a sail area of just over 4,000sq ft, meaning that in favourable conditions she could maintain a speed of about 8 knots.

The exact number of men who sailed out of Plymouth in *Golden Hind* at the start of her voyage is not known, but the fleet of five ships had a combined crew of about 160. Spanish prisoners taken in the Pacific reported that *Golden Hind* had a crew of around eighty to eighty-six, while according to John Drake's evidence she sailed from the Moluccas with sixty men onboard, arriving off the Cape of Good Hope with fifty-nine.[5]

Although da Silva provided no visual image of his floating prison, his comments do give us some insights into the practical aspects of managing such a ship on a long voyage. He notes, for example, that she was well-sheathed, having a sacrificial outer hull as well-fitted as her inner one. The outer one acted as the larder for hungry tropical wood-boring molluscs whose hidden voraciousness could reduce hull timbers to dangerously feeble, riddled weakness. To further protect the hull, a coating of tar and horsehair was used both as a sandwich between the hulls and as a coating for the outer one. Well aware of the risk, Drake stopped several times to careen his ship, scrape off weed, examine her timbers, replace decaying ones and to recoat the hull. This not only protected her against worm, it also kept her robust. Nowhere was his diligence better rewarded than when *Golden Hind* went firmly aground in the Spice Islands.

As they realised that their ship was firmly stuck on a reef, John Fletcher, the priest, got down on his knees, while Drake the professional took more direct action:

> Showing us the way by his own example, first of all the pump was well plied, and the ship freed of water. We found her leaks to be nothing increased. Though it gave us no hope of deliverance, yet it gave us some hope of respite, as it assured us that the hulk was sound [wrote Fletcher, continuing] Which truly we acknowledged to be an immediate providence of God alone, as no strength of wood and iron could possibly have borne so hard and violent a shock as our ship did, dashing herself under full sail against the rocks, except the extraordinary hand of God had supported the same.

In fact, it was the extraordinary day-to-day ship husbandry of Drake that enabled the ship to withstand the shock. Assured of the watertight integrity of the vessel, the captain then set about lightening her by – a hard decision this – throwing overboard 5 tons of spices, which was half of his cargo, and up to eight pieces of ordnance. He would also have lowered his boats and transferred to them any heavy movable items, including some of the crew. After twenty hours aground, a combination of a rising tide and a change in wind direction and speed slid the hull back into deeper water. From then on the voyage continued with little incident, with *Golden Hind* arriving back in Plymouth still in a most seaworthy condition. Yet her seagoing days were over. Taken round to the Thames, she was visited by the queen who, having knighted Drake on her decks, ordered his ship to be preserved for posterity in a dry-dock created specifically for this purpose.

Golden Hind might not have sailed again but her exploits soon encouraged a repeat performance.

The Failure of *Desire*

At 120 tons *Desire*, as well as being much the same size as *Golden Hind*, was built for much the same reason, being ordered by the young Thomas Cavendish specifically to mount an expedition to capture treasure on the Pacific coast of South America. Cavendish sailed from Plymouth in July 1586 in company with the 60-ton *Content* and the 40-ton bark *Hugh Gallant*.[6] With just 123 men embarked, he needed to conserve his crew and was lucky not to lose more than he did following attacks on his shore-parties in both the Canaries and Brazil.

He needed to conserve his ships well, so carried out his first careening in mid December, taking advantage of a good tidal range off Brazil that also produced an abundance of fresh meat in the shape of sea lions. Their passage through the Straits of Magellan was plain sailing and they were able to record that 'in this place we watered and wooded well and quietly.'

Watering continued but not quietly. As they passed up the South American coast, pillaging and burning as they went, they came across larger and better defended settlements. In fighting for the possession of these they were to lose a number of men so that by early June they had to sink *Hugh Gallant* 'for want of men'.

Success came to the remaining two ships when the 700-ton carrack *Santa Anna* was sighted making her Pacific landfall off California. She put up a brave fight, only surrendering when she came in danger of sinking. The wealth unladen from the vessel (and over 500 tons of cargo was not transhipped for lack of space) almost upset the voyage, for the men squabbled over their shares and those onboard the inaptly named *Content* decided to part company and return home via the Straits of Magellan. They were never heard of again. Cavendish, however, navigated *Desire* successfully through the Asian island chains and made a swift and safe passage homeward, just having a storm blow out his sails a few miles short of Plymouth, where he arrived in early September 1588, his arrival by good chance timed so as to avoid falling in with the ships of the Armada.

Desire had proved to be stoutly built, but vessels needed to be as robustly commanded if they were to make successful voyages to the Pacific plunder grounds, as can be shown by the fate of Cavendish's second, and unsuccessful, repeat voyage which began at Plymouth on 26 August 1591. On this occasion *Desire* was commanded by John Davis, while Cavendish sailed in *Galleon Leicester*, with Captain Cocke in *Roebuck*, and two barks keeping company.[7]

Things fell apart from the moment that they arrived in Brazil, giving such forewarning of their intentions at Santos that 'in three days the town that was able to furnish such another fleet with all kinds of necessaries, was left unto us nakedly bare, without people and provisions', so that they sailed 'worse furnished from the town than when we went in.'

A great storm then ensued, scattering the fleet and drawing the laconic remark from the diarist, John Jane, 'that our captain could never get any direction what course to take in such extremities, though many times he had entreated for it.'

Worse was to follow when, snowstorm-bound and ill-victualled in the Magellan Straits, 'all the sick men in *Galleon* were most uncharitably put ashore in the snow, rain and cold, when men of good health could scarcely endure it, where they ended their lives in the highest degree of misery.' The rest survived on mussels, water and seaweed. It could not last. The captains conferred and the men were consulted. Although there were many who wished to continue, Captain Davis was not among them, reporting that *Desire* had 'no more sails than masts, no victual, no ground-tackling, no cordage more than is over head, and among seventy and five persons, there is but the master alone that can order the ship and but fourteen sailors.' They turned back into a ferocious gale, the mariners dying from want while their once gallant ship was also failing as fast. The account records that on 16 May:

> We had a violent storm [in which] perished our main trestle-trees, so that we could no more use our main top-sail, lying most dangerously in the sea. The pinnace likewise received a great leak . . . the 26th our fore-shrouds broke, so that if we had not been near the shore, it had been impossible for us to get out of the sea.

Desire found shelter at Port Desire, named after her on the first voyage, where her crew found that 'our shrouds are all rotten, not having a running rope whereto we may trust, sails all worn, our top-sails not able to abide any stress of weather, neither have we pitch, tar, or nails, nor any store for the supplying of these wants; and we live only on seals and mussels, having but five hogsheads of pork within board, and meal three ounces for a man a day.' There were also large shoals of smelt that could be hooked with a bent pin. Their troubles were far from over, for the suggestion by Captain Davis that he should leave the majority onboard, while he took a trusted few in the pinnace to search for help, almost caused a mutiny with murder in mind. Luckily, the plan was revealed and the ringleaders handled with clemency by the captain. Nevertheless, the crew drafted an account of their circumstances which remains one of the most harrowing tales of the tribulations of ill-victualled mariners.[8]

They were, to all intense and purposes, shipwrecked, but having sunk in despair they resurfaced to repair. A forge was created to make nails, bolts and spikes. A cable was converted into rope for the rigging and, having carried out essential maintenance, they weighed anchor to sail forth towards the Straits and through them into the South Sea. Here they met with storms which kept driving them back to the Straits because they did not dare subject their sails to any stress. Even in comparative shelter their trials were not over, for one of their cables parted causing them to fear being driven aground. The wind died just in time.

Now, 'we unreeved our sheets, tacks, halyards, and other ropes, and moored our ship to the trees close by the rocks.' Unable to recover their lost anchor they found the remaining one had just one fluke, and was secured by a piece of old cable spliced in two places. When the next wind arose they towed themselves out to sea by means of their repaired boat. The anchor came home held by just a solitary strand.

Back at sea they found the weather unimproved, while the precarious state of their rigging limited their options. Their pinnace, under tow, suddenly reared up and drove herself into the ship's side; by morning she had disappeared. Onboard *Desire*, the night's gale split both the foremast and its sail so that the mizzen had to be shifted to serve in its place. Now, every time the ship encountered rough weather a body blow was dealt her; like a boxer weakened by too many rounds, she was inexorably being driven onto her watery canvas. Except, and this speaks volumes for English shipbuilding, she appears to have remained both watertight and upright, so that it would seem to be the precarious state of her masts, rigging and anchors that would decide her fate.

That 'ruinous end' almost came in mid October when, forced once more under bare poles back towards the Straits, they feared that they would be driven ashore before rounding the entrance for 'our sails had not been half an hour aboard but the footrope of our foresail broke, so that nothing held but the eyelet holes'. The seas continually broke over the ship's poop, and flew into the sails with such violence that 'we still expected the tearing of the sails, or oversetting of the ship.' A wrecking seemed inevitable until 'our master veered some of the main sheet; and whether it was by that occasion, or by some current, or by the wonderful power of God, as we verily think it was, the ship quickened her way, and shot past that rock where we think we would have shored.'

If there is a reverse analogy to a cork shooting out of a bottle, this is how *Desire* then entered the Straits for 'we were shot in between the high lands without any inch of sail, we spooned before the sea, three men not able to guide the helm.' Six hours later they anchored and pumped the ship dry then, probably, slept, as best might exhausted men being eaten alive by clusters of lice as big as peas.*

By now, all hope of making the voyage was gone and they returned to the Atlantic and their anchorage at Port Desire, where they ran the ship up on the ooze and secured her firmly with a number of lines. There they had foraged for copious amounts of the aptly-named scurvy grass, which they fried together with penguin

---

* Similar suffering was endured by the crew of the Bristol pirate ship *Delight* whose crew wrote a petition outlining why they had behaved mutinously in the Straits in February 1589.

eggs and fish oil. Without their knowing why, this diet cured them all of the typical swellings and bleedings associated with scurvy. They also took onboard 14,000 dried penguins to supplement their victuals for the estimated six-month voyage home. For this journey, the ration per man was reduced to two ounces and a half of meal twice a week, three spoons of oil three times a week, a pint of peas between four men twice a week, and every day five penguins for four men and six quarts of water per day to be shared by the same four men, thus indicating the importance of the system whereby a small number of men formed their own mess.

Of all the provisions, water was both the most important and the most problematical. They called in at Plancentia in Brazil, their first stop on the outward voyage, not only to take fresh water onboard but, more importantly, to repair their split and leaking casks. The town had been abandoned and, while the overgrown gardens provided some fresh food, the repair of the casks was disrupted by an Indian attack in which thirteen of their number were killed and their weapons seized. They sailed with just 8 tons of water poorly stowed, only for a series of heavy showers to salve their thirst.

Relief was short-lived: in an 'Ancient Mariner'-like incident the equatorial sun caused massive 'worms' to erupt from the bodies of the dried penguins and crawl upon the weak sailors where 'they would eat our flesh, and bite like mosquitoes.' Scurvy also seemed to return with a violence, so that 'they could not draw their breath', while their joints, limbs, breasts and 'cods' all swelled hugely and 'divers grew raging mad, and some died in most loathsome and furious pain.' By the time the ship was able to turn towards the British Isles, just sixteen of her original complement of seventy-six remained alive, of whom just five were capable of working the ship.

They flopped homeward, unable to set a sail, hardly able to handle the sheets, tackle or capstan, and with the captain and master taking watch about on the helm. 'Thus as lost wanderers upon the sea', they drifted into Bearhaven in Ireland on 11 June 1593, where the locals insisted on being paid £10 up front, before agreeing to help secure the vessel whose sorry condition belied the fact that she had withstood an assault on her timbers that would have sunk many larger ships.

Galleon Leicester, Cavendish's flagship, also arrived safe home, but without her commander. Somewhere in mid Atlantic the disillusioned and half-mad leader of the failed expedition lost his will to live and was buried at sea.

Dainty

Information about the tragic happenings on Cavendish's final voyage did not reach England until after Richard Hawkins sailed from the Thames in April 1593 on his own gloriously mismanaged voyage to the South Seas in *Dainty*. The ship had been built at the end of 1588, to voyage, so Hawkins claimed, to Japan, the Philippines and Moluccas by way of the Straits of Magellan, and to make a 'perfect discovery' of those parts and to establish 'the commodities which the countries yielded, and of which they have want', which is as disingenuous a description of piracy as wielded by any pen. *Dainty* was originally named *Repentance* by Hawkins's puritanical stepmother, until Elizabeth sighted her and ordered a name change. She was larger than *Golden Hind*, being of some 350 tons, but she had those same essential attributes, being 'profitable for stowage, good of sail, and well conditioned.'

All of these attributes she seemed to have demonstrated in her brief pirateering career before she sailed for the Pacific in 1593. She was part of the pack that captured the great and richly cargoed Portuguese carrack, *Madre de Dios*, in 1592 and was one of Frobisher's squadron that seized a 600-ton Biscayan laden with iron that same year. Nevertheless, the elder Hawkins considered that she 'never brought but cost, trouble and care', and he had little hesitation in selling her to his son for he was, above all else, a businessman. The younger Hawkins wasted little time in readying her for the voyage for which she was built.

The account of *Dainty*'s Pacific voyage was written wonderfully well in *The Observations of Sir Richard Hawkins*, who proved to be a better raconteur than rover, ultimately losing his ship in a fight with the Spanish. Yet the whole voyage lurched towards this final ignominy with Hawkins always learning lessons after the event, while refreshingly admitting his own culpability in most of the incidents that occurred.

It began on day one, 8 April 1593, when Hawkins saw *Dainty* off from Blackwall, determined to join her himself that night at Gravesend. However, seeing the ship anchored at Barking he rowed out and clambered onboard to be greeted with a tale of near woe. *Dainty* had sailed with her gunports open and they, because the vessel was deeply laden, lay perilously close to the waterline. A sudden fresh wind had caused the ship to heel and water to rush in at the open ports pulling the vessel over. Luckily, once this was noted and the 'sheet flowne, she could hardly be brought upright.' Danger described, Hawkins recommended that ports be shut and caulked, although the example he quotes in evidence is the loss of *Great Harry* at Portsmouth in 1545 not, as it in fact and famously was, *Mary Rose*. It had been a close thing and Hawkins's crew insisted that the ship be lightened before she proceeded into the Channel, so some 6 or 8 tons were duly offloaded into a hoy hired for the purpose.

The passage down-channel was a drearisome one against contrary winds, with *Dainty* having to anchor on the flood tide before weighing to gain westings on the ebb. The ship then ran into fog so dense that for three days they had no sight of land and had to feel their way gingerly down the coast, until a bark from Dartmouth informed them they were not far off the Eddystone, while they thought they were off Exmouth. Cue for another lesson from Sir Richard about navigation in mist when he states that over-shooting 'often happeneth to those that make the land in foggy weather, and use no good diligence by sound, by lying off the land, and other circumstances to search the truth, and is the cause of the loss of many a ship, and the sweet lives of multitudes of men', to which he adds a few lines later the sound advice that, 'I found by experience that one of the principal parts required in a mariner that frequenteth our coasts of England, is to cast his tides, and to know how they set from point to point, with the difference of those in the channel from those of the shore.'

No sooner safe, or so he thought, in Plymouth than fog gave way to gale. Hawkins, who was ashore at the time, found himself unable to regain his ship because of the storm and could only pray and watch as he noticed the mainmast of *Dainty* 'driving by', which must have been a startling experience. Luckily, that loss lightened the vessel and kept her off the rocks. Not so lucky was Hawkins's pinnace, *Fancy*, which was beaten upon the rocks and had to be salvaged over the next few days.

The woes of Hawkins's consort continued, for when they finally got underway from Plymouth, she signalled frantically to Hawkins that they had sprung a great leak and needed to return to the Sound. On examination it was found that the caulkers had left a great seam uncaulked, just running pitch along its length which the sea soon removed, allowing a powerful ingress. As so often in Hawkins's yarn, he no sooner suffered a setback than he quotes a similar example so as to gain the satisfaction of a woe shared. On this occasion it was *Ark Ralegh*, which on her maiden voyage was found to be leaking because a trenail hole had not had a trenail driven home. This embarrassing departure made Hawkins a keen caulker, and when the planks of his ship shrank in the tropical sun, he turned out his whole crew to recaulk all the area that they could reach, both inboard and outboard.

Such good husbandry caused another near fatal accident through fire. One day, the ship's carpenter, supported by the master and against Hawkins's better judgement, heated some caulking pitch in a pot on the galley fire. Unwatched, it bubbled up, spilled over and ignited. The carpenter fled the flames. Another, braver, man put on a double pair of gloves and grabbed the pitch pot, but was forced to drop it, overturning its contents into the fire, which now raged fiercely. Hawkins saved the ship by commanding his men to tie lines around their watch-gowns (garments he had provided them with to keep them warm at night) and to throw the coats overboard until they were soaked. A succession of soaking gowns dampened the blaze, surely a unique way to douse a fire at sea. True to form Hawkins then related that:

> With drinking of tobacco [ie, smoking] it is said that the *Roebuck* was burned at Dartmouth.
>
> The *Primrose of London* was fired with a candle at Tilbury and nothing saved but her keel.
>
> The *Jesus of Lubeck* had her gun-room set on fire with a match, and had been burned without redemption, if that my father, Sir John Hawkins, then general in her, had not commanded her sloppers [scuppers] to be stopped and the men to come to the pumps, whereof she had two, and plying them in a moment, had three or four inches of water on deck . . . which they threw upon the fire.

Along with fire, *Dainty*'s crew were also subject to another of the seamen's fears –
grounding. One day, just as he was about to conduct morning prayers, Hawkins
noticed a change in the colour of the sea, which he thought might indicate that
they were nearing shoals. Being assured by his master, officers and his own
observations that they could not be nearer than two hundred miles from land,
Hawkins continued with the service. But his suspicions were not driven away by
prayer and he ordered soundings to be taken, which showed them to be in fourteen
fathoms of water. Lookouts were quickly sent aloft and continuous soundings taken
and, in a short while, they found themselves just five leagues off the low-lying coast
of Africa. The sudden arrival of shallow water was a common experience, which
most mariners acknowledged was often due to them having no sure way to measure
longitude. Hawkins, while acknowledging this defect in navigation, blamed the,
fallacious, presence of strong but variable ocean currents, which meant that some
'coming from the Indies and looking for the Azores have sight of Spain and some
having looked out for Spain have discovered the Azores.' The suspected presence
of this fickle current was also commented on during Cumberland's return from
Puerto Rico when the narrative relates that:

> though the winde was not worthy to be called so, nor scarce by the name of a
> breath, and besides so narrow, that we stood upon a bowling, yet we were found
> in that last passed artificiall day, to have run above fiftie leagues at the least.[9]

Reading the accounts, and the fact that no such current exists, indicates that the
problem was caused by faulty positional fixing, which is unsurprising given the
inchoate state of knowledge and instrumentation available for celestial navigation.
Whatever the cause, the potential hazard of such errors was best handled by the
keeping of a good lookout which Hawkins, being Hawkins, acknowledged, but did
not enforce.

The cause of another near grounding is shocking, for had it been been common
practice it would have meant many a good ship would have found herself cast up
upon the coast. Tracking along the coast of Brazil one night, content that a steady
wind would keep the ship on track, both Hawkins and his master decided to turn
in for the night, leaving one of the master's mates at the helm. This man was also
overcome by drowsiness and allowed the ship to track more westerly towards the
shore. By one of those inexplicable moments of luck, to which many a seaman will
vouch, the writer included, the master woke with a start, realised all was not well,
went on deck, saw white water to starboard, and ordered the helm put hard over.
When soundings were taken it was discovered that the ship was in just over three
fathoms of water and had been heading directly for the shoals.

In his commentary Hawkins observed that they ordered such things better in
Spain and Portugal, where a seat was provided by the compass in which sat,
throughout the voyage, the master or one of his mates, in the role, as we would
refer to it today, of officer of the watch. Sat here, he would not only keep a check

that the ordered course was being steered, but make sure that the helmsman was 'continually excited' to keep him alert. Whether Hawkins himself adopted this precaution he does not say, but one excellent practice he did follow was to make sure every opportunity to reprovision with fresh food and water was taken. Additionally, like Drake, if a stopover was of any length, he had the ship's company exercise. He had, without realising it, solved the problem of scurvy which so ravaged the crews on most long voyages.

The inevitable grounding took place in the Straits of Magellan, while *Dainty* was being conned by some who thought they knew the waters around Tobias Cove. They did not, and steered the ship onto a rock shortly after a mighty wind blew itself out, giving her a calmer collision than might have been the case. Worryingly, it was found that she was trapped on a pinnacle amidships, so that the weight of bilge-water, both forward and aft, was in danger of weighing her down and breaking her back. Despite trying to wind her off, they had to wait until the next high tide to float clear. Months later, when she was grounded near Panama, they saw that 'a great part of her sheathing was beaten off on both sides in her bilges, and some four foot long and foot square of her false stem, adjoining the keel, rested across, like unto a hog yoke, which hindered her sailing very much.'

Another threat to ships on lengthy voyages through the tropics was an attack on their timbers by worm, *Teredo navalis*, a pest not present in colder northern waters, but a ship destroyer in warmer climes. The remedy was to provide a sacrificial sheathing, such as Nuña da Silva noted was fitted to *Golden Hind*. Indeed, the provision of such sheathing on certain ships was interpreted by spies as an indication that the English were planning voyages of plunder. Hawkins, as ever, provided his expert view, 'for the ignorant', on the dangers of worm which 'enter in no bigger than a Spanish needle, and by little and little their holes become ordinarily greater than a man's finger.' Noting that the Iberians used lead for their sheathing, he dismissed this as too costly, too heavy and too frail. He also dismissed simple double-planking as too heavy and only suitable as a delaying factor as regarded penetration. A method which he did consider efficacious was to burn the outer planks black and then apply pitch, either by itself or mixed with ground glass. Best of all, he thought, was to apply a thin outer sheathing of elm, which of itself was rot-resistant, while between this and the main planking a thick smearing of tar mixed with horsehair was applied. Although he admitted that this method was 'invented by my father', his view that 'experience has taught it to be the best and of least coat' is borne out by the fact that it remained in use until *Dolphin* completed a circumnavigation in 1769, successfully sheathed in copper.

Whether or not Hawkins and *Dainty* would have completed a successful circumnavigation will never be known, for the ship was captured by the Spanish after a lengthy fight in which, true to form, the behaviour of his crew contributed much to their defeat. Yet, in theory, Hawkins knew precisely what was needed among a company to keep a ship safe while at sea. This necessitated: having a knowledgeable captain keeping a watchful eye upon all his men and their works; a watchful pilot; a boatswain to keep the ship clean, and well-rigged and secure; and a carpenter who regularly inspected the ship's sides, pumps, masts, boats. Above all, Hawkins believed:

> Every officer, in his office, ought to be an absolute commander, yet ready in obedience and love, to sacrifice his will to his superior command. This cannot but cause unity; and unity but purchase a happy issue to dutiful travellers.

Unless, of course, they fall foul of a stronger enemy, a circumstance which ended Hawkins's voyage and which Cumberland, often frustrated by the escape of his quarry, was determined to avoid.

The *Scourge of Malice* and her Consorts

So in 1594 that most optimistic and persistent of pirates resolved, in Monson's words, 'to build a ship from the stocks that should equal the middle rank of Her Majesty's and act so noble and rare, it being a thing never undertaken before by a subject that it deserved immortal fame', comments that would have been as appropriate for the earlier *Ark Ralegh*.

Cumberland's desire was to have a ship not only capable of overwhelming the great carracks whose escape from his fleet's clutches in earlier years had so frustrated him, but also one not subject to the queen's caveats against close-quarters engagements, and one that he could crew and victual himself. The result was a four-masted vessel of some 700 tons and a set of ten sails, including topgallants and two lateen sails. Her thirty-eight guns included a number of demi-cannons, sixteen culverins, twelve demi-culverins and eight sakers, a suite that would have enabled her to batter as well as board.

Rather than confiscate her for her own use, as she had done with Ralegh's *Ark*, Elizabeth graciously agreed to be present at the launching of 'the best ship that ever before had been built by any subject', being most content that the name she gave her, *Scourge of Malice*, had an irony that would not be lost on those whom the ship was designed to plunder. In fact she plundered but little, being an unlucky vessel through most of her piratical career despite Elizabeth's early support.

On 28 March 1595 the Queen issued authority for Cumberland to victual and arm for sea the '*Malice Scourge* and such other ships and pinnaces . . . not exceeding six', although she made sure that her own coffers would benefit from the permit by stating that 'all prizes that shall be taken by you or by any person or persons appointed by you are to be brought into the most convenient haven without breaking bulk or making any distribution of shares until our further pleasure is known.'

The earl, having a close relationship with the queen by right of rank rather than, as in Ralegh's case, whim, might well have protested against the stringency of audit as outlined above, for in less than a month he had new documents which instructed him: 'to weaken the force of those who are hostilely disposed against us and to destroy the forces of the subjects of the King of Spain', for which service the earl was allowed 'the value of any prizes taken by them without account saving £10,000 on every carrack bound from Portugal to the Indies or £20,000 on any from the Indies to Portugal.'

Prior to sailing, Cumberland had gained some intelligence as to the timings of the departures of the Indies ships from Portugal, only for him to arrive at Plymouth to discover reports that Hawkins and Drake had stolen a sail on him and had captured just such a carrack, an act and a presence that had led to the cancellation of further sailings that year. Much disgruntled, Cumberland disembarked, sending his squadron on without him. Without his being present, they lacked the drive to achieve much and returned with a limited haul.

In 1596, the year of the Cadiz raid, *Scourge of Malice* appears to have been employed in a supporting and not rewarding ancillary role, being tasked with investigating shipping movements around Ireland and making a show of force off Calais, which the Spaniards had recently captured. Inactivity or absence from the centre did not appeal to Cumberland and in 1597 he offered to lead a fleet in his flagship to 'burn the Spanish Navy [or] impeach them divers ways and hinder them from going to Ireland or pursue them thither.'

Whatever the aim, the weather intervened and a few days out *Scourge* lost her mainmast and had to return to harbour. This assault by the weather should not have surprised observers of Cumberland's sea career, for he seemed to have drawn storms to him like a meteorological magnet and he needed strong ships to ride them out, as is evidenced in the account of a most frightening gale:

Upon Thursday the seventh of September, the gale began to be very fresh and to keepe the sailes stiffe from the Masts, and so continued all that day. Upon Friday it began to speake yet lowder, and to whistle a good in the shrowdes, insomuch that our Master made the Drablers bee taken off, and before night it had blowne the fore-top-saile in pieces by the terrible board; this was taken for the beginning of a storme, which came indeed about the shutting in of the day, with such furie and rage, as none could say it stole upon us unawares. For I am out of doubt that I had never heard any winde so high. One of our Bonnets had beene taken in the evening, and the other was rent off with the furie of the storme. And thus (for our mayne-top-saile was taken in and the top-mast taken downe) bearing onely a bare corse of each, if the ship had not beene exceeding strongly sided, shee could not have indured so rough weather. For oftentimes the Sea would ship in waves into her of three or foure Tunne of water, which (the ship being leakie within board) falling often, was as much as both the pumps were able to cast out againe, though they went continually all night, and till noone the next day were never throughly suckt, so that if any leake had sprung upon us under water, it could not have beene chosen, but shee must have foundered, seeing the pumpes were hardly able to rid the water that was cast in above hatches. The Missen-saile had beene in the evening well furled (for the winde came upon the starboard quarter) and yet the storme had caught it, and with such violence and furie rent it, that with much adoe the Missen-yard was hailed downe, and so the quarter decke and poope saved from danger of renting up. All this was in the night, which made it much more hidious, specially in the fore-end of the night before the Moone got up. The winde continued in this excesse of violence till midnight, and then abated hee something, but then began the effect of his blowing to shew it selfe, for High-swoke then the Sea began to worke, and swell farre higher then before. His Lordships ship is a very goodly one, and yet would shee bee as it were in a pit, and round about vast mountaines of water, higher then our mayne-top. And that (which is strangest) the Sea came upon every point of the Compasse, so that the poore ship, nor they that directed and cunned her, could not tell how to cunne her to bee safe from the breaking of these vast waves upon her. This continued all night: and though the winde fell by little and little, yet the Sea was so light, that all Saturday it was not quieted, so that though out of a storme, yet were wee still in a stormy Sea, insomuch that our mayne-top-mast was broken.[10]

Cumberland was to endure many such storms including one so powerful that 'his Lordships Cabbin, the dining roome, and halfe Decke became all one, and he was forced to seeke a new lodging in the hold.' He may have experienced more extremes of weather than most, but the best description of such conditions was written by the poet, and landlubber, John Donne, whose brief time at sea while serving the earl of Essex on both the Cadiz raid and the Island Voyage, gave rise to his poems 'The Storm' and 'The Calm' (Appendix 3).

Scourge of Malice re-emerged in March 1598, with Cumberland onboard for what was to be his last and in many ways most successful voyage. The plan, as always, was based on the seizing of carracks, this time off the Tagus. The plan, as so often, failed when the fleet was sighted and the carracks stayed. A few small ships were attacked, as Cumberland related:

I ceased not working day nor night, and by Saturday at night was readie to set saile, when within night I heard the Ordnance goe off betwixt me and the shoare, and well knew it was a small ship of Hampton and my little Pinnace the *Skout*, that were in fight with a ship which they chased to windward of mee before night, and fearing their match too hard, as in truth it proved. I, for losing time let slip mine anchor, and soone came to helpe the poore little ones much over-matched. At my first comming up shee shot at me; yet forbare I, and went so neere that I spake to them, and demanding of whence they were? answere was made, of Lisbone. Then assuring my self shee was a Biscaine, and would fight well, I came close to her, and gave her my broad side, which shee so answered that I had three men killed, five or sixe shot, and my ship in sixe or seven places, some of them very dangerous. So I laid her aboard and tooke her, shee proving a ship Ship of Hamburgh, laden with Corne, Copper, Powder, and prohibited commodities. I made the more haste to end this fight, for that I would be out of the sight of the Land before day, which as I desired I was, and there met with a French man laden with Salt.[11]

Knowing that he had been sighted off Iberia, Cumberland attempted to take advantage of his failure by sailing fast to the Indies, leaving the Spanish to believe that he was still lying just over the horizon from Lisbon. The result was that he was able to use surprise, along with flair, daring and bold execution, to take San Juan de Puerto Rico, a feat that had eluded Drake. The reward was little, the loss of life through disease high, but the honour was great, and made the more so, for it was with the shame of that loss fresh in his ears that King Philip of Spain died on 13 July 1598. Had he lingered on he might have been cheered to learn that Cumberland, as so often, had failed to intercept his convoys off the Azores, but he did not, and the war, his war, which had begun to all intent and purpose with the defeat of the pirate John Hawkins at San Juan de Ulua in 1568, had ended for Philip, after the loss of hundreds of ships, thousands of men and millions of ducats, with the victory of the pirate George Clifford at San Juan de Puerto Rico.

Like the *Ark*, the *Scourge* was to prove the professionalism of her Deptford builders by her own longevity. In September 1600, having hung up his sea-boots, Cumberland offered the East India Company first refusal on the purchase of *Malice Scourge*. Following a survey to 'search into all her defects', an offer of £3,000 was made 'for the said ship and all her ordnance, sails, cables, anchors and furnishings, as she now is' (Appendix 4). Cumberland stated he would take not less than £4,000, but the company knew its man and his means, and they settled for £3,700. To prepare her for her long voyage to the Far East, she had her bottom cased in cement to prevent worm, and almost 800ft of timber replaced: much of it 'borrowed out of her Majesty's storehouse at Woolwich.' To oversee the refit and then take command of the vessel, the company appointed the pirate, James Lancaster, who had already already made one voyage to the east, in 1591 in *Edward Bonaventure*. It had been a disastrous voyage. Lancaster had struggled to reach Penang, raiding and trading in equal measure, before turning for home that November. After refreshing his weary and depleted crew at the Cape of Good Hope, he was driven to the Indies where after much hazard he was marooned when, with just six men onboard, his ship sailed away and disappeared forever. Eventually, thanks to a passing French vessel, Lancaster and eleven colleagues managed to land back in England in May 1594. Shortly afterwards his fortune changed when he led a raid on Pernambuco in Brazil, in which so much booty was seized that the pirates could not find sufficient hulls to haul it away.[12]

Lancaster's new command was relaunched in December 1600 and renamed *Red Dragon*. On 13 February 1601 she led a fleet of five ships out from Woolwich on the company's first venture to the East Indies. She returned in September 1603, fully laden with spices, having proved her seaworthiness – just. For, on approaching the Cape on her return journey, *Red Dragon* had been struck by a storm so violent that she lost her rudder, while the mizzenmast, which was taken down to provide substitute steering, was also unshipped. The strain placed on a ship's rudder by heavy seas made these vital components very vulnerable, mounted as they were to the hull only by a number of iron hinges which could rust unnoticed underwater. Frobisher had had a similar incident while returning home from the Labrador coast. Spanish vessels used to rove a line through the rudder, secured to the deck at both ends, so that should the fastenings snap, the rudder could be recovered. Furthermore, many also carried a spare, while the measurements of the rudder were marked out on the deck so it was easy to build a replacement. The English did not adopt these sensible measures, thus committing their rudders to the deep and themselves to the mercy of the elements. Onboard *Red Dragon* the crew demanded that the ship be abandoned and they be transferred to their faithful consort, *Hector*, but Lancaster had faith in the refitted vessel and persuaded them to stay. The next day dawned with a welcome calm and *Red Dragon* came home without further incident. The seamanship that Lancaster had learned as a pirate thus proved to be invaluable to him as a merchant seaman.

Lancaster's stubbornness in the South Atlantic and his faith in *Red Dragon* served the East India Company well, for the ship made five further voyages to the East Indies before ending her days, as a good fighting vessel should, when she was attacked and sunk by a superior Dutch force in October 1619.

Yet stout timbers alone did not make a good ship: what was essential for success was a strong leader able, often by example, to encourage his men, not only in the excitement of the fight, but in the long bitter weeks of a slow homeward journey when provisions were failing. There is little doubt that this quality was possessed by Drake and, because it involved adversity, Cumberland, who met these challenges with bravery and devotion to his crew. Returning from his voyage of 1589, with his numbers inflated by the presence of some captives, he met with heavy weather which kept his *Victory* at sea overlong so that food, but most especially water, had to be severely rationed, Cumberland made sure that there was:

> equall distribution of the small store they had as well to all his prisoners as to his owne people. By this time the lamentable cryes of the sicke and hurt men for drinke was heard in every corner of the ship: for want whereof many perished (ten or twelve every night) then otherwise had miscarried in the whole Voyage . . . His minde was yet undaunted and present, his bodily presence and preventions readie. The last of November hee spake with an English ship, which promised him the next morning two or three tunnes of Wine, but soone after unfortunately came on ground. The next day hee had some supply of Beere, but not sufficient to enable him to undertake for England. Hee therefore put into Ventre Haven [Bantry Bay], in the Westermost part in Ireland, where having well refreshed, the twentieth of December he set sayle for England.

Such experiences might have persuaded a lesser man to return to land management, which Cumberland's neglected estates badly needed, but the earl had a spirit, 'further kindled and enflamed by former disasters' or, as his daughter wrote, 'though the miseries of sickness, death, famine and many other mis-adventures were sufficient to have moved his Lordship to have abjured for ever those marine adventures . . . such was his natural inclination . . . he could not be diverted from attempting another sea voyage.'

The Navy Royal

Far from deprecating the desires of her private, piratically-inclined shipbuilders, Elizabeth was most willing to lend them vessels of her own, to become in fact a joint conspirator and partner. However, the queen had just one caveat when leasing out her vessels to her pirateers, but it was a bit of a stopper, for she decreed that they were not to be used for boarding, for fear of their destruction by fire, or serious injury while grappling. She did, however, also stipulate that any booty seized by her ships would be hers by right, thus requiring the return while denying the means of acquisition. She was also more willing to loan out her older models than the sleek new galleons that John Hawkins was bringing off the stocks.

Thus to Hawkins, in his earlier role as a slave trader, she loaned the old fashioned high-sided carrack *Jesus of Lubeck*, which had plenty of hold room in which to cram slaves. When she proved too unseaworthy to handle the hurricane that hit Hawkins's ships off Cuba in 1568, he was forced to turn back to shelter at San Juan de Ulua, where she received a severe mauling from the Spanish. This was the incident which provided Drake with the excuse to set out on his rampage of revenge and reprisal. If *Jesus* had been a more seaworthy vessel, perhaps, the course of pirate history would have been much altered. A similar 'what if' happened a few years later with another unseaworthy royal ship, *Tyger*.

Tyger had been built as a galleass in 1546, but converted to a ship in 1549. In 1584 she sailed as Grenville's flagship in his voyage to Virginia to establish Ralegh's pirate base at Roanoke. Here, in an attempt to pass through a gap in the Carolinas Outer Banks, 'through the unskilfulness of the Master whose name was Fernando, the Admiral struck ground, and sunk.' In fact she only grounded but, unlike *Golden Hind*, the effect was to split open her timbers, so that 'the salt water came so abundantly into her, that the most part of his corn, salt, meat, rice, biscuit and other provisions that he should have left with them that remained behind him in that country was spoiled.' Also lost was the seed for the crops, meaning that Ralph Lane and his 107 men would not be self-sufficient for their year-long sojourn on the shores of Virginia. This forced them to scrounge from a resentful, hostile, native population, whose subsistence economy could not support the strangers who were then reduced to grubbing roots and gathering shellfish. No wonder they abandoned their settlement when Drake offered them the opportunity so to do, just one year after they had landed so full of hope. Thus did poor ship-husbandry influence the early history of the English in America.[13]

Tyger's grounding did her no permanent harm, for she was finally condemned in 1605, almost sixty years old! Sadly, she was built one year too late to feature in the wonderful, if inaccurate, roll of royal vessels, created by Anthony Anthony, Henry VIII's armourer in 1545.

A year after *Tyger* returned to England, having made the fleet's admiral, Richard Grenville, a fortune when he seized the laggardly unescorted treasure ship *Santa Maria* on the voyage home, Ralegh ordered from the yard at Deptford a flagship for his growing private pirate fleet, the great *Ark Ralegh* which, at 555 tons, would be one of the largest ships constructed in England to that date. Her keel length was 103ft, her beam 37ft and she had a draught of 16ft. A fully rigged, four-masted vessel, she needed a crew of 250 seamen and thirty-two gunners to sail and man her forty-two guns, distributed on two gun decks.

Ironically, but indicatively, *Ark Ralegh* was never deployed as the flagship of her eponymous owner's pirate fleet, nor loaned for any of his pirateering voyages. She was too grand for the queen not to covet and before her maiden voyage, the more elderly maiden, Elizabeth, wheedled it out of Ralegh's possession with the sweetest smile that ever twisted an arm and had her transferred into her own navy, in an arrangement with which Ralegh could only gallantly consent. Renamed *Ark Royal*, she became the first of a many an illustrious Royal Navy ship to bear that name, winning her first battle honours just two years later as Howard's flagship in the fight against the Spanish Armada. The Lord Admiral was in no doubt as to the bargain Elizabeth had procured telling her 'that her money was well given . . . for I think her the odd ship in the world for all conditions; and truly I think that there can be no great ship make me change and go out of her.' The fact that the queen had not paid a single penny for her does not detract from Howard's enthusiasm.

In 1596 Howard again flew his flag in *Ark Royal* when he led the raid on Cadiz, but she saw little action after that date. During the reign of James I she had both a name change, becoming *Anne Royal*, after his Danish queen, and a refit, overseen in 1608 by the famous shipwright Phineas Pett. But her days of glory were over. In 1625 she sailed again to Cadiz as the flagship of Lord Wimbledon on that ignominious failed expedition. After that she remained idle but seaworthy until she stove in her timbers with an unsecured anchor and sank in the Medway in 1636, only to be raised and almost immediately condemned, being broken up in 1638.

The queen's ships that did sail under pirate command had limited success. In 1593 Elizabeth loaned Cumberland several vessels as part of a strong squadron despatched to 'invade, and destroy the powers, forces, preparations and provisions of the King of Spain.' Two of the royal ships, *Golden Lion* and *Bonaventure,* would have been a match for any Spaniard that they encountered. The former, a bulky 560 tons, had been built in 1582 and was fitted with four demi-cannon, eight culverin, fourteen demi-culverin, nine sakers, one minion and eight fowlers. *Bonaventure*, with an 80ft keel length, was 20ft shorter than *Lion*, but carried a similar armament. Both ships had a crew of about 250 men which represented a wage and victualling bill of £379 3s a month, a price that explains why so many vessels sailed poorly provisioned and why Cumberland preferred organising his own supplies. Whoever the supplier, the costs were never negligible and frequently not covered by the residual return once charges and expenses had been met (Appendix 5). Victualling proved not to be a problem on this voyage, for a serious illness led Cumberland to abandon the voyage and return home. Thus the queen's ships missed an opportunity to prove their worth against a Spanish fleet and extract a vengeance for *Revenge*.

Cumberland, being a charmer, a champion and a close relative, benefited greatly from the loan of the queen's ships. In 1591, two years after his horrendous return voyage in her 565-ton *Victory* which was recounted earlier, he sailed with a small squadron to patrol off the coast of Spain while Lord Thomas Howard and Grenville lay in wait for the *flota* off the Azores. Cumberland himself commanded the 600-ton queen's ship, *Garland*, which had a keel length of 95ft, a beam of 33ft and a draught of 17ft. Her impressive armament included sixteen culverins, fourteen demi-culverins, four sakers, two fowlers and two port pieces. In company sailed Cumberland's own *Samson*, *Golden Noble* commanded by Monson as rear admiral, *Allagarta*, and the pinnace *Discovery*. It was on this voyage that Monson was captured, escorting a group of prizes homeward, which were recaptured by the untaken ships in their convoy, with Cumberland unable, for lack of wind and the fact that *Garland* was 'evil of sail', to come to his vice admiral's rescue. As a result Monson spent a year in the galleys and prison before organising his escape, an episode in his career for which he took a while to forgive Cumberland. On the positive side of this voyage, Cumberland dispatched *Discovery* westward to warn Howard of the departure of Admiral Alonso de Bazan's powerful fleet sailing to bring him to battle. As a result, Howard managed to get his ships out of Flores Bay moments before the Spaniards arrived, leaving just Grenville in *Revenge* to stay behind for death and glory, having given a fine, but foolish, demonstration of English firepower.

CHAPTER 4

Arms and Action

Gunners, beat open the ports and out with your lower tier, and bring
me from the weather side to the lee so many pieces as we have ports to
bear upon him. Master, lay him aboard luff for luff. Midships men, see
the tops and yards well manned, with stones, fire-pots and brass balls to
throw among them before we enter, or if we be put off, charge them
with all your great and small shot. In the smoke let us enter them in the
shrouds . . .

Captain John Smith, *A Sea Grammar*, 1627

Just as the craft engaged in piracy varied greatly in size, so did the armament that
each vessel carried. Coastal pirates, often sailing in craft too small to offer a stable
gun platform for mounted artillery, would have relied mainly on handheld weapons
and a fierce assault. The oceangoing professionals with wealthy backers could afford
to deploy a formidable arsenal in their ships and, on occasion, hire royal vessels
such as *Jesus of Lubeck* and *Tyger*, whose guns had been provided from the royal
armoury – this latter luxury much depending on the trust placed in the subject by
the sovereign.

Although the Tudor monarchs were involved in mainland European wars, they
had also to keep a watchful eye and strong arm to react against Scottish and Irish
threats and civil unrest which brought conflict onto their own lands. Such threats
required a careful control on the issue and audit of armament. Rebel ranks might
swell, but as long as they were matching bill and hook against loyal harquebuses and
cannon, then their hope for success soon became forlorn. As the weapons that were
deployed at sea were readily interchangeable with those in use on land, the
government tried to ensure that a register of such weaponry was kept, a policy more
useful when periodic efforts were made to control the spread of piracy by ordering
county vice admirals to stop suspicious vessels departing port in a 'warlike manner'.
Yet the threat of piracy and the move by English merchants into distant seas created
a major problem, in that all peaceful vessels required to be able to defend themselves
and, ergo, needed to be armed appropriately for their burden and crew numbers.
Once so armed, it was a simple matter of turning defence into offence.

Types of Gun

This was an age of introduction and experiment.[1] When Henry VIII came to the throne in 1509, most ship-borne guns had a definite medieval appearance, consisting as they did of a long cylindrical barrel made from wrought-iron staves bound firmly together with a number of iron hoops. The king was instrumental in creating a revolution in the national heavy arms industry when first he bought cast bronze weapons from the Low Countries, and then established his own foundries to make these guns in England. So adept were the English in casting bronze that a flourishing export industry was soon established, while the Elizabethan navy, as Sir John Fortescue proudly remarked in 1593, had changed from being one fitted with iron guns to one armed with modern bronze weapons, as were the more important pirate ships. Even as Sir John was eulogising, the navy was moving back to iron weaponry, having discovered how to cast that material successfully to create cheaper and more reliable muzzle-loading gun barrels. The Alderney wreck, dating back to that time, was fitted with iron minions of the same size and calibre, a far more effective suite than a mix of various weapons.[2]

Of greater significance for naval gunnery was the change in the way in which larger guns were armed. The early iron guns were breech-loaded, having a separate chamber into which the shot and charge was placed, before being lifted up behind the barrel and wedged into place. Cast guns were muzzle-loaded, meaning that they had to be run inboard after firing to be sponged out, and to have their shot and powder rammed down the barrel. For larger weapons this was a far harder evolution to carry out than fitting a chamber, and necessitated having a crew of very well-drilled gunners supporting each weapon if a reasonable rate of fire was to be maintained. Muzzle-loading was awkward and manpower intensive, but it held sway in the fleet until the reintroduction of the breech-loaded weapon in the nineteenth century. Thus the navy of the age of sail reached its apotheosis as a fighting force using weapons that were poorly adapted for the deck of a warship. Although a well-trained crew, such as those in *Revenge* in 1591, could keep up a most commendable rate of fire, when numbers were few and those less qualified (as in many a pirate vessel), lengthy engagements were much to be deprecated.

A century of change, adaptation, experiment and innovation contributed much to the many confusing and contradictory classifications of the weapons on a gun deck. The earliest English attempt to describe this artillery was William Bourne's *The Art of Shooting in Great Ordnance* which was written in 1572, although not published until 1587. Then in 1628 Robert Norton produced a work entitled *The Great Gunner*. Between the publication dates of these significant works lies the period of state piracy with which this book is concerned.

Main Armament

The introduction of bronze ordnance brought with it a description of the various weapons, their size, calibre, purpose and possible combinations thereof, which

Corbett described as a violation of every system of nomenclature. This included at least twelve types of culverin (large, small, ordinary, extraordinary, bastard, special, etc), five types of demi–cannon, five types of saker, and a multitude of others, often with exotic or zoomorphic names such as falcons, robinets, pelicans, sparrows, basilisks, lizards, fowlers, minions, murderers and double-murderers, serpentines, drakes (dragons), syrens, apostles, and even shrimps.[3] However, this multitude could be mustered into four main groups: the cannon, the culverin, the short-barrelled perriers, and the mortar. Of these, it was the culverin class which was the weapon found most frequently at sea, until in the latter part of the seventeenth century the battering power of the cannon made it the preferred naval gun.

Table 1. Characteristics of ship's armament

Name	Bore (in)	Weight of Shot (lbs)	Length/Weight Gun (ft)	(lbs)
Cannon-royal	8	63	12	8,000
Cannon	7	39	11	7,000
Demi–cannon	6.5	30	10	6,000
Culverin	5	15	9	4,300
Demi–culverin	4.5	10.5	8	2,400
Saker	3.5	5	9	1,550
Minion	3	3	7.5	1,200
Falcon	2.75	2	7	700
Falconet	2.25	1.2	6	500
Rabinet	1.5	0.75	4	300
Base	1.25	0.5	3	200

Cannon

Eventually, nearly all large muzzle-loading guns were referred to as cannon. In part, this marks the same process by which all vacuum cleaners became referred to as 'Hoovers', but it also marked the end of the age of experimentation in ship fits, and the acknowledgement that a reduced suite of weapons, with a standardised bore, improved fighting efficiency far more than a large number of guns with little in common.

Cannon could be reasonably described as short, fat weapons that fired a large ship-timber-crushing shot. Their bore was around 8in and their calibre (the ratio of bore to length) between about 12 and 15, out of which barrel they discharged a shot of approximately 60 pounds (lbs). The shorter barrel made for easier reloading when the gun was run in following its recoil. Given their weight, some 5,000lbs, and use, hull smashing, they tended to be placed low down in a ship, from where such a force delivered horizontally could exert the most obvious and most worrying damage. Richard Hawkins had little doubt as to the value of the short-bore cannon, even after *Dainty* had to surrender to her Spanish opponents in 1594. He wrote:

Although their artillery was longer, weightier and many more than ours, and in truth did pierce with greater violence; yet ours being of greater bore and carrying weightier and greater shot, was of more importance and of greater effect for sinking and spoiling, for the smaller shot passeth through and maketh but his hole and harmeth that which lieth in the way; but the greater shaketh and shivereth all it meeteth, and with the splinters, or that which it encountered, many times doth hurt more with his proper circumference.[4]

Pirate Hawkins was, without realising it, highlighting a dilemma faced by all who wished to prey in hostile waters. Faced with a well-drilled, well-armed enemy determined to overpower his vessel, the pirate captain would wish to deal out a shot-shattering assault on his foe, desiring most heartedly to sink his attacker. Yet a similar weight of shot fired at a potential prize might see the reward for his investment disappear beneath the waves, taking with it some dismembered gentry for whom, safe and well, a ransom might be raised. On such a voyage a good lookout and a rapid recognition of a closing sail was essential to ensure both survival and success, through discretion or the manning of the most appropriate weapons in the suite.

Culverin

For those pirates who could afford the purchase price, the main armament of choice was one of the culverin class, which Norton considered to be, as well as the culverin itself, the saker, falcon, falconet, robinet and base. These, Norton stated could 'shoot further and pierce deeper' than cannon but, most importantly, they were not ship sinking weapons, piercing rather than shattering their target's hull.

The culverin was a long-barrelled gun, having an average length of 14ft with a bore ranging from 4–6in, from which it discharged cast iron shot averaging about 15lbs weight. Mounted on its carriage it was a heavy weapon of almost 1,500lbs, capable of firing its medium-weight shot a greater distance than could its shorter-barrelled, heavier partner, the cannon. Eventually, however, the fact that less metal was required to cast a cannon told in the latter's favour and the culverin was destined for a short but beautiful life.

For if ever a weapon of war deserves to be described as a work of art, uniting in its fine form the artisan and the craftsman's skills, then the beautifully proportioned brass culverins of Tudor England warrant such an accolade. Unknown in England before Henry VIII's time, they came to prominence through his establishment of bronze weapon foundries in England. With such royal interest it was not long before home-cast brass ordnance equalled and then, possibly, surpassed those being made in the more experienced works of Flanders and Venice.

Luckily, thanks to the disaster that sunk *Mary Rose* in 1545, and the skill and perspicacity of those who found her wreck and raised her, we have several examples of the naval culverin at the height of its ornate majesty, for bronze-cast guns brought the craftsman's pride to the fore. Whereas their successors with their limited and uniform adornment were early indicators of an age of industrial mass production, each bronze culverin was a unique casting which reflected the pride of its creator. They were thus embellished with lion heads on the trunnions, patterns of shells, fleur-de-lys or acanthus columns, coats of arms and the monarch and maker's name no better summarised than in the words inscribed on one of *Mary Rose*'s bastard culverins:*

ROBERT AND JOHN OWYN BRETHERYN BORNE IN THE CYTE OF LONDON THE SOMNNES OF AN INGLISH MADE THYS BASTARD ANNO DNI 1537

Saker

The saker, a weapon with a bore of 3–4in and a length of 9ft, firing a 5lb shot, was to become one of the most commonly fitted guns aboard ship. Lighter than cannon or culverin, but still weighty enough to deliver a powerful punch, it was more easily manned and deployed than its weightier cousins, and would not create problems of stability in vessels of less tonnage than that of major warships. It was probably the weapon carried on the gun deck of *Golden Hind* during Drake's circumnavigation.

A fine example of a saker, cast by the great Italian gun-founder Alberghetti, was discovered off Teignmouth in 1975. It bore the coat of arms of the de Molin family, giving rise to the belief that it formed part of the armament of the *Sao Paulo*, which was sunk by pirates in 1603 while carrying the luggage of the Venetian ambassador to England, Nicola de Molin, a most embarrassing illustration of the presence of these robbers to King James I, who had arrived in England stating his determination to rid his waters of this plague. The restored gun can now be seen in the Henrician castle of St Mawes, which guards the eastern side of the entrance to Falmouth harbour.

Minion and Falcon

Lighter weapons such as the minion and falcon were naturally cheaper and easier to obtain for smaller vessels, but they had a role on larger ships, in that they could be placed up higher without fear that their weight would affect the ship's stability in the way that the great guns would. As it was, many a captain voyaging to patrol for prizes several months out from home would stow his guns in the hold to give his ship greater stability and handling qualities during the voyage. It was then fervently hoped that a good lookout and a good suite of sails would prevent the embarrassment of having to go into action with one's main armament still below decks.

---

*One in which the barrel length was shorter than normal when measured in calibres.

Accidents

One of the reasons why muzzle-loaded bronze weapons were preferred by gunners was that they were far less likely to blow up in the face of the crew than their breech-loaded iron predecessors, of which Lucar, writing as late as 1588, advised:

> Put into every chamber so much powder as his piece requireth for a due charge, and with a rammer beat a tompion of soft wood down upon the gunpowder. Moreover, put a big wad into the peece at that end where the mouth of the chamber must goe in, and after that wadde thrust into the peece at the sayde end a fitte pellet, & when you have done all this, put the chamber into the lowest end of the peece, lock them fast together an cause the saide tompion to lie hard uppon the powder in the sayde chamber, and the pellet to tooch the tompion, and the wadde to lie close by the pellet.

> . . . and when a Gunner will give fire to a chamber peece, he ought not to stand upon that side of the peece where a wedge of yron is put to locke the chamber in the peece, because the sayde wedge may through the discharge of the peece flie out and kill the Gunner.

In 1602 when the pirate ship *Lyon* rejoined Sir Thomas Shirley's fleet in Falmouth and discharged 'a piece to salute the Castle, the same break and killed two of her men, hurt divers others, tore her decks and brake her main-yard.'

A few years earlier a similar salute by James Lancaster, returning from his pirateering raid to Brazil, and anchoring in The Downs, caused chaos when:

> The gunner being careless, as they are many time of their powder in discharging certain pieces in the gunroom, set a barrel of powder on fire, which blew up the admiral's cabin, slew the gunner with 2 others outright, and hurt 20 more, of which 4 or 5 died. This powder made such a smoke in the ship with the fire that burnt in the gunroom, that no man at first wist what to do. But recalling back their fear (for the Queen's ships now and also the other ships that were in our company came presently to help) that, God be praised, we put out the fire and saved all.[5]

Such accidents occurred despite the fact that rules for the loading and discharge of weapons and the care of powder were commonplace. Some powder horns even had a spring mechanism behind the spout so that it would shut off as soon as the gunner removed his finger. This not only prevented powder spilling out, but meant that by the use of a simple count while the horn was in use, the gunner could fill the vent with a precise and identical charge of powder each time.

Even small arms incorrectly loaded could produce undesired effects on discharge. Richard Hawkins records in his *Observations* that:

> After we opened the bay and port of Arica; but seeing it clean without shipping, we haled the coast alongst and going aboard to visit the bigger prize, my company saluted me with a volley of small shot. Amongst them, one musket brake, and

carried away the hand of him that shut it, through his own default, which for that I have seen to happen many times, I think it necessary to note in this place, that others may take warning by his harm. The cause of the muskets breaking was the charging with two bullets, the powder being ordained to carry but the weight of one, and the musket not to suffer two charges of powder or shot. By this oversight, the fire is restrained with the overplus of the weight of shot, and not being able to force both of them out, breaketh all to pieces . . .

Proof-firing

In an effort to reduce the number of guns that split asunder on firing, many guns were proof-fired before being sold or issued. This was necessary in part because, although the English became masters in the science of casting both bronze and iron guns, their product did not always stand the test of usage. Norton reported that:

Some and a great many pieces are come forth of the furnaces, spongy, or full of honey-combs and flaws, by reason that the metal runneth not fine, or that the moulds are not thoroughly dried, or well nealed: whereby either the Gunner that serveth with them is much endangered, they being as bad or worse to serve with, as those that are too weak and poor in metal: for if they be loaded with so much powder as is ordinary for those sorts . . . they will either break, split, or blowing spring their metal.[6]

To guard against such weapons failing it was standard practice to test each weapon at the foundry with a charge double that which the gunner was expected to load during action.

But even proof-firing had its detractors. Richard Hawkins, who could be guaranteed to examine all relevant topics with sobriety, stated that:

I am of opinion, that it is a great error to prove great ordnance, or small shot, with double charges of powder or shot; my reason is, for that ordinarily the metal is proportioned to the weight of the shot which the piece is to bear, and the powder correspondent to the weight of the bullet; and this being granted, I see no reason why any man should require to prove his piece with more than is belonging to it of right: for I have seen many goodly pieces broken with such trials, being clean without any combs, cracks, flaws, or other perceivable blemish, which no doubt, with their ordinary allowance, would have served many years . . . It seems quite possible that a piece may bear the proof, and yet the particles be so disarranged, that it fail afterwards.[7]

Anti-personnel Guns

The primary ambition of the attacking pirate vessel was to board his opponent with the minimum of opposition. In many cases he relied on stealth to swing alongside an unsuspicious ship but even then, once his purpose was made clear, he could expect an attempt be made to repel his boarders. In these circumstances small-bore, rapidly reloaded guns firing several types of anti-personnel shot were essential. These did not have to kill: maiming or driving below was sufficient for purpose. Thus these weapons could be manned and trained by one man by means of a 'tiller', while swivelled on a spigot fitted into holes on the ship's side to bring to bear where required. Such swivel guns appear to have been referred to as 'bases' and were considered to fire dice-shot by way of a chamber, ie they were breech-loaded. Several were recovered from *Mary Rose* and preserved in such a condition as to reveal their design.

Another type of anti-personnel gun was the handheld hailshot piece which scattered a dozen or more dice-shaped shot on a broad front created by the bore resembling a letter-box mouth in shape, commonly being referred to as 'flukemouthed'.

Richard Hawkins admired such weapons greatly 'for that their execution and speedy charging and discharging is of great moment.'[8]

Ship Fit

In 1565 Martin Frobisher sailed out of the Tyne in the 100-ton *Mary Flower* which was carrying a saker, two quarter-slings, six bases, two falcons, twenty corselets, ten bows and several dozen pikes, a suite of weapons ideal for clearing the decks of any potential prize and repelling any would-be boarders.[9] The weapons had been provided by the master of the queen's ordnance at Newcastle.

Some twelve years later Drake's *Golden Hind* was described by his Portuguese captive pilot, Nuña da Silva, as having 'seven armed port-holes on each side, and inside she carries eighteen pieces of artillery, thirteen being of bronze, the rest of cast-iron'. The actual calibre of the weapons is nowhere described. Expert opinion ranges from these being represented by eight demi-culverins, six sakers and four falcons, while another presumes fourteen sakers and four falcons; a third proposes twelve demi-culverins, two sakers and four falcons, while a fourth suggestion is four culverins, eight demi-culverins, two sakers and four falcons. Given the size and tonnage of *Golden Hind* she may well have carried fowlers on her upper deck and sakers below, while for close-quarters work there were many swivel bases which would have been brought up and mounted on the ship's side when needed. As far as her size was concerned *Golden Hind* was not dissimilar to the queen's *Scout*, a bark of slightly greater tonnage, built in 1577, which carried eight sakers, two minions, eight falcons and falconets, two fowlers and four bases. Drake, who took great pride in his vessel, used to give those he captured a tour of the ship so that they could see his major weapons as well as the harquebuses, pistols, pikes, fire-bomb and bows and arrows which he carried onboard. Once released, he relied on these one-time captives to dismay the authorities ashore, and awe those sent to pursue him, with their description of his warlike weapon fit.

The lifting of restrictions on the issue of letters of reprisal led to a significant increase in the suite of weapons carried by pirateering vessels. Indeed, one clear indication as to how the growth of organised piracy took hold of the nation can be evidenced from the weapons with which the principal pirates equipped their ships. Just seven years after the 18-gun *Golden Hind* returned from her circumnavigation in 1580, Walter Ralegh, with the queen's full knowledge, launched as the flagship of his already formidable pirate fleet, *Ark Ralegh*, a 555-ton galleon carrying some fifty-five guns, consisting of four demi-cannon, four cannon perrier, twelve culverin, twelve demi-culverin, six saker, two fowler and four port-pieces, with the rest being made up of smaller calibre weapons such as swivel-pieces.

To avoid such weaponry being sold to foreign fleets, in June 1574 the Privy Council issued a number of controlling directives. The overarching requirement was for armament foundries to be licensed and for all their output to be brought to Tower Wharf for sale, and once there for it 'to be sold unto English merchants or to such strangers as dwell in this realm and are owners . . . and they only buy them for the furniture of English ships and not make sale of them unto any strangers out of the realm'. Moreover, 'owners of every ship shall . . . be bound to be answerable for all such pieces as be aboard their ships and to bring them to England again, either whole or broken, or else perfect certificate where they have

Table 2. Weapon fit of selected vessels

Ship	Jesus of Lubeck	Golden Hind	Ark Ralegh	Scourge of Malice
Tonnage	700	120	555	600
Guns of Brass				
Cannon	2			
Demi-cannon			4	2
Cannon perrier			4	
Culverin	2		12	16
Demi-culverin			12	12
Sakers	2	14	6	8
Minions				
Falcons			4	
Falconets				
Fowlers				2
Guns of Iron				
Port pieces	4			
Slings	10			
Demi-slings				
Quarter-slings				
Fowler	4			
Minions	12			
Bases		?	?	?
Top pieces	2	?	?	?
Hailshot pieces	20	?	?	?
Hand guns	20	?	?	?
Total	82	18	40	38

been lost'. Harbour authorities were required to record what number of pieces were onboard each vessel 'as well as their going as their coming', an early example of counting them all out and counting them all back in.[10]

One cannot but presume that such close control was more frequently breached than honoured, and that fleets such as that owned by Ralegh and Cumberland had no problem ignoring the directives.

An indication of the gun-suite of lesser vessels might be gauged from a High Court of Admiralty inventory of 119 ships seized between 1579 and 1590. Over half of these ships, most under 150 tons, were armed, with the most common weapons being falconets, falcons and minions, while a few carried sakers.[11]

The debate as to what mix of gun was ideal was not one that appeared to have been solved with consensus. So often personnel experience influenced belief, as in the case of the defeated but defiant Richard Hawkins; recalling his fight in *Dainty* against three Spanish ships in 1594 he wrote:

> Doubtless it is most proper for shippes to have short ordnance, except in the steme or chase. The reasons are many: viz. – easier charging, ease of the shippes side, better traversing, and mounting j yea, greater security of the artillery, and consequently of the ship. For the longer the peece is, the greater is the retention of the fire, and so the torment and danger of the peece the greater. But here will be contradiction by many, that dare avouch that longer peeces are to be preferred, for that they burne their powder better, and carrie the shott further, and so necessarily of better execution; whereas the short artillery many times spend much of their powder without burning, and workes thereby the slenderer effect. To which I answere, that for land service, fortes, or castles, the long peeces are to bee preferred: but for shipping, the shorter are much more serviceable. And the powder in them, being such as it ought to, will be all fiered long before the shott can come forth; and to reach farre in fights at sea, is to little effect. For he that purposeth to annoy his enemie, must not shoot at randome, nor at point blanke, if hee purpose to accomplish with his devoire, nether must hee spend his shott nor powder, but where a pot-gun may reach his contrary; how much the neerer, so much the better: and this duel executed, the short artillery will worke its effect as well as the long; otherwise, neither short nor long are of much importance: but here my meaning is not to approve the overshort peeces, devised by some persons, which at every shott they make, daunce out of their carriages, but those of indifferent length, and which keep the mean, betwixt seven and eight foot.[12]

Further considerations in the positioning of weapons were given by Bourne who suggested that:

> The shorter ordnance is best to be placed out at the ship side for two or three causes, viz.
>
> First, for the ease of the ship, for their shortness they are lighter: and also, if that the ship should heel with the bearing of a sail, you must shut the ports,

especially if the ordnance be upon the lower orlop, and then the shorter piece is the easier to be taken in, both for shortness and the weight also.

In like manner, the shorter the piece lieth out of the ship side, the less it shall annoy them in tackling of the ship's sail, for if the piece do lie very far out of the ship's side, then the sheets and tacks, or bowlines, will always be foul of the ordnance, whereby it may much annoy them in foul weather . . .[13]

Bourne also recommends that both bow and stern chasers should protrude a good distance out of their ports for fear of damaging, or setting light to, the overhanging structures when they were fired.

Shot

At some stage towards the end of the century it was realised that the carrying of a mixed suite of weapons, few of which had the same or a standard bore, was inefficient – and even dangerous if guns had to fall silent for want of the right-sized shot. Such non-conformity must have vexed many a master gunner: too small a shot or charge and the target would not be reached; too great and it could destroy the gun from which it was fired and its crew as well. Good gunners were those who ensured the safety of their crew first and foremost.

If uniformity was a virtue for the queen's ships, sailing close to home and in company, as the desperate need to rearm during the running battle with the Armada demonstrated, then it was even more important for pirate ships operating singly and very far from friendly shore-support. Thus the value of a limited suite of standard-sized weapons might have been demonstrated through the experience of pirates.

Although the larger guns were designed primarily to fire iron or stone shot, there were occasions when tactics required other ordnance to be fired; for example, to bring down rigging, or rip apart sails or sailors. Canister-shot was ideal for the latter task, consisting as it did of two loosely bound hollowed-out tubes of wood into which were placed, in John Smith's words, 'any kind of small bullets, nails, old iron or the like . . . to shoot out of the ordnances or murderers. These will do much mischief when we lie aboard . . . to shoot down masts, yards, shrouds, tear the sails, spoil the men, or anything that is above decks.'[14]

For the destruction of rigging and sails, ships carried several forms of chain-shot (two balls linked together by chain) and cross-bar shot, which was a ball through which a spike had been inserted. An idea of the importance of this type of shot can be gauged from that provided for Cumberland's *Red Dragon*, also known as *Sampson*, at Portsmouth in July 1588 as she provisioned to sail to join the attack on the Armada. This consisted of:

8 cross-bar shot for demi-culverins	10 cross-bars for falcons
70 cross-bars for sakers	47 shackled (chain) shot for sakers
70 cross-bars for minions	50 round shot for sakers.[15]

Gun Crews

It might be assumed that in matters such as gunnery, those serving in the Navy Royal would be better-trained and more professional than their piratical cousins. However, there is no evidence to support this and, given the small amount of shot carried per gun in naval vessels, the lack of commonality between weapons along the gun deck, and the time ships spent alongside or in engagement-free patrols, it is probable that the freebooting, or even merchant naval, gunnery teams could match or exceed their naval counterparts in firing drills.

The art of gunnery was also going through a scientific renaissance, with much work being done to limit the inevitable inaccuracy caused by propelling through a smooth bore, with variable strength powder, a shot with at least a quarter of an inch 'windage', from a deck that was moving in three directions, whilst aiming at a target that was also moving, and whose range was both variable and unknown. One could add to this the delay between applying the lighted linstock to the vent hole and the actual explosion of the gunpowder beneath; akin to, and as frustrating as, trying to capture a moving image such as a child's face with a digital camera. Nevertheless, rules were written with accompanying tables and instruments, such as the 'gunner's quadrant', produced. This, by means of a graduated set square to which was attached a plumb line, enabled the gunner to read off and adjust his elevation.

Yet as gunnery moved from art to science, so there arose a shortage of men trained and available to fill master gunner roles onboard ship. In 1582 the Privy Council was asked to renew and increase the scope of the charter of the Fraternity of Artillery, so that they could examine all those wishing to qualify as master gunners. It was further indicated that ships should be provided with trained men at the rate of one gunner per 20 tons, and that a list of all qualified men should be kept in an annually updated register. At the same time, it was felt that all merchantmen should carry one qualified gunner for every two guns they shipped, and that an allowance for powder be made available by the government for training purposes. Nevertheless, when the nation was in greatest danger, awaiting the Spanish Armada, Effingham invited Walsingham to write to Drake to request him to desist from wasting powder by carrying out firing drills.

The year before, William Bourne had produced his treatise on gunnery, in which he stated:

> . . . we Englishmen have not been considered but of late day to become good Gunners, and the principal point that hath caused English men to be counted good Gunners, hath been, for that they are hardy or without fear about their ordnance: but for the knowledge in it, other nations and countries have tasted better thereof as the Italians French and Spaniards, for that English men have had but little instructions but that they have learned of the Dutchmen or Flemings in the time of King Henry the eight. And the chiefest cause that English men are thought to be good Gunners is this, for that they are handsome about their Ordnance in ships on the Sea etc.[16]

This ease in weapon handling can only have been achieved by crews being well-drilled by efficient master gunners. Not all ships were so well-versed – not surprisingly, *Dainty* providing an example of the worst case in her fight in the Bay of Atacama, about which Hawkins remarked ruefully:

> Doubtless, had our gunner been the man he was reputed to be, and as the world sold him to me, he [the Spaniard] had received great hurt by that manner of boarding. But contrary to all expectation, our stem pieces were un-primed, and so were all those which we had to lee-ward, save half one in the quarter, which discharged, wrought that effect in our contraries as that they had five or six foot of water in hold, before they suspected it.
>
> Hereby all men are to take warning by me, not to trust any man in such extremities, when he himself may see it done: and coming to fight, let the chieftain himself be sure to have all his artillery in a readiness upon all occasions. This was my oversight, this my overthrow . . . leaving the artillery, and other instruments of fire, to the gunners dispose and order, with the rest of his mates and adherents; which, as I said, was part of our perdition. For bearing me ever in hand, that he had five hundred cartridges in a readiness, within one hour's fight we were forced to occupy three persons only in making and filling cartridges; and of five hundred ells of canvas and other cloth given him for that purpose at sundry times, not one yard was to be found. For this we have no excuse, and therefore could not avoid the danger, to charge and discharge with the ladle, especially in so hot a fight. And coming now to put in execution the sinking of the ship, as he promised, he seemed a man without life or soul. So the admiral coming close unto us, I myself, and the master of our ship, were forced to play the gunners.
>
> Those instruments of fire wherein he made me to spend excessively, before our going to sea, now appeared not; neither the brass balls of artificial fire, to be shot with slur bows (whereof I had six bows, and two hundredth balls and which are of great account and service, either by sea or land); he had stowed them in such manner, though in double barrels, as the salt water had spoiled them all; so that coming to use them, not one was serviceable . . . Few of our pieces were clear, when we came to use them, and some had the shot first put in, and after the powder.[17]

After voicing his suspicions that the man was a spy or traitor and before, noble-hearted that he was, accepting the blame for the disaster through his failure to check on the man, Hawkins stated wryly that, 'I am sure all in general gave him an ill report, and that he in whose hands the chief execution of the whole fight consisted, executed nothing as was promised and expected.'

Boarding and Hand Weapons

The main desire of any pirate was to board his prize as soon as the opportunity presented itself, which meant driving its crew from the upper decks either by canister-shot from alongside or cutlass once on deck, in a method well described by John Smith at the head of this chapter.

Not forgotten was that far more ancient yet more accurate weapon, the bow and arrow. *Golden Hind* carried a quantity of these which, given the fact that arrows could be more easily replenished than shot and required no gunpowder, was a sensible measure for those on lengthy deployments. Drake used his archers in combination with his firearms both in his boarding of *Cacafuego* in 1579, and in the taking of *Rosario* in 1588. Longbows were also carried in reserve by shore parties armed with harquebuses which, relying on a match to spark off the charge, was not a weapon of total reliability after a journey through the surf, or a march in pouring rain.

There were two main uses for hand weapons onboard a pirate ship. The first was to repel enemy boarders, while the second was to be used when boarding a vessel oneself. The need was different. An enemy waiting to swing over the side, or even clamber up it, was best dealt with at longer than arm's length. A pike was ideal for this purpose, but of no use for those endeavouring to scramble onboard their foe, when it could be guaranteed to trip one up or get snarled in rigging, as well as being too long in a close-quarters situation. For this the pirate needed his famous cutlass, or other sword, and a dirk. Because scrambling violently around a ship's deck was an occupation requiring at least one free hand, it is doubtful whether boarding parties carried shields of any description. They might have held a pistol to fire a shot on arrival, but it is unlikely the fight allowed time to reload: instead they would have relied on carefully aimed musket shots from their own deck to dispose of any enemy taking aim at them.

The repelling of boarders, after two ships were grappled together, was based around control of the target ship's waist, the upper-deck amidships. For passive defence many vessels stretched anti-boarding netting across the waist, fragments of one being recovered from the wreck of the *Mary Rose*. Should this fail to deter, most of the elderly large carracks had swivel guns mounted in their fore and after castles, so as to bring fire down upon those swarming onto that deck. The castles themselves could be turned into 'close-fights', being protected against small arms fire and closed athwartships by heavy bulkheads known as 'cubbridge-heads'.[18]

William Monson, pirate turned naval officer, gave a good description of the taking of the first legal prize in the Spanish war that began in 1585 when, that September, Sir George's Carey's vessels *Muscat* and *Marlyn* took a Biscayan fishing boat after a fierce fight:

At about eight a-clock in the evening, being upon the coast of Spain . . . we met and boarded a Spanish vessel of three hundred tons burden, well manned and armed. All our men with one consent entered her, and were left fighting aboard her all night, the seas being so grown that our barks were forced to ungrapple and fall off. The Spaniards betook themselves to their close fights, and gave two attempts by trains of powder to blow up their decks on which we were, but we happily prevented it by fire-pikes. Thus continued the fight till seven in the morning when the Spaniards found the death and spoil of their men so great as they were forced to yield. When we came to take a view of our men we found few left alive but could shew a wound they received in the fight. The spectacle, as well of us as the Spaniards, was woeful to behold; and I dare say that in the whole of the war there was not so rare a manner of fight, or so great a spoil of so few men.[19]

In 1592 Thomas White in *Amity* returned to London with two Spanish prizes, worth £707,000, that his crew of forty-three had overpowered, despite their foe having almost four times as many men. Hakluyt's lively description of the incident shows how such actions relied on the teamwork between master, seamen and gunners, and the use of both cunning and bluff:

> The enemy having placed themselves in warlike order, one cable's length from the other *Amity* began the fight, in which our men continued as fast as they were able to charge and discharge for the space of five hours, being never a cable's length from either.
>
> In this time they received divers shot both in the hull of the ship, masts and sails to the number of 32 great, besides 500 musket shot and harquebuses a crock at least. And because they perceived the enemy to be stout, our men thought good to board the Biscayan which was head on to the other, where lying onboard about an hour and playing their ordnance, in the end they stowed all the enemy's men. Then the other in the flyboat, thinking our men had entered their fellow, bare room with *Amity* meaning to have laid her aboard and so entrapped her between them both. But *Amity*, quitting herself of the enemy, hoisted top sails and weathered them both. Then coming hard about the flyboat with her ordnance prepared, gave her whole broadside and slew several so that our men saw the blood running out at the scupper holes. After that, they cast about, new charged all ordnance and, coming upon them again, willed them to yield or else they would sink them . . .[20]

Although the larger Iberian treasure ships retained their high freeboard with towering castles fore and aft, during the latter part of the sixteenth century, under Hawkins's leadership, English warships became flush-decked, while the height of both their castles was much reduced. This created a superior sailing vessel which was able to come alongside a prize beneath the tier of its lowest guns. However, this new design had 'the grave defect that the waist no longer afforded a trap for boarders and the deck could not be enfiladed from protected bulkheads.'[21]

Fire

Fire was a deadly weapon to use at sea, and even deadlier if unleashed without intention. As a weapon of war its most effective but erratic deployment was through the use of fire-ships. The Spanish had drifted such vessels down upon John Hawkins's fleet moored at San Juan de Ulua in 1568 with limited effect. Twenty years later Hawkins witnessed his revenge at Calais when the majority of the

Spanish fleet panicked, cut their cables and scattered at the appearance of fire-ships which passed harmlessly through their anchorage and burnt out on the sands.

The Spanish believed that incendiaries were a major weapon in the English arsenal. In the inquisition of John Butler, Oxenham's captured pilot, carried out as a matter of urgency by the Spanish authorities in Lima once they had been alerted to Drake's presence on their coast, the investigators wanted to know, first, if he was capable of forging guns, of which they had a great deficit and secondly, whether he could explain how to make incendiaries, either for use in setting fire to sails or, when fitted with nails, for lighting the wooden decks themselves. Butler explained that, 'the necessary ingredients . . . are powder, oil, pitch and sulphur', to which could be added 'to make them very effective, camphor and spirits.' This was made into a paste which was stuck onto the projectile. A hole was then made, into which dry powder was poured and then lit. Butler also spoke of incendiary grenades, but these were unlikely weapons for a pirate to use when assaulting a ship that he wished to keep intact.[22]

For a fired ship would soon be a failed prize, unless everyone ceased fighting and united to fight the fire. The greatest loss from fire was the carrack, *Las Cinque Llagas* (The Five Wounds), a 2,000-ton giant to whose flanks Cumberland's squadron of *Sampson, Mayflower* and *Royal Exchange* attached themselves in June 1594 off the Azores. With no hope of subterfuge leading to success, the pirates maintained an assault with 'great and small shot' which succeeded in ripping some of her sails to shreds, thus limiting her speed and manoeuvrability. During the night the English lay off to confer, agreeing to return with boarding in mind, from three directions simultaneously, in the morning. This plan went somewhat awry. Captain Anthony of *Mayflower* was slain and, in drifting away, his ship was damaged by colliding with the carrack. George Cave, the admiral in *Royal Exchange*, was also shot through both his legs and his crew seemed reluctant to storm onboard the fiercely defended prize, the crew of which used firebrands to dismay the boarders. Repulsed by such an unusual and effective tactic, the attackers foolishly fired a mat on the carrack's beak-head which spread to forecastle and sails, and then abetted her eventual doom by shooting at those that came to quench the flames. The blaze increased in ferocity so that both *Sampson* and *Mayflower*'s own sails caught fire, while *Royal Exchange* had to break off the fight just to dowse her own sails and decks. *Samson* almost shared the same pyre as the carrack, for the two ships were intertwined through their spars and rigging. Luckily, the fire itself, by burning though the cordage, separated the two ships. However, seeing what seemed to be their shared predicament, a Spanish grandee called for a flag of truce and then, seeing the 'fiery flames increasing more forcible both afore and aft . . .' besought the Captain General to yield unto the Englishmen, thereby to save their own lives.'

But the captain had a bit of the Richard Grenville about him and was 'nothing willing so to do, for a long time withstood their entreaty.' Then, when he too was convinced that salvation lay only in surrender, his carpenter stated that he might still be able to put out the fires. More delay, while the English, safely astern of this flaming torch, watched in wonderment and sadness as their prize and her riches burnt down towards the waterline.

An examination of the survivors revealed that *Las Cinque Llagas* had been carrying inflammable Benjamin gum in the forepeak, along with a quantity of oil, which explained why the conflagration took hold so easily. All that day and night the abandoned vessel burnt, until at dawn the next day the flames reached her store of sixty barrels of gunpowder and she blew apart.

The ever vigilant Venetian ambassador in Spain produced a pithy report on the incident, which covered a number of issues unknown to the English. However, in view of the Spanish interest in the use of incendiaries at sea, it is interesting to note that the Venetians also believed this to be an English weapon of choice despite the obvious shortcomings linked to its use:

> The trouble caused by the English is felt more acutely every day at Lisbon. A ship, the richest that ever sailed from East India port, was lost the other day. The affair happened thus. This ship, the largest of the four or five that were expected from the East Indies, and also the best armed, was laden with a cargo worth upwards of two millions of gold, not only in pepper and drugs, but in a large quantity of oriental pearls and jewels and other precious goods. The ship made out her journey happily, when the captain, tempted by greed, took on board four hundred blacks, whom he intended to sell in Spain. The heat and overcrowding brought on the plague, of which upwards of five hundred persons died in ten days; for besides the blacks above mentioned there were on board three hundred passengers, chiefly Italian and Portuguese merchants. After this terrible mortality, the ship began to draw near to the Azores, where she was exposed to the fire of three English corsairs, who followed her up for two whole days with a heavy cannonade. The English drew close and managed to board her with twenty-five men, but these were all cut to bits. Seeing that there was no hope of capturing her, as she was now in sight of the Azores, the English resolved to fire her with Greek fire, which was applied to many parts of the ship at once, and then uniting made a tremendous flame, in the midst of which she went down with crew and cargo, and not a thing came into the hands of the English. I hear that the loss of four only among the merchants amounts to six hundred thousand ducats. His Majesty's loss is three hundred thousand ducats, and the total reaches two millions.[23]

Dismayed at having lost twenty-five men as well as their prize, but not yet downhearted, the three English ships continued their patrol and on the last day of June they came across another mighty carrack, the 1,500-ton *San Philip*, which they closed. However, with Captain Cave grievously wounded, the assault on this carrack lacked a co-ordinated plan and the attack was delivered at range rather than closing to board. The carrack could have sustained such damage for days, but when it fell calm the English sent a boat over to parley, stating that the Spaniard should yield to the queen of England and her good subject the earl of Cumberland or else abide the hazards of war by sinking, killing, burning or drowning. Yet again they met with a stout heart, with the carrack captain informing them that he had been present at the taking of *Revenge* and that, 'let him do as much as he can for his Queen, I will do as much for my King.'

True to his word, no sooner had the parley boat been recovered than *San Philip* opened up with a broadside directed at *Mayflower*. She responded in the traditional way, firing her guns on one side and then, it still being calm, using her skiff to pull her head round, so she could fire again from the other side. This was the last exchange, for the wind got up and the carrack got underway, closely followed by the vigilant English. But overnight the pursuers lost sight of *Sampson* and, in searching for her, fell too far astern of the carrack to catch her up before she arrived home. Thus did Cumberland's fleet fail to take two of the richest prizes ever to come within the grasp of the piratocrats.

The gallant Captain Cave lingered on long enough to be landed in England, where he died in early December. Although his infected wound was blamed on poisoned bullets, in all likelihood, like Frobisher, he probably died from gangrene as a result of having an uncleansed wound.

Surprise and Fear

Every intelligent pirate captain's aim would have been to seize a prize without having to fire a shot, thus saving his weaponry for another occasion. For this reason, stealth, deception and surprise were honoured weapons in the armoury, being backed up at the last moment by the fear-induced panic when a presumed friendly hull revealed its true colours moments before coming alongside.

Drake was a good deployer of these non firing or minimum-firing tactics. During his circumnavigation he took full advantage of the fact that lightly-armed Spanish ships did not even suspect that a Protestant fox had entered their pacific hen- (or golden goose-) house. On 5 December 1578, giving every appearance of friendship, he anchored in Valparaiso harbour close to a well-stocked merchant ship. To this lightly manned vessel, Tom Moon rowed over with every sign of boarding for a friendly visit. Instead, in an instant, the incredulous crew was bundled below with cries of '*Abaxo, perro!*' 'Down below, dogs!'

Drake's main target in these halcyon days was *Nuestra Señora de la Concepción*, a richly-laden cargo ship that had left Callao a fortnight ahead of her pursuer. Her nickname *Cacafuego (Spitfire* or, less politely, *Shitfire)* indicated to Drake that, unusually for these seas, she was reasonably well armed. Drake crowded on sail to catch up, but gave himself time to take other prizes that crossed his path.

Once *Cacafuego* had been sighted, Drake did not press on at best speed. Instead, keeping all sails set, he streamed out astern a number of empty wine jars which, filling with water, acted as a sheet-anchor and made *Golden Hind* appear to be a heavily-laden merchant ship. Glad of such company on her lone voyage, *Cacafuego* altered course towards her. Only as their hulls touched did Drake reveal himself, when his men, hidden until now, appeared aiming their bows and harquebuses at Juan de Anton and his crew. Two gunshots brought down her mizzen and, seconds later, over her gunwale on the opposite side clambered a boarding party which had crept around her stern in Drake's pinnace. She surrendered without further resistance, giving Drake access to a treasure, while a sea-fight against such a foe might have brought him naught but wreckage.

Eventually, at the height of his fame, Drake used his very name as a primary weapon in his arsenal. In 1588 during the first day of the English and Spanish fleets' close encounter, the up-channel-bound Armada had to leave in their wake *Rosario* which, as a result of a close encounter with one of her own kind, had lost bowsprit, foremast and mainmast. That evening, Drake in *Revenge* was given the vital task of acting as the guide for the pursuing English, keeping his ship, at whose stern he was to burn a lantern, in the van, so that none woke up to find that they had closed the enemy too closely overnight. But Drake's pirate itch got the better of him and, ordering the light to be extinguished, he flanked the English fleet and, with his instinctive navigational skills, arrived near dawn close to *Rosario*.[24] Onboard the crippled vessel that senior Spanish Don, Pedro de Valdés, prepared to sell his and his crew's life dearly but, on enquiring as to who commanded *Revenge* and being informed it was *El Draque*, he decided that surrender was not only discreet but honourable. Like the gentlemen they were, Drake and de Valdés exchanged pleasantries onboard the captured ship before, without having fired one shot, Drake relieved the Spaniard of his command and 55,000 gold ducats, then ordering *Rosario* to be escorted as a prize into Torbay by *Roebuck*.

If subterfuge failed, the attackers had to be ready to fight immediately. In June 1586 two of Ralegh's pirate ships, *Serpent* and *Mary Spark*, sailed for the Azores and encountered a lone Spanish vessel which:

> . . . we would not be known of what nation we were, we displayed a white silk ensign in our main top, which they seeing, made account that we had been some of the king of Spain's Armadas, lying in wait for English men of war: but when we came within shot of her, we took down our white flag, and spread abroad the Cross of Saint George, which when they saw, it made them to fly as fast as they might, but all their haste was in vain, for our ships were swifter of sail then they, which they fearing, did presently cast their ordnance and small shot with many letters . . . into the Sea.[25]

The English pirates thus followed neither written fighting instructions, nor a predictable method of attack. Successful piracy required the seizing of the initiative as much as it did the deployment of superior firepower. In 1574 Don Luis De Requesens y Zuñiga, the Spanish governor of the Netherlands, had written that in a future clash between the English and Spanish fleets:

If the fleets came to hostilities it would be well to give orders when they approach them, that the ordnance flush with the water should be at once discharged broadside on, and so damage their hulls and confuse them with the smoke. This is their own way of fighting, and I have many times seen them do it to the French 30 years ago. I advise his Majesty's ships to be beforehand with them, and they will then send to the bottom all that are opposed to them. This is a most important piece of advice. I am also advised that, if they find the Spanish fleet powerful and prepared, one of the principal instructions given to the captains is that they are not to attack but to go to Normandy or Guyenne, where they may find the best shelter.

As it was, the bold proposal of the Spanish to seize the Scilly Islands and blockade the Western Approaches ended with the death of that fleet's admiral, Don Pero Menéndez de Avilés, and the clash foreseen by Zuñiga never took place. If it had done, Zuñiga's tactics might have held true, for at the time he was writing, Edward Fiennes, Lord Clinton, was the Lord Admiral, and his ships were commanded by inexperienced naval men. When the delayed meeting took place in 1588, experienced pirates, not gentlemen, commanded the English fleet. They knew how to attack and how to keep clear of broadsides.

CHAPTER 5

Piracy in the Pacific

'With the counsels, consent, and help of my father, Sir John Hawkins, I resolved a voyage to be made to the Islands of Japan, of the Philippines and Moluccas, the kingdoms of China, and East Indies, by way of the Straits of Magellan and the South Seas.'
Sir Richard Hawkins, *Voyage into the South Seas,* 1595

The short period of English state-approved piracy made its grand debut not in the waters around England's coast, but in the Pacific, the reaching of which alone required an almost superhuman effort of seamanship. Only two expeditions managed to sail there with the right mix of ships, manpower, victuals, leadership and resolve, but each received a rich reward. They also established a tradition of naval circumnavigation that endured like a long-distance relay race through the following four hundred years.

Prior to Drake's famous circumnavigation, from 1577 to 1580, a desire for peace with Spain which, like Portugal, was ever jealous of foreign intrusions into waters over which it claimed sole rights, scuppered a plan to sail into the Pacific which had been proposed in 1574 by Sir Richard Grenville, with the supposed aim of discovering the great southern continent of *Terra Australis* which, importantly, was alleged to lie beyond the land already possessed by any Christian prince.[1] However, both the queen and the Spanish suspected that piracy was the real motive behind the expedition, which opinion was validated by the fact that Grenville's flagship was to be the 240-ton *Castle of Comfort*, which in 1566 had fought off a combined assault of seven Portuguese ships, and was armed to enhance her reputation. An unknown spy even reported that, 'They say they are taking with them a store hulk of 600-tons, with provisions, but I believe it is more likely to carry their plunder than to take stores.'[2]

Such concerns did not worry Grenville, but for a while they did the queen. Elizabeth's foreign policy was flexible or inconsistent, depending on the viewpoint of the observer. It so happens that 1574 was a year in which she, encouraged by her merchants, wished to establish peaceful dealings with Spain. This led to the signing of the Convention of Bristol, in which the English agreed to return Alba's gold and to no longer issue letters of reprisal to English seamen authorising the seizure of Spanish vessels. The November following, the court received a request from merchants who were trading with Spain and Portugal to be incorporated with the restoration of past privileges, an opportunity to which several newcomers also desired inclusion.[3] Thus was rejected the proposal of the renowned 'hothead' Grenville, despite his claim that, 'we seek no possession of interest; but only, if occasion be free, to traffic with them and their subjects which is as lawful and as much without injury as for the merchants in Portugal or Spain.'[4] Meanwhile, at court, Burghley was determined to keep the hopes of peace alive. In December 1575 he produced a pamphlet arguing against the 'prudence' of breaking off relations with Spain, 'which he objected to on the grounds of infirmity in finance, military, and naval resources and useful allies, recommending that the Prince of Orange and the Low Countries should be secretly succoured.'[5]

However, if the hierarchy were endeavouring to show restraint, the 'lowerarchy' were not. When Drake had first clapped eyes on the Pacific in February 1573, John Oxenham, a fellow pirate, had been standing next to him and shared his desire to return one day to those waters. Grenville had tried to recruit him for his voyage which, given that the man was a pirate specialising in the Caribbean, is another indicator that Grenville's intentions were not as innocent as his stated aims.

Oxenham had little patience with such subtleties, preferring the direct approach to the source of treasure. The year 1576 found him anchoring in a hidden harbour close to Nombre de Dios, from where he led an expedition across the Isthmus to another secluded bay where he constructed a pinnace with which to swoop upon unsuspecting treasure ships. As his boat floated off, so Oxenham became the first Englishman to set sail upon the waters of the Pacific.

Initially, this bold intrusion was rewarded handsomely. Two ships were taken with ease, yielding a cargo of 60lbs weight of gold and 100,000 pesos of silver, a haul both rich enough to satisfy Oxenham's crew and heavy enough to require several trips back through the jungle. Yet Oxenham was not satisfied and greed was to become his downfall. Near his hideaway lay a native pearl fishery and this he raided, turning the otherwise supportive locals against him. They reported his presence to the governor of Panama who, unlike many of his compatriots, responded vigorously to the threat. The anchorage was discovered, the ships were retaken; the pinnace was also seized. When Oxenham appeared, despite his numbers being swelled with two hundred *cimaroons*, he was bested and forced to flee empty-handed, leaving eleven English dead and seven prisoners behind. Once back on the Caribbean coast he found his own ship in Spanish hands. He fled inland but failed to shake off his pursuers, finally surrendering after his hideout was betrayed by a *cimaroon*. Spanish justice was swift, selective and severe. The seamen were hanged. The execution of Oxenham, Butler, his ship master and a few others was delayed in the hope that robust questioning might yield up valuable information about future English plans.[6]

Oxenham's private venture could, of course, be disowned by the English authorities whose agreements with Spain and Portugal in 1574 and '76 had suspended the issue of letters of reprisal and outlined ways to re-establish trade and suppress piracy. Just over a year later, in early 1578, Drake captured and ransacked three Spanish and several Portuguese vessels, thus breaking the terms of the treaties with both those nations. What is more, he justified his behaviour, and future plans, by claiming that he was carrying the queen's commission for a piratical voyage which had also been approved by Walsingham. To have behaved in such a fashion, without knowing that he had approval at the highest level, would have been equivalent to offering himself up for execution on the mudflats at Wapping. Drake's character and careful preparations for this voyage indicate that he was not gambling so recklessly with his life, and yet the only evidence that exists to indicate the nature of the voyage is a barely decipherable note by Walsingham which stated that:

[He] . . . shall enter the Strait of Magellan lying in 52 degrees of the pole, and having passed therefrom into the South Sea then he is to sail so far to the northwards as thirty degrees seeking along the said coast aforementioned like as of the other to find out places meet to have traffic for the venting of commodities of those of her Majesty's realms. Whereas at present they are not under the obedience of any Christian prince, so is there great hope of gold, silver, spices, drugs, cochineal and divers other special commodities, such as may enrich her Highness's dominions, and also put shipping a work greatly. And having gotten up as aforesaid in the thirty degrees in the South Sea (if it shall be thought meet by the afore named Francis Drake to proceed so far) then he is to return by the same way homewards as he went out. Which voyaging by God's favour is to be performed in twelve months although he should spend five months in tarrying upon the coast, to get knowledge of the princes and countries there.[7]

Very little of the above document made practical sense: the short length of the voyage, the trading opportunities along the barren coast, the type of commodities to be expected, all showed either a lack of understanding, or a desire to have a disclaimer available should Drake exceed his brief in such a way, or at such a time, which meant it would be politic to disown him.

Walsingham's note is all the indication that exists to show that Drake might have sailed with a commission from the queen. By contrast, under examination by their captors Butler and Oxenham opined that, because of the existing treaties with Spain, the 'Queen will not, as long as she lives, grant the licence' to Drake to pass through the Straits of Magellan, but that 'after the Queen's death there will certainly be someone who will come to the Straits.'[8] Neither was the planned voyage welcomed by all of Elizabeth's councillors, several of whom, like Burghley, gave the returning Drake a welcome many degrees colder than that shown by his sovereign. Yet if such a commission was granted, its wording would have marked the moment that Elizabeth moved from being a persecutor to a patron of pirates, at least of those of whom she approved.

Burghley and the peace party's lack of enthusiasm for approving Drake's piratical plans might explain the one blot on the newly knighted Drake's escutcheon as he knelt on the deck of *Golden Hind* to receive the queen's approval, following his richly rewarding voyage round the world.

This had begun on 15 November 1577 when, after years of preparation, Drake sailed from Plymouth with a fleet of five small ships, including his own purpose-built vessel, the 120-ton *Pelican* (later rechristened *Golden Hind*), the 80-ton *Elizabeth*, which was to be commanded by John Wynter, the son of George, one of his sponsors, the 30-ton *Marigold*, the 50-ton store ship *Swan* and the pinnace *Benedict* (later renamed *Christopher*). Of these, just *Golden Hind* completed the voyage. *Swan,* her task done and her slow speed becoming a mighty hindrance, was burnt at Port Desire while *Christopher* was scuttled off Port St Julian, mainly to reduce the risk of the spread of disgruntlement among the crews. Then *Elizabeth* turned back, having been battered by the same storm that sank *Marigold* shortly after the three remaining ships entered the Pacific.

Although many of the 160 men and boys who signed on for the voyage had sailed with Drake before, he had not informed them that he was heading for the Pacific but, for security reasons, let it be known that the Mediterranean was their destination. This disinformation was mainly for the benefit of Spanish spies, but the true purpose of the voyage was kept secret, it appears, even from members of the Privy Council, many of whom were keen not to offend Spain, preferring trade to war. Along with the professional seamen, Drake also took with him a small group of gentlemen, of whom the most senior was Thomas Doughty, whose acquaintance Drake had made in Ireland when both men were serving the earl of Essex. Whatever the reason for including this sophisticated courtier amongst his company, it turned out to be a mistake, with Doughty believing his breeding gave him a right to challenge Drake's authority and plans.

Drake was very clear as to the purpose of his voyage stating, when challenged by Doughty, that the queen herself had invested in his voyage and told him, in private, 'Drake, so it is I would gladly be revenged on the King of Spain, for divers injuries that I have received.' What Drake did not mention was to what 'injuries' the queen was referring to for, in 1577, she had little of which to complain. 'Revenge through roving' was obviously Drake's understanding of his mission, and he showed his contempt for Walsingham's written aims by carrying just £50 in value of goods for barter. Nevertheless, he was playing a dangerous game.

For, with initiatives being taken at the highest level for the suppression of piracy, specifically such as involved the shipping of Spain and Portugal, Drake needed to ensure that his authority to take such actions would be unquestioned both during his voyage and on his return. Wisely, he prepared for his voyage quietly in Plymouth, aware that Burghley was adamant in his opposition to piratical acts being committed against England's Iberian trading partners. So much so that Drake claimed Thomas Doughty was guilty of treason by, on his own admission, discussing the voyage with the secretary, contrary to the queen's direct instruction that the latter should not be told anything about the expedition, a caveat of whose existence the unlucky Doughty would not have known.

Yet it is the presence of Doughty onboard that indicates an incongruity. Drake was never more comfortable when sailing in company with his friends and relatives; his prickly, easily slighted nature made this a most evident fact. Yet here he was, sailing on the grandest voyage of his life, risking that very life, both at sea and on his return home, with a man who was both landlubber and gentleman, two character defects of which Drake did not approve.

The piracy began early. Off the coast of Africa, Drake seized vessels belonging to both Spain and Portugal and relieved them of their cargoes, mainly wine and fish, both of which were vital to the wellbeing of the long-distance travellers. These seizures John Wynter, less certain of his authority than Drake, carefully recorded, along with his own reluctance to take part in the prize-taking. Then in January 1578, off the Cape Verde Islands, the fleet took a much more significant vessel, the 100-ton Portuguese merchant ship, *Santa Maria* (or plain *Mary* as the Protestant Drake rechristened her) laden with trade goods destined for Brazil. These included, along with some high quality wines, linen, canvas, rapiers, cork, hats, skins, combs, fish-hooks, nails, cloth, thread and knives, just the sort of goods essential to both new colonists and sailors alike. Indeed, Francis Fletcher, Drake's chaplain and diarist, thought that these goods, 'served us in that stead that she was the life of our voyage the neck whereof otherwise had been broken for the shortness of our provisions.'

The most valuable prize taken out of *Santa Maria* was in fact a human one in the form of the ship's pilot, Nuño da Silva, who knew well the seas into which Drake was venturing for the first time. During his enforced service he and Drake grew close from a respect based on their mutual professionalism. Much of what we know about the voyage comes, in fact, from the detailed account da Silva gave to the Inquisition during his lengthy interrogation. Indeed, it is from his record that we have the only extant description of *Golden Hind* and life onboard.[9]

The voyage to South America passed smoothly, apart from Drake's concern that Thomas Doughty was stirring up trouble. Finally, after various attempts to control his vexatious gentleman companion, Drake had Doughty arrested and tried for mutiny before all the members of the expedition gathered in a hollow square on an island at Port St Julian, south of the River Plate.

Doughty, no fool, quickly got to the crux of the matter, which was to question Drake's authority. In the belief that he could prove his trial to be unlawful, he invited Drake to 'make sure your commission is sufficient.'

'You may be sure that it is,' responded Drake.

'I pray you then,' said Doughty, 'let us see it. It is necessary for it to be shown.'

It was a fair question and request to which Drake seemed to have no answer. He blustered, telling Doughty that he would not see it, then appointing a jury to listen to the charges. They seemed to have little of serious substance in them until Drake asked one of his men, Ned Bright, to recount a conversation he had had with Doughty in which, so Bright claimed, Doughty had told Bright that 'my Lord Treasurer knew the real purpose of the voyage.'

Drake gently opened the jaws of a trap, asking Doughty how Burghley could possibly have known this. Doughty replied, 'He had it from me.'

In those five short words he condemned himself, for Drake, with angry glee, thrust home. 'Lo, my masters, what this fellow hath done. God will have all his treachery known, for Her Majesty gave me special commandment that of all men my Lord Treasurer should not know it. See how his own mouth hath betrayed him.'

From that moment the verdict and the punishment were inescapable and, on 2 July, having dined with Drake, Doughty was rowed ashore where the assembled crews watched his execution. Drake marched forward to grasp the severed head stating, as he raised it up, 'Lo! This is the end to traitors.'

Yet it was a strange form of treachery, to inform the queen's most long-serving, senior and trusted adviser of the true purpose of a voyage in which the queen herself had invested. Besides which, why should the busy Lord Treasurer have spared the time to discuss such issues with a man of such inconsequence as Doughty? Given the fact that Burghley wished to avoid aggravating Spain through acts of piracy, a far more likely scenario is that Burghley summoned Doughty and appointed him as his 'eyes and ears', and even as his authority on the voyage to ensure that Drake adhered to the one plan which was committed to writing, a trading voyage towards *Terra Australis*. This planting of his own men seems more likely in that Doughty did not sail alone: he was accompanied by his brother, John, and, most significantly, a lawyer, Leonard Vicary. Here would be sufficient legal witness to give evidence should any misdemeanours occur on the voyage that would give rise to a hearing in the Court of Admiralty, as did happen when Wynter arrived home, having abandoned the voyage, with *Elizabeth's* hold filled with seized Portuguese goods. Drake was not prepared to risk such a challenge to his authority, purpose or prizes, either on the voyage or once it was over. The trial and execution of Doughty made that perfectly clear. It also made clear that the expedition planners had tied themselves in a knot of such Gordian proportions so as to disguise their purpose and avoid recrimination that it needed a man of Alexander's directness to cut through the contradictions, most drastically at Port St Julian. Once by his drastic measures disencumbered from such machinations, Drake made sure that everyone understood where sole authority lay. He did this, bluntly, by dismissing all the masters from their ships, challenging them to query his right so to do, before restoring them to their positions, and then, more memorably, by a speech that was to become part of the naval tradition when he said:

Thus it is, my masters, that we are very far from our country and friends, we are compassed in on every side with our enemies, wherefore we are not to make small reckoning of a man, for we cannot have a man if we would give for him ten thousand pounds. Wherefore, we must have these mutinies and discords that are grown amongst us redressed, for by the love of God it doth even take my wits from me to think on it; here is such controversy between the sailors and the gentlemen, and such stomaching between the gentlemen and the sailors, that it doth even make me mad to hear of it. I must have it left, for I must have the gentlemen to haul and draw with the mariner, and the mariner with the gentlemen. What, let us show ourselves to be all of one company, and let us not give occasion to the enemy to rejoice at our decay and overthrow. I would know him that would refuse to set his hand to a rope, but I know there is not any such here; and as gentlemen are very necessary for government's sake in the voyage, so have I shipped them for that, and to some further intent, and yet though I know sailors to be the most envious people of the world, and so unruly without government, yet may I not be without them.

Then he gave them the political argument as if he was the *agent provocateur* of the Privy Council's war party, saying:

Let us consider what we have done. We have now set together by the ears three mighty princes, as first her Majesty, the Kings of Spain and Portugal, and if this voyage should not have good success, we should not only be a scorning or reproachful laughing stock unto our enemies, but also a great blot to our whole country forever. And what triumph would it be to Spain and Portugal! And the like would never again be attempted.

Only a man knowing that he had the full support of his queen for what he was about to achieve could have uttered those words, which voiced a purpose so contrary to the policy that Burghley wished to pursue. But Drake also had his supporters in Council, as the Spanish ambassador made clear, telling his king that several of the councillors, including Walsingham, 'affirmed that nothing would suit them so well as to make a supreme effort to trouble and disturb you on all hands.'[10]

Drake produced no evidence to show that the queen had stated that Burghley was not to be informed about the voyage, yet it was possible. In 1591 Elizabeth wrote to Cumberland approving his forthcoming piratical voyage, but including an injunction that he should not tell the earl of Leicester about their correspondence. The only difference was that had her great favourite learned of the letter, no one would have been accused of treason for letting the information slip out.[11]

Even without the commission, Drake had great authority vested in him simply by being the expedition's commander. This power over life and death was common to all navies, be they English, Spanish or Dutch: Medina Sidonia sentenced two subordinate Armada commanders to death for being slow to obey a signalled order, and Drake's powers of punishment, although slightly less draconian, would have been similar to that given by the Prince of Orange to Dutch pirateering commanders in 1582 (Appendix 6). Yet neither those powers, nor his resounding words at Port St Julian, stiffened every sinew present. On 6 September, having passed through the Straits of Magellan in just sixteen days, Drake's fleet entered the Pacific and sailed into a monstrous and persistent gale which drove them south and swallowed up the diminutive *Marigold*. In the face of such an onslaught, John Wynter returned to shelter *Elizabeth* inside the Straits. Once there, according to him, his crew voted to return home rather than sail to 30° South, their rendezvous point, and he, fearing mutiny as the alternative, gave way.

Drake, however, managed to weather the storm and on 1 November he sailed northward. It was soon obvious that they were in a sea unknown to da Silva for, expecting the coast to run northwest, they held to this course until they realised that they were miles from land and had to turn sharply back towards the shore. By this time the crew was starving, thirsty and scrofulous, while the ship herself was much in need of a bottom scouring to restore the sailing qualities required by a pirate vessel. At the earliest likely-looking spot, Drake closed the shore and anchored off Mocha Island.

At first the natives appeared friendly, welcoming the new arrivals with much needed gifts of fresh meat, fruit and vegetables. The place seemed ideal for Drake to careen the newly named *Golden Hind* and to allow his men some days for relaxation and recuperation well south of the land known to be occupied by the Spanish. Besides which, he thought, the missing *Marigold* and *Elizabeth* might well reappear on track for the rendezvous at 30° South. So the next day he had himself rowed ashore with a dozen men to negotiate their stay with the still smiling welcoming party. Thomas Flood and Thomas Brewer were the first ashore, jumping in the water to secure the boat's painter to a rock or tree. Then, as they stepped onto the beach, they were seized and dragged away, while from all sides a volley of arrows was unleashed on the unsuspecting English. All were struck, some several times, and it was only because one sailor cut through the painter with his sword that the boat's crew was saved from annihilation. Fending off attackers who were wading towards them, they backed water until they could pull away to the safety of the ship. Although they all managed to scramble onboard, the gunner, Great Nele, died of his wounds, while the horrific end of the captured men could only be imagined.

Refreshed but saddened, Drake now demonstrated that he felt in no way restrained by any orders to remain clear of Spanish interests. His one attempt to establish relations with the people dwelling south of 30° had ended in an exchange of fire, the death from wounds of two of his party and the savage butchery of two others. So much for trade. Now, after just one month in the designated region, Drake was to spend the next four concentrating on what he had really come to do, plundering Spanish ships.

Golden Hind weighed anchor and continued northward, but both she and the crew did need to find a place of safety soon. This could have proved problematic, for they were soon level with the Spanish port towns of Concepción and Valparaiso. Then, fifteen miles beyond Valparaiso, they sighted a sheltered and apparently empty bay. In they steered, to be greeted this time by a couple of local people who were not only relaxed in their company, but informed them that there was one great ship, *Capitana Grande de Los Reyes*, in Valparaiso along with several smaller vessels. Drake's predatory olfactory senses smelt loot. Delaying the ship's careening (after all, a smooth hull was not necessary to attack vessels in port) and with one of the Indians as a guide, Drake retraced his track to the port town of the Spanish capital, Santiago.

He entered the harbour on 6 December to find it unguarded, so that Tom Moon was able to row over and seize *Capitana* with ease. The alarm was, however, raised ashore and on hearing it the population fled before the small group of devilish-looking Englishmen. The freedom to ravage the houses resulted in little reward; as so often during this period, the real riches lay afloat and *Capitana*, which by local standards was not well laden, yielded sufficient bounty to 'make' the voyage by herself.

Her main cargo was of sweet-smelling cedar timber and Chilean wine, some 1,770 jars worth of which, if any of it survived the journey to England, would have marked the beginning of a trade that only became established in the late twentieth century. Almost unnoticed at first glance were four treasure chests filled with Valdivian gold, of which one, at least, judging by the way it was secreted away, was being smuggled. The owner of the vessel estimated the value of the gold as 24,000 pesos, but the official bottom line was 200,000 pesos.

As with *Mary* so many months earlier, *Capitana* also carried a valuable human treasure, another pilot, a Greek, Juan Griego, whom Drake retained, having released the other members of *Capitana*'s crew. As for the ship itself she was pressed into Drake's service and began the voyage under her new owner in a leisurely way while Drake, oblivious or uncaring about the alarm his exploit had raised, continued northward to look for a site for his delayed careening.

On 18 December he selected the wrong site, too close to the town of Coquimbo, from where a squadron of mounted soldiery charged down upon the shore party before, alerted by the ship's lookout, they could re-embark. Richard Minivy, in command of the party, turned to face the foe, giving his companions a chance to pull away. In this they were successful, but Minivy was shot dead and then horribly mutilated, his head and right hand being cut off, before his heart was plucked out and his torso pincushioned with arrows.

Now caution took a hold and it was not until 22 December that Drake took the risk of hauling *Golden Hind* ashore in Salada Bay. This time the English were more tactically competent. Most of *Golden Hind*'s cargo was transferred to *Capitana* to lighten the former and make it easier for her to be careened and graved. The prize was also anchored offshore to warn of the approach of any enemy shipping. Onshore, to cover the working party and his flagship, lying helpless as a beached whale, Drake sent out reconnaissance parties to forewarn of any approaching troops, although it is unlikely that with his few defenders he would have been able to protect, let alone relaunch, *Golden Hind*, in the face of a determined onslaught. In this eventuality *Capitana*, already stored and victualled, would have been the Englishmen's only hope of avoiding capture and returning home. As a further precaution, each night the men returned onboard *Capitana*, leaving just a few sentinels behind on the beach. If a sudden attack under cover of darkness did occur, most of the crew would be able to sail away, abandoning just a few of their number to, at best, incarceration or the galleys, at worst, a heretic's death in the flames. While these preparations were taking place, Drake assembled a pinnace from the prefabricated kit he was carrying onboard *Golden Hind*. With suitable armament she could well deter any approach by local vessels hunting for him, for his intelligence suggested few were anything other than lightly armed. The pinnace also had another use. Once she was completed, Drake himself took command and sailed away to search for his two missing consorts, only to be driven back by strong winds.

Disturbed only by a few inquisitive natives and a small group of Spaniards who were frightened away by a couple of shots, the stinking, sweaty, back-breaking task of cleaning *Golden Hind* continued apace. The outer hull was scraped free of barnacles and weed and all the bore-holes made by teredo worms drilled and filled. Loose strips of caulking were prized away, and fresh oakum driven into the gaps between timbers. Once both captain and carpenters were satisfied with the clean lines of the hull, the exposed side was recaulked, tarred and greased. Then the ship was refloated, turned around and dragged ashore once more for the other side to receive the same treatment. While all this was going on, an unfortunate few laboured deep in the hold, scooping out the faecal material, slime and general stinking slops that had sluiced downward during the course of the voyage. Then, before the ship was refloated, fresh ballast had to be spread evenly across the hold to await the fresh drizzle of detritus.

With the careening complete, Drake felt able to leave behind much of his store of tar, feeling that his men would benefit from its replacement with Chilean wine. On 19 January the squadron of three ships weighed and turned north. The wine proved useful on this leg, as they were sailing along one of the most barren coasts in the world, and even the pinnace, deployed inshore to seek out fresh water, had little success. For a while, although they were approaching the latitude in which the fabulously rich silver mountain of Potosi lay, they came across few Spaniards. The few native craft that crossed their path they boarded and relieved of their catch of fish.

One day they made a farcical catch of their own. Sighting a small Indian settlement, Drake sent a small 'fishing' party ashore to see if there was anything worth taking. The village was abandoned, but in one hut they found an exhausted

Spaniard snoring beside thirteen bars of silver he was carrying to the coast. This was removed without disturbing the sleeper. Then, a few miles up the coast, they sighted a man and a boy leading eight pack llamas down a track. On reaching them it was found that each llama was carrying two bags full of refined silver, a grand total of 800lbs weight in all, providing the pirates with both food and another small fortune.

Small, for other reasons, would be Drake's haul over the next few days, when he had expected that it should have yielded most, for he had arrived at the great silver trans-shipment port of Arica. Partly, it was the timing; the fleet arrived to find just two ships in port, only one of which had any cargo worth taking, and that just thirty-five bars of silver and a chest of coins. Warning had also been passed ashore, giving the Aricans all night to assemble a formidable reception party. With his numbers much depleted, Drake could not afford to mount an opposed landing – he withdrew.

A similar disappointment awaited him at Chule. True, a large treasure ship lay at anchor, but her sides were glistening, indicating that her cargo had just been unloaded; indeed, a baggage train of llamas could be seen slowly plodding up the track, away from the town whose jubilant and jeering population yelled to Drake that he had just missed seizing five hundred bars of silver. In a few days the hopes of the voyagers must have taken a tumble. It was obvious that, as they journeyed north, along the land routes news of their passage was preceding them. Speed suddenly became important once again and although unable to match swift mounted messengers ashore, Drake knew he had the fleetest ship in those tranquil waters. By now he also had a number of prizes which not only were difficult to man properly but were lethargic sailers, a fault that outweighed their usefulness as treasure chests. After a thorough sort-out of cargo, they were all abandoned while Drake pressed onward, unfettered by this flock.

The few ships taken on the days that followed added little to their haul. Then, on Friday, 13 February, off Callao, Drake learned that a very well-laden treasure ship, *Nuestra Señora de la Concepción*, had departed that port a fortnight earlier for the long voyage to Panama. Even then, the calculating admiral did not cram on all sail in pursuit. Deciding Callao ought to be worth investigating he lay out of sight until nightfall, before nosing his way into the harbour – a minor feat of competent pilotage. Empty vessels and angry townspeople greeted him. The viceroy of Peru, Don Francisco Alvarez de Toledo, one of those aroused, rushed down to the harbour and ordered a pursuit. Two ships were commandeered, filled with soldiery and dispatched, only to lose heart slightly before losing sight of the pirate whom they discovered to be the notorious 'El Draco' only after they had sailed. Of course they had their excuses ready on their return, stating that their ships, being unballasted, 'with the movements of the people and being narrow were awkward and unable to carry much sail, responding like drunken men and handling badly [so that] many of the gentlemen were seasick and too ill to fight.' In addition, they had sailed so swiftly that they were carrying insufficient food, no cannon, few harquebuses, and no 'engines to throw fire'. This latter seems to have been a local obsession, and on 20 February John Butler was hauled before the Inquisition in Lima to explain just how such a weapon could be manufactured.[12]

Embarrassed and furious, Toledo turned from tactics to strategy. A bark was to be sent to warn all coastal settlements between Callao and Panama of Drake's presence. The two treasure ships at sea were to be overhauled and ordered to make for the nearest port where their cargo could be unloaded. Two armed merchant ships were to be sent to intercept the pirate, while a galley at Guayaquil was ordered to carry out a search of all possible creeks and inlets where Drake might be laid up.[13]

It was not until 27 February that the two pursuing ships departed carrying 120 soldiers, under command of Don Luis de Toledo, the viceroy's son. Drake, meanwhile, was closing in on *Cacafuego*. As he advanced, Drake sought out information from the crews of captured ships, most of which yielded few goods of value, but all of whom gave him some inkling as to his quarry's progress. One vessel, belonging to Benito Diaz Bravo, appeared to be laden only with tackle, maize, salt pork and hams, flour, sugar and other stores destined for Panama, most of which would have been welcomed by the hungry English. Yet the well-dressed passengers made Drake suspect that more lay hidden. So first, like so many robbers, he demanded that his captives empty their pockets and their cabins. Delighted but not content with the haul he informed them: 'Gentlemen, in a few moments . . . my men will search your vessel . . . If they discover any hidden items . . . I shall have you all hung.' The deck rang with dropped rings and the heap of riches rose rapidly.

The next day, having stripped the vessel of all that would be of use to him, Drake returned the ship to Diaz Bravo, who estimated that he had lost 18,000 pesos in gold and silver, with a further 4,000 pesos damage done to the ship and her stores.

Drake and the pinnace sailed on. Knowing that he must soon sight his prey, the captain offered a reward to whoever sighted her first. It was to be his cousin, John Drake, peering with his bright young eyes from the crow's nest who claimed it, when he saw her sails just twelve miles ahead.

Rather than race after *Cacafuego* and thereby cause alarm, Drake crowded on his sails but, at the same time, slowed his progress by trailing a sea-anchor consisting of water-filled wine jars. This deception worked well for, far from being suspicious, San Juan de Anton, captain of *Cacafuego*, glad of the chance of some company on his dreary lonely voyage, put his helm over and closed the other ship. As he came within hailing distance he heard, to his astonishment, a call for him to strike sail and surrender. Entering in to the spirit of the joke San Juan issued his own invitation: 'What England is this that orders me to strike sail? Come onboard and strike sail yourself?' The pirates needed no further invitation. In the words of San Juan's testimony:

> They blew a whistle on the English ship and the trumpet responded. Then a volley of what seemed to be about sixty harquebuses was shot, followed by many arrows, which struck the side of the ship, and chain-balls shot from a heavy piece

of ordnance carried away the mizzen and sent it into the sea with its sail and lateen yard. After this the English shot another great gun . . . and, simultaneously, a pinnace laid aboard to port and about forty archers climbed up the channels of the shrouds . . . while at the opposite side the English ship laid aboard. It was thus that they forced San Juan's ship to surrender.[14]

Drake, as always, was courteous in victory, embracing San Juan and commiserating with him, saying, 'Have patience, for such is the usage of war,' although, with their nations at peace, it was his own private war to which he referred.

The rewards of this war were great. Drake asked for an inventory of *Cacafuego*'s cargo and then had his men search the ship to match the amount registered. Up from below they brought 1,300 bars of silver, fourteen chests of silver coin, 80lbs of gold, and a great deal of jewellery, to the value of 362,000 pesos, to which could be added a further 40,000 pesos in unregistered cargo. This, at an exchange rate of eight shillings to the peso, meant that Drake had taken a cargo valued at over £125,000, the equivalent of half a year's income for the Crown!

Over the next few days Drake revealed to San Juan how much he was driven by the defeat at San Juan de Ulua. Jestingly, he stated that since that date the king of Spain had been his treasurer for the sum that he had lost that day. For this reason, 'he now wished to act as treasurer of the king's estate', taking the king's silver for his own as compensation, while the rest of the treasure would be passed on to his queen.

A fallacy lies within that joke that made a legal farce of all letters of reprisal. Hawkins's inflated demand for compensation for his losses at San Juan de Ulua had totalled £30,000, including £5,000 for *Jesus of Lubeck*, £9,120 for the slaves, and £900 for lost property. Drake was now claiming roughly that amount, some £37,000, from King Philip's property alone onboard *Cacafuego*: legally, he had no right to the remainder of her super-rich cargo. However, he was in the position to claim, in defence of his actions, if charged with piracy on arrival home, that he just wished to retain fair repayment for his losses while the government was free to do what they would with the remainder. Far better defence, of course, was the vast amount of treasure that he would now have to lay at his queen's feet.

Drake was satisfied. Departing from the unladen *Cacafuego* at night, he sailed north again, knowing that his only remaining major challenge was to find a safe route home. There were four alternatives which San Juan de Anton summarised as being, 'by the way of Good Hope and India; by Norway; by the Straits of Magellan, and the fourth he would not name', but which might well have been a passage through the Straits of Anian over the top of North America. Before selecting one of these options Drake needed to careen the ship for, whichever route he chose, a good speed would be essential to ensure the survival of the crew. He began the operation off Costa Rica, but with *Golden Hind* now being so deep-draughted, he could only scrape off the weed to just below the waterline. What he needed was a convenient hull into which his heavy guns and cargo could be shifted, so that *Golden Hind* could be hauled over and cleaned. On 17 March his pinnace, patrolling while the mother ship was being scraped, came across a bark which, having offered an initial resistance, surrendered. Onboard the bark, they found a cargo which, at that moment, could have been far more valuable to Drake than another hoard of treasure. This was an elderly pilot, Alonso Sanchez Colchero, who had been selected to accompany the new governor of the Philippines to Manila and had with him all the charts and rutters necessary for that purpose. Drake dispossessed Colchero of the charts, but could not remove his dignity. Faced with threats and then with actual hanging until close to death, Colchero simply refused to become a traitor and abettor of this English pirate. While Drake continued his rough wooing of Colchero, guns and goods were transferred to the captured bark and ashore to expose as much of the seaweed shrubbery which was accompanying *Golden Hind*. Then with the assistance of the tides the ship was hauled over for a good bottom scrape. By 24 March the work was complete and they departed once more northward.

A few days later Drake decided that, with his raid successfully completed, the captured bark was of more use for the next leg than the diminutive pinnace. He therefore transferred most of his recent prisoners into the pinnace, provided them with food and water, and dispatched them coastward. Colchero he kept, still convinced he could turn the pilot to his service. He could not, but a few days later he took another ship, one of whose passengers, Francisco de Zarate, Drake's most senior captive, gave a vivid account of the capture of the ship in which he was sailing:

> On the fourth of April, about half an hour before dawn, we sighted in the moonlight a ship very close to our own. Our steersmen shouted at her to get out of our way and not to come alongside but to this they made no answer, pretending to be asleep. The steersmen then shouted louder asking what ship it was, to which they replied, 'From Peru,' and that she was 'of Miguel Angel', which is the name of a well-known captain on that route . . . The ship of the adversary carried her bark at her prow as if she was being towed. Suddenly, in a moment, she crossed our poop, ordered us 'to strike sail' and shot seven or eight harquebus shots at us. We thought that this was a joke but soon it turned out to be serious. On our part there was no resistance, nor had we more than six of our men awake on the whole boat, so they entered our ship with as little risk to themselves as if they were friends.[15]

There was no violence shown to the captured crew and passengers. Drake was his assured, charming self, although he wanted to know if the ship was carrying any gold or silver, and any relative or goods belonging to Don Martin Enriquez, the viceroy, and Drake's hated adversary from the fight at San Juan de Ulua, stating that he would not stop his plundering until, 'I collect two millions which my cousin, John Hawkins, lost at San Juan de Ulua.'

Within a few days Zarate and his companions, including the adamantine Colchero, were handed back their ship, and released to sail to the port of Realejo, from where the nobleman was able to write and inform Enriquez of his close encounter with the viceroy's sworn but courteous enemy.

As if the proximity of his hated enemy still rankled, Drake then risked all on an unnecessary raid on the port of Guatalco, vandalising the little settlement and its church, before sailing away after dumping, unceremoniously and callously, his long-term but no longer useful captive Nuño da Silva, knowing that he would be likely to face an intense, unsympathetic grilling from the Inquisition.

Drake was still uncertain as to the selection of his homeward route. He was, however, already on the western coast of North America which, cartographers claimed, led into the Straits of Anian and eastward back into the Atlantic. What Drake also knew was that April was not a good month in which to begin a trans-Pacific passage, for it would mean that the ship would arrive in the Philippines during the typhoon season. There was, therefore, nothing to be lost in using up the time to search for the mythical straits. The *Golden Hind* headed north.

But soon Drake, with his instinctive grasp of navigation, sensed that the Anian option was wrong. Not only did the coast not trend in the direction suggested by the cartographers, but the weather was turning incredibly cold. The passage, even if it existed, would take several months and Drake realised that he could be risking the whole expedition by sailing into an icy wilderness. Somewhere around 48° North he turned back to seek a safe anchorage in California, where he could careen and store up for the long passage westward.

On 17 June, after many weeks at sea, Drake brought *Golden Hind* to anchor in a bay at about 38° North. Here he was to stay until he left America for good on 23 July, establishing friendly relations with the Indians whose land he claimed for his queen, naming it Nova Albion, nearly forty years before Captain John Smith applied the same term, New England, to northern Virginia.

Piracy now ceased and, except for one foolish challenge of a Portuguese carrack near the Philippines, Drake behaved like a peaceful trader in his dealings with the native rulers of the East Indies, loading his already crammed ship with tons of cloves and other spices.

Because *Golden Hind*'s Pacific crossing passed without incident, little comment has been passed on what was an incredible feat of both navigation and victualling. Drake did have Colchero's charts, but they would have had both inaccuracies and omissions, so much so that he could not have been certain as to how long the open ocean passage might take. Although the men had taken and salted down both seal and bird meat from the Farallones Islands near San Francisco, they had been living in an arid land whose people had a subsistence economy with scarce enough food to feed themselves, let alone provide surplus for strangers. Nevertheless, by 21 October, which was the first date on which the English could take on supplies of fresh water and food unmolested, not one of the company appears to have suffered a serious attack of scurvy. In years to come, Drake was frequently criticised for his lack of attention to victualling his ships before a long voyage. His Pacific crossing indicates that he could be little short of brilliant in this essential activity.

The most notable and serious event over the next eleven months was the grounding of the deeply laden *Golden Hind* upon 'Hard and pinching rocks', which has been discussed earlier. Triumphantly refloated after that perilous accident, the ship crossed 140° of latitude before, on 26 September 1580, she nosed her way into her home port. The quality of her reception depended on many things: was the country at peace or war; what was the present policy concerning pirates; which courtiers were the most influential of the moment; what foreign policy was in force? All of which could be summarised in Drake's first question to those who rowed out to meet him: 'Does the queen still live?'

She did, and soon became a fervent supporter of Drake and those who wished to sail in his wake. As for the Spanish ambassador, Bernard de Mendoza's warning that she should disown the pirate or suffer the wrath of his master, to him Elizabeth turned deaf ears, appreciating more the full coffers that Drake laid before her than the empty threats from Spain. Drake had returned with a cargo valued at £25 million, in modern terms, far more than the English national debt. He was quick to send the most impressive trinkets off to London where they so delighted that there was not even a question of him not 'breaking bulk' until an official audit of his haul had been made. In the years to come this would become an ungranted privilege, but in 1580 Drake was the hero of the moment.

What is more, he was a master at using flattery as added value, as Mendoza reported to Philip the following January:

> Drake is squandering more money than any man in England, and, propor-
> tionately, all those who came with him are doing the same. He gave to the Queen
> the crown which I described in a former letter as having been made here. She
> wore it on New Year's Day. It has in it five emeralds, three of them almost as long
> as a little finger, whilst the two round ones are valued at 20,000 crowns, coming,
> as they do, from Peru. He has also given the Queen a diamond cross as a New
> Year's gift, as is the custom here, of the value of 5,000 crowns. He offered to
> Burghley ten bars of fine gold worth 300 crowns each, which however he refused,
> saying that he did not know how his conscience would allow him to accept a
> present from Drake, who had stolen all he had.

As for the queen, Mendoza reported that she showed.

> Extraordinary favour to Drake and never fails to speak to him when she goes out
> in public, conversing with him for a long time. She says that she will knight him
> on the day she goes to see his ship. She has ordered the ship itself to be brought
> ashore and placed in her arsenal near Greenwich as a curiosity.[16]

There, on 1 April 1581, Mendoza was able to report that the corsair, in full view of large crowds, had entertained his queen onboard *Golden Hind* and been knighted after dinner.

Although *Golden Hind* was then laid up as a public attraction, there was no intention of calling a halt to the enterprises for which she had been built, and others soon planned to repeat Drake's voyage.

The first endeavour ended in disaster and, for Drake, a personal tragedy. In May 1582 Edward Fenton sailed from Plymouth in *Leicester Galleon*, accompanied by *Edward Bonaventure*, *Elizabeth*, and the bark *Francis*, commanded by Drake's close cousin and companion on the circumnavigation, the twenty-year-old John Drake.[17] Even before they sailed, it was obvious that the force lacked victuals, tackle and leadership, and a fixed aim, although it was proposed to make a trading voyage to the East Indies. Following a fight with Spanish vessels off Brazil and a failure to find victuals, Fenton turned back. John Drake, however, persuaded his company that they should travel and triumph in his uncle's footsteps. Their first step on their own saw them shipwrecked in the estuary of the River Plate, where the survivors were either killed by Indians or captured by the Spanish. The latter was the fate of young John. He never saw England again, being last reported as a frail old man shuffling along in an auto-da-fé held in Cartagena in December 1650.

Then, on 21 July 1586, a comparative amateur navigator, Thomas Cavendish, left Plymouth for the South Seas with just three ships: the 120-ton *Desire*, the 60-ton *Content* and the bark *Hugh Gallant* of 40 tons, very similar in size to Drake's vessels, as was his company of 123 men.

The account of Cavendish's voyage in Hakluyt is an early anthropological gem, notable most of all for its detailed description of the native population with whom they came in contact, and the wild animals on which they fed. Also there emerges a coarser side of pirateering, in contrast to the more gentlemanly approach by Drake. For example the account states that:

> On Sunday 28 the general sent some of his company on shore, and they played and danced all the forenoon among the Negroes.
>
> On Monday morning, our general landed with 70 men or thereabouts, and went up to their town, where we burnt two or three houses and took what spoil we would.

A similar rough treatment was meted out to Spanish captives. In an effort to obtain some minor intelligence from the crew of a small bark, Cavendish

> was fain to cause them to be tormented with their thumbs in a wrench, and to continue them at several times with extreme pain. Also he made the old Fleming believe that he would hang him; and the rope being about his neck he was pulled up a little . . . but he would not confess.

Which last torture, to be fair, was exactly what Drake had performed upon Colchero, the Pacific pilot, and with exactly the same result.

During their passage through the Straits of Magellan, Cavendish's force came across the sorry remnant of the garrison of four hundred Spaniards who had been sent thither to prevent the use of the passage by the English. After three years of starvation and Indian attacks, just twenty-three of them remained, plodding along the shoreline, foraging for limpets and mussels, in an endeavour to reach the river Plate and civilisation.

Cavendish's squadron passed through the Straits into a welcoming March storm that kept them at the pumps for three whole days. Thereafter they made their way up the coast, skirmishing and being repulsed for little reward, but losing sufficient of their company that by June they had to sink *Hugh Gallant* 'for want of men'. They did take two ships with a cargo of 'sugar, molasses, maize, skins, montego de porco, many packs of pintados, Indian coats, some marmalade and a thousand hens', sufficient to provide several good breakfasts but no fortune.

So it continued, all the way up to the coast of California, by which time many must have felt that they voyaged in vain. Then on 4 November they sighted a sail which proved to be *Santa Anna*, a 700-ton carrack, bound for Panama from Manila. The Spanish crew, although outgunned, offered a strong resistance from 'fights fore and aft', hurling lances, javelins, and 'innumerable sort of great stones' upon the heads of the boarding party, whom they greatly outnumbered. Cavendish had little option but to stand off and batter his target into submission, a risky business for a pirate not wishing to sink his prize and, indeed, it was the rising water in the hold that persuaded the master to yield. Onboard the English found, 122,000 *pesos de oro*, wrapped around with silks, satins, damasks, and a rich, varied and extensive pantry of victuals. The voyage was made. The 190 Spaniards were set ashore, well-armed and provisioned, and with their own sails with which to erect shelter. While they came to terms with their fate, the anchored English argued about the division of the spoils and the journey home. Cavendish had retained from the prize a couple of Japanese youths and three young Filipinos but, more usefully, an elderly Spanish pilot with knowledge of the Pacific crossing, for he was determined to follow Drake's route home. This journey did not, however, appeal to the crew of the misnamed *Content*, who, having been handed their share, parted company overnight, presumably planning to return through the Straits. They were never heard of again.

Desire's voyage home involved many opportunities for describing the habits, some most peculiar, of the peoples with whom the crew came in contact, but was incident-free. In June she called at St Helena for refreshment, lingering there almost a fortnight before starting on the final leg of their voyage. On 3 September 1588, six days out from Plymouth, she met with a Flemish hulk which gave them news of the Spanish Armada into whose path, had it not been for their leisurely stopover in St Helena, she might have fallen. Cavendish's luck had held to the last and he was soon a very rich man indeed.

He was also, in not much longer a time, poor again, having spent his share of the prize money trying to impress at court. In August 1591, in an effort to restore his fortune, he led *Galleon Leicester*, *Roebuck*, his old ship *Desire* and two barks out of Plymouth, in a disastrous attempt to repeat his previous voyage. Storms in the Straits were a prelude for hunger and mutiny, disease and loss of life, the account of which reads like the tale of the Ancient Mariner. They endured most of the deprivations any crew could suffer and live to tell the tale. Few did. Cavendish took his own life. *Desire*, with just the captain and master fit enough to take turns at the helm, limped into Bearhaven, southern Ireland, where she was run upon the shore, her five crawling and eleven bedridden survivors too weak to lower her sails.[18]

In between Cavendish's voyages, the Bristol ship *Delight* had endeavoured to sail into the Pacific, only for the voyage to come to grief in the Straits of Magellan, with the crew complaining about being starved by a captain who kept all the rations to himself. Once again, the importance of leadership and shared hardship on voyages such as these comes vividly apparent.[19]

The accounts of the two voyages of Thomas Cavendish are wonderful works of maritime prose. Yet alongside them, even surpassing them, must be placed *The Observations of Sir Richard Hawkins, Knt in his Voyage into the South Seas in the Year 1593*.[20] This is a classic, informative and candid account of the last Elizabethan attempt to wrestle prizes from the Pacific, and there was much which Hawkins, the son of Sir John, could be candid about, for misfortune, mostly of his own making, dogged his entire voyage in the 350-ton *Dainty*, which he had bought from his father expressly for a Pacific endeavour.

The voyage was authorised by a royal commission, although John Hawkins had to pester Robert Cecil for its issue which, when it came in October 1593, gave him permission to:

> attempt some enterprise with a ship, bark, and pinnace against the King of Spain, his subjects and adherents, upon the coast of the West Indies, Brazil, Africa, America, or the South Seas, granting him and his patrons whatever he shall take, reserving to the crown one-fifth part of all treasure, jewels, and pearls.[21]

The ship and her armament have been a motif throughout this work, so it suffices to say that Hawkins's voyage provides an excellent illustration, by its shortcomings, just how much planning was needed to prepare for a successful circumnavigation. It is no wonder that the journey ended when a Spanish squadron seized *Dainty* in May 1594 and imprisoned her crew. Yet even then, fortune favoured the hapless mariner: he was soon on his way home in a ship that was almost captured by Ralegh during his failed Island Voyage of 1596. When Hawkins eventually reached England, he discovered a far easier way of making money, through getting appointed to the office of vice admiral of Devon, a post he held from 1603 to 1610, apart from a short spell in 1606/7 when he was suspended for his too-obvious corrupt dealings with pirates.

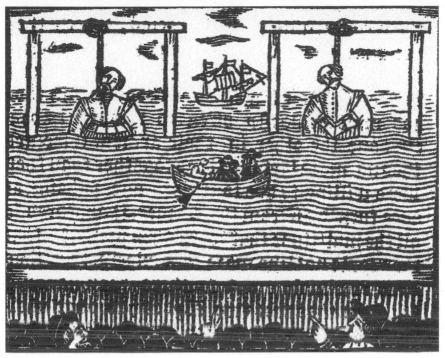

With the punishment for piracy being to be hanged in chains at Wapping, most practitioners were either foolhardy, desperate or the possessor of influential friends. (Author collection)

Before the English established trading links with the Far East, their preferred method of acquiring oriental exotica was to forcibly remove it from returning merchantmen like the ones depicted here. (© National Maritime Museum, Greenwich, London)

Without the need for wharfage or alongside berths, pirates were able to unload while anchored in any friendly, quiet cove or creek. This picture purports to show the return of Sir Edward Michaelbourne, after a piratical, interloping voyage to the Far East in 1606. (© National Maritime Museum, Greenwich, London)

The circumnavigators Drake and Cavendish and the doyen of English transoceanic travel, John Hawkins, all relied on piracy to replenish their ships and return a profit. (Author collection)

The Portuguese trading fort of San Jorge da Mina provided an open prison for Frobisher and later a point of contact for Hawkins when he entered the slave trading business. (Author collection)

Contrary to Victorian romantic notions, Ralegh's boyhood was not spent listening to salty tales of adventure, but in a household that practised piracy. (Author collection)

LEFT: Until Hawkins, Drake and their fellow pirateers learned the art of navigation, there would have been no Englishman qualified to pose for portraits such as this, showing a professional navigating officer with globe and dividers. (© National Maritime Museum, Greenwich, London)

BELOW: This drawing of *Golden Hind* reflects both the smallness of the vessel and its movement even in a modest sea. (© National Maritime Museum, Greenwich, London)

By the time that the queen loaned *Jesus of Lubeck* to John Hawkins, the ship was an old and cranky vessel; nonetheless, its presence in his fleet indicated her open approval of both piracy and slave-trading. (Peter Kirsch)

Ark Ralegh was too magnificent a vessel for the commoner, Ralegh, to retain as his pirate flagship, and he was soon forced to donate her to the queen. (Author collection)

Pirate ships deployed far from home needed to find secluded harbours where their ships could have their bottoms, scraped clean of weed, inspected for worm, and be tarred and caulked. (Author collection)

Scourge of Malice, as magnificent a ship as Ralegh's *Ark*, remained in the earl of Cumberland's fleet until he sold it to the East India Company, in whose service, renamed *Red Dragon*, and commanded by Lancaster, an ex-pirate, she continued her career of attacking Portuguese carracks, as this contemporary print shows. (RN Museum, Portsmouth)

A replica of *Elizabeth* that sailed with Grenville to establish the pirate base at Roanoke that became England's first, but short-lived, settlement in the Americas. (Author collection)

In 1607 the ex-pirate, Christopher Newport, in *Susan Constant*, led a small fleet of three ships into the Chesapeake and founded Jamestown, England's first permanent settlement in America. (Author collection)

The culverin or demi-culverin was the professional pirate's heavy weapon of choice, although it could only be carried in larger vessels whose exploits were, probably, state-approved. (Mary Rose Trust)

This saker, at St Mawes Fort, Cornwall, is presumed to have come from the ship carrying the goods of the incoming Venetian ambassador to London. Most embarrassingly, it was sunk by pirates. (Author collection)

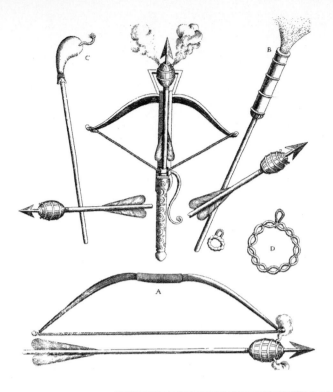

ABOVE: Bows and arrows, spears and grenades, such as those shown here, could be modified to hurl incendiaries into a potential prize. Unfortunately for prey and predator alike the resulting conflagration could easily get out of control, destroying the former and threatening the latter. (Author collection)

RIGHT: The upper deck of the replica *Golden Hind* at Brixham, showing the small-calibre guns that could be safely carried higher up in a light vessel. (Author collection)

The penetration of the Pacific by a handful of pirates was a short-lived episode: Oxenham first floated his boat on its waters in 1576; Drake disembogued from the Straits of Magellan on 6 September 1578; Cavendish set sail on one successful voyage in 1586 and one disastrous one in 1591; while Richard Hawkins surrendered to his Spanish foes in May 1594. In between those dates few other voyages rewarded England and irritated Spain so much. Given the rich rewards brought home, it might be wondered why more did not attempt the voyage, but the fact is that Drake's success represented a triumph many wished to emulate but few were able to imitate, for the ease of his genius disguised the effort of his endeavour, which made his triumphant circumnavigation one of the greatest voyages ever undertaken by man.

The planning necessary to travel successfully to those rewarding waters and, more importantly, to return safe home, was a challenge that daunted even the most well-organised of pirate adventurers. So it is not surprising that few attempted the passage and of those few a fair number failed either to depart, reach their destination, or return.

Logistics and leadership were the twin keys. The ships were sturdy enough for the great trek across three oceans; the seamanship and navigation competent for the task; the vessels well enough armed for the task, and the seamen willing to accept the challenge with its promise of rich reward. Things went awry, and swiftly, if a lack of food added to the discomfort of cramped quarters and sodden, cold clothing. The latter were considered as unavoidable, but empty bellies represented a betrayal, while the unfair distribution of scarce victuals encouraged mutiny.[22]

So, the ideal vessels for these voyages had to be neither too large nor too small. Large vessels would require too great a crew to victual and if, as would inevitably happen, disease and fighting reduced that number, the commander might find himself with too few fit men to man his vessel.

On the other hand, too few crew allowed little leeway once losses began to mount or when the requirement arose to man a rich or useful prize. Many a vessel on a long sea voyage limped back to the British Isles with only a handful of men to handle her. This was not a return befitting a pirate prince, nor would it persuade the court of the efficacy of such operations. The answer, as Drake realised, was to set sail with a number of vessels, some of which would be abandoned once they had fulfilled their task of carrying extra victuals, with their crew being used to augment those in the remaining ships. A victualling ship was vital at the start, for the pirates would be pariahs in any port at which they called, only able to replenish by force not peaceful persuasion.

Another essential was the presence of a pilot with local knowledge, even if their services had to be obtained by force. The pirate crew needed to be brave, professional, energetic, hard-working, reliable and well willing to attack larger vessels, while enduring setbacks without bitterness or mutiny. To keep them keen they needed to trust their commander and he them. Hauling and drawing together must have helped; so, probably, did a sense of humour. Leadership, its successes and failures, is most evident in those tales of the Pacific voyages. Those less able to contemplate or command such a lengthy voyage continued to seek for success on the waters of the Atlantic.

CHAPTER 6

The American Dream

That this western voyage will be a great bridle to the Indies of the King
of Spain and a means that we may arrest at our pleasure for the space of
ten weeks or three months every year, one or two hundred sail of his
subjects ships . . .

Richard Hakluyt, *Discourse of Western Planting*, 1584

Drake had demonstrated that riches could be stolen from both Central and South
America. However, the English were also looking for other ways to gain wealth from
the far side of the Atlantic. Their plans were designed to bypass the stipulations of
the Treaty of Tordisillas, which banished nations other than Spain and Portugal
from the world's wealthy middle. Justification for ignoring the terms of the treaty
were provided, first by the polymath Dr John Dee, who argued in his *Limits of the
British Empire* that, geographically, the line only stretched between 54° South and
45° North, leaving lands beyond those latitudes free for others to explore and claim
and that, historically, the English had already established a presence in the northern
part of the America. His views won support from Richard Hakluyt, the travel writer,
who, being an Anglican priest, also argued in his 1584, *Discourse of Western Planting*,
that 'no Pope has any lawful authority to give any such donation.'[1]

But before the English challenged the Spanish right to ownership of all of North
America, they endeavoured to circumvent that presence by passing over the top of
the continent to find a short route to the riches of Cathay, thus not only avoiding
the waters which the Iberians claimed for their own, but also the temptations to
seize prizes contrary to the treaties with Spain and Portugal of 1574 and 1576.
These had little effect on Drake's plans for his piratical voyage to the Pacific, but
the queen could claim that his was an independent venture, whereas her approval
was sought and granted for the northern voyages of which Dee, who was also a
cosmographer and astrologist, was a keen supporter and adviser.

First underway were three voyages commanded by the piratocrat, Martin
Frobisher. These began with a plan, prepared by a London merchant, Michael
Lok, to enter the Pacific from the north by a route, the Straits of Anian, which Dee
persuaded Lok existed as a navigable channel, and which was shown on a map in

Sir Humphrey Gilbert's 1576 edition of his *Discourse of the Discovery of a New Passage to Cathay*, which also stated that any ship transiting this strait would not be infringing the rights of the king of Spain, who had neither laid claim nor established possession to these northern lands.

So, in 1576, armed with this inaccurate map, Frobisher set sail. Reaching Labrador, he peered along its icy passageways and came home, but not before he had fossicked up some glittering rocks from an island lying off Baffin Island. From that moment geology took precedence over geography, and Frobisher's next two voyages were dispatched to mine more of this 'gold', with all plans for sailing to Cathay being shelved. The expeditions returned with over a thousand tons of this ore, which was soon shown to be but a worthless aggregate, an outcome which did not amuse Elizabeth, who had invested £1,000 in the enterprise. Once this inglorious fact was confirmed by the assayers, it is neither surprising that Michael Lok was imprisoned for debt, nor that Frobisher, true to pirate principles, blamed others for the farce rather than himself. Thus by the time that Drake was beginning his voyage along the Pacific coast of South America, the queen had invested in two transoceanic enterprises undertaken by her pirates. One had ended in the total destruction of her ship, *Jesus of Lubeck*, at San Juan de Ulua, along with the loss of many men and most of the cargo. The other had ended in the import of Frobisher's worthless rocks. So with trade with the Central America proving problematical, and voyages of discovery and mining to *Ultima Thule* proving useless, Elizabeth was persuaded to license those who would dwell about the middle part of that continent.

The origins of this initiative lay in another pamphlet written by the belligerent Devonian Sir Humphrey Gilbert, and entitled *A Discourse on how Her Majesty Might Annoy the King of Spain*. It had landed on Elizabeth's reading desk on 4 November 1577, just as Drake was fretting in Plymouth for want of a favourable wind. In his tract Gilbert proposed that the state should establish a settlement in Newfoundland, from where raids could be made upon the Spanish treasure fleets. As with Drake's voyage, Gilbert suggested that the true purpose of such a venture could be disguised and legitimised by issuing letters patent indicating a colonising and exploratory purpose.

On first reading, it would seem that Gilbert's choice of Newfoundland as a location for the establishment of a pirate colony from which to descend upon the Caribbean might have been somewhat perverse, save for the fact that it lay not too many days sailing from the West Country, along a route well known to the fishermen from those parts. Yet behind the site selection lay knowledge of a more southern tragedy.

During his trading at Borburata in modern Venezuela in 1564, Hawkins had teamed up momentarily with a French slaver and pirate, Jean Bontemps. From him he learned of the newly established French Huguenot colony, Fort Caroline, on the Rio de Mayo in Florida and it was to here he detoured on his return journey. The

English were welcomed amicably and able to give some service to the hungry colonists and their leader René de Laudonnière, to whom Hawkins sold a small ship after the French had refused his offer to evacuate them home. It was a decision they would die to regret.

For, shortly after Hawkins departed, the French, deciding that they should have sailed with him, embarked in their own vessels, but were prevented from sailing by adverse winds which, however, blew the French pirate Jean Ribault into the harbour with his resupply fleet of seven ships and hundreds of new colonists. Amidst much rejoicing everyone disembarked and began the rebuilding of their dilapidated fortifications. It was too late: those same winds brought an armada, commanded by the newly appointed governor of Florida, Pedro Menéndez, to the coast, where he tried to engage the French ships, which cut their cables and ran south, only to return the next day to warn the settlement of the imminent danger. Ribault, contrary to the advice of Laudonnière, embarked to engage the Spanish at sea. Instead, he sailed into a hurricane which wrecked all his fleet on the coast well south of Fort Caroline.

The experienced Menéndez had anticipated the storm's onset and disembarked his forces at a sheltered inlet he named St Augustine. From here his men turned north and, after a three-day, rain-bedraggled march, fell upon the colony at dawn. His magnanimity stretched to sparing fifty of the defenders, the rest he slaughtered, except for fifty who managed to escape, twenty-six being later killed, while the survivors embarked on two of the vessels that Ribault had left behind. Among these lucky ones were Laudonnière and the artist Le Moyne; from their survival posterity has benefited from a first-hand account of the colony and a folio of early colonial drawings that rival those of England's John White.

Hearing of the disaster that had befallen Ribault, Menéndez turned back south until he found the 120 survivors of Ribault's fleet huddled together on an exposed sandbank. Negotiations were never going to be successful and, having surrendered unconditionally, the French were ferried over the creek ten at a time, led behind a convenient dune and put to the sword. The same gory process was repeated with Ribault and a further two hundred survivors who were rounded up twelve days later.[2]

Albeit this was a massacre of an isolated settlement on a distant shore, the news was not long travelling back to Europe. Indeed, the Spanish were desirous that all should be aware of what treatment awaited any rash enough to settle in their domains. Humphrey Gilbert, Walter Ralegh and Richard Hakluyt, the proselytisers of plantations, would thus have known that a robust reception awaited any who wished to establish a settlement just some few hundred miles north of Fort Caroline. Newfoundland was far enough north not to wave a red rag of trespass before the Spanish bull.

In the same month that Gilbert delivered his latest tract, John Dee arrived at court with another of his writings. He was by this time the nation's most respected mapmaker and geographer, a man whom all those wishing to sail into the unknown considered it prudent to consult. But he was not only a cosmographer, cartographer and mathematician, he was also a man who believed strongly in England's manifest destiny to seek out and occupy new lands. It is he who is credited with coining the term 'British Empire', and he who proposed practical ways of achieving this. In August 1578 Dee presented to Elizabeth his study, *The Limits of the British Empire*, which justified England's ingress into lands claimed by Spain and provided a good defence against accusations of trespass. He was also summoned, shortly after Drake's return from his circumnavigation, to brief both Burghley and the queen on an intellectual justification of the pirate's behaviour that would overmatch Mendoza's outrage.

A short while later the queen, presented with many options as how best to continue the exploitation of northern America, selected for that purpose neither merchant adventurer nor explorer but Gilbert, another pirate whose business plan was one based on deception and deprivation of the goods of a nation with whom England was at peace. Yet the canny queen was not going to give her European neighbours cause to complain about her championing of corsairs for, just two months before she approved Gilbert's voyage, she issued an order in April 1578 'for the remedy of spoils and depredations committed by English pirates on the subjects of foreign princes in amity.'[3] This was followed on 11 June 1578 by her signing of letters patent in which she granted to her 'trusty and well-beloved servant, Sir Humphrey Gilbert, licence, to discover, find, search out and view such remote, heathen and barbarous lands, countries and territories *not actually possessed of any Christian prince or people' (author's italics)*, which, having been first discovered and then conquered, Gilbert and his heirs were authorised 'to hold, occupy, and enjoy', as long as they took possession of the land within six years. And what an estate was to be Gilbert's to enjoy, for the patent gave him authority to hold the land within two hundred leagues of his first settlement – a stretch of land equivalent to one that stretched from Land's End to beyond the Arctic Circle or, in North American terms, from Florida to Newfoundland. True to Gilbert's brief, the authorisation made no mention that the true purpose of the voyage was an assault on the Spanish Indies and its fleets, but Gilbert's aims were more apparent in the ships and men he selected to sail with him from Dartmouth, where in the summer of 1578 he gathered his fleet.

It was a well-chosen haven. For one thing, Dartmouth lay conveniently close to Gilbert's home at Compton Castle. For another, Dartmouth understood the ways of Gilbert and his men. In April 1578, as part of another nationwide crackdown on lesser pirates, Adrian Gilbert, the deputy of the port of Dartmouth, had been invited to take action against several citizens of that town over matters of piracy, including its mayor, Robert Plomley.[4] With a relative supervising the port and a sympathetic mayor in charge of the town, Humphrey Gilbert could have prepared for piracy quietly without complaint, had it not been for the behaviour of some of his captains, and the fact that several of his vessels were either known pirate ships or prizes taken by pirates.

Among the latter was Henry Knollys, son of the treasurer of the Royal Household, a relationship which he must have felt protected him from prosecution as a pirate. Quite openly, he allied himself with the notorious pirate John Callice and, even before the voyage got underway, sallied out into the Channel to take some prizes. Soon he and Gilbert fell out over Knollys's refusal to hand over two of his men for trial as murderers. As a result, Knollys and Callice, with several vessels in company, departed to go a-pirating off Ireland and Spain, their depredations being laid at Gilbert's door.

Meanwhile, Mendoza was following Gilbert's preparations with interest although, unusual for him, being confused as to its aim. Realising this, in an audacious move he reported to his king that he had infiltrated a spy onboard to sail with Gilbert and to make a full report on his return.[5]

It would have been a short report. Gilbert got to sea on 26 September 1578, only for his fleet to be blown into Plymouth by a strong equinoctial gale which kept them in shelter until 19 November, when they ventured out only to be forced immediately back to Dartmouth, where the voyage was abandoned. Only the novitiate, Ralegh, remained at sea, taking the queen's ship *Falcon* into the Bay of Biscay, where he attacked the first Spaniard he came across and received a severe pasting for his pains.

Although Gilbert saw this debacle as merely a delay, the queen and Privy Council viewed it as a clear indication of incompetence by a loose cannon who needed securing before he caused more damage. In a wonderful example of early bureaucratic language the Council wrote to Sir John Gilbert that:

> Whereas heretofore their Lordships wrote their letters to his brother Sir Humphrey, that either he would in respect of divers misfortunes wherewith he had been crossed forbear to proceed any further in his intended voyage, or else put in good bonds and sureties to her Majesty's use for his and his company's good behaviour on the seas; by letters of his of the 7th of this present and Sir Humphrey's of the 8th their Lordships having understood that before the receipt therefore having repaired to the sea, and could not without great loss stay, did not perform the said order accordingly, in the mean time the said Sir John assured his Lordships that his brother and his company were clear of such complaints as were made of spoils and injuries to be by them committed, and did undertake to be answerable for them; howbeit since that time complaints have been brought before their Lordships of the like disorders committed by his brother or his company, and that since the date of the said letters he hath a good while remained on that coast, and hath not put in bonds accordingly, and amongst the rest it is complained by Gonzala de Levilia, a Spaniard that the 4th of this present his brother as it is said being at his house at Greenway which is the very same date on which he writeth to his brother to be departed for the seas, a certain bark being

laden with oranges and lemons lying at anchor was by some of his brother's company taken out of her Majesty's streams . . . he is to see the said Spaniard returned to his bark and stores or otherwise sufficiently recompensed; and for that their Lordships are advertised that his brother Sir Humphrey has not yet departed and his brother, Walter Ralegh has not yet returned to Dartmouth, like as their Lordships have written to the Sheriff, Vice admiral and Justices of that county, to command them both to say so he is required friendly so to advise them to surcease from proceeding any further and to remain at home and answer such as have been by their company damaged.[6]

To emphasise their determination to control such acts of piracy, the Council sent by the same post a letter to the county worthies mentioned above, directing them to 'order that no person or shipping pass to the seas in warlike manner, although the parties would put in bonds and sureties'. This directive, they confirmed, applied especially to Gilbert and Ralegh, who were to 'remain on land' and to 'surcease to proceed in that their enterprized journey.' Finally, the authorities were tasked with tracking down the oranges and lemons and organising the recompense for their disposal and, presumably, consumption.

The Council was not prepared to let the matter rest. A little while later the authorities in Devon were told to 'make diligent enquiries of all piracies by seas and robberies by land committed by any such person' who 'pretended to accompany' Gilbert and Ralegh in their voyage and to commit them to prison or to paying a bond to guarantee their appearance in court to answer charges. Not that the Gilbert gang were being uniquely outrageous: the Council went on to demand the suppression of the many pirates operating in the area, singling out Torbay, a large and sheltered anchorage close to Dartmouth, as a special haven for these miscreants.

In June the Privy Council wrote one letter to the Devon dignitaries, thanking them for their diligence in the apprehension of pirates, and another to the authorities in Kings Lynn, asking them to investigate whether a bark that had arrived there was the same one as had been seized off Devon with her cargo of oranges and lemons, from which it would appear that those particular pirates had felt it best to leave the West Country until the situation returned to favourable normality.

Justice for Gonzago de Levilia was soon arranged by the Council who, having restored his bark, invited the Lord Lieutenant for Devon and Cornwall, the earl of Bedford, who was, incidentally, Drake's godfather, to load it with grain in lieu of the lost fruit. This arrangement was how both letters of reprisal and the Admiralty Court were meant to work, restoring goods to the value of those stolen if piracy could be proved.

Piracy was not the only activity with which Gilbert was associated, for later in 1579 a very stern order was issued by the Council requiring him to answer charges that members of his company were responsible for the murder of one of the retainers of Sir Owen O'Sullivan and for 'wounding his brother almost to death.'

Meanwhile, Gilbert remained free to plan his second voyage to the Americas. This was a much more sombre and, at first, successful affair, for he sailed from Cawsand Bay on 11 June 1583 and arrived off Newfoundland on 30 July, a journey of just seven weeks, having been abandoned by only one ship, Ralegh's bark *Ralegh*. This time Gilbert had issued very clear instructions to his fleet of five as to how they should behave as an organised body, but in discussions as to whether or not they should sail north or south about to reach their destination he betrayed his piratical instincts stating that, as a shortage of victuals might hinder a southern approach, they should sail direct for the Great Banks where 'a multitude of ships repairing there for fish, we should be relieved abundantly with many necessaries, which, after the fishing ended, they might well spare and freely impart unto us.' The true interpretation of this sentiment was demonstrated by the behaviour of the crew of *Swallow*, herself a prize, who, pleading with a well-stocked fishing bark for some supplies, boarded and ransacked her of both tackle and victuals.

On 3 August the downward spiral began with Gilbert grounding in the approaches to the harbour of St John's, Newfoundland, much to the amusement of the previously bemused fishermen gathered there, and deflating the pomposity with which Gilbert had planned to claim the land for his queen. The fishermen did, however, provide him with sufficient victuals to send him on his way. He left, having sent *Swallow* home with his sick. He retained her pirate captain and crew, only for most of them to perish when *Delight*, into which they had transferred, ran headlong onto the rocks in foul and misty weather, while *Golden Hind* (not Drake's) and *Swallow*, following blindly astern, were barely able to claw their way back into deeper water.

With the loss of *Delight* went the desire to continue the voyage so, on 31 August, the two remaining ships turned back for England. The stormy passage revealed one of the main weaknesses in the over-arming of pirate vessels, for *Squirrel*, 'which was overcharged upon the decks with fights, nettings and small artillery, too cumbersome for so small a boat that was to pass through the ocean', foundered with the loss of Gilbert and his entire ship's company. Gilbert left an eternal image of his last moments for when *Golden Hind* approached *Squirrel* on the previous day they saw the admiral seated calmly in the stern reading a book, while above the storm he was heard to shout, 'We are as near to heaven by sea as by land.'

So for a number of years Drake was the only one of Elizabeth's adventurers who had returned with anything to show for his efforts and her faith. Frobisher had imported hard core, while Gilbert had not even made it to the shore beyond which Her Majesty had been generous to grant him overlordship. Had Frobisher found a route to Cathay or a mine of great worth; had Gilbert returned with tales of a brave new world, then Drake might well have been disowned as an embarrassment to a queen wishing not to go to war with Spain. Elizabeth was, however, still willing to put her trust in one of her inexperienced favourites, a faith for which she was rewarded by the flop of Ralegh's Roanoke expedition. In so doing she was also encouraged by a brave new voice, a man whose gift with prose was the equal of Shakespeare's in verse. This was Richard Hakluyt the younger, who in 1584 published his *Discourse on Western Planting*, which was a brief collection of 'certain reasons to induce her Majesty and the state to take in hand the western voyage and the planting there.' Among the articles were those that suggested:

> All other English Trades grow beggarly or dangerous, especially in all the king of Spain's Dominions, where our men are driven to fling their Bibles and prayer books into the sea, and to forswear and renounce their religion and conscience and consequently their obedience to her Majesty.
>
> This voyage will be a great bridle to the Indies of the king of Spain and a means that we may arrest at our pleasure for the space of time weeks or three months every year, one or two hundred sail of his subjects ships at the fishing in Newfoundland.
>
> The richness that the Indian Treasure wrought in time of Charles the late Emperor father to the Spanish king, is to be had in consideration of the Queen, most excellent Majesty, lest the continual coming of the like treasure from thence to his son, work the unrecoverable annoy of this Realm, whereof already we have had very dangerous experience.
>
> What special means may bring king Phillip from his high Throne, and make him equal to the Princes his neighbours, wherewithal is showed his weakness in the west Indies.
>
> The Spaniards have executed most outrageous and more then Turkish cruelties in all the west Indies, whereby they are everywhere there, become most odious unto them, who would join with us or any other most willingly to shake of their most intolerable yoke, and have begun to do it already in divers places where they were Lords heretofore.
>
> The Queen of England's title to all the West Indies, or at the least to as much as is from Florida to the Circle arctic, is more lawful and right than the Spaniards or any other Christian Princes.

Arrogant, avaricious, adventurous and ambitious, Walter Ralegh had all the necessary attributes to take up the cause championed by Hakluyt, especially as he was obvious heir to the licence granted to his drowned half-brother. When added to this potent mix was the admiration, indeed infatuation, of the queen for this handsome young courtier, then his suit was going to be unstoppable. In a very short time he had obtained a charter to continue Gilbert's unfinished work. This granted him dominion over an area of America far larger than that controlled by any other of Elizabeth's subjects, along with the right to sell huge estates over there to others to help pay for his expeditions. The only catch was that the land needed to be settled, if only in part, within six years of the grant date of 25 March 1584.

Ralegh thus acted with speed but not before, unusually for an Elizabethan courtier, drawing up a strategic plan based on the ideas put forward by both Gilbert and Richard Hakluyt.

There was only one impediment to this vision facilitating a significant exodus of free-born Englishmen to the shores of America. This was the simple fact that few free-born Englishmen wished to emigrate. That this was apparent to Hakluyt, even as his pen raced enthusiastically across his parchment, can be seen in that he saw 'That this enterprise will be for the manifold employment of numbers of idle men, and for breeding of many sufficient . . .' This implication that volunteers might not be numerous was made clear in practical terms when Ralegh was granted a right to impress men in the West Country to man his expeditionary forces, the first of which sailed just one month after the queen had signed his charter.

Such a speedy departure indicated that Ralegh's plans were well advanced by the time that he received official approval. They were, befittingly, both ambitious and economically opportunistic. Ralegh well knew that to obtain financial support for his venture he needed wealthy backers, the queen being a notorious skinflint, and that such investors would only be encouraged to make advances should there be an almost certain opportunity for a reasonable return. This, short of stumbling on either a gold mine or a passage to Cathay, his settlers could not guarantee, so for the moment the opportunities were said to lie offshore in piratical raids on Spanish shipping, as Hakluyt had made clear, stating that:

> If you touch Philip [in the Indies] you touch the apple of his eye; for remove his treasure, which is *nevus belli* and which he hath almost completely out of his West Indies, his old band of soldiers will soon be dissolved, his purpose defeated, his powers and strength diminished, his pride abated, and his tyranny suppressed.[7]

To neutralise, or even eradicate, the benefits that Philip was accruing from the Indies, the English needed to cut off the supply, most easily at its source. In short, it was necessary to establish a suitably sited settlement, from which the English could plunder both north for fish and south for gold, thus overcoming many of the disadvantages that plunderers based so far away in England experienced. Hakluyt, very much an admirer of, and adviser to, Ralegh, most definitely considered that here was the man for the job, giving him every encouragement to establish a pirate base in America. Ralegh's plan was supported by four pillars each of which essential to stop the project from wobbling or collapsing. They were:

> First, the despatch of a reconnaissance party to discover a suitable site.
> Secondly, the occupation and fortification of the chosen site to deter or repulse attackers.
> Thirdly, the reinforcement and re-provision of this site.
> Fourthly, the establishment of a civilian settlement to encourage self-sufficiency, ship-husbandry, and to seek, plant and develop export goods to send back to England.

Even before the reconnaissance party was despatched, Ralegh sought advice as to where a suitable pirate haven might lie. The aim almost dictated the geographic location, for if its ships were to attack both north and south, a point almost equidistant between the *flotas* and the fishing boats seemed ideal, especially as this would still displace the English settlement a sufficient distance from the Indies to deter the Spanish from mounting all but a major expedition against the interlopers.

The key lay, therefore, in finding whether or not such a well-sheltered harbour existed in such an ideal location. According to Ralegh's cartographical adviser, John Dee, it did. In 1580 he produced a very long chart depicting the North American seaboard from Newfoundland to the Caribbean.[8] It was a most comprehensive map, its construction based on correspondence with Ortelius and Mercator, the foremost mapmakers of the time, and enhanced by discussions with some, such as the Portuguese pilot Fernando, who had sailed along that coast. It could thus claim to be the most up-to-date and accurate map available, its reliability enforced by the provision of lines of latitude and longitude. And, behold, just where the ideal site for a pirate base might lie, Dee showed a circular bay, Bahia de Santa Maria, its entrance protected by a double row of three islands. Dust that vellum roll and it might even be possible to detect Ralegh's index fingerprint as it struck that point of the map and he declared that this was what he was looking for.

To find the bay, he despatched two ships, the names of which we do not know, commanded by Philip Amadas and Arthur Barlowe, both of whom, as well as being members of Ralegh's extensive household, had received up-to-date navigational instruction from a third member of the household, Thomas Herriot, one of the great brains of his generation.

The two ships seemed to have covered the long southern passage, via the Canaries to the West Indies, without incident, and emerged from the Florida Passage to find themselves, in early July, sailing along a continental sandbank that seemed to stretch without breach hundreds of miles to the north. After several days passage the captains, convincing themselves that a few narrow, shallow gaps in the banks were Dee's bay, managed to enter the inner lagoon that separated the banks from the mainland and found themselves so kindly welcomed by the native people that Amadas felt compelled to write, 'We found the people most gentle, loving and faithful, void of all guile and treason, and such as live after the manner of the golden age.' As for the possibility of resistance to an English settlement, well, Amadas reported that, 'when we discharged any piece they would tremble threat for very fear, and for the strangeness of the same: for the weapons which themselves use are bows and arrows: the arrows are but small canes, headed with a sharp shell or tooth of a fish sufficient to kill a naked man. Their swords be of wood hardened: likewise they use wooden breastplates for their defence.'

The natives, in other words, could be discounted as a threat. Which left the Spaniards, of whose massacre of the French at Fort Caroline no one needed reminding. So somewhere on the landward side of this sheltered lagoon, where sheltering ships and a small settlement could be hidden and protected by the Outer Banks, seemed ideal, and a few days after they arrived Amadas and Barlowe were ferried to a site that they felt answered these requirements and at which the local chief was content for them to establish their settlement. This was Roanoke Island and, in accepting the offer, the two captains made a decision that day which was to doom all the rest of Ralegh's initiative to failure, for neither of them noted that entry into the Sound could only be made by ships of a very limited draught and then only in good weather.

It is easy to criticise Amadas and Barlowe for their decision, but they had been at sea for many days and still could see no end to the great sandbanks that ran along the American littoral. They were, in fact, just sixty miles short of the great sheltered haven of Chesapeake Bay, to where future settlers in Virginia would be directed and which, it would appear, coincided with Dee's Bahia de Santa Maria, for its entrance lay at latitude 37° North, while St John's, Newfoundland was sited at 47.5° North and the exit from the Florida Channel, the route that the *flotas* took to enter the Atlantic homeward bound, lay at 27° North. Thus, by just sixty miles out of a journey of nearly four thousand, did Ralegh's reconnaissance party fail to found a city on other than sand.

They were back in England by mid September. The captains even brought with them the name for this new-found land. It was Wingandacoa, later translated as 'what fine clothes you are wearing', which, as such, might have suited the sartorially elegant Ralegh, but he did not have a reputation as a subtle schemer for nothing. Addressing his queen he suggested that, rather than keep referring to 'her' new empire with an unpronounceable heathen name, from henceforward the land should be named, in her honour, Virginia. And so it was that, although Ralegh failed to inveigle Her Majesty's investment, he succeed in hooking her heart.

Stage two of the grand piratical plan was launched on 14 September 1585 when, with Sir Richard Grenville as both admiral and general onboard the 140-ton queen's ship *Tyger*, a fleet of seven ships sailed from Plymouth with a company of soldiers under the command of Colonel Ralph Lane, embarked to build a fort at Roanoke. Along with *Tyger* sailed the 100-ton *Lion*, and Ralegh's *Roebuck*, with this beastly trio accompanied by the more ladylike *Elizabeth* and *Dorothy* and two pinnaces for inshore work, one of which was lost on the crossing.[9]

It would be thought that for such a delicate operation a clandestine passage would have been appropriate. But clandestine was not Grenville's way. A man whose party-trick was to eat the glass from which he had drunk his wine was not going to worry about disturbing dastardly Spanish Papists. The fleet, which had soon lost contact with the admiral, rendezvoused off Puerto Rico, where Ralph Lane, deliberately selected for his military engineering skills, built two forts at two separate sites, both of which drew the local Spaniards' attention to the expedition. Grenville then captured two ships, before inviting himself to dinner at the governor's residence at Isabella, the town that Columbus had founded. Indeed, just to show how well provisioned his party was, Grenville had:

> our men provide two banqueting houses covered with green boughs, the one for the gentlemen, the other for the servants, and a sumptuous banquet was brought in served by us all on plate, with the sounds of trumpets, and consort of music, wherewith the Spaniards were more than delighted.

Following dinner, the governor laid on a three-hour-long bullfight in which both sides took part. After which entertainment, even avoiding the possibility of *in vino veritas*, it is unlikely that the governor had much doubt about Grenville's intentions. Any suspicions would have been confirmed the following day when Grenville's party traded for 'horses, mares, kine, bulls, goats, swine, sheep', as well as the more saleable items such as sugar, ginger and pearls. Once the English departed, their presence and surmised intentions were passed along the reporting chain all the way to Philip, crouching like a hunched black spider at the centre of his web in the Escorial. From these documents there seemed little doubt that the piratical plan had been let out of the bag. The fate of the settlement hung, for a while, on Philip's response to the several reports.

In the meantime, the English, who sailed from Hispaniola on 7 June, almost solved the Spanish problem for them by arriving too early on the American coast, when a navigational error by the Portuguese pilot, Fernando, brought them to a dangerous proximity of the aptly named Cape Fear. They hauled away from this danger only, again through a misjudgement by Fernando, for *Tyger* to run aground in an entrance to the Sound that lay inside the Outer Banks. The ship was refloated and repaired, but the damage that counted was not to the ship but to her cargo. For some reason *Tyger* was carrying not only most of the provisions, but also all the seed for planting. Nearly all of this was spoiled beyond recovery, leaving Lane's party, who were eventually landed well beyond the end of the growing season, short of victuals before they had even begun their settlement. Nevertheless, the 107 men left behind when Grenville sailed for home on 27 August seemed to regard their immediate future with equanimity, confident in the belief that fresh supplies were already on their way.

The source of these supplies was, in accordance with Ralegh's master plan, Drake's brother, Bernard, who was meant to sail for the colony later that year. However, the Council now intervened for, while Grenville was in the Indies, the Spanish authorities had decided to embargo all English ships entering Spanish ports. Word of this decision swiftly reached England and spread rapidly to the ports, thus preventing many a merchant from sailing into captivity. It was unlikely, however, that the news would filter over to the English fishing fleet off Newfoundland, many of whom intended to land their catch in Spain. To warn them of this danger, Bernard Drake was ordered to sail for Newfoundland rather than Virginia. This change of plan proved advantageous for him, for he seized sufficient cargo to 'make' the voyage. What he did not do was proceed onward to Roanoke, preferring to return directly home. The first nail in the colonial coffin had been hammered home.

Grenville, like Bernard Drake, but in his usual idiosyncratic way, had also 'made' his voyage, to the immense relief of Ralegh and the investors. And, as befitted the grand plan, this was not wealth won in the wooded wilderness of Wingandacoa, but through piracy on the high seas, a clear indication that Ralegh's predatory plans could pay dividends.

A few days sailing from the Outer Banks, Grenville sighted a tall ship, gave chase and overhauled her through 'goodness of sail'. She was the *Santa Maria* of St Vincent, the flagship of the San Domingo *flota*, which had sailed as a convoy of thirty three ships, but had been scattered into smaller and smaller groups by incessant inclement weather until *Santa Maria* found herself a mother hen without any chicks. Indeed, far from 'goodness of sail' resulting in her being overhauled, she had deliberately reduced sail in order for the other ship to close her, believing that it was one of the missing convoy. Several salvoes from *Tyger*'s guns soon destroyed that illusion, along with much of her rigging and several of her crew. When two shots holed her close to the waterline, the captain decided to surrender.

Grenville was now in a quandary. He had a prize drifting close to him, but he had left the ship's boat behind with Lane to allow the latter to explore the Sound. A rummage through the ship produced some timber which the carpenter swiftly nailed together, so that Grenville crossed over, 'with a boat made with boards of chest, which fell asunder, and sunk at the ship's side as soon as ever he and his men were out of it.'[10]

The farcical ferrying proved most worthwhile.[11] The passengers onboard the prize turned out to be wealthy, returning to Spain with goods stowed in their chests to the value of 40,000 ducats. Besides this, in the hold, were 200 boxes of sugar, 7,000 calf-hides, 1,000 quintals of ginger and sundry other items, valued at 120,000 ducats. Grenville spun a different story about the taking of the prize and its apparent value. In a disingenuous letter to Walsingham, justifying his behaviour, he wrote, almost dismissively:

> In my way homewards I was encountered by a Spanish ship, whom assaulting me and offering me violence, God be thanked, with defence and safety of myself and all my company, after some fight I overcame and brought into England with me; her lading is ginger and sugar.

As for the rumours of a far richer cargo, Grenville continued:

> I do assure your honour that I have found but little; neither doth any such quantity pass from St Domingo from whence they came to Spain. That which was here belonged only to private persons who were passengers into Spain . . . And the same when the ship yielded was embezzled by the company.

Which was their right for, by law and custom of the sea, the possessions of private persons became the property of those that seized them.

Strange then, if the cargo was of so little value, that Grenville decided to travel home in her, sending *Tyger* on ahead, thus separating the prize from those who had a right to a percentage of her value. For a while the *Santa Marians* had a tight time of it for, although he kept her cargo onboard, Grenville had most of her victual transferred to the short-rationed *Tyger*. To rectify the shortage, Grenville sailed his prize to Flores where, hiding his crew below decks, he had the Spanish captives call out for a boat with supplies to be brought out to them. Discovery of the true nationality of the ship's crew led to a stand-off, which Grenville resolved with his usual charm and bluster by actually paying for his provisions.

Returning to England Grenville was able to dissemble and cloak his good fortune without much difficulty, for even his reduced estimate of value guaranteed the investors a good return.

Ralegh had thus proved that western planting could be made to pay and he made ready for the next two stages of his grand plan – the resupply of Lane and the despatch of the civilian community that would settle around the fort. It was now that the scheme, already frayed, began to unravel towards its tragic and mysterious bitter end.

The spoliation of the victuals when *Tyger* ran aground had meant that, as winter approached, Lane's party had to rely more and more on the generosity of the local population who, as is common to all subsistence groups in temperate lands, could barely store enough to support their own folk through the winter. However kind and welcoming they might be to sojourners like Amadas and Barlowe, they had neither the ability nor the intention of supporting a group who behaved like bullying beggars.

Given these circumstances, Lane did remarkably well to keep his men both fit and alive. He led by example, eating the scarcely warm innards of his slaughtered pet mastiff as if they were the best *foie gras*. Others were more picky. To avoid starvation Lane sent several groups down to the coast to survive on clams and other crustaceans, while he hunkered down to repel or frustrate the anticipated Indian assault. In this he was as successful as he was in keeping his men alive: on that criterion alone, Lane was by far the most successful of the early colonial leaders. Indeed, his group would have overcome the non-arrival of Bernard Drake's fleet had Ralegh's relief vessel or Grenville's reinforcement and resupply fleet returned on time and as promised.

As far as the latter was concerned, Lane might have had misgivings. Not only had he quarrelled openly with Grenville, but in letters sent home 'from the new fort in Virginia' he wrote a blistering criticism of the proud pirate, probably aware that Grenville would be made aware of the content. Did Lane, every day that Grenville failed to reappear, wonder if he might have been more circumspect? Eventually a fleet did anchor off the coast, but this one was that of Francis Drake, whose presence takes us back to the original concept of the settlement as a pirate base.

A fly alighted on an arras in the plushly furnished apartments of Ralegh's Durham House had more access to the ideas being aired and the schemes being hatched in that room than we can ever gain from archival material. It is easy to forget that the spoken truth often escapes heavenward on insubstantial airs and is not, especially in the case of the risky or inglorious, always captured in ink on fly-paper pages. That having been said, the Tudors did record, recount and report many views that might today be only disclosed through the Freedom of Information Act. Yet they knew how to avoid being trapped by written indiscretions, as Henry Howard, condemned to death through such evidence recorded during Henry VIII's reign, stated:

> Although a man sometimes in speech utters that which is not so well to be allowed, yet speech be easier forgotten. What a man . . . commits to writing, wherein there is any error, it is ever open evidence of a man's folly.[12]

So, although the propaganda published to encourage the English to establish a presence across the Atlantic to 'annoy' Spain is freely available, we have to surmise some of the related machinations which were being hatched by the piratical-minded Ralegh and his coterie of talented supporters and were not written down. An example of this may well be the route followed by Drake on his way home from his West Indies raid of 1585/86, for although there is no documentary evidence to link Drake's voyage with Ralegh's plans, the fly on the arras probably knew more than the records show.

Drake had sailed from England on 14 September 1585 with the appointed task of securing the release of the English merchant ships being held in Spanish ports. For this task Drake's force consisted of the queen's ships *Elizabeth Bonaventure* and *Aid*, several privately-owned pirate ships belonging to Hawkins and Drake, and a strong contingent of merchantmen, among which was *Primrose*, the one ship that had escaped Spanish clutches and raised the alarm about the embargo. As long as he achieved the main aim, the queen appeared to be relaxed about what Drake then did with his powerful flotilla, as long as she could not be held responsible for his actions. She had, however, invested £10,000 in the expedition, excluding the value of the ships, so certainly expected some return. Drake was also sailing with some twelve companies of soldiers under the command of Christopher Carleill, and they certainly were not embarked to provide idle mouths for Drake to feed once he had sailed away from Galicia.

Drake was after plunder, especially that being transported across the Atlantic but, as so often in piratical planning, he went about it in just the wrong way. Making haste for the Spanish Biscayan coast, he soon discovered that orders had already been given for the release of the English ships. Yet, instead of putting on all sail to make his interceptions, Drake dawdled just to irritate, without income, the Spanish port authorities. He left Cape Finisterre astern on 9 October, unaware that the Mexican *flota* had passed the mouth of the Guadalquivir two weeks earlier, the immensely rich treasure fleet being welcomed home at about the same time as Drake turned south.

Deprived of his prey, and knowing that no rich convoys remained at sea, Drake was forced to turn from piracy to plunder. A series of raids ensued, beginning, after being repulsed off Madeira, with an assault on Santiago in the Cape Verde Islands, which produced victuals but not valuables, and a virulent fever that killed some three hundred men and left many more weakened or incapacitated.

The sacking of Santo Domingo in Hispaniola came next. The occupied town, held to ransom for a million ducats, eventually yielded the attackers just 25,000. The disappointed fleet sailed on to arrive off Cartagena on 9 February 1586. This was a major settlement, but one that relied much on the natural defences of swamp and creek to protect it from assault. The English went straight into the attack, with Frobisher and the pinnaces endeavouring to break into the harbour, but being kept back by the defender in the Boquerón fort, while Carleill led a brilliant assault along the narrow spit of land on which the town lay. Once the inhabitants fled, negotiations for the return of their town began, agreement being reached for what was also a disappointingly low sum, 107,000 ducats.

With his holds empty, Drake considered the options available to him. There had been talk of holding onto Cartagena, but his force was now too weak to attempt this. Likewise, an assault on Panama was considered too risky for too little potential reward. The ships had been at sea for a long time, on a voyage that had been a financial failure, and one that had resulted in major loss of life through sickness, casualties and accidents. All the more reason then for Drake to lead his force through the Florida Channel and head for home. Yet he did not do this, and his actions indicate that he had no intention so to do, for while at Cartagena he embarked into his poorly-victualled ships some two hundred released galley and field slaves, and encouraged up to three hundred native Indians to join them for a passage north. Now, given the state of the English ships, and the skills necessary to sail them, this group did not represent an impressment of seamen essential to get the ships back to England. No, this group was destined for one place only, Roanoke, where they could augment the small force established there by Lane.

Drake's actions very much indicate that he had discussed and approved Ralegh's plans for Virginia, for his first port of call on the homeward leg was the Spanish settlement of St Augustine, whose town and fort he put to the flame, seeing it, quite rightly, as a threat to England's more northerly base. To this he sailed on, discovering its whereabouts without much difficulty, which rather belied the careful plan to conceal it. Leaving that point to one side, Drake must have been dismayed by what he found. He had anticipated entering a harbour defended from both the enemy and the weather, a harbour in which his pirate ships could be safely careened and his men be allowed to stroll ashore. Instead, he found he had to keep them onboard, because he had to anchor in the open ocean a safe league or so from land.

For a moment, Drake thought that all was not lost. Lane too had appreciated that Amadas and Barlowe had stopped just sixty miles short of one of the world's largest and most secure anchorages and he had conceived a plan to move his men to that safer haven. Drake, impressed, offered him sufficient hulls and victuals to achieve this aim and get Ralegh's scheme back on track. Then the weather intervened. The skies darkened, the winds and waves rose up, and the English fleet found itself being forced to run out to sea by a great hurricane.[13] Days later, broken-masted and storm-stained, the survivors and stragglers returned – but not all of them. Several of the pinnaces were wrecked and some of the ships, including the 70-ton *Francis* which Drake had offered to leave behind to transport the settlers to the Chesapeake, allowed the storm to blow them towards England.

Drake offered Lane another vessel, but it was considered not fit for the task and Lane, probably in isolated reluctance, accepted the admiral's alternative offer to go home with him. The fort was abandoned. This left the men and women whom Drake had embarked in Cartagena. They were offloaded onto the Outer Banks. Nothing is known of them thereafter, but it can be surmised that their fate was unpleasant and their life short. Grenville's much delayed resupply convoy arrived just after Drake's sails had dipped below the horizon.

Drake, with the colonists embarked, reached Portsmouth on 28 July. His voyage had cost the lives of 750 men, the majority of whom died from disease. To set against this, he landed goods assessed at £60,000, which did not equal the initial investment. Neither had he managed to intercept either of the *flotas* that crossed the Atlantic while he was at sea. This costly failure brought into sharp focus the benefits to be gained from Ralegh's alternative operation, the establishment of a permanent pirate base in the Americas, yet the early success of this well-planned project was also ripening sour as Ralegh failed to adapt to events as they unfolded.

Of these, the most telling was the return of Lane and his men. When the colonel reported to Ralegh, the latter knew not what success Grenville might be having in re-establishing the abandoned fort. By the time it was known that Grenville had sailed away from Roanoke, in vain pursuit of a *flota*, leaving behind, inconceivably, just Sergeant Coffin and fourteen soldiers, far too few to hold the fort against hostile attack, Ralegh had already committed himself to the fourth stage of his plan – the despatch of the civilian settlers. Thus began the process that was to lead to the failure of Roanoke and the tragic disappearance of the second group of colonists for, ironically, the Spanish were to deal the crippling blow to Ralegh's scheme, not through a savage descent on the colony, but through a campaign against England itself, the Armada which, although ending in total failure, nevertheless as a by-blow destroyed a settlement over three thousand miles away from that fleet's journey.

That new settlement was a family affair: eighty-nine men, seventeen women, two of whom were pregnant, and eleven children, forming fourteen families, were embarked onboard *Lion* when she sailed out of Plymouth on 8 May 1587. With this village-sized community Ralegh was hoping to found the modestly named City of Ralegh. If, in 1585, he had intended to conquer America with a company, now he desired to build a civilisation with a group of villagers. The ineptness of his thinking is no more obvious than in the choice of the recently returned John White as the group's governor. White, the highly competent official artist on Lane's expedition, was no way near as skilled as a leader. Consistently, during the new voyage he found himself, quite rightly, but injudiciously, at odds with the sea commander, Fernando, the same pilot who had run *Tyger* aground. This time Fernando misidentified shore-marks and sites for collecting salt and sheep. Then, as cruel as it was uncalled for, Fernando forced the passengers to disembark at Roanoke, rather than taking them into the Chesapeake, claiming that the date, 22 July was too late in the season to risk the onward passage – of eighty miles! Fernando even brazenly disproved his own reasoning by remaining off the Outer Banks until 27 August, even after he had been driven out to sea by a storm. When he did sail it was with White in company, but onboard the little flyboat; Fernando had no wish to share his ship with the governor whom the colonists had elected to return to tell Ralegh of their perilous position. The two ships soon parted company with Lane, in a vessel that had lost both anchors and men, having a poor crossing home, while Fernando went a-pirating, his favoured occupation.

In his despatch of White's settlers with no military support force, Ralegh almost certainly condemned his colonists to death, while also abandoning his still feasible idea of establishing a pirate base. His contemporaneous scheme to establish a similar plantation in Munster, far nearer home, probably influenced his decision, while occupying more of his attention. Certainly, his Irish estates were foremost in his mind when the flustered White finally reached him in mid November 1587, with a tale of shipwreck, sickness and starvation to add to the drama of his desperate colony.

Ralegh did all the right things, except one. He mustered supplies; he 'appointed a pinnace to be sent thither with all such necessaries as he understood they stood in need of, and also wrote his letters unto them, promising that a relief expedition should be with them the summer following.' Yet he did not, in their dire distress, take himself down to the port to personally ensure that the said pinnace was stored, manned and despatched. Neither, as far as can be ascertained, did he call on his queen to acquaint her with the situation and evoke her sympathy. Bad weather delayed the pinnace from sailing and, with rumour of the imminent departure of the Armada from Spain, in March 1588 the Privy Council ordered Grenville's latest resupply fleet not to depart. Transatlantic travel was embargoed for as long as the invasion threat was a real and present danger.

There the story of the American pirate base should end; the disappearance of the abandoned settlers is a sadness this account is not subject to, except for one fact. When White did attempt to return he was frustrated from so doing by the pirates with whom he sailed.

The first attempt was made in two ships, *Brave* and *Roe*, released from Grenville's force as being of too little strength to offer much in the fight against the Armada. With White, and some stores embarked, they set sail for Virginia, or were meant so to do. Sadly, they were commanded by the pirate Arthur Facy who, as soon as they had sailed, set out in pursuit of prizes. After a few days of lucky encounters, the diminutive fleet sighted a number of sails, which turned out to be two large Frenchmen who, contrary to Facy's plans, boarded *Brave* and took all the new world supplies with them, only sparing the company as they recognised Facy as a rogue with whom they had had prior dealings. Storeless and battered, there was no point in continuing the voyage and the disheartened White once again returned home alone. He was to do so once more when he sailed with a squadron of pirate vessels belonging to the wealthy merchant, John Watts. At the proposed time of departure, January 1590, another embargo had been placed on ships' departing England's shores as a new Armada was expected. This time, under encouragement from White, Ralegh did get a licence to depart for Watts's ships, provided that they called at Roanoke. Watts's men demonstrated their gratitude by refusing to embark any supplies destined for the colony, and insisting that White travelled alone.

Yet again the hope of treasure in the Indies delayed the fleet's arrival off Roanoke, and it was not until 17 August that White, after losing several men in the surf, found himself, at last, back at the settlement. It had been abandoned. The only indication that the colonists might have moved elsewhere was the word CROATOAN (the name of a friendly southern settlement) carved on a timber and the fact that there were no signs of distress. Naturally, White favoured a passage down to this more southern isle, but the weather intervened. The strong winds which had earlier overturned the boat blew fiercer, and drove *Hopewell* and *Moonlight* south, well beyond the latitude of Croatoan Island, and by the time it was possible to go about, the captains had decided neither to return nor to winter in the Caribbean, England was to be their next port of call and here, yet again, the despondent White disembarked alone and for the last time.

The failure in Virginia did nothing to dent either Ralegh's optimism or egotism: if he could not succeed in North America, then he would turn his attention to South America. In 1586 two of his pirate ships, *Serpent* and *Mary Sparke*, returned from a successful voyage to the Azores, having captured a Spanish grandee, Don Pedro Sarmiento de Gamboa. During his enforced stay as Ralegh's guest, Don Pedro entertained his host with stories of a city of gold, El Dorado, which lay up the Orinoco River in Guiana. Ralegh was hooked and, with all ideas for Virginia forgotten, he put together an expedition to take possession of this territory. Elizabeth, still willing to indulge her one-time favourite, granted him a charter which included a desire that he did everything in his power to annoy and enfeeble the king of Spain and capture any of his shipping that trespassed into this new domain. Ralegh sailed in February 1595, taking the usual selection of pirates to be his partners. By September they were back, having spent a fruitless month on station and returning with nothing other than the draft of a best-selling travel book, *The Discovery of the Large, Rich and Beautiful Empire of Guiana with a Relation of the Great and Golden City of Manoa*, a lengthy title in which, if the first half was true, the second part was all fabrication.

Ralegh, refusing to believe the evidence of his own eyes, foolishly sailed again to Guiana in June 1617, but as a prisoner of James I on remand. This time he turned failure into disaster. His son, Wat, was killed attacking a Spanish fort, an act which by itself gave James the excuse finally to execute Walter soon after his return in November 1617. James's virulent hatred of the elderly rover was fired up by both Count Gondomar, the Spanish ambassador in London, and several of Ralegh's company, who perjured themselves with tales of piracy encouraged by their leader rather than confess to this crime.[14] George Carew, who knew Ralegh better than most opined that, 'there is a doubtful opinion held of Sir Walter and those that malice him boldly affirm him to be a pirate.' He might not have been on this occasion, but he had been one for all his adult life. Hubris, fed by arrogance, had been his downfall, for he had an urge to exceed the successes of his peers. This trait he acknowledged his in the account of his voyage to Guiana, stating that:

> It became not the former fortune, in which I once lived, to go journeys of picory (marauding); it had sorted ill with the offices of honour, which by her Majesty's grace I hold this day in England, to run from cape to cape and from place to place, for the pillage of ordinary prizes.[15]

In fact, for almost forty years England's enterprises in the Americas had been commanded by pirates, with their bold but careless approach and their short-term desire for gain. This was the shared characteristic of all Elizabeth's piratocracy, and because of it they did not deliver what the sound argument advanced by John Dee and Richard Hakluyt suggested was possible. Frobisher failed to find both a northwest passage and gold; Ralegh's pirate lair in Virginia and dream of El Dorado were stillborn; even Drake, following his individual successes in the 1570s, could not return triumphantly when entrusted with a royal commission. By putting her faith in state-sponsored rovers, Elizabeth threw away the opportunity to challenge Spain in the Americas and lay the foundation for what John Dee termed the British Empire.[16]

Ironically, after forty years of failure, when the English returned to the region of the Chesapeake in 1607, the seaman in command of the three ships was Christopher Newport, the one-armed pirate who had been present at the seizing of *Madre Dios*, but by now, with England at peace with Spain, the gold that he was sent to search for would have to be mined rather than stolen. Before then, however, the failure in Virginia left the piratocracy seeking new ways in which to intercept the richly loaded hulls of Spain.

CHAPTER 7

The Azores and the First Battle
of the Atlantic

Gallant, in faith, since three o'clock last noon,
Until this morning, fifteen hours by course,
We have maintained stout war and still undone,
Our foes assault, and drove them to the worse.
Fifteen *armados*, boarding have not won,
Content or ease, but been repelled by force,
Eight hundred cannon shot against our side,
Have not our hearts in coward colours dyed.

Anon, *The Most Honourable Tragedy
of Sir Richard Grenville, Kt*, 1595

John Hawkins had backed his son Richard's attempt to plunder in the Pacific, but he was one of those who believed that the rewards from piracy could be delivered far closer to home. So, having abandoned his own slaving voyages to the West Indies, he decided to seek for a new fortune in the waters around the Azores, which lay like a broken bracelet on the blue baize of the Atlantic. The islands had become a vital provisioning and protected stopover for Portuguese vessels heading to and from Brazil and the East Indies, and Spanish treasure fleets crossing to Seville from the Caribbean. By Elizabeth's time, the greatest portable portion of the world's wealth passed this way and thus the island waters became the natural focus for those privateering vessels whose limited horizons and poor communications made scouring empty oceans in search of prey a most costly alternative.

In 1567 George Fenner, having been repulsed off the Cape Verde Islands, sailed his *Castle of Comfort* to the Azores, where he trailed a Portuguese vessel, looking for an opportunity to board. She, however, led him into the offing of a squadron consisting of a galleon and two carvels. Thus began one of the first naval gun, as opposed to boarding, engagements. It lasted well over a day, with Fenner at one time fighting a combined force of seven Portuguese ships. These he repulsed and made his escape under cover of darkness.[1]

By 1576 it was clear to Hawkins that rich pickings were waiting to be plucked in the waters off the Azores, so he proposed to Burghley that he put together a squadron of the queen's ships, *Dreadnought*, *Foresight* and *Bull*, with five merchant ships which he just happened to have available, to sail and intercept the Spanish treasure fleet. It would, Hawkins estimated, cost just £3,750 to get such fleet to sea, a sum that would pale when set against the profit. However, as Burghley was the one member of Elizabeth's inner circle who was urging caution in her dealings with Spain, the scheme did not progress. In 1579, armed with examples of Spanish misdeeds and a belief that the queen would not be repatriating whatever Spanish treasure Sir Francis Drake might be returning with from his circumnavigation, Hawkins tried again. This time he proposed the despatch of the royal vessels *Lyon*, *Philip and Mary* (later renamed, less embarrassingly, *Nonpareil*), *Swallow* and *Aide*, which would be sheathed at a cost of £1,000 each, and accompanied by five merchant ships and eleven pinnaces. 'The booty that is of ordinary to be struck upon the Indies fleet is £2,000,000,' wrote the almost slathering Hawkins, who was convinced of total victory so that 'there need not to be suffered one ship, bark, frigate, or galley, to stay untaken.' His boast was not to be tested, although later experience would deem it over-optimistic.

While Drake was away on his circumnavigation, the king of Portugal died with no male issue. This led to the legal unification of the Spanish and Portuguese crowns under King Philip II of Spain, whose ambivalent attitude to his new domain was summed up in his phrase, 'I inherited it, I bought it, I conquered it.' Although Philip's succession was legitimate, many Portuguese resented their loss of independence, and objected to the fact that Philip enforced his claim by sending troops to occupy his neighbour's territory. This gave an opportunity for a pretender, Dom Antonio, to claim the throne. Sadly for his supporters, Dom Antonio was no dashing cavalier, but a middle-aged monk, the illegitimate cousin of Sebastian, the last but one in the Portuguese royal line who had died, along with many of his nobles, fighting the Moroccans in the disastrous battle of Alcazarquivir. With limited charisma, little wealth and no mainland power-base from which to rally support, Dom Antonio rebelled, rose and ran to seek foreign aid. The English were tempted and Hawkins saw an opportunity which was further enhanced when, with the typical islanders' independence of thought, the Azoreans declared for Dom Antonio. Back in Spain Philip was taking no chances, writing in November 1580 to Mendoza:

> The victory of Oporto having completely crushed Don Antonio's rising, the Pretender has escaped. Use the most unceasing vigilance to learn whether he arrives in England. If so, give a full account of the circumstances of the rebellion to the Queen, and request her to arrest Don Antonio as a rebel and surrender him to me a prisoner. Assure her how deep will be my obligation to her if she does so, and how just, my cause of offence if she refuse, which I cannot believe she will.[2]

He was wrong: she did, stating that she 'did not know yet whether she should help Dom Antonio or not, but she would not arrest or surrender anyone to be killed.' When reminded that her treaty obligations included an extradition clause for the surrender of a rebel or traitor, Elizabeth responded that such a request could only be considered if it was submitted in writing, monarch to monarch.[3]

So although Dom Antonio arrived in England, a mendicant relying on foreign charity, a fact that he failed to disguise by conspicuous tipping, he was listened to by those in authority, being invited, according to Mendoza, to an operational planning meeting with 'Leicester and Walsingham; and Captains Drake, Winter, and Hawkins, who are pirates and seamen.'[4]

That meeting led to a proposal both to send a fleet to the Azores and to recognise letters of marque issued by Dom Antonio against the subjects of the king of Spain.[5] Control of the Azores was the shared desire, although for vastly different reasons: for Dom Antonio they represented a toehold for his return, although they were too distant, too poor and too sparsely populated, certainly with soldiers, to back any armed landing on the Portuguese coast, but for the English these islands were the key to access the passing richly-laden ships of both Spain and Portugal, which were worth far more than all the promises made by the impoverished pretender. The English therefore drafted their 'First Enterprise', a plan to seize the Azores and base a fleet at Terceira to prey on the passing *flotas*. In this double aim lay the dominating weakness of English maritime strategy for the next two decades. Whereas Elizabeth was funding costly wars against Spain in France and the Netherlands from which she anticipated little return, she saw naval expeditions as potential money-making ventures to replenish her empty coffers. No government-supported naval force would sail during her reign without its main aim being weakened by having several additional objectives, of which the primary one was always to return with sufficient booty to, at the least, pay its expenses. A major opportunity to do this lay in the holds of cargo ships transiting the Azores.

In December 1580 Mendoza informed Philip that the queen was urging the islanders to stand firm for Don Antonio, a situation reinforced when, much to Mendoza's alarm, there arrived from the Azores a delegation begging for English support and promising to pay for 'all the arms, munitions, and stores, which may be sent to them', an offer which led to the purchase of weaponry, including 'a thousand harquebuses and muskets' from Antwerp.[6]

Mendoza attempted to discourage the Azores voyage by spreading rumours that Philip had despatched a force of forty galleons to recover Terceira and await the arrival of the Anglo-French fleet. He also gave out some geography lessons explaining how poor were the anchorages off the islands, meaning that an English fleet could not be relied upon to be present to repulse a retributive landing.[7] Perhaps his greatest diplomatic ploy was to convince English merchants trading with Spain to petition the queen and Walsingham, aided by the promise of a

10,000-crown bribe for the latter, that the planned assault was not in their and Her Majesty's best interest. This suggestion, Mendoza claimed, delayed Drake's planned date of departure, leaving Terceira undefended against a Spanish expeditionary force.[8]

Drake's strategic plan was to land at Terceira and construct fortifications. Then, leaving a strong party behind, he proposed to take his fleet a-hunting for the *flota*. If he failed to intercept the treasure fleet, he intended to sail westward to carry out a raid on the West Indies before returning to Terceira. Wet-lipped at the prospect of loot, many a merchant venture volunteered a ship to add to Drake's fleet, until twenty-five vessels were being fitted out to join the task force. But someone was keeping a running total of the costs, much of which, including Dom Antonio's contribution, was on credit. As the figure passed the £13,000 mark, the weight of cautionary and counter-argument tipped the scales so rapidly that by August the expedition was all but cancelled. The lack of funding and absence of any certain return was only the first of several discrediting issues. As the date of departure drew near, so the threats from Spain seemed to become substantial rather than hollow. These were an invasion of Ireland; a trade embargo; a seizure of shipping; and even a declaration of war. Philip, well aware of the emerging English concerns, forwarded through Mendoza two letters to the queen, one more placatory than the other; both making clear that Spain would not lie dormant should an English force land in the Azores. Diplomatic niceties were still observed with the king 'requesting' Elizabeth to surrender Dom Antonio to him, while praising his ambassador for 'frightening them with the fleets that have sailed from here, and so checking the corsairs, who are fitting out in England.' Philip urged his ambassador to impress upon the queen how great a favour the arrest and return of Dom Antonio would be, but added, 'if you cannot get her to accede to my request you may tell the Queen that, even though she does not wish to break with me, if Dom Antonio leaves her country for any of my dominions, or to injure any of my subjects, I shall understand it to be a declaration of war.'

A few days later the king tried his hand at good-cop/bad-cop correspondence, sending a further two letters to Mendoza, leaving his ambassador to decide which, the conciliatory or the threatening one, would be the most appropriate in the changing circumstances to present to Elizabeth. However, even without Spanish threats, Mendoza noted that the desire to support Dom Antonio was waning, with preparations becoming notably half-hearted and desultory. Ultimately, the ambassador, stated, it came down to a matter of wages, with few of the captains and men having any faith in the belief that they would be paid for their services. By now, knowing the English seamen's mindset well, Mendoza said, 'the evident intention of most of the Englishmen is simply to plunder under the name of Dom Antonio as, indeed, they openly state.' What is more, they were quite prepared to change sides, and capture the property of Flemish rebels, if Mendoza would give them permits to enter Spanish ports with their booty.

Piracy and plunder, not politics, were still the main interest of the English seamen, so that the ambassador was in little doubt that 'most of the men contracted by Dom Antonio will leave him for the other side, which offers a more assured profit than he can do.'[9]

The perspicacious genius of Mendoza was soon to be proved right when, with the growing certainty that her guest was approaching insolvency, the queen became reluctant to commit openly to an act of aggression. Protesting too much that events were being planned to which she was not privy, a standard royal ploy, she issued an order that none of her 'people were to enter the service of Dom Antonio.' Then she brought the curtains down on English involvement in the enterprise, in slow and deliberate stages. First, she limited the expedition to eight ships, four of Drake's and four which Dom Antonio had purchased or hired. Then she withdrew Drake and his ships, while still giving Dom Antonio a daily audience, during which the pretender could not fail but to notice that the 'Queen is cooling towards him', as were the ships' companies, with Mendoza reporting that:

> Nearly all the mariners and soldiers left glad of the opportunity, in consequence of the hunger by which they were pressed. The captains alone remained, as they wrote to the Council, in order not to abandon the ships until they knew who had to pay them the wages that were due.[10]

Soon afterwards, Mendoza was able to report on the rescinding of the letters of marque issued under Dom Antonio's authority.[11] Thus ended the first alliance between the pretender and the privateer: they would unite again in 1589 with, as far as placing the former on the throne of Portugal, a similar outcome

Yet if Elizabeth had withdrawn her support for an assault on the Azores, the dowager-queen in France had not. Very aware that Dom Antonio's presence in England had given Elizabeth a tactical advantage, in the spring of 1582 Catherine de' Medici ordered an invasion force of her own to sail to the islands. Sensing an opportunity, or not wishing to be denied one, Elizabeth tucked three of her ships on to the tail of Admiral Strozzi's fleet of sixty ships carrying seven thousand soldiers.

The French preparations did not pass unnoticed and Philip ordered his own admiral, Alvaro de Bazan, to sail and intercept the French. Bazan's own force comprised two Portuguese warships, nineteen armed merchantmen and ten troop transports. The mix was significant, for Philip did not possess a fighting fleet of his own, and would not do so until the shock of the failure of the Armada in 1588 spurred him to found a navy.

The opposing forces met on 24 July 1582 in an inconclusive encounter, renewing their acquaintance on 26 July some twenty miles south of Punta Delgada. At first, it seemed that the Spanish would be outmanoeuvred and outgunned by the French. But then Bazan closed in to engage in an old-fashioned, galley-style, action of boarding and wielding Toledo steel. Bravely, he allowed himself to be surrounded by some seven French ships, including Strozzi's own flagship, and these his men boarded and captured. When Strozzi died of his wounds, total victory could be declared.

Bazan sailed home, only to return the following year with an even larger force to subdue the islands successfully. He had not failed to notice that during the battle of Punta Delgada, the English ships had at first held back and then fled. Such Protestant hens were unlikely to provide, he surmised, a serious threat to any bravely-led Spanish fleet, and he told his master so.

Thus, from the Battle of Ponta Delgada, the two future enemies learned lessons that would dominate their strategic thinking for the rest of the century. Philip's great efforts to control the islands indicated to Hawkins and his group how vital a hub they were for the valuable trading voyagers while, for Philip and his naval advisers, the poor performance of the English ships indicated that an armada against England was a strategic feasibility. Philip thus called for plans to mount an invasion, while Hawkins developed his scheme to place a permanent patrol off the Azores. Both men's plans were to prove failures.

While such grand plans required government approval, there was nothing to prevent independent pirates from having a go themselves. In June 1586 Walter Ralegh sent two of his pirate ships, the 35-ton *Serpent* and the 50-ton *Mary Sparke*, to cruise the Azores. Their first prize was a small bark, which just happened to be carrying the governor of San Miguel onboard – a lucky bargaining chip. On another captured vessel they found Don Pedro Sarmiento de Gamboa, the governor of the ill-fated settlement placed in the Straits of Magellan to impede Drake's homeward passage in 1578 and to deter further English voyages to the South Seas. They then chased a pair of ships which came to anchor under the guns of the fort on Graciosa. Undeterred, the English piled into their boats with muskets and calivers, exchanging fire as soon as they came in range while, at the same time, bending to their oars, the wind being contrary, in an endeavour to arrive before the Spanish managed to offload their stores ashore. The first ship they boarded had been abandoned and was taken back to sea by a prize crew of just two, while the other seven men headed for the second ship. After an unopposed boarding, the crew having fled save for one negro slave, the English cut her cable and hoisted her sails only to find that the wind had died, leaving them at the mercy of a crowd of about one hundred and fifty who had gathered ashore to hurl stones and insults at the pirates. Tumbling back into their boat, they escaped by towing away their prize, but not before the narrator, John Evesham, killed the gunner of the fort with a musket shot at range, just before the latter fired a great gun at them which would have blown them out of the water – or so he alleged!

After this, having seized some fish and taken a mast to replace one of their own, they seem to have felt their voyage had been made, for they went about and sailed for home. Then, first one, then another, then ten, finally some twenty-four sails were sighted and closed in pursuit. They had stumbled across every pirate's dream, a treasure fleet. However, the disparity in vessel size was enormous. The narrator of this account reckoned their targets included two carracks of 1,200 and 1,000 tons, ten galleons and some lesser but well-laden merchantmen. The diminutive duo tried to manoeuvre around the protective carracks to pick on someone their own size but, with just sixty men left onboard and after thirty-two hours of engagement in which they had expended most of their ammunition without a successful boarding, they decided to retire. Back at Plymouth they were given the usual roisterous welcome, the arrival of their prizes on the previous tide having whetted the appetite of the townsfolk – who were probably disappointed when the fleet set sail again, its bulk unbroken, for Southampton – where Walter Ralegh, ever wary of his rights, came to welcome them and view the booty of such exotics as 'sugars, Elephants teeth, waxe, hides, rice, and brasill.'

In August 1586 Hawkins, at last, led his own fleet out of Plymouth. His flagship, the 500-ton *Nonpareil* was accompanied by the similarly sized *Lion*, in which his good friend, and shortly Drake's great enemy, William Borough, sailed as vice admiral. *Revenge*, *Hope* and *Tramontana* completed the squadron. Prey fell early to the group, which on one day in early September captured four ships homeward bound from Brazil with valuable, but not rich, cargoes. With their booty onboard, Hawkins altered course for the Azores, planning to intercept the treasure fleet.[12] But the weather thought otherwise and, scattered and driven back by adverse strong winds, Hawkins's fleet came home in November, having failed to sight the islands, let alone any passing plunder. That December the London merchant Robert Flicke was also licensed to send a fleet to the Azores to intercept the *flota*, but he also failed to take any prizes.

It was to be Drake who would show that his cousin's vision could be realised. The following year he sailed from England on the voyage that would make him a legend in England, and confirm his status as a supreme corsair in Spain. Both countries knew that all-out war was not far away, and England, behind her moat, knew that Spain could only hurt her through mounting an invasion. When it became evident that this was precisely what Philip intended, an English fleet commanded by Drake was despatched on a spoiling raid, with plunder being its equal aim. Drake's triumphantly successful 'singeing of the king of Spain's beard' in Cadiz harbour has been much written about, being as it was the opening salvo in a two-year sea battle that climaxed with the passage of the Armada up the English Channel, and petered out with Drake's less successful return to the coast of Spain in 1589. The story of the Cadiz assault lies outside the scope of this book, although Drake's prickly relationship with his vice admiral, William Borough, who had the temerity, and the right, to question his commander's decisions, gives an insight into the study of pirates as naval commanders. Following his success at Cadiz, Drake sailed to blockade Lisbon in whose harbour, safe but impotent, lay Bazan, the Armada's admiral, now elevated to being the Marques de Santa Cruz. Realising that his fleet could not match the battle-trained English challenging him to sail towards their guns, he stayed put, allowing Drake to detach some of his fleet to head homeward, while he hauled over to the Azores with nine vessels, perhaps having intelligence (delivered by the devil, so the Spanish claimed) to suggest that a rich cargo was due in those waters. The strength of his force would indicate that he did not wish to suffer the embarrassing indignity of Ralegh's two vessels. In fact he took his prize, the East Indies carrack *San Felipe*, with great ease, although her tonnage was three times as great as his own *Elizabeth Bonaventure*. But the English benefited from that disparity, being able to run alongside the carrack's sides beneath her own gun ports, which is what three of them did. After six Portuguese had been killed, the captain surrendered, and Drake boarded to view a cargo almost as valuable as that he had taken from *Cacafuego*. Indeed, it was a far richer prize than can have been anticipated, for she had onboard, as well as her own cargo, that of the galleon *San Lorenzo*, which had been unable to proceed homeward beyond Mozambique.

Drake, having placed his prize-crew onboard, behaved with his normal courtesy to both his men and the captured ship's crew. The latter, with wounds bound, were placed onboard another well-victualled prize and sent home; then Drake assured his men that each of them would 'have a sufficient reward for his travail.'

The capture of *San Felipe* created the usual flurry of paperwork in both England and Spain, in which one nation endeavoured to assess the losses, while the other tried to audit and allocate her gains. From Spain, where the capture of a ship bearing the royal name was seen as an ill-omen, the king wrote to Mendoza, exiled in Paris for his scheming on behalf of Mary, Queen of Scots, informing him of swift Spanish countermeasures in the form of a thirty to forty sail fleet despatched under the command of the veteran Santa Cruz, with orders to 'sweep the corsairs from the seas' and to give Drake 'what he deserves.'[13] This being the same Santa Cruz who had refused Drake's challenge at Lisbon a few months earlier!

Spanish spies in London did little to calm the exasperated Philip; indeed, they made the link between Drake's prize and the planned return of Dom Antonio, informing the king that 300,000 crowns found onboard *San Felipe* were going to be invested in an expedition to 'take Dom Antonio to Portugal.' The pretender's hopes were soon dashed. A few weeks later the same source was reporting to Philip that Dom Antonio had not received anything from the plunder.[14]

Drake arrived back in Plymouth on 26 June and, as was his custom, sent a short report of proceedings to London ahead of his own journey to the capital. He also took care to ingratiate himself with his monarch, who by 1 July had already appointed commissioners to audit the cargo. Drake, wishing to ensure he was allocated a fair share, selected for the queen a choice present. On 11 July the state papers made note of:

> A small casket with divers jewels viewed in the town of Saltash; the said casket being varnished with gold, with two keys and a small chain of gold to the same. The which casket and jewels Sir Francis Drake hath taken charge to deliver unto Her Majesty with his own hands.[15]

Drake could afford to be generous. The lengthy inventory of the prize lists gold canteens of cutlery, gold chains and chests of jewels and ivory which, when all was added up, came to a total worth of £112,000. The bulk was also incredible, for it was stated that it took seventeen ships to ferry it round to London, where its sale lasted a full year. October was a busy month for this business, with Burghley deciding that 'the best mode of effecting the sale of the carrack taken by Sir Francis Drake' was to establish a market at Leadenhall, where the pepper and other commodities taken could be 'sold by wholesale.' At this stage the inventoried value was put at £108,049 13s 11d, the Elizabethans liking to be precise, if not accurate. Once sales and distributions were complete, the queen was richer by £50,000 and Drake by £20,000.[16] The importance of the royal reward can be seen when measured against such extraordinary items of expenditure racked up by the Cadiz raid such as '£12,512 11s 8d expended on victualling Her Majesty's ships to the seas.'

Sugden, in his excellent book, *Sir Francis Drake*, says of the Azores diversion that 'Some historians have been strongly critical of Drake's voyage to the Azores, and cited it as an example of his alleged willingness to subordinate the national interest in naked profit-seeking.'[17] Yet in the pirate state that England had become, 'national interest' and 'naked profit-seeking' were as one. Given an avariciously-minded but poorly-financed state that desired both to challenge and defend itself against a mighty global empire, Elizabeth wisely let her pirates perform both tasks to their mutual benefit. The need for this public/pirate partnership is made pithily obvious in the State Papers Domestic for the period 1587 to 1588. Over those twenty-four months the main subject discussed was the manning, victualling and equipping of naval vessels and expeditions to counter the threat of Spain. Occasionally this massive expenditure was offset by an entry under income: Drake provided such an entry. His contribution was much appreciated by Walsingham who opined, to the still cautious Burghley, that Drake should sail again for the Azores to interdict more Spanish treasure ships, as the best way 'to bridle their malice is the interruption of the Indian fleets.'[18]

The taking of *San Felipe* added strength to Hawkins's proposal of December 1587 to station a fleet off the Azores to intercept even more Iberian shipping.[19] None of the plans hatched previously to seize the treasure fleet had a greater guarantee of success than the serendipity of sighting a sail while loitering with intent. Hawkins's problem was how best to execute a good idea for, rather like a tennis player stretching desperately for a ball flying just out of reach, so the distance between Plymouth and the Azores proved too great a gap to control with a small fleet unable to be reliably victualled. To cover this wide court Hawkins now proposed to play doubles, with one fleet close to the islands, while the other paced the baseline of the Iberian coast to intercept that which escaped the first group.

However, the Armada campaign put on hold all other plans by the English pirates, both to assault the *flota* and to replenish Roanoke. There then followed Drake's unfortunate voyage of 1589 with its hydra-headed aim to attack the remnants of the Armada in northern Spanish ports; seize Lisbon and place Dom Antonio on the throne; and to pay for it all by sailing to the Azores to capture treasure ships. By the time that the Lisbon assault had ended in failure, Drake was in receipt of letters from his sovereign, voicing great displeasure that he had not destroyed the Spanish shipping and had dawdled, profitless, at Corunna. More than ever the corsair needed a rich prize to placate his queen. But time wasted and adverse winds meant that this opportunity for salvaging both a reputation and financial return by a successful foray to the Azores was lost, and Drake for once had to return with little reward for his efforts and the queen's expenditure. Worse was to follow, when it was reported that of the few prizes that were taken, 'two-thirds parts of all the lading were spoiled and embezzled by the men-of-war and mariners at sea, before they were brought into Plymouth, and that one half of the third remaining was purloined and scattered since the arrival of the ships in that haven.'[20]

While the English plans were being frustrated by poor intelligence and execution, the Spanish were improving their chances of slipping past any intercepting fleet stationed off the Azores. Their new class of ship, the *gallizabras*, were designed to outsail any heavily-armed enemy and outfight any lighter, faster foe. Sailing independently, they were able to skim past the Azores without stopping and discharge their silver cargo safely in Seville. The introduction of *gallizabras* did not mean the end of the convoys, but their defences were much improved in the years after 1588 by the building of a new Spanish fleet of warships whose most famous class was to be the 'Twelve Apostles', construction of which began shortly after the Armada limped home. By the end of the century Spain had increased its naval forces by some twenty ships, augmented by double that number of hired merchantmen.

Yet in 1589, before the Spanish had mastered how best to deploy their new strength, the Hawkins plan was executed with Frobisher acting as the back-stop off Spain, while the earl of Cumberland sailed to the Azores, in his own words, 'to pilfer'. He embarked in the queen's ship *Victory*, taking along the unseaworthy *Margaret*, and two other vessels, one of which was commanded by William Monson as vice admiral. Capturing vessels while on passage, this small fleet arrived off San Miguel in August, taking four small prizes just offshore. They then sailed on to Flores to water and seek out intelligence. On being informed that some carracks were lying at Terceira, to there they sailed, capturing several more prizes off the port. The lack of any resistance emboldened Cumberland to launch an assault upon Fayal, of which town the narrator of the expedition, the cartographer Edward Wright, provided Hakluyt with a detailed description for his *Voyages*. The town was ransomed for 2,000 ducats, paid mainly in church plate, and Cumberland sailed away, leaving behind a reputation for gentlemanly conduct. A similar descent on Graciosa was called off when Cumberland decided that it was too risky. Instead, the governor was bluffed into releasing sixty tuns of wine and some fresh victuals.

The final assault, on a fort on Saint Mary's, ended in failure with Cumberland himself being severely wounded by shot, but they took two more rich prizes a few days later, just as they turned for home, expecting to make landfall before Christmas. As the richest prize, according to Monson, was worth some £100,000 and the spices they had captured a further £7,000,[21] a reasonable return looked likely, although Linschoten, an island resident, reported that the English failed to capture a vessel that sunk beneath the boarding party, taking some 200,000 ducats worth of gold, silver and pearls to the bottom. If this were true it would be typical of Cumberland's luck, which was about to get worse.

For gales prevented them from entering the Channel, and even held them off the coast of Ireland so long that they were in danger of dying of thirst. All the severely rationed water was drunk, hailstones were gathered up which 'we did eat more pleasantly than if they had been the sweetest comfits in the world.' On the rare occasions when it did rain, every napkin and cloth was held out to be thoroughly soaked and then sucked dry. The crew collected around the scuppers with jars and cans, even drinking the muddy, reeking bilge-water as it was pumped up. The men sucked bullets to slake their thirst, but 'every day some were cast overboard.' To add to their misery, a great storm sprung up and threatened to overwhelm the ships. A replacement mainsail was ripped overboard and only gathered safely in by the enormous courage of the ship's master, William Anthony, who crawled along the lowered main yard to gather the sodden sail from the sea.

When they eventually made Ireland, Cumberland was able to procure fresh provisions ashore and set off once again for England, but contrary winds meant that they 'kept a cold Christmas with the Bishop and his Clerks that lie to the west of the Scillies.' Eventually, the survivors made landfall in Falmouth where, to add to their discomfiture, they learned that the richest of their prizes had foundered off Cornwall with the loss of Captain Lister and all but six of his crew.

Back in the Azores their misfortune was still being talked about, for a few days after Cumberland's departure the two richest vessels of the treasure fleet limped, storm-shattered into Terceira, in no condition to have repulsed an assault by Cumberland should they have met him. Indeed, the crew reported that they would have surrendered to the pirate to save their lives. Linschoten witnessed them unloading 5 million ducats of silver 'so that the whole quay lay covered in plates and chest of silver', besides pearls, gold and other stones which were not registered. Apparently the admiral, Alvaro Flores de Quiniones, had valuables of his own worth 50,000 ducats; other passengers would have been almost as well endowed.[22]

Unlucky in pilfering Cumberland may have been, but he was more than lucky in the freedom with which he was allowed to patrol the Azorean waters, for there is no record of a single sighting of a Spanish ship of war at sea: two years later he would send a pinnace hastening to the Azores to report the imminent arrival of fifty-three such vessels.

That year, 1591, marked a major change in the balance of power at sea. In March, Lord Thomas Howard sailed for the Azores while Cumberland patrolled the

Iberian coast. Here he had the embarrassment of losing Monson, who was taken onboard a ship he had captured when her consorts closed in, leaving Cumberland upwind and unable to come to his subordinate's assistance. Monson was flung into jail and then the galleys, but was wily enough to escape in 1592. It took him a while longer to forgive Cumberland.

With Howard, and heading for immortality in command of *Revenge*, sailed the fourth member of the quartet of pirate kings, Richard Grenville. Their fleet arrived off the Azores in May and very soon, rather than seeking out a rich *flota*, they were preoccupied with managing a virulent sickness that meant the fleet had to put into Flores to 'rummage' all of the vessels that remained, clearing out the ballast and scrubbing the whole of each ship with disinfecting vinegar. While this major cleansing was taking place, a solitary pinnace was kept on station to the westward to warn of the approaching *flota*, but it was a pinnace from the east that alerted them, not to rich pickings but to a revengeful fighting force, led by Alonso de Bazan, the experienced brother of the late great Santa Cruz. With just sufficient warning, Howard hauled his fleet to sea and safety, leaving behind Grenville in *Revenge*, who decided to fight rather than flee, to seek fame rather than infamy in his battle of one against fifty-three. Wonderful accounts were written of the last fight of *Revenge*. Ralegh penned the panegyric for his friend in his pamphlet, *A Report of the Truth of the Fight about the Isles of the Azores*. The Spanish wrote a 'Relation' giving their side of the story that is well summarised by Rowse.[23] However, the conversion of Ralegh's report into epic poetry by Alfred, Lord Tennyson, is by far the best account for those who would be uplifted by one of the founding events in British naval tradition and, as such, it is reproduced at Appendix 7.

From Grenville's heroic, foolish fight, three things emerge quite clearly; first, that the English stand-off tactics during the Armada campaign had been correct: Grenville may have sunk several of the enemy, but in 1588 England could not have afforded to risk any of her floating defences; secondly, Howard behaved as the custodian of the queen's wooden wealth, responsible for keeping her fleet in being, rather than as a fighting admiral given the opportunity to engage the enemy more closely; thirdly, it demonstrated that England was no longer the sole master of the ocean for, at last, Spain was able to meet the challenge to her trade routes.

Able she might have been, but her treasure fleet was still at risk, for the loss of *Revenge* had not daunted the desire of the piratocracy for wealth and, in the year following the sinking of *Revenge*, they took their greatest prize when a consortium of merchant ships combined with Ralegh and Cumberland's fleets to seize the mighty 1,600-ton Portuguese carrack, *Madre de Dios*. Only one of the queen's ships, *Foresight*, was present at the prize-taking, for the loss of *Revenge* had made the Lord Admiral cautious, and Cumberland convinced that the royal caveat, 'not to lay any Spanish ship aboard with her ships, lest both might together be destroyed by fire', too restrictive. However, its presence paid off handsomely, allowing the queen to claim a lion's share of the takings, despite her very limited involvement.

Cumberland had hired the 600-ton *Tyger* as his flagship, with his own 300-ton *Sampson*, the 160-ton *Golden Noble*, and two 50-ton barks and a pinnace as her escorts. Adverse weather delayed their departure by three months, at the end of which Cumberland decided to abandon the voyage himself, transferring command to Captain Norton, whom he ordered off to the Azores. Here Norton fell in with a fleet assembled by Ralegh, under the command of Sir John Burgh, whose intentions to assault Panama had also been frustrated by sailing delays. The fleets agreed to combine to attack the carrack *Santa Croce*, which they had espied but she, to avoid capture, ran herself ashore and set herself ablaze after her portable wealth had been carted away, only for some of it to be intercepted on the road to safety by English landing parties.[24] Shortly after this, the English fleet was joined by a group of vessels under the command of Christopher Newport, who had set sail in the 150-ton *Golden Dragon*, with her consorts *Prudence*, *Margaret* and *Virgin*, to capture, loot and ransom the Spanish town of La Yaguana in Hispaniola, only to find it abandoned, the townsfolk having been forewarned. Content with what they had captured, Newport sent his storm-surviving prizes directly home, escorted by *Margaret* and *Virgin*, while the other two ships detoured to the Azores, capturing a ship loaded with pigs and tobacco, which must have provided them with many a contemplative hog roast.

Newport agreed to remain on station with Burgh in expectation of capturing some prizes – a decision that turned a voyage that had scarcely been 'made' into the most spectacular financial triumph ever, for on 3 August they sighted *Madre de Dios*, and gave chase.

The swifter sailers, *Golden Dragon* and *Dainty*, came first in range and when Sir John joined them, they boarded the towering vessel simultaneously from both bows and the quarter. The fight was fierce. The captain of *Dragon*, along with three of his men, was soon slain, while 'divers others [were] very sore hurt in fighte', in a fight which became controversial, as every group exaggerated the part that they had played so as to assert their rights for a greater share of her enormous treasure.

Thus it was recounted that *Foresight* and *Roebuck* were so fiercely engaged that they had to withdraw for fear of sinking, although Sir Robert Crosse in the former managed to return alongside in time to thwart the carrack's master from driving his ship ashore. By this time *Tiger* and *Samson* had joined the fray, which lasted for a further three hours until, overrun by boarders from all the ships clamped to her side, the prize, like a bison brought down by wolves, surrendered to her fate. She had fought bravely, as a description of her state by Hakluyt indicates: 'No man could almost step but upon a dead carcase or a bloody floor but specially about the helm where very many of them fell suddenly from stirring to dying.' Little compassion was shown initially by the boarding parties vying with each other to loot the loose goods on the upper deck and to relieve the passengers of their possessions, as was their right. This changed the next morning when Sir John, content that he had saved *Roebuck* from foundering, boarded with his own barber-surgeon, 'denying [the wounded] no possible help or relief that he or any of his company could afford them.'

Sir John also summoned up *Grace of Dover* to act as a hospital ship to ferry the survivors homeward, although their trials did not end there, for that bark herself was boarded by *Bond* of Weymouth and her passengers, fiercely frisked, forced to hand over 50,000 ducats of diamonds that they had previously kept hidden.

In another act, very typical of the pirateers, Sir John unchained four hundred slaves from *Madre de Dios*'s hold and released them on the beach at Flores where, one can only sadly surmise, they were recaptured. Sir John also made a swift audit of the goods being carried in the carrack, estimating that she held £102,000 of pepper, and pearls, amber and musk worth 400,000 crusadoes.[25]

Despite her battering, *Madre de Dios* remained seaworthy, although a looter had upset a candle and caused a fire to spring up close to where the ship's gunpowder was stored. When that was quenched and the clearing-up completed, Newport transferred out of the much damaged *Dragon* to sail her to Dartmouth, whose narrow entrance the great ship must have filled when she arrived, a massive and early Christmas present for many on 7 September.

Her looting became as infamous as her capture was renowned. Much had already been removed, contrary to the rule of distribution laid down by the Lord Admiral, which required that the bulk cargo be not disturbed until officially parcelled out, but *Madre de Dios*, registered as departing Cochin with a draught of 31ft entered Dartmouth drawing just 26ft. Even that represented holds deep enough for those ashore to greatly benefit. On arrival the cargo was considered to comprise: 500 tons of mixed spices, 8,500cwt of pepper, 900cwt of cloves, 700cwt of cinnamon; 500cwt of cochineal, 59cwt of mace and nutmeg, as well as frankincense, galingale, camphor, ginger. There was also 15 tons of ebony, and a wealth of gold, silver, ivory, tapestries, jewels, silks, calicoes, damasks, taffetas, towels, quilts, carpets, porcelain, coconuts and, of course, diamonds. Eager, canny, traders flocked into the town ready to relieve the sailors of the contents of their pockets and chests for insufficient but ready money. It was, of course, a cargo the loss of which had little effect on Spain's ability to manage her military campaigns.

The capture of *Madre de Dios* encouraged Cumberland to continue roving and in 1593 he persuaded the queen to provide him with two hulls, *Golden Lyon* and *Bonaventure*, which he crewed and victualled himself, believing that to leave such arrangements to Their Lordships left him open to surrendering too much of his gains. The royal ships were joined by seven private vessels with Monson, now reconciled, sailing as a commander. Success came early with the capture of two very rich French ships from St Malo and the overpowering, after a fierce engagement, of twelve hulks carrying powder and ammunition to Spain. The fleet then headed over to the Azores, where they soon sighted a convoy of twenty-four vessels. Having closed and prepared for action, Cumberland decided that the enemy was too powerful to overcome and withdrew, hoping for an easier opportunity. However, it is clear that one of the reasons for this decision was that the earl himself was ill and, in order to treat the patient, Monson, who had been badly injured while avoiding being captured, yet again onboard a prize vessel, hobbled ashore at Corvo to ask for a pail of milk for his commander – he returned with the whole cow.

They had missed, however, the golden calf, for the Venetian ambassador to Spain, Francesco Vendramin, provided a detailed list of the valuables unloaded at Seville on 28 August that year which totalled some 475,301 ducats (Appendix 8).[26]

There was more besides. Cumberland had detached three of his vessels to the West Indies, where news of their success led to the Spanish sending a squadron in pursuit. By the time it arrived on station the English were back in Plymouth. However, during their voyage one of the English vessels, the 250-ton *Anthony*, engaged seven Spanish ships, all above 180 tons, and in a severe fight defeated them and captured several, a clear indication that the pirateering spirit of Grenville was not unique.

Two years after the taking of *Madre de Dios*, Cumberland let an even larger fortune escape his grasp. His own *Sampson*, accompanied by *Mayflower* and *Royal Exchange*, both London vessels, sailed from Plymouth in April 1594 and were on patrol off St Michael's by mid May. On 2 June they sighted the great carrack *Las Cinque Chagas* and closed in for the attack (described in Chapter 3) only to watch her burn out.

By the mid 1590s the piratocracy had proved their worth, although the majority of their cargoes were valued as far less than that seized from the great carracks (Appendix 9) They had also earned respect from the besting of a formidable enemy fleet. Yet they had had their misfortunes as well, such as Drake's unsuccessful assault on Lisbon in 1589 and subsequent years of disgrace. That failure led the queen to believe that she did not have to entrust future expeditions to the command of her experienced seamen.

While the English rethought their strategy, the *flotas* continued to bring enormous wealth into Spain, although it was seldom a journey accomplished without some loss through shipwreck, disease or piracy. On 9 May 1595 the Venetian ambassador at Madrid reported that:

> The arrival of the India fleet is delayed. The people of Seville are alarmed, for the whole month of April has been stormy. Although it is said that the English are not as strong as reported, yet forty ships have sailed from England; and as it is known that two thousand persons have died on board the Spanish fleet owing to the hardships of the journey, they say it will be no such easy matter to resist these forty.

Four days later he reported a change of mood in Seville when, 'after long labour and great danger of going to the bottom', the West India fleet arrived in port with goods valued at 'twenty-two millions of gold'.[27] What is more, several ships were still missing and if they were safe, the ambassador reckoned that 'in the course of five or six months thirty millions of gold will have been brought into the country.'

England's finest could not be expected to lie at anchor while such wealth was ferried unchallenged across the Atlantic. In 1595 Drake and Hawkins joined forces, the first time since San Juan de Ulua, with a poor but approved plan to plunder Panama, to which they added a detour to the Indies to seize one of the treasure ships that had failed to make the crossing. This was *Begona*, the flagship, which had lost both her rudder and masts in a storm, and put into Puerto Rico on 30 March for repairs, with 2.5 million ducats of treasure in her holds. Yet the English raiding party, jointly commanded by these two elderly pirates, did not get underway until 28 August and, for a variety of avoidable diversions, did not arrive off the alerted and well-defended Puerto Rico until 12 November, when Sir John promptly died. Drake burnt a few ships, fired at a few forts, and then retreated, sailing on towards Panama, the seizure of which had been another objective in this multi-aimed voyage, dying himself off Porto Bello on 28 January.

There were no more Drakes. To lead the next voyage to the Azores in 1597, the unwise decision was made to appoint the inexperienced Essex in command, with his rival courtier, Ralegh, as his subordinate. To appoint such popinjays as commanders in a joint venture courted trouble and proved to be a marriage made in Hades. As Henry Howard was later to remark, 'The Queen did never yet love man that failed in a project of importance put into his hand.'[28]

The two men had served together under the Lord Admiral in the 1596 raid on Cadiz, managing to fall out, openly, on several occasions, only for the eldest man's conciliatory nature to smooth over the fissures, possibly too well, for now Essex and Ralegh found themselves with no superior to control the former's petulance or the latter's pride. Lord Thomas Howard, less authoritative and noble than either his relative the Lord Admiral or the queen's two favourites, formed the lesser member of the triumvirate, although he was the only one with serious sea experience.

The original plan had been to land an army of six thousand at The Groyne (Finisterre) to do serious damage to the Spanish fleet and fortifications. This was a project felt both to be worthy and within the capability of the two commanders who had, after all, succeeded at Cadiz, but foul weather prevented the execution of this strategic objective and, after landing the soldiers back in England, and without consulting the queen, the two men abandoned an attack by fire-ships on Ferrol and led their fleets towards the Azores to intercept the *flota*. From a military campaign that demanded limited tactical appreciation, the expedition had turned into one requiring planning, co-ordination, logistical support, intelligence-gathering, and an appreciation and knowledge of ocean winds and currents: skills of which neither man had a grasp. Disaster threatened as surely as the storms that blew the squadrons apart, and when Essex found Ralegh's ships had left the Spanish coast for the Azores ahead of him, he suspected that the latter was seeking to gain for himself the glory of seizing the treasure fleet.

On 15 September 1597 the two squadrons anchored off Flores, where the less recently provisioned Ralegh wished to stay to victual and water ship. Essex reluctantly agreed but then weighed anchor himself, sending a message back to Ralegh ordering him to sail with all dispatch to join him at Fayal. Ralegh obeyed, only to find no sign of Essex at the rendezvous. Knowing his colleague's temperament, Ralegh waited five days before launching an assault on the town which fell, mainly due to his leadership by example. Essex reappeared at the moment of triumph and, charging Ralegh with proceeding without his commander's explicit instructions, threatened to court-martial and execute him.

Ralegh responded that the order to which Essex referred applied only to ships' captains, of which he was not one and, furthermore, he had been following Essex's orders to replenish at Fayal. Matching bluster with bravado, the Westcountryman then threatened to engage Essex's forces with his own if the commander did not reinstate those of Ralegh's officers whom he had summarily dismissed. The youth rescinded and Thomas Howard managed to negotiate a truce.

Having demonstrated his incompetence as a commander, Essex compounded his inabilities by ordering the fleet to fall back to the east of Terceira to which the *flota* would be heading from the west. The bulk of the English sailed away, but Monson in *Rainbow*, with *Dreadnought*, *Garland* and *Mary Rose*, failed to comply with the order. Three hours after Essex departed, the still-present Monson found himself alone in company with twenty-five of the incoming *flota*. His challenge to them was spurned and his signal for reinforcements unheard and unseen, until *Mary Rose* and *Dreadnought*, steering towards the sound of gunfire, arrived too late to prevent the treasure fleet entering the well-guarded roadstead at Terceira. When Essex eventually responded to Monson's urgent message, he had the fortune to come across a treasure ship belonging to the governor of Havana and her two escorts. These he took easily, adding some 100,000 ducats to the expedition's otherwise meagre haul. But there was, by this time, no chance of taking the main fleet. It lay well-protected under the guns of the castle of San Sebastian. After an argument between Essex's soldiers, in favour of an assault, and Ralegh's seamen, opposed to making a landing, the fleet accepted the inevitable and sailed off to St Michael for Essex's final incompetence.

The English error had a strange witness. Onboard one of the Spanish ships was Richard Hawkins, being returned home after his capture off the coast of South America. In a salt-rubbing note to Essex, he wrote of the events, 'if you had been amongst the fifteen ships which had us in the midst of them – three ahead, three astern and nine on the broadside – I had been your prisoner, and twelve million that came in six ships of 250 and 300 tons apiece.'

Now Ralegh was ordered to act as a decoy while Essex landed, but failed to take Villa Franca. The mood lightened among Ralegh's squadron when they sighted a great carrack of some 2,000 tons heading towards the bay, believing the fleet at anchor to be of its own kind. If deception could be maintained its capture was certain. Ralegh ordered the lowering of national flags and the holding of fire until it was too late for the enemy captain to go about. All waited and watched their prey as she slowly approached the bay. Then an impetuous Dutchman, anxious to stake a major claim, weighed and opened fire just before the carrack lowered her sails. With just sufficient way on to alter course, the gallant Spanish captain drove his vessel onto the rocks and set fire to his cargo. As this was mainly molasses, it burnt too fiercely to enable the English boats crews to close for salvage.

Thus ended the unsuccessful 'Island Voyage' led by men who had behaved not like naval commanders, but as arrogant, envious and jealous courtiers.

Cumberland would have been a far better choice of leader, but he was already at sea and thus not available for the task. He too returned empty-handed from the Azores, but not from total incompetence, nor poor leadership. His original target had been the carracks sailing from Lisbon but they, having got warning of his arrival, stayed put. The thwarted commander then tried his hand at kidnapping and capture at Lanzarote in the Canaries, again without success. By this time the unrewarded seamen were starting to grumble, their mood assisted by copious consumption of the local wine. Cumberland, allowing sufficient time for a return to sobriety, then summoned them, reread his commission, imposed some new rules and regulations and reminded them of the penalties available to him for infringement. But then he did not rant and rave, but unveiled his plans to take San Juan de Puerto Rico, a feat that had recently eluded Drake, and released each ship from keeping close company to range wide and capture what they could as long as they made the appointed rendezvous in a timely manner. It was a brilliant display of leadership, showing a skill totally lacking in Essex, and barely discernible in Ralegh. Then, just to show that he was not a soft touch, Cumberland issued the following instruction, of which Drake himself would have been proud:

> Let the warning I now give you drive these thoughts out of their thoughts that hold them . . . my overpatient humour is now shaken off and I will neither oversee nor suffer to pass unpunished ill deserts. The sum of it all is that as you shall look from me to be commanded for your good so will I have you pay me all obedience and then we will be partners in all either profit or honour that is got.[29]

San Juan, when it fell thanks to Cumberland's inspired initiatives, and enthusiastic and loyal followers, yielded more honour than profit, and when tropical diseases decimated his men he headed homeward via the Azores for 'the final string left in his Bow.' When long periods of calm and fierce moments of storm deprived him of the chance of falling in with the Spanish fleet and left his own ships ill-provisioned, he landed on the islands under a flag of truce, his impeccable manners earning him a supply sufficient to bring them safe home to England.

By now the English, aware that the Spanish had sufficient galleons to escort the treasure fleets through the danger point of the Azores and back to Spain, were showing signs of abandoning this regular deployment that had always relied on serendipity rather than strategy to bring home a prize. However, intelligence reports that the Spanish fleet had been severely battered by storms on the voyage from the Azores to Lisbon led the English to plan for one further expedition to those islands in search of what they thought would be a poorly defended *flota*. After years of recruiting all and sundry to join their pirateering voyages, and thus having no chance of keeping their intentions hidden from Spain, in 1600 the English, after years of war, finally produced a plan that had some resemblance to that required to mount a purely naval expedition. First, it had one aim: the capture of the treasure fleet; secondly, it had one, professional, commander, Richard Leveson; thirdly, it was based around a small, strong squadron of galleons: *Repulse*, *Warspite* and *Vanguard*, and a few pinnaces, including *Lion's Whelp*, although some merchant vessels were included, possibly as victuallers. Yet the most important point of all was that the voyage was planned using a weapon strange to all previous deployments, secrecy. Leveson's fleet was already at sea, gainfully employed off Dunkirk. In their absence, victualling stores were assembled quietly at Plymouth, to be loaded swiftly onboard the fleet as it called in on its way westward at the end of June.

Nevertheless, a Spanish fleet of five galleons, with supporting minor vessels, also sailed for the Azores that month under the command of Don Diego Brochero, one of Spain's less successful Almirante Generals. Widespread rumour indicated that this was a fleet manned by the sweepings from the seaport gutters, but Leveson, a cautious commander, decided that rather than risk an engagement he would intercept the *flota* to the west of the Azores. He didn't, returning to England in early October without catching sight of a single Spanish sail.

This incident didn't cover Leveson in glory and there were those who felt that he owed his command to the fact that at the age of seventeen he married Margaret Howard, the daughter of the Lord Admiral. It must have been an unstoppable love-match, for Leveson's father, William, was a rogue, and his son had at this stage no obvious prospects. Like son, like father, for shortly afterwards William married Susan Vernon, the cousin of the earl of Essex.

Shortly after the empty episode described above, Leveson seized his moment for glory when he was appointed to command the naval forces to challenge the Spanish landings in Ireland. While supporting the siege of Kinsale, Leveson was informed that a Spanish fleet, commanded by Pedro de Zubiaur, had disembarked at Castlehaven. Losing little time Leveson warped *Warspite*, *Defiance*, *Swiftsure*, *Crane*, *Merlin* and two support vessels out into the teeth of a continuing gale and bounced his way to Castlehaven.

The entrance to the haven is narrow and, as its name suggests, commanded by a castle which Zubiaur's men had already taken. He had also established a battery of eight guns to support the hundreds of musketeers he had landed to repulse a relief force coming from the sea. Inside the haven, their guns pointing seaward, lay Zubiaur's own squadron of six well-armed vessels.

If Drake's blood flowed through any of his successor's veins it did so in Leveson that day. Sending his gallant pinnace ahead to sound out the approach, he sailed straight in to the harbour through the barrage of shot from left, right and in front of him. His crew gave better than they got. Within five hours Zubiaur's squadron was no more. Yet with the job done, Leveson could not depart: the wind that had blown him lustily straight into the haven now denied him any opportunity to exit. For three days he lay in easy range of the enemy's artillery, once even grounding in his eagerness to engage at close quarters. *Warspite* became a pepperpot before Leveson, his job done, withdrew rather than 'fight against rocks'.[30]

Returning to England, Leveson's force was almost immediately redeployed to cause mischief off the coast of Spain and, incidentally, to take the treasure fleet, the leitmotif of all such deployments. In support he was promised a Dutch fleet, long anticipated but longer in coming, and a squadron under his vice admiral, the pen-pushing pirate William Monson.

Leveson was ordered to blockade the Spanish fleet in port, while tempting it out to meet its fate before the English guns. A large dollop of water was mixed into this heady brew by the statement, no doubt inspired by the admiral's reckless zeal at Castlehaven, that although he might attempt an assault, he could only do so without putting the queen's ships in danger. A more harmful dilution was made with the addition of the piratical tendency. Leveson was ordered to sail early in the hope that he might intercept the silver fleet hurrying home from the Azores and to consider making an attempt on both the outward and homeward East Indian carracks or, if that was not successful, to sail from Lisbon to meet the arriving West Indian fleet.

Leveson's command consisted of eight galleons: *Repulse*, in which he flew his flag, *Garland*, with Monson as his vice admiral, *Defiance*, *Nonpareil*, *Warspite*, *Mary Rose*, *Dreadnought* and *Adventure*, a few supporting vessels, and the absent Dutch. Intelligence about the movement of the silver fleet meant haste was essential and on 19 March Leveson hauled out of Plymouth with six ships, leaving Monson to catch up when he had manned the remaining vessels. This the vice admiral failed to do until he was shooed to sea by the silver-hungry Cecil on 26 March.

While Monson endeavoured to find his admiral, Leveson himself had carried out the first and only interception during the war of a complete treasure fleet. But the days of unescorted *flotas* were long past: growling around the wealthy flock were at least sixteen fighting ships, each of which was a match for Leveson. Still, buoyed by his success at Castlehaven, Leveson waited until dark and, disregarding a tempestuous sea, boarded the ship nearest to him, realising that his powerful assault might mean that he was 'more doubtful of sinking than of winning her.' He described the next few hours vividly, writing:

Here was my misery. The night was exceeding dark, and the sea did suddenly grow so high, as I was neither able to make her fast, nor my people able to enter her, unless it were some few of my valiantest, which between the ships (I fear) were unfortunately lost. Four several times my ship fell off, and four times I boarded her again . . . Though our fortune in this might seem to be crooked and adverse, yet it was God's will to dispose all for the best, for this fleet was so strong (which at that instant was unknown to me) as if I had taken the least ship of theirs, I must either have engaged all the Queen's ships, with danger to have kept her, or else have lost her the next day following, with grief and dishonour.[31]

With morning dawned the Englishmen's realisation that they were in the presence of an overwhelming force. Leveson summoned his captains, who agreed that they had fought a good fight but were not in a position to claim the prize. So, reluctantly, they left her 'with as much discontent as man can imagine to see so much wealth without power to take it. Yet I followed the fleet into the shore that day and the next night, in hope of a straggler, but the weather growing to be very fair, would not yield me such a benefit.'

However, a pearl of high price was lying not far away to compensate. Shortly after Monson and Leveson were at last united off the Tagus, information arrived that a fabulously well-laden but storm-shattered carrack lay beneath the protecting guns of Cezimbra Castle, having been unable through lack of a fit crew to enter the Tagus. She was not, however, lacking in protection. Frederico Spinola, sailing with his galley fleet of eight for Flanders, was diverted to Cezimbra and reinforced by three more galleys commanded by the new marquis of Santa Cruz. This was a formidable opposition and, during his commanders' conference, Leveson's plan of attack was received without enthusiasm, except by the piratically trained Monson, who was all for challenging the galleys. The decision was made to sail in the next day and attack, galleys, castle and carrack in one great rush, repeating the tactic which Leveson had proved to be so effective at Castlehaven. Now the experience of two maritime traditions fused wonderfully well for, if Castlehaven was carried out with all the confidence of a naval officer at the peak of his profession, Cezimbra was to be a classic example of a cutting out operation carried out with all the cunning of a corsair.

Leveson's report of the operation is a good summary:

1602, June 5. It is my purpose to let your Honours know that it has pleased God to give me the possession of a very great and, I hope, a very rich carrack, which I did fetch out of Cezimbra Road, being guarded there with 8 pieces of artillery upon the shore, and 11 galleys, whereof the Marquis of St Cruz and Signor Spinola, being both there in person, were principal commanders. The galleys were lodged to the westward of the road, behind a point of rocks, having bent their prows somewhat dangerously to receive us at our first coming in. But the *Warspite* and *Garland*, luffing up near unto the rocks and coming to anchor, displaced the galleys within a short time out of their cove. The *Nonperille*, *Dreadnought* and *Adventure*, keeping it up under a sail, chased the galleys,

131

sometimes to the eastward and sometimes to the westward. To be short, the Marquis, being very soundly beaten, ran his way, and Signor Spinola followed him with no less haste. It was my good fortune to surprise with boats two of Spinola his principal galleys, the one being his vice-admiral, and both being laden with powder and oil for the Low Countries, which I sacrificed to the fire, having no leisure to heave it out. And I protest unto your Honours that two other of his galleys were coming unto me to have yielded themselves, but I, having then a fairer object in mine eye, and being ready to give the attempt upon the carrack, would not stay to receive them.

The course which I held with the carrack was this: first, I thought it no discretion to board her with any of her Majesty's ships, because the Spaniards might at any time burn her, being no longer able to defend her, and then fly to the shore. I did therefore prepare a hulk of the east country, which I had taken about three days before, with fireworks. I put into her 20 of my gallantest men, with direction to board her in the 'hauss,' and to cut cable if it were possible that she might drive out to sea; if not, then to burn her, and come away in their boats. Now you shall perceive how fortunately this fell out. The hulk, going to board the carrack, was taken upon the stays by ill steerage, and having a leeward tide was not able to fetch her again within any short space. My purpose being thus defeated, I had then no other shift but to let our guns go off roundly, as well at the carrack as at the fort, purposing indeed to have sunk her, but within 2 hours' space we had so well quieted both the fort and the carrack as I received but sometimes a 'faynty' shot from them. Then I sent off my boat with a flag of truce, and the Spaniards entertained the parley, sent some gentlemen to treat with me, and I did the like. In the interim, I got up my hulk again to windward, and anchored her right in the hausse of the carrack, within half caliver shot. The meaning of the Spaniard was no other than to protract time that they might be able to send some of their principal men and wealth to the shore, and then burn the ship. But being thus well provided with my hulk, I showed them my fireworks. I laid open all my purposes, with protestation that if they would not presently resolve to yield, they should all presently resolve to burn. Hereupon the carrack was delivered up unto me.[32]

Leveson's luck, however, ran out once he had safely delivered his valuable cargo home. He was accused of removing goods from the ship for his own use, a charge that was pursued with much vigour even after his death and was not settled until 1623.

The Azores strategy had resulted in a few successes such as *San Felipe* and *Madre de Dios*; a few failures, such as *Las Cinque Chagas*; but these were all Portuguese carracks. Throughout all these years of lying in wait, the Spanish treasure fleets eluded the English net and avoided capture. There were many reasons for this, but an inability to stay on station long enough and with sufficient intelligence to guarantee an interception were major failings, as was the choice and mix of commanders. Yet the task was not an impossible one. On 26 November 1628 Piet Hein, admiral of the Dutch West India Company, anchored in Falmouth Roads, that great pirate lair, bringing along with him the entire Spanish silver *flota* which he had captured off Havana. Did a wave from that attack roll slowly southerly and ripple over the skeleton slung between the round shot off San Juan de Puerto Rico?

CHAPTER 8

A Preference for Pirates – The Failure of the Spanish Armada

> When news of the departure of the Armada arrived the Pope said to several Cardinals, who were at audience, that he had done all he could to persuade the Queen to return to the Catholic Church; and offering to grant her a new investiture of her kingdom in spite of the deprivation pronounced by Pius V, and to give her the Bishops she might approve; to which the Queen had replied that the Pope would do well to give her some of his money.
>
> Giovanni Gritti, Venetian Ambassador in Rome,
> to the Doge and Senate, July 1588[1]

In January 1586 a list of seventy-six potential sea captains was drawn up in preparation for the arrival of the Spanish invasion fleet. It included six 'Drakes', that is Sir Francis, Bernard, Richard, Thomas, Hugh and one just recorded as Drake, gentleman.[2] These six of one family were matched by half a dozen of another, the Howards for, along with the Lord Admiral, there sailed to meet the Armada his cousin, Lord Thomas Howard, his nephew, Edmund Sheffield, his brother-in-law, Lord Henry Seymour, and his son-in-law Sir Robert Southwell, to all of whom were given commands, while the eighteen-year old-likely lad, Richard Leveson, newly married to Howard's daughter, Margaret, served as a volunteer in *Ark Royal*, under his father-in-law's watchful eye.

The 1586 list had been drawn up in order of social rank and those so listed might have expected to be appointed to sea command in a seniority that reflected their social status, but nothing indicates more clearly the primacy of the piratocracy than the fact that in 1588, with the nation in the gravest danger, command and control of its foremost fighting force was given to the professional pirates, regardless of their social standing. What is more, the aristocrats, even those with sea experience and related to the Lord Admiral, accepted their position without demur for, by the time that the Armada was sighted off the Lizard on 19 July 1588, all the piratocracy had made the move from criminal to courtier class, but without making a commensurate career change. Now their Channel commands would confirm them as respected senior servants of a pirate queen proud to acknowledge them as hers, along with her own kith and kin.

The Spanish readily appreciated that the hour of the corsair had arrived and that Drake, returning triumphant from his assault on Cadiz and the taking of the richly-laden *San Felipe*, was not only the hero of the moment but England's supreme fighting strategist. The letters written to Philip by Mendoza speak mainly of Drake and the piratocracy, not the Lord Admiral. In June 1587 Mendoza informed Philip that Drake:

> Had victualled his ships for more than six months with the biscuit and wine he had captured from your Majesty's vessels, and he would distribute the meat and other stores so that they should last the same length of time . . . it was decided that four out of the eight ships the Queen had guarding the west end of the Channel should be sent to Drake, and that 10 merchantmen, of from 80 to 100 tons burden, should be fitted out in Bristol and the West-country . . . It was uncertain whether they would be commanded by Grenville, a gentleman who has been sailing as a pirate, or Frobisher, who they thought would agree with Drake better than the other.[3]

The Spanish had no problem with identifying Grenville as a pirate. In a long letter to Mendoza listing a horrific series of ship seizures by the English, the writer, who was interested in organising a prisoner exchange, wrote of:

> The poor pilots who were captured by Richard Grenville of Cornwall, and are now held prisoners by him. He is a pirate and brought to England 22 Spaniards whom he treated as slaves, making them carry stones on their backs all day for some building operations of his, and chaining them up all night. Twenty of them have died or escaped, but he still keeps the two pilots.[4]

The supposed importance of Grenville in the English naval preparations is again mentioned by Mendoza in a note of February 1588 in which he reported that Drake would shortly be back at sea and that:

> The Queen had ordered Grenville (an Englishman, who, as I have informed your Majesty, has several times gone on plundering voyages, and was lately on the coast of Spain) to remain with 20 merchantmen and pirate ships on the English coast opposite Ireland.[5]

Grenville was, however, to play a less significant role in the upcoming engagement than that imagined either by Mendoza, or by Grenville himself, for he was confined to the West Country, where he received directions from the Privy Council not only to stay those vessels that he had prepared to dispatch for the relief of the Virginia settlement, but also to gather up a flotilla that could be sent round to Plymouth to join Drake, this despite Grenville informing their lordships that he would patrol the seas between 'Cape of Cornwall or the Scillies for commodity of wind, to be better able upon any occasion to repair where most use might be made of his service.'[6] He was, Their Lordships felt, better employed ashore where, because of his knowledge and experience in martial affairs, he was ordered to remain to give assistance and advice to the Lords Lieutenant of Devon and Cornwall.[7]

It was only when the danger had passed, in September 1588 while Armada vessels were struggling home or still being wrecked on the Irish coast, that Grenville was ordered to sea to 'destroy the Spaniard's ships' that might be discharging soldiers at Irish ports. They weren't and he didn't.

Ralegh was similarly confined to the land, although he did manage to join Howard's fleet off Calais, as the queen's messenger to invite the admiral to 'attack the Armada in some way, or to engage it if he could not burn it', belated advice which Howard probably dismissed with disdain.

Grenville and Ralegh could be consigned to the coast because Howard had plenty of other piratically inclined seamen available, without risking command cohesion by employing the arrogant Ralegh or the irascible Grenville, both of whom, to be fair, were amphibians able to exercise command ashore as well as afloat. Apart from John Hawkins and Frobisher, soon assigned, Howard had the four Fenner brothers at his disposal. Among these was Thomas, whom Corbett described as 'one of the most daring and experienced officers of that time'. He had sailed with Drake on the West Indies expedition of 1585, proving his courage during the boat attack on Cartagena which he and Frobisher pressed home with success. In 1587 he commanded *Dreadnought* in the assault on Cadiz and in 1588 he was to serve as Drake's vice admiral in command of *Nonpareil*.

George Fenner was another most daring pirate, whose greatest achievement was in *Castle of Comfort* in 1567 off the Azores when he fought alone against seven Portuguese ships in an engagement which Corbett considered 'as the earliest revelation to English seamen of the power their superiority in gunnery was to give them.'[8] Certainly, apropos of future fighting instructions, tactics and the armament suite of warships, Fenner's experience was more relevant than that of Hawkins and Drake and their harbour action at San Juan de Ulua the following year. George's career from then on was typical of those merchants who combined piratical opportunism with legitimate trading. He appeared as both litigant and defender in cases of pillage, seemingly concentrating his full attention in this area, for he did not renew his fighting career until his appointment to command *Galleon Leicester* in the Armada campaign. Edward commanding *Swiftsure* and William in command in *Aid* completed this pirateering quartet.

The ascendancy of Drake and his fellow pirates has overshadowed the fact that in 1588 the Navy Royal did have its own officers with many years' sea experience between them. Such a one was Sir Henry Palmer who, at the age of twenty-six, in 1576 was appointed in command of a squadron of queen's ships off Flanders, a year when the English and the Dutch had a minor spat at sea. In 1586 he was appointed Admiral of the Narrow Seas, flying his flag in *Foresight*. These were waters that he knew well, for he had also had responsibility for the development and protection of Dover harbour. This connection was to prove most useful after the Armada anchored off Calais, for it was Sir Henry who sailed away to collect a number of boats from Dover, 'laden with bavins and pitch for firing the Spanish fleet'. However, the thirty boats, the rapid provision of which earned the Cinque Ports much praise, were returned in one piece, as by the time they had crossed the Channel the Spanish fleet had already fled the earlier attack by fire-ships organised by Howard.[9]

As the Spanish threat materialised, Palmer was transferred to *Antelope* as just one of the eastern squadron captains. There is a hint why, cometh the hour he was not the man, in the gossipy and sometimes inaccurate work of Richard Hawkins, who wrote:

> Sir Henry Palmer, a wise and valiant gentleman, a great commander, and of much experience in sea causes, being appointed by the queen's majesty's council, to go for general of a fleet for the coast of Spain, in 1583, submitting himself to their lordships pleasure, excused the charge, saying that his training, had been in the narrow seas; and that of the other he had little experience: and therefore was in duty bound to entreat their honours to make choice of some other person, that was better acquainted and experimented in those seas; that her majesty and their lordships might be better served.[10]

Hawkins applauded Palmer's integrity, but for the queen and Howard, now committed to a fight for survival, this admiral's attitude had all the appearance of that of a 'Protestant hen', the taunt aimed at her fleet as they wafted the Armada up Channel while keeping out of range. Palmer, having failed to take his tide at the flood, spent the remainder of his career in the shallows, ending up Comptroller of the Navy in succession to another naval man whom Howard might have considered appointing to high command, the much experienced William Borough.

The younger brother of the great navigator, Stephen, William went to sea in 1553 at the age of sixteen and had walked decks ever since. For ten years he passaged to and from northern Scandinavia and Muscovy, voyages that honed and tested the skill of any ship's master and not only their navigational skills. The waters in the Gulf of Finland held a congregation of corsairs, whose supremacy could only be challenged by well-armed vessels travelling in convoy. This Borough did and in 1570, as the 'captain general' of a fleet of thirteen ships, he successfully drove off an attack by six Danish 'freebooters'. His services on this trade route, including his drawing up of hydrographical information, brought him to the attention of both Burghley and Walsingham, and it can be assumed that it was through them that he transferred to royal naval tasks. It also led to his first unfortunate clash with the piratocracy, when he sued Michael Lok, Frobisher's sponsor for the Labrador voyages, over the sale of the bark *Judith*. As a result, Borough was one of those whose claims led to Lok's imprisonment in 1579 for debt, a fact that Frobisher, who collected slights, would not have forgiven.

In 1583 Borough was appointed Comptroller of the Navy, and thus a colleague of both Howard and Hawkins, but he was soon back at sea on anti-piracy patrol charged with 'apprehending certain sea-rovers'. Borough's two barks, despite early reports of their discomfiture, returned triumphant with ten sail taken. This success was turned into a spectator event when ten of the pirate leaders were hanged at Wapping on 30 August. The condemned men themselves added to the spectacle by having themselves attired in the most flamboyant of clothing which was cut off and distributed to their supporters before they swung.

Following this success, Borough might well have anticipated naval preferment. That this was likely is shown by his appointment as Drake's vice admiral for the Cadiz raid of 1587. Borough sailed in *Golden Lion*, and later, presumably, wished that he had not. The attack on Cadiz was a timely and definite success but, in Drake's modest appraisal, it succeeded only in 'singeing the king of Spain's beard' – embarrassing, irritating, but soon unnoticeable.

The English fleet was a mighty one, with the usual mix of the three seagoing fleets. There were six queen's ships, eleven City of London merchant hulls, including four heavily-armed Levanters, led by the company admiral, Captain Robert Flicke, Drake's rear admiral, four of Drake's own pirate vessels and two ships belonging to Lord Admiral Howard, which would also have been licensed to rove by spurious letters of reprisal. Anxious to be at sea before Elizabeth changed her mind, Drake left Plymouth on 2 April recording, with one more of his notable phrases, 'the wind commands me away . . .'

A speedy passage brought the undetected fleet to the entrance to Cadiz harbour on 19 April. Without pausing to summon his captains, Drake led his ships into the outer harbour. The crews of the principal harbour defence, the fourteen royal galleys, hastily scrambled onboard and rowed out to meet the intruders. Precedent would have favoured their chances. Ever since a previous Lord Admiral Howard, Sir Edward, had died in leading an attack on moored galleys, near Brest in 1513, the English had feared these warships, especially in confined waters. However, under the enthusiastic governance of Hawkins, a new type of English vessel had been created in recent years: the race-built galleon, which was not only capable of delivering a weighty salvo ahead, but had a massive punch available from her broadside armament. Drake was commanding one such ship, the 600-ton *Elizabeth Bonaventure*, which although purchased in 1567 had been rebuilt as a galleon in 1581.

Drake had also directed that *Bonaventure* be rearmed according to his requirements for his West Indies expedition of 1585. It is this rearmament which indicates his transition from high-seas pirate to royal raider, for he offloaded all the ship's close-range boarding weaponry in favour of weight of shot for pounding both shore defences and ships' hulls.[11]

Table 3. The Armament of *Elizabeth Bonaventure*

Armament	Demi-cannon	Cannon Perrier	Culverin	Demi-culverin	Saker	Minion	Falcon	Port Piece	Fowler	Base
Pre-1585	4	2	6	8	6	2	2	4	6	12
Drake's list	4	4	8	12	6	1	3	–	–	–

If *Bonaventure*, which Cumberland captained during the Armada campaign, carried a weapon fit that was typical of the other galleons, then it is no wonder that the pirate commanders in 1588 chose not to attempt boarding the Spanish vessels, whose soldiers alone carried sufficient small arms to repulse such attempts.

Drake was thus fitted with the firepower best suited to thrash his foes. They consisted, apart from the galleys, of about sixty vessels representing the expected mix in a naval and commercial port preparing for a major expedition. The two on-duty harbour guard galleys who had nosed out to challenge the new arrivals limped to safety, holed and broken. The seven others that rowed out in line abreast like a seaborne cavalry were similarly dispersed by an English broadside and sought shelter behind the Las Puercas shoal, which lay close to the shore at the southern side of the outer harbour entrance. The remaining challenger was a Genoese galleon, but she was hemmed in by other vessels and unable to bring her own guns to bear effectively, and so was pounded until she sank. That, effectively, ended the floating resistance, leaving Drake at liberty to anchor and to select his prizes at leisure.

Once the shipping in the outer harbour was destroyed, Drake turned his attention to the inner harbour, which was crowded with vessels, including the galleon selected by Santa Cruz to be his flagship for the Armada expedition. Knowing that *Bonaventure* drew too much water to pass into that shelter, Drake transferred his flag to the smaller *Merchant Royal* and led a dawn raid to capture that ship and destroy those that floated around her. Once the prize had been towed out, Drake returned to *Bonaventure*, where his anxious vice admiral found him.

Borough was annoyed by the fact that, contrary to naval fighting instructions, Drake had not summoned a council before charging in to Cadiz, a tactic that made absolute sense to the experienced pirate, but was contrary to the beliefs of the cautious comptroller. With every hour spent within the confines of the harbour, Borough's anxiety grew the more. He pleaded with Drake to depart, but the pirate in Drake saw booty all around him and felt the necessity both to replenish his ships and the coffers of the merchants who had funded his force. He dismissed Borough and continued offloading. Borough returned to *Golden Lion*, where he almost witnessed the wisdom of his own advice, for the wind dropped, becalming the English and making them sitting targets for the re-sited Spanish shore-batteries and a fleet of fire-ships which were sent to drift down on the English on the ebb-tide. This last tactic failed when Drake had his boats haul the blazing boats away to safety, while using the light from their flames to assist the night-time emptying of the prizes. His act was also witnessed by the Duke of Medina Sidonia, not yet appointed as commander of the Armada. The memory of it must have added to his chagrin, when the boats' crews he had deployed off Calais in 1588 to neutralise the English fire-ships panicked at their approach, and caused his fleet to cut their cables to escape a threat which fizzled out harmlessly on the sands.

Drake departed Cadiz in the early hours of the following morning, having destroyed or captured thirty-seven ships and transferred much cargo to his own fleet. His next decision, for he was not a man to make proposals, was to take the fort at Sagres, which commanded a sheltered bay near Cape St Vincent, and from here to assail passing shipping. Borough, misjudging his commander completely, put in writing (well, he was by now a bureaucrat) his objections, along with many other criticisms of his commander. Drake, never one to enjoy criticism or a challenge to his authority, responded by ordering Borough's arrest onboard *Golden Lion*, sending Captain John Marchant over to that ship as his replacement. It did not work out quite as Drake had anticipated, for the crew of *Golden Lion* objected, released Borough, sent Marchant back, and sailed home independently, claiming a lack of victuals in defence of their action.

When Drake, who never saw a sleeping dog without having the urge to kick it, returned home, he insisted that Borough be court-martialled for cowardice and disobedience, for which he demanded his execution. Accusation and counter-accusation ended with Borough's life being spared, but his character being assassinated to such an extent that when commands for the Armada campaign were authorised, this experienced fighting seaman was ordered to patrol the Thames in *Bonavolia*, a galley of 180 tons with a crew of twenty, many of whom were felons.

Appointing Borough to an inshore galley might have been a cruel revenge exacted by Drake, especially as at Cadiz his subordinate commander may well have had logic on his side, while Drake was served by luck. Drake had, after all, not sunk the galleys, but merely forced them to retreat, and when they did they took shelter under the city guns close to the exit from the harbour, from where they could have sailed to challenge the departing English. Borough had anchored *Golden Lion* opposite them, from where he could respond to any attempt they made to re-enter the fray. Far from seeking to avoid action, the vice admiral was placing himself closest to the only remaining serious threat. Rather than withdrawing from the fray, he was ensuring that his commander had a free hand to complete his work of destruction. The galleys responded by sailing to attack Borough, in support of whom Drake despatched *Rainbow* and five merchant ships, a sizeable force for what was being dismissed as a threat of little consequence. The rumble of more broadsides caused another galley retreat and this time they stayed behind their shoal until the English departure whereupon:

> ten of the galleys that were in the Road came out, as it were in disdain of us, to
> make some pastime with their ordnance, at which time the wind turned on us,

whereupon we cast about again and stood in with the shore, and came to an anchor within a league of the tow: where the said galleys, for all their former bragging, at length suffered us to ride quietly. We now have had experience of galley-fights, wherein I can assure you that only these four of her Majesty's ships will make no account of twenty galleys, if they may be alone and not busied to guard others. There were never galleys that had better place and fitter opportunity for their advantage to fight with ships: but they were forced to retire.[12]

After seventy-four years, the fear of the galleys was laid to rest through the combined efforts of a headstrong pirate and a cautious naval officer. The same combination would lead to its final removal as a threat in the early years of the next century.

The supremacy of the pirates reflected the state's belief that they were the nation's most experienced sea-warriors. Of the twenty royal ships that formed the western squadron in the anti-Armada fleet disposition, no less than twelve were commanded by those involved with piracy. By contrast, the fourteen ships of the eastern squadron, which was not expected to be in the thick of the fighting, were commanded mostly by career naval officers, including several members of the aristocracy.

From Henry VIII's time this inexperienced coterie had been selected for naval command, with the Howards providing that king's first two appointments as Lord Admiral, the brothers Edward and Thomas. Senior commanders also tended to come from aristocratic families, but by 1585 when Charles Howard, Elizabeth's uncle, was appointed Lord Admiral, the aristocratic leavening of royal commands, unless they were relatives of Howard, had ceased to be significant, so that in 1588 such as were appointed had to be content with subordinate roles. These included Cumberland and Lords Thomas Howard and Edmund Sheffield, Howard's cousin and nephew respectively, and Sir Robert Southwell, Howard's son-in-law, in the western squadron. There was one aristocratic throwback in the choice of commander for the eastern squadron. Up until Howard's departure for the West Country, the modest Henry Palmer, as the Admiral of the Narrow Seas, held and might have expected to continue to hold, this post, but suddenly he found Lord Henry Seymour assuming the admiral's billet with Sir William Wynter as his vice admiral. The latter was the more experienced of the two, having been both a fighting sailor and Master of Naval Ordnance. Seymour, on the other hand, as well as being Howard's brother-in law, could also claim preferment through pedigree, for he was the younger son of Edward Seymour, the 1st Duke of Somerset, who had been both Lord Admiral and then Protector during Edward VI's reign, before, in a strange tradition of ex-Lord Admirals, losing his head on the block.

Wynter had served his apprenticeship not in tropical trading or slaving, but with his merchant father and in the Navy Royal, seeing his first action in 1544 during the amphibious assault on Leith and Edinburgh. That experience he recalled in 1588 when, having been asked his opinion as to the size of Parma's fleet, reassuringly observed that if his strength was thirty thousand soldiers he would need a minimum of three hundred ships to transport them:

> For I well remember that in the journey to Scotland . . . there was in that expedition two hundred and sixty sail of ships and yet we were not able to land above eleven thousand men and we then were in fear of none that could impeach us at sea.[13]

In 1545 Wynter was present in the inconclusive confrontation with the French fleet in the Solent, during which *Mary Rose* capsized and sank. In 1547 he was back in Scottish waters, where the Lord Protector despatched him to assist in the harrowing of the Firths. His presence was noted and by 1549 Wynter had shown himself competent enough to be appointed Surveyor of the Navy. This did not bring his sea career to an end, for that same year, while in command of *Minion*, he captured the French ship *Black Galley*, and a few years later sailed to the Mediterranean. In 1557 he was appointed Master of Ordnance but, yet again, this shore appointment did not interfere with his sea career for he was present at the razing of Le Conquet in 1558, while in December 1559 he was commanded by the new Queen Elizabeth 'to act as though on his own initiative, in intercepting French ships' suspected of ferrying troops to Scotland and to 'pick a quarrel'.[14] It is in this latter duty that he showed his mettle, overcoming the wild weather of the season whose name he shared to cut the French lines of communication.

Wynter's war with Spain, prior to the Armada, was focused around Ireland, where he was responsible for blockading the invading Spanish force in Smerwick Castle in 1580, giving the defenders no option other than to surrender, on terms, to Lord Gray, who slaughtered them all. In 1586 he and Drake were linked in the command of a squadron planned to sail for Spain and for which charges were raised, 'for the grounding, ransacking, dubbing and caulking', but the older man seems to have been withdrawn before this turned into the raid on Cadiz.[15]

In the year that the Armada hove into sight, Wynter celebrated his sixtieth birthday. He was thus, by the standards of the time, an elderly man, but his actions in the campaign through his spirited assault of the Armada off Gravelines as vice admiral in *Vanguard*, and his vigorous reporting of the same, indicate clearly that he was still able to fight and to command. After all, the captain of *Dreadnought* in that action, George Beeston, was reputed to be eighty-nine when he joined his ship, and he earned a knighthood from Howard for his gallantry. Nevertheless, Wynter had also been sidelined to allow the main battle fleet to be commanded by the pirates. A year later he was dead.

More important than appointments was the influence that the piratocracy had over strategic and tactical decisions, for nothing indicates more Drake's influence and inexperience as a naval commander than his persuading Howard to sail in search of their foe as he assembled in the ports of northern Spain. This strategy was summed up in words that Drake penned to the Privy Council on 30 March 1588:

> My very good lords, next under God's mighty protection, the advantage and gain of time and place will be the only and chief means for our good; wherein I most humbly beseech your good Lordships to persevere as you have begun, for that with fifty sail of shipping, we shall do more good upon their own coast than a great many more will do here at home, and the sooner we are gone the better we shall be able to impeach them.[16]

The language recalls his note to Walsingham of almost one year earlier in which, on 2 April 1587, he wrote:

> The wind commands me away. Our ship is under sail. God grant that we may live in His fear as the enemy may have cause to say that God doth fight for Her Majesty as well abroad as at home . . . Haste![17]

It is but one sentiment, but for two differing circumstances. In 1587 the Armada – or that section of it at Cadiz, for Drake did not attack the main body at Lisbon – was neither fully prepared nor expecting an assault. One year later it was a seagoing force. It was sailing 'confidently in hope of a miracle', but the winds that were to overcome it at its end were to play a subtler, crueller trick at the start of its voyage by denying Drake the engagement for which he prayed.

Drake's desire to deploy to the Spanish coast to engage the enemy at his earliest opportunity was explained in a letter to Elizabeth on 13 April, but it posed several questions for which he had no answer. To her he wrote:

> If the fleet come out of Lisbon, as long as we have victual to live withal upon that coast they shall be fought with . . . in such a sort as shall hinder his quiet passage into England . . . The advantage of time and place in all martial actions is half the victory, which being lost is irrecoverable. Wherefore, if her Majesty will command me away with those ships which are here already, and the rest to follow with all possible expedition, I hold it in my poor opinion the surest and best course; and that they bring with them victuals sufficient for themselves and us, to the intent the service be not utterly lost for want thereof.[18]

Many have commented ill on the Council's stodgy alternative, which was to have both a western and eastern squadron and to squash the Armada in between them. Most criticism is based around the dangers inherent in dividing the fleet, but Drake was proposing to do just this, sailing with those ships which were ready for sea, and to let the rest in draggled line astern link up with him where and when they found him. Elizabeth, upbraided for her hesitancy, had it about right when she told Leicester, an advocate of a forward policy, that 'my ships have left to put to sea and if any evil fortune should befall them all would be lost, for I shall have lost the walls of my realm!' Drake's proposal was to move those walls that were tight and impenetrable in the Channel to where, like unlinked fence-posts, they could be brushed aside, especially if they ran out of victuals and ammunition. In his desire to sail south, Drake also seems to have forgotten that he had already declined the opportunity to attack the Armada as it lay within the protection of Lisbon harbour, and that many of the northern ports to which in which it might seek shelter, such as Santander, offered an equally formidable approach to an enemy.

Yet Drake's enthusiasm won the day and by 13 June the previously sceptical Howard was writing to Walsingham, proclaiming his conversion to the forward strategy and stating that:

> The opinion of Sir Francis Drake, Mr Hawkins, Mr Frobisher, and others that be men of greatest judgment and experience, as also my concurring with them the same, is that the surest way to meet with the Spanish fleet is upon their own coast or in any harbour of their own and there defeat them.

Thus spake the pirates to the pirate lord who had no other seamen of great judgement to advise or restrain him, for they were all sitting in ships of the eastern squadron awaiting either Parma's punts, an unlikely occurrence, or the shot-shattered, storm-scattered, stragglers from an already defeated fleet. With no counsel but that of his corsairs, Howard stored his ships as best he could, for victuals were scarce in the West Country that year, and sailed south.

The English made several attempts to reach the coast of Spain, all the time recognising the problem that the Armada could not sail if the north winds blew favourably for the English, while a southern wind blowing the Spanish north could well keep the English trapped in Plymouth. There was also the chance, as Elizabeth feared, that the English might sail south without sighting the Channel-bound Armada, thus leaving the West Country beaches open for invasion, a situation which again threatened to materialise when Essex led his fleet south in 1596.

The attempt to take the fight south ended after a series of wind-assisted frustrations, during which not one English ship even managed to sight the peaks of the high mountains of northern Spain. After weeks of wasted effort, Howard was forced to return to Plymouth to await the Armada's delivery to his doorstep.

If the winds had not been so fickle, there is a strong possibility that the battle between these two great fleets might have taken place in the broad waters of the Bay of Biscay rather than the close confines of the Channel. Had it done so the result might have been very different. John Sugden quite rightly states that 'speculation about the possible outcome of the conflict is specious',[19] but that great naval historian and admirer of Drake, Sir Julian Corbett, was convinced that his desire to attack the Armada off its own coast was a sign of his genius, writing of that strategy that in the 'final swoop for Spain at the eleventh hour, no more brilliant or daring movement was ever executed by naval commander.'[20]

Drake's plan cannot be treated both ways, but dismissing the great risk that he was taking with the nation's only sure defence as inconsequential does no service to our understanding of the man. So without considering the outcome it is worth examining the odds. First, the greatest feat of fleet command and control of the whole campaign was the way in which the Armada held to its crescent formation all the way up the Channel and even managed to restore it after the pounding at Gravesend. There is little reason to assume that the English could have broken it up significantly during its open seas passage. Secondly, the English expended so much powder and shot during the days of contact that the ships that tailed the Spanish to the Scottish border had little or no ammunition left. Indeed, listening to the boom of guns from the Isle of Wight, his pirate fiefdom, Sir George Carey was to report that 'it might rather have been a skirmish with small shot on land than a fight with great shot at sea', so, knowing from the experience of his own pirates how quickly ammunition could be expended in such frays, he needed little encouragement to dispatch boatloads of munitions to the fleet as it sailed slowly by.

Should those skirmishes have started several days earlier, there is every chance that the English would have re-entered the Channel very short of powder and shot. Indeed, the commanders complained of the lack of resupply, having received just 60,000lbs of powder during their passage, and this while their vessels were in sight of their own country. How adequate provision would have been made to a fleet in action many leagues from land is hard to imagine. The Spanish were not stupid. They would have realised that if they could absorb the blows from English guns, mostly delivered at range, for a few days, then the periodicity and efficacy of such attacks would diminish, giving them more freedom to address their mission. Of course, that was mission impossible, for Parma would not have got his boats to sea whatever the circumstances, and Medina Sidonia might not have used his own initiative to have made a landing at Margate, but had he done so there is little likelihood that the English forces, commanded from the other bank of the Thames at Tilbury, would have defeated the professional soldiers of Spain. Both sides knew their enemy's strengths and weaknesses: both sides were purblind to their own inadequacies. Principal amongst these was the English inability to appreciate that the forces that it could call upon to repel a Spanish army once it had landed were amateur, inadequate, ill-trained, ill-armed and potentially badly-led. Only the nation's seamen, especially her pirates, could prevent such an unequal contest, but then only if they were present when most needed. Drake's belief in offence as the best form of defence almost deprived the country of that presence.

Most of all, the perennial problem of victualling would have played a major part. As it turned out, the English fleet, which famously warped out of Plymouth on 29 July, drifted into Margate Roads on or around 18 August with its crews so famished that many died onboard ship or while begging in Margate's streets. An engagement with the Armada many leagues south of Ushant would have left the English fleet starving by the time the battle drifted past Plymouth.

What seems evident is that Drake, having given voice to a sound strategy, intended to apply it in unsafe circumstances. In the end, it was the wind, not his wisdom, that brought the English back to where they were best suited to engage the Armada – in the well-known waters off their own shores, where resupply was available, as was a second, fully-stored fleet, which made a great contribution to the dispersal of the Armada off Gravelines. If Drake had met the Armada where he desired, it is quite possible that he would have spent his shot well before that decisive engagement. As it was, before that fight all Howard managed to do, from his place of advantage astern, was 'pluck their feathers one by one', an adequate, although not exciting, operation. But pirates were not content to pluck, certainly not Drake.

The first major damage that the Armada sustained was self-inflicted, when the 950-ton *San Salvador* blew up, possibly as a result of sabotage. Wounded, she drifted away from the safety of the flock, encouraging both Howard and Medina Sidonia to close her, only for both to withdraw rather than risk an early action. *San Salvador* was left to her suffering and abandoned overnight.

There had been an earlier encounter involving that most experienced Spanish admiral, Recalde, and his flagship *Santa Ana*, during which, in a two-hour engagement, the Spanish vessel had sustained damage serious enough for Recalde to call for assistance later in the day. Both *Santa Catalina* and Pedro de Valdéz's *Rosario* responded, only for the latter to ram the former and in so doing lose her bowsprit. When that sheared off, the forestay and foretopmast stay parted allowing the foremast itself to tumble down, fouling the mainmast as it did so. Once again Medina Sidonia, in *San Martin*, bringing a galleass and a galleon with him, fell back to offer support, this time in the form of a tow, but the commander's naval adviser rebuked him for this rashness, reminding him of his duty to command the whole fleet and not to be diverted by one of his sheep who had gone astray. Leaving the two smaller vessels to succour the 1,150-ton cripple, Medina Sidonia sailed away. In the gloaming, *Rosario* was approached by the 200-ton merchant ship *Margaret and John*, more out of curiosity than with a view to conquest, but the presence of this diminutive vessel spooked the escorts who, thinking that more English ships were on their way, cast off the towlines and rejoined the main force. Like *San Salvador*, *Rosario* was left to face the night alone.

Meanwhile, onboard *Ark Royal* Howard ended his council of war by ordering Drake to lead the fleet through the night in the wake of the Armada, a task which naturally required *Revenge* to burn a lantern at her stern. Both fleets settled down for a meal and a quiet few hours of passage. Not so Drake.

Drake knew that drifting over the western horizon lay a mighty prize. *Rosario* was a large flagship with the stores, weapons, money and very ransomable entourage befitting her station. Shame if she either escaped or fell to some less-worthy freebooter. At midnight *Revenge*'s stern light was doused. At dawn the watch on *Rosario*'s deck saw a well-equipped enemy warship closing down on their wallowing hull. They hailed their closing foe and, on hearing that it was Drake himself who was challenging them, had no hesitation in surrendering. Yet again,

Drake's most effective weapon had been the fear of his name. It was an easy victory, which realised some 55,000 gold ducats stowed in the cabins, a further £35,000 from Pedro de Valdéz's personal possessions and, five years later, an additional £3,000 in ransom money for the release of Don Pedro, which was paid to the Esher branch of the Drake family, who had taken care of the hostage. Nor did Drake retain the booty for himself as he was accused of doing, in violent language by Frobisher and more measured tones by some later historians. In fact, as Sugden makes clear, Drake surrendered 25,300 ducats of it to Howard, some of which was shared around the fleet, along with the captured ordnance, some forty-six guns.[21] The contents of the ship were plundered at Dartmouth, to where she was towed by Ralegh's *Roebuck*, before the mayor, a known pirate supporter, established his authority. Sadly, *Rosario* herself, undamaged apart from her masts, proved to be of no use to the English. She was towed around to Chatham where she lay unloved until 1622 when she was broken up.

Drake had broken every rule of behaviour that might have been expected of a senior admiral in close contact with the enemy. He made up a lame excuse about sighting some strange sails heading west in the night, but even those did not justify his action, which left Howard finding himself uncomfortably close to the Spanish rearguard when dawn broke. Had Drake been Howard and Howard, Drake, there can be little doubt that the prodigal pilot would have been facing a court-martial at the least. Howard seemed merely to have invited his deputy to resume his post. He had not been the only pirate reverting to type that day. The sinking *San Salvador* had attracted the attention of John Hawkins in *Victory*. So often more unlucky than his cousin, he boarded her only to find that her treasure had been transferred, along with most of her crew, leaving behind eighteen cannon, 2,246 cannon balls, and 6 firkins of musket shot and 132 barrels of unexploded powder, useful in the circumstances but not rewarding.

So far the third pirate, Frobisher, had seen little of the action, but on 2 August his *Triumph*, the largest warship on either side, was sighted anchored off Portland Bill along with five smaller escorts, where she could threaten any Spanish attempt to land in Weymouth Bay. Sidonia dispatched four galleasses to attack this group, but they were unable to close because of the state of the tide and the fierce run of the Portland Race as it seethed over the Shamble Bank. Frustrated, Sidonia made a move towards Frobisher and in turn attracted the attention of *Ark Royal* and her escorts. The two commanders-in-chief exchanged fire at close quarters before Sidonia withdrew to assist Recalde, who was engaging Drake, and Howard broke off to resume his position of advantage to windward of the Armada. Seeing their admiral depart, the galleasses also retired, freeing Frobisher to rejoin the fleet. It had been a frustrating day of fighting in which neither side could claim any significant success, but Howard, impressed by the way the individual Spanish squadrons and their commanders were able to act either independently or concertedly depending on the tactical circumstances, decided to adopt their ideas.

The apotheosis of the Elizabethan piratocracy occurred on 3 August 1588, when the Lord Admiral summoned his senior men and divided his fleet into four squadrons to be commanded by himself, Drake, Hawkins and Frobisher, thus placing the fate of the nation in the hands of pirates and pirate profiteers. Yet, a few weeks earlier, if the winds had blown differently, those soon to be lionised for humbling the Armada might have been guilty of throwing away England's only reliable defences, their ships. Even now, after three days in close contact, the pirates had demonstrated only their ability to irritate rather than attack their enemy. Tucked in astern they had managed neither to unship a rudder nor rip apart any rigging: nothing, in short, that would have prevented the Armada coming to anchor unscathed off Margate. Howard was, however, content. A few days later, after further desultory fighting off the Isle of Wight, he used his evening quarters to knight both Frobisher and Hawkins, along with his own relations, Lord Thomas Howard and Lord Sheffield and the nonagenarian captain of *Dreadnought*, George Beeston.

So far, for all their claims to superiority in ship and weapon handling, the English had done little damage to Sidonia's fleet. Now, as the channel narrowed, and the Armada's destination came closer, drastic action was demanded to disassemble that fleet in being. As it was, the English merely had to wait for the illogical aspects of Philip's grand plan to unwind, for the king had sent his magnificent force down a cul-de-sac, at the end of which lay sandbanks and shoals, not succour in the shape of the Duke of Parma. On 6 August the Armada came to its inevitable juddering halt as anchor after anchor was let go with the ships lying in the same tight formation that had protected them at sea, but which was now to leave them immobile and vulnerable to attack in the shallows off Calais.

Two hundred years later, on 1 August 1798, with the French anchored in a similar situation in Aboukir Bay, Nelson defied both the onset of night and the shallows to sail in and inflict on them the most overwhelming defeat in the long history of the age of sail. Now, at the dawn of that age, Howard had neither the experience nor the need to do likewise. Hawkins and Drake knew precisely what to do next. In the confined waters of both San Juan de Ulua and Cadiz the Spanish had drifted fire-ships down on their squadrons and, although no damage had been caused, the pirates realised that the time for revenge had arrived.

Fire-ships were not the weapons of a well-trained, confident and well-armed fleet, but the advantage of their use at Calais was that they posed no risk to Howard's force. By deploying them he could keep his fleet in being while, hopefully, to mix elements, flushing the Spanish out in some disarray. By now, Sidonia appreciated both his predicament and his failure, for he knew that it would be impossible for him to carry out an opposed landing by boat on a hostile shore with an enemy fleet in attendance. However, the decision as to what he might next do was made for him when, during the night of 7 August, eight fire-ships were seen drifting towards his fleet. The duke had prepared for such an attack, posting boats with long hooks upstream of his vulnerable fleet, but the fiery, exploding hulks unmanned them and they fled, leaving the flaming vessels to drift on unchecked. Sidonia, Recalde and the senior commanders weighed anchor and shifted to a safe berth. They were right to do so, for all eight vessels washed up on the sands and burnt themselves out without even scorching a Spanish sail. However, fear not fire, wrought the greater damage, for most of the Spanish fleet cut its cables and made for the open water, except for the flag galleass, *San Lorenzo*, which, following a collision which unshipped her rudder, drifted ashore beneath the guns of the fort at Calais. The lack of anchors would inflict a greater loss on the Spanish fleet than did English ordnance, for it left many a vessel without the means to avoid being driven ashore on the hostile coast of Ireland.

At dawn, Sidonia saw his flock scattered and, as a dutiful captain-general, he weighed to round them up before the inevitable battle. At dawn, Howard saw *San Lorenzo* and, infected by the pirate bacillus, sallied away from his fleet to claim her as a prize. He spent three hours endeavouring to seize her, only to have to abandon the attempt when the captain of Calais made a counter-claim backed up by his heavy weapons.

Luckily, the English did not need their errant leader, for they were well-placed to harry the foe which was, amazingly, soon assembled in its crescent-moon formation, despite having to manoeuvre with caution to keep clear of the Zeeland shoals. Accounts indicate that on this occasion the English engaged the enemy more closely than hitherto. Perhaps they saw this as their last opportunity to inflict meaningful damage before they ran out of ammunition, victuals and a retiring foe. There might have been another influence.

The eastern squadron had waited patiently for its opportunity to participate in the battle, but it had joined up with Howard on the 6 August, the very day that the Armada had anchored off Calais. Monday, 8 August thus represented the first opportunity for the career naval officers to show their mettle. They did so with relish, with Wynter boasting to Walsingham that:

> Out of my ship there was shot 500 shot of demi-cannon, culverin, and demi-culverin; and when I was furthest off in discharging any of the pieces, I was not out of shot of their harquebus, and most of the times within speech one of another . . .When every man was weary with labour, and our cartridges spent and munitions wasted . . . we ceased and followed the enemy.[22]

A Spanish account supports Wynter's, in that it refers to the fleets as being just 'a pike's length asunder'. Although not close enough to board, it was more than near enough to batter, and for the first time during the exchange of fire the Spanish hulls splintered and sprang. After a gallant and isolated fight, both *San Mateo* and *San Felipe* had to be abandoned and left to drift ashore. That gallantry was ever present in Sidonia's *San Martin*, which was handled with skill and fought with competence, it being reported that the captain-general, 'kept luffing up continually upon the enemy's fleet, transfigured and shrouded in the smoke of his guns, which he ordered to be fired with the greatest rapidity and diligence.'

Yet it was not Wynter who should have been where the fight lay thickest. With Howard absent for reasons of greed, it was Drake, as the second in command, who should have been lying alongside the Spanish flagship. This he set out to do, it being reported that he fired on *San Martin* with his bow guns as he approached and then raked her with a broadside as he moved past. Tactics would suggest that he should have then gone about and resumed the engagement with the weapons on his opposite side – but he did not. Instead, he departed from the written account with some suggesting, with little evidence to support the argument, that he sailed onward to 'break up a threat which he could see developing ahead', which was the sight of scattered ships rejoining to reform the Armada's crescent formation.[23] But why should the commander disengage from hacking off the head to try and lop off a few fingers?

Frobisher, a colic witness, was highly suspicious, accusing Drake of 'Bragging up at first, and giving them his prow and his broadside; and then kept his luff and was glad he was gone again like a cowardly knave or traitor – I rest doubtful which – but the one I will swear.' Drake, a man ever jealous of his honour, does not seem to have responded to this verbal cannonade, but Hakluyt's account states that *Revenge* was pierced with shot some forty times and that the admiral's cabin was twice shot through to the discomfort and miraculous survival of several weary gentlemen at rest. There is no mention of damage to masts, spars, rigging or sail, or any loss of life: *Revenge,* for the flagship of England's premier fighting admiral, seems to have been almost unscathed. Is there a chance, just a chance, that Drake's piratical instincts once more got the better of him and he went a-hunting for easier prey more willing to surrender at the sound of his name than would have been Medina Sidonia and his gallant flag-captains? Even if this were not so, all the evidence, certainly from Wynter and Frobisher's accounts, indicates that it was the ships commanded by naval men and not pirates that engaged the enemy most closely.

The guns of both fleets, their number, type, quality and use, have been a matter of much conjecture by historians for over a century. As far as the rate of fire is concerned, there is general agreement that the English could reload and discharge anything up to three times as fast as their opponents. Bourne, in his 1587 *Arte of Shooting Great Ordnance*, noted that the English were considered good gunners, because 'they are handsome about their ordnance in ships on the sea.' Yet despite this remark, N A M Rodger estimated that it would have taken one and a half hours to reload each of Wynter's thirty-four guns, which seems to defy both logic and the first-hand accounts of the exchanges.[24] More significant than the rate of fire was the range at which the enemy was engaged. Before Gravelines, the English were firing at too great a range to cause much damage, despite expending a great deal of shot. Howard even managed to remark on the fact that the stern lantern of one the Armada ships was seen bobbing past. The stern lantern! Now if it had been the main- or mizzenmast, or even more importantly the rudder, then he would have had something worthy of record. Many contemporary commentators were critical of long-range firings, Richard Hawkins, serving in *Swallow*, considering, 'How much the nearer, so much the better,' while Monson dismissively remarked, 'he that shooteth far off at sea has as good not shoot at all.' Firing from far-off was not only ineffective against a good stout hull, but the trajectory of the shot precluded it from doing damage to the rigging. If, and it seems likely that it was a major consideration, the English considered the Armada vessels too heavily manned, and too high in the water, to risk boarding, then their best option for breaking up the formation was to cripple the ships one by one by bringing down their masts and rigging.[25] *Rosario* demonstrated on the first day how crippled and vulnerable a ship rapidly became once her rigging went awry, but from then on all the reports are of firing into the hulls of the enemy, a tactic so ineffective that only one ship, *La Maria Juan*, could be claimed to be a victim of gunfire, sunk by the privateer Robert Crosse in *Hope*, and even then some claim that she sank after a collision with *San Juan de Sicilia*.

There is one other issue that might have affected the way that the English fought on the first few days. The ships' captains would have taken their cue from their commanders, and these were the pirates with a pirate's way of looking at things. For them a ship sunk was a prize lost: they relied as much on shock, awe and surprise to board and take an opponent as they did on broadsides which used up their limited ammunition. The awe in which Drake's name was held led to the surrender of *Rosario* without a shot being fired, but no other commander in sight of the captain-general was going to be so willing to surrender. Untrained in the art either of sinking ships or massacring crews, the English behaved in perfect analogy with a pack of wolves pursuing a herd of heavy bison; they snapped at their heels, taking care not to get hurt, and waited for the inevitable moment when the weakest would be exposed to their fangs. If the herd could not drive off their tormentors, then losses were inevitable.

Medina Sidonia knew this and, along with his excellent and realistic summaries of the strategic position into which he was sailing and the tactics behind the adoption of the *lunula*, informed his king and Parma of the frustrations caused by the English unwillingness to attempt any boarding:

> The enemy's ships have continued to bombard us, and we were obliged to turn and face them, so that the firing continued on most days from dawn to dark; but the enemy has resolutely avoided coming to close quarters with our ships, although I have tried my hardest to make him do so. I have given him so many opportunities that sometimes some of our vessels have been in the very midst of the enemy's fleet, to induce one of his ships to grapple and begin the fight; but all to no purpose, as his ships are very light, and mine very heavy.[26]

The conclusion from this succinct summary must be that English gunnery was a secondary factor in influencing the outcome. The primary reason for Sidonia's failure was his inability to board and take any of the enemy ships. To the English, his belief that he might do so in a significant way would have come as a surprise, but this would not have been so for one brought up with a galley culture. Spain's greatest victories at sea, Lepanto and Terceira, had both involved a melee of ships ramming and boarding in such a crush that soldiers played as vital a role as seamen. In the galley-unfriendly waters of the Channel, such a close clash was never going to happen. There were two notable occasions on which the English did lock sides with Spanish warships. At Flores in the Azores in 1591, when it took four Spanish ships a day and a night to overcome their grappled target, *Revenge*, and off the Pacific coast of Central America in 1594, when it took two Spanish ships three days and nights to overcome Richard Hawkins's *Dainty*. If that experience is transferred to the fleet strengths in the Channel in 1588, then Sidonia's aim to subdue over fifty well-armed warships with such tactics was unrealisable. This was Sidonia's tragedy; it was Hawkins's triumph. It was he, above all of those present, who had been responsible for the conversion of most of Elizabeth's navy into fleet-footed 'race galleons'. It is true that this newer design, ironically developed from the Spanish galleons of Mary's time, had heavier armament carried lower in the hull and also bow-chasers to drive away galleys without offering a broadside profile, but in 1588 these were not their vital virtues.

What was important in that summer dispute that lasted the length of the Channel was not the type of guns that the English carried or how they brought them to bear, but that they were fleet-footed enough to keep clear of the enemy's clutches. Relevant here is that the one English vessel which appeared threatened by Sidonia's forces was Frobisher's unmodified, high-castled, ungainly *Triumph*, which was 'rescued' by Howard's group of galleons. Yet Howard was the hero of the campaign, not for leading an attack, but for imposing an order that we have no record of his issuing which was that no English ship was to close and board any of the enemy whatever the temptation or opportunity so to do – only he, Drake and Hawkins disobeyed that edict! In this area Howard defied pressure from his queen who, admitting that the Armada included some mighty vessels, remained puzzled that no attempt was made to have 'boarded divers of the meaner ships'. Finally, the English nation owed an enormous debt to the unknown masters of their fleet who managed their vessels so well that they were able to dance out of harm's way whenever the bulkier Spanish lumbered in their direction.

In a very telling few lines towards the end of his study *The Successors to Drake*, Julian Corbett highlighted the fact that 'we see dwindling almost to nothing the gap between the ships of Drake's prime and those in which Nelson learned his art', going on to say that, 'between the natures of the guns that won Gravelines, and of those that proclaimed the final triumph of Trafalgar, the difference except in weight of metal and more accurate boring are barely perceptible.' Any visitor to *Mary Rose* and *Victory*, conveniently berthed beside each other in Portsmouth Historic Dockyard, can confirm Corbett's opinion, for there is far more in common between

ABOVE: More than a whole library of books, a replica of *Golden Hind* in Brixham brings home what conditions must have been like on the ship in which Drake circumnavigated the globe and captured the rich prize, *Cacafuego*. (Author collection)

LEFT: A print showing the moment that Drake's circumnavigation became a financial triumph with his capture of the *Cacafuego*. (Author collection)

The rewards of booty – Drake's home at Buckland Abbey, purchased from another pirate, Richard Grenville. (Author collection)

The sandbanks of the Carolinas coastal strip seem to stretch on forever. In frustration, Ralegh's reconnaissance party and Grenville's main group turned in through shallow gaps to establish an unsuitable base at Roanoke rather than press on for another sixty miles to the magnificent inlet of the Chesapeake where Jamestown was founded in 1607. (Author collection)

LEFT: It was a hurricane such as Isobel, shown here striking the Carolinas in 2003, that showed Drake and the Roanoke settlers, how unsuitable was the site that they had selected for their settlement. It was abandoned. (Author collection)

BOTTOM LEFT: Richly laden, great Portuguese carracks such as the *Santa Catarina* shown here often sailed homeward from the East Indies alone, relying on their size and armament to dissuade attack. Although the English were to claim several successful encounters, more often they were frustrated in their attempts to seize these ships and their cargo. (© National Maritime Museum, Greenwich, London)

BOTTOM RIGHT: The Spanish fleet assembling for the 1582 Azores expedition. The high-sided galleon in the foreground portrays a design that the English had moved away from with their race-built, swifter and more manoeuvrable warships. (Author collection)

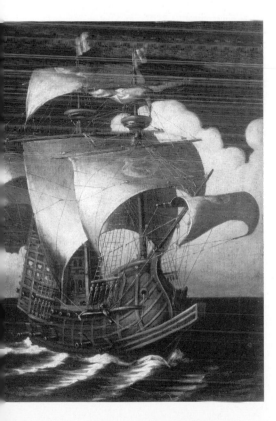

The last great carrack taken in the war was seized by Leveson and Monson close to the shore off Portugal. Its capture marked the acme of Leveson's career, but was the cause of his fall from grace when questions about his disposal of the prize goods were raised. (Author collection)

The Spanish fleet assembling for the 1582 Azores expedition. The high-sided galleon in the foreground portrays a design that the English had moved away from with their race-built, swifter and better manoeuvrable warships. (Author collection)

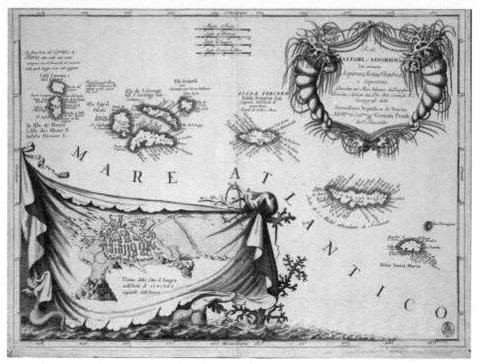

ABOVE: This chart of the Azores shows the islands where the English played cat and mouse with both Spanish treasure fleets and Portuguese carracks. The inset shows the fort at Angra on Terceira, under whose friendly guns many an endangered Iberian escaped from English pirates. (© National Maritime Museum, Greenwich, London)

RIGHT: Caught red-handed. While the Armada at its most vulnerable endeavours to regroup after the fire-ship attack, it is pursued by elements of the English fleet whose commander-in-chief, Howard, can be seen off Calais trying to take the stranded *San Lorenzo* for a prize. (© National Maritime Museum, Greenwich, London)

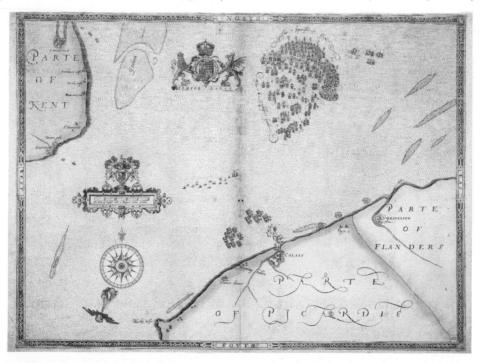

This near-contemporary painting shows the English fire-ships drifting towards the Spanish fleet off Calais. than was the reality during the campaign. (Author collection)

In the foreground, the artist has depicted an English galleon and a Spanish galleasse in closer contact

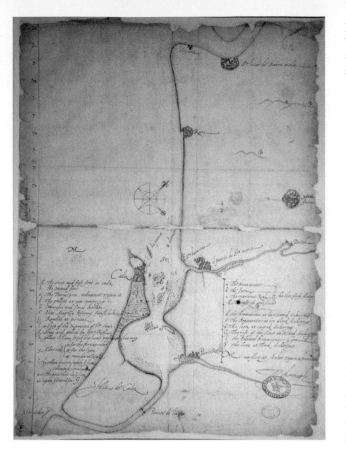

LEFT: A sketch map of Cadiz signed by William Borough and showing the disgraced vice admiral's view of the 1587 action. (Author collection)

BELOW: *Golden Lion* was Lord Thomas Howard's flagship during the Armada campaign and was loaned the following year to the earl of Cumberland for his pirateering voyage to the Spanish coast. (Author collection)

these two ships, built almost three hundred years apart, than there are differences; Howard and Drake's flagships that faced the Armada would have had even more in common with that of Nelson. Yet the latter destroyed the French fleet, not once but twice, while Howard and Drake plucked feathers. If the ships had such similarities, then the difference in outcome must be due to reasons other than weight of shot or armament suite. Tactics, training and experience should have had a major role to play but, whatever, the individual bravery of its commanders, the western Elizabethan fleet consisted of a collection of ships unused to operating together as a battle group. They were capable of managing a close encounter with the enemy, but not necessarily a close engagement. It would be almost another hundred years before that essential element of naval warfare was achieved. That this limitation of Elizabeth's pirate fleet failed to turn into a tactical inadequacy owed much to the fact that their opposition were labouring under an even more deadly curse, that of a unrealistic strategy. Only at Gravelines with the arrival of Wynter and the navy men did a true sea battle take place.

After Gravelines the Armada lacked further opportunity to threaten England, while the English lacked sufficient ammunition to thwart its onward passage towards the more adamantine threat of Irish rocks, which would rip more of its hulls apart than could the English fleet. Contact between the two fleets was broken off on 12 August. Howard was anchored off Margate by 18 August, his concerns now being the care of his starving, ragged ships' companies. Yet that was not all that exercised his mind, for on 27 August he was writing to Walsingham, in a letter brought up to London by Drake himself, on plans to send a force to the Azores to intercept the Spanish treasure fleet, although he admitted there would not be sufficient ships serviceable until they had been 'grounded and repaired at Chatham'.[21]

The threat had been met, managed and ameliorated: it had been dispersed, but not by force of arms defeated. Yet soon and ever subsequently, the campaign came to be referred to as 'the defeat of the Spanish Armada'. This is to apply a victor's gloss to the picture, for from Cornwall to Calais the Spanish lost just a couple of ships through the inevitable accidents that holding to their tight and undisrupted fighting formation would involve. They almost made their rendezvous with Parma and achieved an amazing coherent formation even after their battering at Gravelines. What they did not achieve was their unrealistic objective, but this was not the fault of their commanders, but of he who sent them. Thus a fairer phrase to summarise the result of the fortnight's fight would be to refer to it as 'the failure of the Spanish Armada'. This would not only do greater justice to Medina Sidonia, but it would also reflect fairly on the inchoate tactics and management of gunnery that were present in an English fleet commanded by pirates with pirate priorities and fighting preferences.

On 18 February 1653 Robert Blake with eighty warships met and engaged off Portland a similarly-sized Dutch squadron commanded by Maarten Tromp, who was endeavouring to escort one hundred and fifty merchantmen back to the United Provinces. The three-day battle took the fighting fleets up the Channel once more to Gravelines. Hostilities commenced with Tromp blasting Blake's flagship *Triumph* with three broadsides, which persuaded the English admiral to continue the fight at longer range. Nevertheless, the largest English vessel *Prosperity* was boarded and surrendered. Despite the Dutch ferocity, when the engagement was broken off, Blake was left controlling the Channel having, for the loss of one ship, captured forty-three prizes and taken or destroyed twelve enemy warships. This is a battle of no renown, but it was in actions like this, rather than the Armada, that the English navy learned to fight as a navy rather than just a collection of ships. As significant was the administration and management by the authorities ashore. A few extracts from the State Papers serve to illustrate the gap between 1588 and 1653:

> 19 February 1653, Portsmouth.
> Captain Edwin, commander of the *Oak*, has come on shore, who was in the engagement yesterday until 2pm, they beginning at the break of day, and he having his masts maimed and his guns dismounted, was forced to come away, leaving them at it at night. The *Assistance*, rear-admiral of the Blue, having lost her mainmast, has also come in I cannot learn that any of our ships, except the *Sampson*, have miscarried. Captain Edwin saw six of the Dutch ships on fire before he left.
>
> The *Advice* also has just arrived much hurt, after an engagement with five Dutch men-of-war, but another of our vessels coming up, three of them left her, and she sank the other two, with all their crew except seven. They have flung 30 dead men overboard, and have 40 wounded.

> 20 February, Portsmouth.
> I want orders as to disposing of the very many Dutch prisoners, many of whom are dangerously wounded, as also to send the wounded English to the hospitals in London. What is to be allowed a day for the Dutch prisoners, and what done for their care?

> 22 February.
> Petition of Elizabeth Alkin, for the place of nurse to the maimed seamen at Dover. Has been faithful and serviceable to the State upon all occasions in the late wars, in which she day and night hazarded her life, and was a great help to the imprisoned and maimed soldiers.
>
> The Admiralty Committee to take care that physicians and surgeons be dispatched to Dover and Portsmouth, to take care of the sick and wounded. Also to move Parliament to consider the families of those slain in the engagement, some being already known, and further particulars hourly expected.
>
> To write to Mr Willoughby at Portsmouth to take care that nothing be wanting to the sick and wounded brought in there, and to allow the prisoners a reasonable maintenance.

23 February
Council of State.
The Commissioners for Dutch Prizes to allow 6d a day to all the Dutch prisoners
brought into Dover.

Navy Office.
We have dispatched surgeons to Portsmouth, Dover, Deal, and Sandwich with
medicaments, and a further supply is preparing. We want much money to remove
the present clamours for want of pay.[28]

The contrast between the two armada engagements and their management is very
evident, and detrimental to the Elizabethans. Their priorities were soon apparent
in the decisions that were made to take advantage of the Spanish failure.

The obvious strategy was for the Lord Admiral to instruct Grenville to intercept
the weakened and separated ships of the Armada as they straggled down the coast
of Ireland, even to send reinforcements to support him in this action. Secondly, it
would have been to prepare a fleet to destroy the surviving ships as they sheltered,
unmanned and undefended, in the harbours of northern Spain. This was certainly
the option that the astute Venetian ambassador to Spain, Hieronimo Lippomano,
thought likely, warning that, along with an attack on the 'Peruvian fleet': 'No small
trouble would arise now if Drake should sail and descend on the Spanish coast,
for here he would find no obstruction to his depredations and might even burn the
ships that have returned, for they are lying scattered in various harbours.'[29]

Instead, the Lord Admiral had his mind set on prizes, and it was left to Elizabeth
and her Council to issue the next strategic objective to her fleet, the destruction of
the surviving Armada shipping. Unfortunately, as so often, opportunistic and
potentially richly rewarding additions were appended to this financially
unrewarding aim. These were to storm Lisbon and put the pretender Dom Antonio
on the throne and then to seize the Azores, as a base from which to intercept the
flotas. With Drake appointed commander, it is no wonder that, with his piratical
instincts, he paid little heed to the strategic imperative and concentrated on the
latter two objectives, to his disgrace and the expedition's failure. If the Armada
campaign had illustrated the shortcomings of Philip's tight leash, then the English
Counter Armada of 1589 demonstrated the weaknesses in Elizabeth's policy of
giving her piratocracy a free rein.

Drake was as roundly disowned by his monarch as a national treasure could
be and sent to play the reluctant domestic back in Devon. He returned to sea in
1595 in harness with Hawkins to chase the chimera of a richly-laden galleon
lying helpless in the Indies. Both men were to die in this vain attempt to show
that the swashbuckling behaviour of their prime years could still be applied
against a foe who had increased in wisdom, while the English remained wedded
to the idea of 'haphazard commerce raiding', as Andrews so succinctly
summarises their strategy.[30]

What the English needed to do in their war with Spain was to blockade her ports and sever her transatlantic trade routes, along the lines that Hawkins had proposed in 1587. But to do so effectively would have required the presence of a permanent force of naval vessels whose cost could not be guaranteed to be deferred by the taking of prizes. This Elizabeth would not do, with the result that even before the age of reliance on state-sponsored piracy ended in 1603, the nation had been deprived of competent, experienced naval officers, the lack of whom was to be embarrassingly apparent for generations to come until a powerful new enemy, the Dutch, made it necessary to send generals to sea to teach the navy how to fight.

PECULATION AND THE PIRATOCRACY

CHAPTER 9

The Land Rats

But ships are but boards, sailors but men: there be land-rats
and water-rats, water-thieves and land-thieves – I mean pi-rats.
Shylock, *The Merchant of Venice*

While at sea Elizabeth's Protestant pirates brought a new meaning and proof of
the supremacy of 'cannon' law, ashore their supporters amended the tenet of the
Lutheran faith to support the concept of justification by force. In so doing they
showed that they believed not so much in the rule of law, but in the law of ruling,
not so much as being on the side of the law, but as having the law on their side. By
1590 their creed of greed which sent poor petitioners hungry away, while filling the
rich and powerful with good things, had more ardent adherents amongst the ruling
elite than did the Protestant religion. This abuse of power began where the means
of controlling piracy were most immediate, relevant and available: the small ports
and havens of England and Wales, ruled as fiefdoms by local families. All the while
this coterie of gentry supported their own pirate fleets, rottenness was the
inevitable, widespread result. A few samples fished from a trawl along the south-
west coast, where the pirates shoaled most copiously, indicates how well-established
and how tenacious was their dominance of those waters.

The Falmouth Franchise
The Killigrews were one of Tudor Cornwall's oldest and most disreputable
families. In 1403 they acquired the manor of Arwennack in the Fal estuary as a
most suitable base for their maritime interests. Given such a local presence and
knowledge, Henry VIII appointed Sir John Killigrew as the first governor of
Pendennis Castle, which was built during the invasion scare of 1542. This provided
the piratically inclined clan with a strong base out of which to sally to prey on
transient neighbours. Such deprivations might have remained locally notorious,
but nationally unnoticed, had it not been for the family's ardently-held belief that
opposition to the succession of the Catholic Mary in 1553 might bring about an
earthly reward. In July 1556, in response to a report that the Killigrews were at
sea with 'four or five barks and have taken good prizes',[1] the queen sent

159

Vice Admiral William Tyrell with a fleet of seven ships from Portsmouth with orders to intercept and capture them.[2] The pursuit ended one-sidedly off Plymouth with six pirate ships being seized, including those of Peter Killigrew, the family's admiral, and the two John Killigrews. The latter were released on the payment of a £2,000 bond, holding them to answer charges of piracy brought by a Spanish merchant. Then, while twenty-four of his fellows were hung, Peter, the leader, was released, even after intense interrogation revealed his support for a rebel plan to invade England with French support, an act of treachery for which most men would have been hung, drawn and quartered.[3]

Peter might have been spared because the state valued his skills and knowledge of the southern Channel coast. On 1 January 1558 Calais was seized by the French and, having failed to support the fortress before it fell, the English assembled a fleet to make a face-saving assault on Brittany. A list of the fifty-five captains appointed shows William Tyrell and his one-time prey, Peter Killigrew, serving together 'at the seas in the King's and Queen's Majesties ships'.

The family's opposition to Mary found favour with Elizabeth, a fact which the family patriarch, John, put to his own notorious use, rustling cattle onshore and seizing shipping offshore. His appointment to the piracy commission caused him no crisis of conscience, for he was content to use his authority to advance his illegal business interests, rather than reform his behaviour. Controlling large areas of land on both sides of the Fal estuary gave him a private haven from which to operate, land, handle, market and hide stolen goods. Peter, having tasted legitimacy, resumed his past practices, joining Frobisher in 1563 for a pirate voyage, the unravelling of which was described earlier.

Frustration caused the blind at last to see and in 1565, the same year as the commission for piracy was established, an investigation was ordered into John Killigrew's malpractice. However, nothing came of the inquiry, as no one was prepared to give evidence against a local magnate who could claim, as did others of an earlier time, 'In my own country my family upholds the law, and the law is what we care to uphold.'[4]

Unconcerned as to the direction of the wind, the Killigrews sailed illegally onward. In June 1568 some citizens of Antwerp sent a letter to Arwennack asking Peter to return or pay half the value for 184 rubies he had seized from one of their ships, but John Killigrew threatened the messenger, refused to sign for the letter and failed to inform on the whereabouts of his son.[5]

In March 1569 a 36-ton Flemish flyboat, laden with herring, put into Falmouth where it was visited by Killigrew, who surveyed their vessel with a critical and approving eye, and received with gratitude the gift of two cheeses. On sailing the next day, the flyboat was followed by a well-manned pirate ship whose crew boarded and 'robbed them of every farthing', and escorted the boat back to Falmouth, stating that this prize would make a fine ship for the admiral's use. On arrival in Falmouth the crew were forced ashore, 'to beg before church doors' for crusts, but 'never got a penny', and were saved from starvation by the compassion of a lady from Flushing who raised 8 sous for fodder. The captain and two of the crew then headed off to London, to seek redress, but 'during the journey could scarce get straw to sleep upon or a morsel of bread to eat.'[6]

Despite such incidents, the Privy Council continued to treat Killigrew as an upright Commissioner for Piracy in Cornwall. In April 1575 they asked him to investigate what appeared to be a simple case of lawful reprisal. A French ship had been seized and her captain imprisoned in Penrhyn by the trader/pirate John Cocke, in response to the seizure of his own vessel by the Frenchman John Lestonbeck. Cocke was demanding an exchange of corn, which that year was plentiful in the West Country, for salt, which his prisoner felt unable to arrange due to the scarcity of that commodity in Brittany. The Council directed Lower and Killigrew to hear the case and arrange for the prisoner to be released and, if they felt Cocke had acted wrongly, to issue a bond for his appearance before them.

Having carried out his legal duties, the following year saw Killigrew reverting to his normal practice. Three ships from Flushing had been seized and brought into Falmouth where their arrival was reported by the Admiralty agent. Despite submitting their inventories to the court, William Lower, the vice admiral of Cornwall, failed to account for the goods. In a letter addressed to Killigrew, Their Lordships thanked him for the work he had done regarding the vessels but went on to say that:

> As the said ships be not yet delivered as was appointed but do remain spoiled and decayed and the goods that were in them contained in the inventories . . . are not forthcoming, they are eftsoons required . . . to take some pains therein, to the end that the said ships and goods may be delivered in sort as they ought to be.

Indeed Killigrew was ordered to appoint someone to conduct a further audit to ascertain what goods remained, thus tacitly acknowledging their illegal removal.[7]

The following year the Privy Council wrote to Lower, inviting him to investigate a claim that Killigrew had bought some stolen wine from a known pirate, Hicks. The vice admiral was informed that the lawful owners had stated that they were content not to press charges if Killigrew and his associates were prepared to pay the going rate of £10 the tonne, but as they had only been offered £6, the full rigour of the law was to be applied.

Cornwall and its vice admiral were not alone in their flexible approach to felony. At about the same time the Privy Council summoned to appear before them John Dye, the deputy vice admiral of Bristol, accusing him of supporting pirates and taking bribes to release them from custody. Killigrew himself avoided such an appearance when summoned by the simple expedient of dying in March 1584. The fact that he died intestate indicates both his style of living and the fact that piracy at a local level was never a great or reliable money earner.

More unusual for the times than having a pirate as the commissioner for piracy was the fact that the Killigrew ladies were equally adept at purloining goods from merchant ships. Lady Mary, the wife of Sir Henry, began her career with an error, when the owner of a ship she seized and sold in 1570 turned out to be a friend of Queen Elizabeth. But Mary had a locally more important friend in the magistracy, and thus escaped any meaningful punishment.

Elizabeth, wife of Sir John, was a feisty lady who managed the illegal activities of the family. Her most notorious act was perpetrated in 1582 when she led a boarding party out to seize *Marie de San Sebastian*, a large merchant ship that was sheltering from foul weather in Falmouth. The crew responded fiercely and in the fray a factor was murdered, a crime which could not be easily covered up by the local authorities. The sixty-year-old Elizabeth was arrested, tried and condemned to death, while the rest of her family received lesser sentences. However, her plight touched her sovereign's heart and, after the sentence was commuted to imprisonment, Lady Elizabeth returned to Falmouth, leaving a bribe behind her.

The Hawkins's Haven

Corruption was not confined to Cornwall. Just over the border in Plymouth, the Hawkins family used their control over shipping and wharfage to ensure that the opportunity to profit from the mismanagement of suspect goods was never overlooked. Even in 1589, while the Spanish threat remained high, Sir John Norreys was writing to Walsingham about losses from the sale of the prize goods brought in from the ships captured during the Armada campaign. This he attributed to Hawkins and the mayor of Plymouth who had depressed the sale price so that they might purchase them for their own use. In addition, according to Norreys, 'the Mayor and Mr Hawkins have received £12,000 for victuals and pay of the debts, of which their army had not received above the value of £1,000.'[8]

The Plymouth merchants even knew how to twist the law so that those authorised to claim recompense were thwarted at the very moment they might have thought justice was being delivered to them. In 1593 *Tiger*, a pirate vessel commanded by William Holliday, sailing without a commission, seized several Dutch ships belonging to a Michael Leeman, and carried the goods to 'Barbary' where they sold them, sinking one of the ships on the voyage and, allegedly, throwing many of the crew overboard. As the outcry in the United Provinces threatened both the goods and lives of English merchants based there, an order was issued that any future prizes brought in by Holliday should be stayed and the goods sold for the satisfaction of the aggrieved merchants. The opportunity to right the wrong came in 1597 when *Tiger* entered Plymouth with a Spanish carvel laden with ginger, sugar and spices and other valuables. On hearing the news the Privy Council sent Leeman down to Plymouth to claim his compensation payment. He was paid less than 2s in the pound and even this was counterclaimed successfully by Holliday, who thus also succeeded in obtaining the release of some of his crew under sentence of death for piracy.[9]

Devon's greatest opportunity for pilfering from prizes came when the three great carracks that the English seized during the course of the war with Spain were brought home. Of these, Drake's *San Felipe* seemed to have a reasonably well-ordered unloading, but the response to the arrival of *Madre de Dios* at Dartmouth in 1592 was a ransacking so overt that Robert Cecil and Walter Ralegh had to be despatched post-haste westward to restore order and prevent a complete looting. Nine years later Plymouth welcomed the great carrack that Richard Leveson had captured in the Cezimbra roads near Lisbon. To ensure that her goods were accounted for, the Council sent Fulke Greville down to the city, in his words, to 'watch, restrain and punish stealth and traffic universally, a distasteful course alike to fleet, strangers and inhabitants, and all sorts of men in these parts.'

Carey's Kingdom

Closer to the queen than Killigrew in distance and in kinship was Sir George Carey, later Lord Hunsdon, who was appointed captain-general of the Isle of Wight in 1582, with just enough time for him to realise and release the piratical opportunities of that strategically placed island before the issue by the Privy Council, in July 1585, of regulations for seagoers having letters of marque and reprisal for the capture of Spanish ships, a document that for all practical purposes doubled up as a declaration of war.

Carey did not need start-up funding for the pirateering opportunities that the Isle of Wight offered him. Situated conveniently for those interested in watching merchant shipping movements through the Solent and up to Southampton lay the anchorage of Mead's Hole, now called Osborne Bay, in tribute to the residence established on its shores by Queen Victoria. Here Carey oversaw an entrepôt port for stolen goods, without asking too many awkward questions about the nationality of any of the prize vessels brought there. In December 1584 he even refused to hand over a cargo of woad and cork from a French ship that had been driven ashore on the island, ignoring the several suits that were brought against him.[10]

Earlier that year, the French ambassador was to complain, *Lion d'or*, a French ship loaded with satin, velvet and leather had been taken to the Isle of Wight, stripped and, although restitution seems to have been made after some protest, Carey was obviously willing to benefit from this illegal seizure as he was when *Bon Temps* of Dieppe was brought to the island, where 'Sir George Carey, before giving up the ship, made them pay him the fifth, and kept two pieces of artillery which he has never restored', as well as distributing the goods to his friends in high places. Once again restitution was eventually made but not, of course, by a willing Carey.[11] It was not his way, as the prince of Condé noted when writing to Walsingham in 1586 about a ship laden with wine that had been taken to the Isle of Wight where 'the governor would lend no favour or aid to the factors and servants of the said receiver, or give them justice for the robbery.' In a vain attempt to emphasise the gravity of the offence, Condé went on to write that 'if this act was left unpunished, it would hinder the accustomed free commerce between the merchants of the two nations.' He then prayed that Walsingham would use his influence with the queen to obtain restitution of the wine and a fitting punishment for the robbers. He didn't, it wasn't, and Carey was allowed to continue using Mead's Hole as a pirate entrepôt port.

Early in 1585 Ralegh's *Roebuck* seized a French vessel cargoed with cloth and, although the vessel was released, the cloth was given to the pirate John Challice for disposal. Carey, through the offices of his steward and the Customer of Southampton, Thomas Heaton, came into possession of some of the undeclared cloth, which he then sold on to Martin Parker, a servant of the Customer of London, for £238. The French owners sought redress in the Admiralty Court, failing to realise that Judge Caesar had already accepted a bribe directed into his palm by Carey, who then wrote to the judge that:

> Whereas I am informed that one Martin Parker is entered into great trouble for buying certain cloth in this island, by the means of a bankrupt vermin and a caterpillar named Fitzwilliams, in respect it is a matter wherewith I was partly acquainted, and that the concealment of my knowledge therein may breed question of my good or bad dealing.

Presumably, the dealing with Caesar, of which he then reminded the judge:

> I wrote upon Challice's first offer of his service to me, that I had persuaded him, for your hereafter good friendship to him, to present you with two packs of cloth, which he yielded unto . . . but he desired you would be content with £50, which you were to receive of the money paid by Parker to my own use.

One can almost see Carey laying down his pen with great satisfaction and, in his mind, challenging Caesar to wriggle out of that!

Such activity and contacts meant that later that year, when a general issue of letters of reprisal was authorised, the first ships to sea to take advantage of this free-for-all were Carey's barks, *Muscat* and *Marlyn*. Their first target was a Biscayan fisherman, which put up such an almighty struggle that it seems strange to believe that the crew were only protecting their cod. Just cod, it might have been, but its capture created a stink, for ownership was claimed by some French merchants, and their case seemed to have been accepted, initially, by Julius Caesar. Carey wrote an oleaginous letter to the judge stating that the latter's 'friendly favouring of my rightful cause' would not pass by unrecognised. He then reported making a near loss on the transaction, which included valuing the captured vessel at a mere £200. His plea, or bribe, must have worked, for the next we hear of the prize is that, as the renamed *Commander*, she was considered well-suited to act as the admiral when Carey sent three of his ships on a raid to the West Indies in 1587.

Carey's lack of concern for legal niceties continued. In 1586 the Admiralty Court made an order for restitution after two French ships, laden with salt for the king's storehouses, were taken to the Isle of Wight for disposal. As with so many cases, the order for the ships to be restored and the salt, or its equivalent value, to be delivered to the ambassador is no indication of the wrong being righted.[12] Carey continued to profit and, rather than see himself reproached, he was elevated to the title of Lord Hunsdon and became a patron of William Shakespeare.

Letters of Reprisal

Letters of reprisal were issued originally to allow a merchant to take the law into his own hands by seizing goods from those individuals, ports or states, up to the value of the cargo which they had plundered from him. Naturally, no merchant underestimated his loss, but by and large this system of justice was recognised by all parties as pragmatic and fair, far better the the launch of indiscriminate naval attacks on innocent ships sailing under the same flag as the miscreant. The move towards the issue of general letters of reprisal began in June 1585 when Philip impounded English ships in Spanish ports, many of which had sailed there with cargoes of wheat to relieve an Iberian famine. As well as impounding the ships and their cargoes, Philip also ordered that their weapons be confiscated and their crews imprisoned. One ship, *Primrose*, shook off her boarders and sailed for England to report the news.

The reaction was immediate. Drake was commissioned to sail south and release, by force if necessary, the ships and their crews. At the same time letters of reprisal were issued, first to those merchants who could show that they had suffered loss, or convince the Admiralty that they had. Thus one London syndicate claimed £39,100, Ipswich £29,000 and Bristol £29,300, while other ports submitted losses amounting to £22,300. By 9 July letters of reprisal were issued irrespective of any loss claimed. Nor, in a similar disregard of convention, did the release of the ships curtail the letters of reprisal, which were soon being issued to all who applied for them with no proof of loss and with no time limit attached. For example, the London syndicate that owned *Amity*, a heavily armed 100-ton merchantman engaged in the Barbary trade, was issued with a letter of reprisal that continued in force to at least 1594, during which time the ship, and her consorts, continually returned to the Thames with prizes. Her most successful voyage in 1592 resulted in two large Spanish prizes being unloaded in London of 1,400 chests of quicksilver and a hundred tons of wine, valued at £20,000. The great London merchant John Watts, who had claimed £15,000 of losses in 1585, used the issue of a letter of reprisal to equip his fleet for both trade and plunder, taking prizes well beyond his original loss, mainly in the West Indies and Caribbean. Few could resist an assault by these dual-purpose vessels: a middle-of-the-range ship such as the 130-ton *Golden Dragon* carried two demi-culverin, six sakers, seven minions, four falcons, thirty-one muskets, three harqubuses and plenty of swords and pistols to distribute between her crew of eighty men, far more than a peaceful trader needed, but more than sufficient to bring three prizes home.[13]

The general issue of letters of reprisal caused enduring problems, mostly regarding the legitimacy of prizes taken. One year after their introduction, English merchants in Rouen were complaining to the English ambassador in Paris, Sir Edward Stafford, that their goods had been seized by 'men of evil fame' as a compensation for 40,000 francs of goods taken by Englishmen holding letters of marque. Not only, stated the merchants, was the claim an exaggerated one but it was illegal as 'letters of recompense are never granted to be executed but at the seas, and against the town who had committed the piracy.'[14] However, from the French point of view, their merchants were acting lawfully, having been granted their own letters of marque in an attempt to end a grievance which the English Admiralty Court had for many years ignored. This was the seizure and sale in 1576 of five of their vessels by the notorious English pirates Callice and Court.[15]

The October following the Rouen seizures, Henry III of France wrote to Elizabeth as her '*bon frère et cousin*' that:

> one Philip Destailleur, a burgess and sheriff of Calais, had laden in two English ships at Hamburg for Calais 36 lasts of wheat and 30 of rye for that place, the same in the way was taken by one Captain [Henry] Griffin an Englishman, and conveyed into Zeeland, where, notwithstanding the [English] Lord Admiral's letters, it was declared good prize and sold, without restitution of money or goods made. And for that the merchant requireth letters of reprisal upon the Zeelanders or any of those countries or confederates thereof, until he may recover his said wheat or the value, amounting to 1500 pounds, he [the King] hath thought good to acquaint her Majesty withal first, that he may have restitution . . . wherein he hath written to his ambassador to solicit her Majesty.[16]

The argument with the French over numerous instances of piracy continued for several years with the judge of the Admiralty finding many ingenious reasons to explain to the French ambassador why he was neither imprisoning the perpetrators nor indemnifying the wronged merchants, counterclaiming in one instance that the French had only themselves to blame, because 'in their whole suit they have found as speedy and favourable justice in England as they could desire, and if it has had no favourable issue, it is because they are not diligent in their own cause' and, what is more, that 'the French King cannot (without open wrong and breach both of his league with her Majesty and his own law) grant reprisals to these men to seize the ships and goods of English merchants trafficking into France.'[17]

The affair showed all the signs of escalating into a major trade dispute and in November 1586, in an attempt to avoid this, the splendidly named Monsieur De L'Aubespine-Chateauneuf wrote to Burghley and '*Messieurs les Grand Tresorier et Admiral d'Angleterre*', asking for them to intervene, as he had been informed that the goods of French merchants in London were in danger of being confiscated, by way of reprisal, by their English counterparts.[18]

Stafford, hoping to avoid a similar and more justifiable response in France, had to deploy all his diplomatic skills to persuade the French king to lift a stay on English ships in French ports, informing the king that the queen had held a conference with the French ambassador, at which a mutually acceptable way forward had been agreed. As a result Stafford asked that: 'the rigorous sentence given in his Privy Council against certain English merchants trading to Rouen be lifted', and that 'all things in like case may pass before those ordained by both their Majesties to see execution of justice on both sides.'[19]

The agreement provides an example as to how prize disputes could be rectified with minimum fuss. Published in May 1587 its edicts can be summarised thus:

1. Restitution of trade between the ports.
2. Release of all relevant miscreants and the settlements of disputes.
3. The appointment of commissioners to settle disputes and to present a united front against pirates from Holland and Zeeland.
4. The prohibition of French victuals being transported to any part of the Low Countries possessed by the King of Spain.
5. Regularisation of Spaniards claiming naturalisation and thus trading as French citizens.[20]

Yet lists of French ships seized or plundered continued to be presented to the Privy Council. On the other side of the Channel, Stafford was asked to make representation, not only because few impounded English ships had been released, but because French warships had attacked three English ships and killed several of the crew, with others being left 'most barbarously upon certain rocks, to the end they might perish . . . for want of succour.'[21]

As his queen, Stafford told the French, 'cannot endure such treatment, she hopes it is not the King's meaning to leave it unpunished; with whom you are to deal earnestly in her name for justice and speedy satisfaction'; letting him understand that 'as the said men of war were not common pirates, but . . . set forth by himself for his service, she the more expects that he shall give her due redress.'

Thus a lengthy disagreement, conducted at the highest level, exposed with clarity the gulf between written agreement and willing action. The English and French continued to plunder each others' vessels, knowing full well that sea water washed away the ink on any international agreements.

The Breaking of Bulk

If the state was relaxed as to what and whose ships were seized at sea, it jealously guarded its claims on all that was landed from such activities, making sure that proper audits were made and its officials provided with the intelligence and authority necessary to limit the valuables being illicitly removed by those by whose efforts the goods had first been won. Indeed, the Privy Council attached more importance to this issue than it did to the administration of Admiralty justice and the physical wellbeing of its own mariners.

The great offence was the breaking of bulk, which was the removal of any of a ship's below decks cargo. The realisation of how valuable these cargoes might be dawned with sufficient slowness for Drake to land the valuables from his circumnavigation with circumspection, but as the value of goods in the hold of returning raiders increased, so did the temptations for pillaging, alongside the superior authorities' fear of loss of that which they regarded as their own. Drake, as always, managed to avoid much of the careful scrutiny of his booty. Even when he brought in the rich *San Felipe* in 1587, it seems to have been left to local administrators to audit her cargo which was valued, with suspicious exactitude, at £108,049 13s 11d.[22]

A few days later, Drake submitted his expenses of £7,407 0s 3d, presumably to be offset from the value of the carrack, following that invoice, post-haste, with some additional expenses and an explanation as to how the sale of the carrack's goods had been organised. Then, a day later, an aggrieved Portuguese merchant, Luis Fernandez, resident in Antwerp, began his quest for compensation for his goods taken in the carrack. The Privy Council, however, were concerned with organising a profitable wholesale of the goods, so that the London merchants could control the amount they released to the public and thus keep the price high.[23]

Drake had appointed William Stallenge, the receiver of customs at Plymouth, to value the prize and its goods and to apportion shares to the queen and other investors in the voyage. This put Stallenge in a strong position regarding the handling of such issues, so that he was able to provide great service, not only to the Plymouth merchants, but also to the Crown and Robert Cecil when the secretary dabbled with pirateering in later years. Most returning ships had their prizes appraised by local worthies. This was the case with *Equina*, whose inventory was approved by Caesar on 13 October 1591 (Appendix 8), but a few days later the return of Lord Thomas Howard's fleet from the Azores caused a flurry of excitement in the Council, much of it based on the erroneous assumption that the English had captured many prizes from both the East and West Indies fleets. To handle such a mouth-watering bounty, on 25 October Sir Thomas Gorges and Mr Carmarthen were sent down to Plymouth to prevent any mariners from coming ashore until the ships had been visited and the goods inventoried, in case 'the sailors embezzle or take away short ends and such things as they may come by.'[24] Two days later, disorderly embezzlement was reported from Dartmouth, where two prizes had arrived in the hope of a quiet disposal of their goods. In this instance, no less a person than Francis Drake was despatched by the Council to 'restrain the contempts and to recover suspect parcels or portions.'[25]

The Council's response might have been too little too late, for by the end of December they had received reports that many of the merchant ships that had sailed with Howard had 'carried their prizes into remote ports and havens and there enriched themselves by rifling the prizes.' Her Majesty, so the Council opined, was not prepared to suffer such behaviour and a proclamation was sent to the southwestern counties, 'charging all that have received any foreign coin, bullion of gold or silver, jewels, pearls, stones, musk, wrought or raw silk, cochineal, indigo or other merchandise' to declare it, or to 'be held fast as felons and abettors of pirates.'[26]

Howard's return was, however, a dress-rehearsal for the arrival at Dartmouth on 7 September 1592 of the greatest prize of them all, the Portuguese carrack, *Madre de Dios*, whose capture has been described earlier. Her cargo was an embezzler's delight, including as it did diamonds and other gems which could be swiftly placed in a pocket, making a treasury of sailors' trousers.

Even before the carrack arrived in Dartmouth, private arrangements were being made to benefit from her cornucopia. On 4 September Lord Buckhurst wrote to the commissioners for the carrack that he was sending a servant 'to make choice of such pearls, stones, and other goods brought in the carrack as are appointed and appraised to be sold, and shall be thought fit for him to buy.' Requesting preferment, he strengthened his case by offering to 'give notice to them of all such as are come down contrary to the order and are the most likely men to buy such wares of pearls and stones', a case of shopping others to safeguard one's own interests.

Buckhurst had been well-informed. The carrack's inventory taken at Dartmouth listed diamonds, jewellery, gold and silver objects, precious stones, strings of pearls, peppers, cloves, nutmeg, ginger, silks, damascenes, carpets, quilts, ivory, porcelain and such exotics as coconuts, together valued at £150,000. As the vessel drew near to Dartmouth, her loot-laden escorts drew away for quieter landings, while from the river mouth boatloads of merchants sailed out to board and offer pennies for rich pickings from gullible sailors. Ashore the taverns did a roaring trade, accepting jewels for drinks – party time. But not in London, where the queen ordered Robert Cecil west, and then released the disgraced Walter Ralegh from the Tower to back up Cecil's integrity with his local influence. Cecil was ordered 'to cause all the lading to be viewed and entered in registers, especially to search out all the precious things, and also to hire sufficient ships to bring such lading into the Thames, but the lighter sort of great price, such as spices, cochineal, etc may be sent by land, if the adventurers think good.'

Cecil was further instructed to order all goods released to be brought to Greenwich because of 'contagion' in London, while at the same time taking due care to check over such items as were claimed by right of 'pillage'. Cecil travelled down not a moment too soon for:

> Every one he met within seven miles of Exeter, that either had anything in a cloak,
> bag, or mail which did but smell of the prizes, either at Dartmouth or Plymouth

(for he could well smell them almost, such has been the spoils of amber and musk amongst them), he brought back to Exeter; stayed any who might carry news to Dartmouth and Plymouth at the gates of the town; compelled them also to tell him where any trunks or malles were, and, finding the people stubborn, committed two innkeepers to prison, which example would have won the Queen £20,000 a week past. Has found, in a Londoner's shop, bag of seed pearl, pieces of damask, cipreses, and calicoes, a very great pot of musk, certain tassels of pearl, and divers other things, which have been registered in the presence of the Mayor, Mr Myddleton, and More, the Surveyor of Exeter.[27]

Sea-green incorruptible, at this time Cecil was not afraid to use strong-arm tactics. But he felt, despite ordering 'the search of every bag or mail coming from the west', that 'the birds be flown for jewels, pearls, and amber, yet doubts not to save Her Majesty, in recovering the pillage, which is almost all desperate, what shall be worth his journey.'[28] It certainly was, for of the £28,500 estimated to have been pilfered, Cecil recovered sufficient to be sold for £13,505.

Part of this came about from his 'rough dealing' with Exeter's mayor, who in return reported recovering from Alonso Gomys, one of Cumberland's sailors, '£42 in gold coin, 320 sparks of diamonds, a collar of a threefold roll of pearl, with 6 tags of crystal garnished with gold, a small string of pearl, with a pelican of gold, a small round pearl garnished with gold, also two chains of two fold pearl, with buttons of gold, and two small jewels hanging unto the ends thereof'. All of these he had handed over to the safe custody of William Stallenge.[29] Gomys sought relief by squealing on others, stating in evidence before Cecil and Drake that the master of the *Sampson* had 150 diamonds, worth 10,000 crusados (£2,500), while a corporal Tonks in *Tiger* 'did take one packet which certainly were rubies'.

Others were taking precautionary measures and issuing warnings. Captain Robert Crosse, who had commanded *Foresight* in the action to take the carrack, wrote to his brother John Crosse on 20 September that:

> The lords of the Council will send for you, I think, to know what men you set ashore of the 'portengales,' and what things you carried to the Isle of Wight in a barque, which I have already said things of mine, 10 bags of anylle and 2 bags of cloves, with some casts of armoury and other things, I know not what, and that you left it with a friend of yours; you must name Mr Cotten. If you can, come presently to me at London to my house. All my things are stayed and seized, and so tell Sir Walter Raleigh if he be not good to me, I shall be the worse by this voyage.[30]

Anthony Moon wrote to John Bedford, master of *Roebuck*, asking for the two pieces of silk he had been promised, but also drawing the latter's attention to the report of a missing great jewel which had been valued at half a million ducats which 'If Bedford please, he may signify this much to their lord and master; otherwise let him conceal it to himself.'

Stallenge, in the meantime, was collecting evidence on the pilfering undertaken by Sir John Borough and his men in Ralegh's *Roebuck*, being among the first to board the carrack, although her captain, in his deposition, stated that Sir John was 'the first that boarded me and he that best fought and took nothing from the prize; for that, when he came to the carrack, she was rifled of all.'[31] However, Stallenge soon received a note listing from Robert Gregory, one of Her Majesty's 'searchers' of 'such money, jewels and merchandizes, as was landed off the barque *Band* in Weymouth and Melcombe Regis, which was taken from the ship by order of Sir John Borough and others.' It included, besides much coin, a fortune in diamonds, rubies, sapphires, rings and spices.[32]

Sir John was in trouble, a position further entrenched when twenty-two of Cumberland's men gave evidence that he and his men had pillaged the carrack immediately after she was taken. One Thomas Favell reported on the seizure of 'a chain of pearls orient, two rest of gold, four very great pearls of the bigness of a fair pea, four forks of crystal and four spoons of crystal set with gold and stones, and two cods of musk.'

By 9 October pilfered goods were readily available in London. A trader, or fence, William Broadbent, on arrest confessed that he gone down to Gravesend and purchased for £130 some 1,330 'small sparks' and 'others there were of somewhat bigger sort, but how many I cannot justly remember. Also there was sixty-one or such a number of small rubies, sixteen ounces of ambergris, with two or three necklaces of small pearls, other two strings pearls, with two or three other trifles of very small value, and one chain of gold of eight ounces.' A few days later Broadbent sold them on as a job lot for £200, giving the Dutch purchaser a very great bargain.[33] Justice was, however, in pursuit and as so often in Elizabethan England, the threat of chastisement soon had the accused singing. In this case the man to whom Broadbent first offered the goods, referred to as Shorry, stated:

Where I have given your Honour to know of certain treasure that hath been taken from the Carrack of late, and as it is informed to you by the contrary party that I have not told you the truth, but like a bad and a perjured man, as he saith, I have slandered him. If I had the wealth that he hath, I would be a little more honester than he, for I would be ashamed to be put in trust by Her Majesty and the Council, as he was, to execute the truth in their behalf, and then to be found contrary to the oath and allegiance of his prince, by favouring and detaining such things as he knows would breed danger.

I will lay forth the truth to your Honour so near as I can. About six days before I came to your Honour, I did see in the hands of Mr Bradbent, of Gravesend, about 1,800 diamonds of divers sorts, and I think 200 or 300 of rubies and 16 ounces and better of ambergris, and I think to the value of £40 worth of gold in chain and jewels for ears, and some four ounces of pearl, and I did value and weigh the parcels, and he did set down every particular in a note with his own hand. He did ask me if I could get him one that would buy them, and give him reason for them, and to know where that they were best in request beyond the sea, whether at Frankfort or at Venice. I said that I would give him money for them, if he would warrant me that I should not come into danger, and that he would stand to the hazard of them if that they should not be well come by. I told him I would give him £5 in every £100 more than any other should, and for him to see where he could get the most. He swore that no man should have them before me, and that I should have them £5 in £100 better cheap better than another in consideration of my painstaking, but he proved perjured himself. A day after I saw this Francis in Lombard Street, and have met with divers other sailors in communication together, and they all went to Bradbent's house, and then the Saturday, as I think, the two brothers came down. On the Sunday at noon they went to London from Bradbent's house in a wherry, very close. The next day I did reason with Bradbent about them, and he said that he was £200 offered more than I valued them at, and I said I would give him as much as any. He said that they would not be sold under three times as much as I offered for them, and then I knew that they were gone, and I told him that they had them, and at the last he could not deny that they had some of them.[34]

Broadbent, however, proved more resilient to questioning when he appeared before magistrates in November, refusing to take the oath and then claiming that it was unlawful for him to answer any questions while not on oath, a position that allowed him to disclaim any knowledge of handling rubies, diamonds and other jewels in the past month.[35]

Broadbent and Shory were not the only ones to be netted by the investigation. Richard Goodwyn, dwelling at the Three Cups in Harwich, was reported to have 'bought out of *Dainty* of Sir John Hawkins so many calicoes, silks and spices as came to £100, all which were taken out of the carrack.' While at Limehouse it was stated a merchant 'hath had and has good store of calicoes, &c', whom he will examine and advertise him further. Lists of offenders continued to be drawn up with one detailing 'those that went down to the Carrack after warning given by Her Majesty and the Council to the contrary, which is disobedience and rebellion.' London was full of under-the-counter traders, whose activities were spied upon:

> The one of the brothers at 'the Bottle' in Fenchurch Street; his name is Francis. He hath had good store of fair rubies and diamonds. One Scote in Fenchurch Street and one of the principallest man that goes about those affairs, and Hannibal Gaman in Cheapside, a goldsmith, and a great doer in those matters. Young Howe, a goldsmith, that by report hath bought so much below at the price that he fears taking in question, that he hath shut up his shop and is gone, but hath been seen in strangers' houses in London, that are jewellers; and Conywayes, in Lombard Street, at the sign of the Bull's Head his shop is and not his house. One Barker in Tower Street, over against Barking Church, one of my Lord Cumberland's men, and one that was there from the first to the last delivery of the Carrick. It is reported that Dutchmen and Frenchmen, jewellers, have bought

for a great deal of money in stones, and have got a great deal of them in secret. One Robert Brocke, in Lombard Street, hath in his hands and hath sold divers diamonds, and it is thought that they are his at 'the Bottle', and Whiskings, a sailor and a master of one of the ships that took the Carrick, hath by report half a peck of pearls in a bag that he took away from one of the company, I heard say as many as contained a whole peck.[36]

And this was all before the convoy of vessels bearing the carrack's cargo had even entered the Thames. Once it had arrived, petty pilfering continued, but with little effect on the Treasury, as the queen took her share of the profit by sequestering the whole of the 725,000lbs of pepper. This was not a great move as it took many years to release it onto the market at an acceptable price, with the bulk being traded for £90,000, payable in instalments.

Cecil's strong-arm tactics did not go uncriticised, with the queen receiving a letter written by many of those present at the taking of *Madre de Dios* who wished:

To make your Majesty acquainted with, to prove that it will be no way beneficial to your Majesty, and very harmful to us, to have any but your ordinary officers deal with her, by your appointment.

First, your Majesty's services, of most importance, both for your own profit and annoying of your enemies by sea, those exceeding chargeable if the faithful free hearts of your subjects did not most times defray them, which no doubt shall still continue, if for their adventure they may receive and enjoy such shares as of due they ought. But if of that in any sort they be restrained, it will so wholly discharge them that hereafter they will be found unwilling, and the whole charge must come, out of your Majesty's coffers If you will have anything attempted.

Secondly, for the fear may be had of concealing anything from your Highness, there is two things in our opinion may easily clear it. The first, the number of your officers in every port, from whom it is impossible to convey much without their knowledge. The second, the small judgement that shall be in us, to adventure the loss of twenty parts clearly our own, to deceive your Majesty of one, besides the touch of our credits, which we have held long with better respect than now to lose to so little purpose.

Thirdly, it being your Majesty's purpose to have but the utmost of your Highness' due for custom, this course shall mightily harm you, for the mariners when they shall hear of any extraordinary appointed, will fear the like course which in the late taken Carrack was used with them, and perhaps not so well remember themselves, as in duty they ought, but carry the ship where they may make their best profit; and so your Majesty and we that are adventurers lose the good, which otherwise it might please God to send us. But if it happen that the commanders have so great power as to keep them from that desperate and dishonest course, yet we assure ourselves it will make them filch, with all extremity, whatsoever they may come by.

Lastly, our acquaintance with the people abroad, our long experience in these causes, the great interest we have in what is to come, be all such as with good reason we may prove, that not any can so well find out, or have so good reason to bring to light whatsoever conveyed as ourselves. And we little doubt but our readiness at all times to do your Highness service in any degree that hath been wished, hath in reason drawn as good a conceit of trust to us from your Highness as your Majesty hath to any such as in this case you will employ.[37]

They received little support; Robert Cecil had proved himself to be the golden boy in waiting, and servants of the queen with his attributes were most unusual. Elizabeth also knew full well that, whatever system of controls she introduced to discourage pilfering, her mariners would not depart a prize without a reasonable return in their pouches.

Yet some, like Cumberland, felt that they should be treated differently because of the service they had rendered and the rank that they held. He had been most grumpy about the thorough going-over his vessels had received on their return to Portsmouth in May 1594 (Appendix 7) and said so in a letter to the Lord Admiral and Cecil complaining that:

I have received your Honours' letters and perceive Her Majesty hath given direction that all such ships [as] are any way brought in for me, shall be, by such as she hath appointed, duly looked into, to the end that all things contained in the same ships and prizes may be truly certified. There hath many more than I can now write, richer come into England, not one of them wherein I was not interested thus searched, but sith it is my hap only to be made an example of these unusual courses, I will content myself with knowing I have better deserved assurance. In time, Her Majesty will blame them that to this advised her, and resolution to bear with patience all burdens shall be by Her Highness laid upon me. Those who adventure with me I know by proof do trust me, your lordship for your tenths I doubt not will, and if Her Majesty do not for so little a part as her custom, I have lived to an unhappy hour and hazarded my estate and life very vainly. Your lordship writeth this is done for my good: I could answer, but that I will forbear till I see her to whom when I have uttered what I am bound in duty, I will wish myself with Him that only knows what will be the end of these courses.[38]

The restraining orders continued. In August 1594 a proclamation was issued against all those who secretly bought or sold prize goods before they were 'customed' and valued. To deter such behaviour it was ordered that those apprehended should not only forfeit the goods but be committed to prison for an indefinite term until the Privy Council ordered them to be released. Additionally, Custom House officials were ordered to board and remain with any prize until all the goods had been discharged.[39]

This was indeed the welcome that awaited those returning from the second assault on Cadiz in August 1596. They were met on the quayside by the usual auditors, and with very good reason, as the instructions issued by the Lord Treasurer made clear by telling the inspectors that:

The Queen and her subjects have at great charge fitted out a navy against the Spaniards, which has now returned or is returning to Plymouth and the neighbouring forts, with great riches. It was always intended that Queen and subjects should be recompensed with the rich prizes taken, which must therefore be valued, and the mariners and soldiers dismissed. You are therefore to repair to Plymouth, or wherever the ships come in, and order the custom house officers to search them under your direction . . . you are therefore to recover all prize goods brought in, acting in conjunction with any agents of the city of London who may be sent to enquire, and none are to be taken away by any adventurer, but to be brought to the appointed staple.

As formerly merchants of London or residents in the ports have privily bought from the passengers, soldiers, or mariners, goods of great value but small bulk, and carried them away secretly, inquisition is to be made therein, and any merchants suspected of much intentions to be ordered to depart, on pain of imprisonment. All corners of ships where any jewels might be hid are to be searched. You shall enquire what has become of the goods from the 15 ships already arrived at Plymouth, and try to recover any that have been carried away.[40]

Both Essex, privily, by the queen, and Howard, openly, by the Privy Council, were also made fully aware of the queen's views, the latter being commanded to make a good search of all the ships in his fleet as 'it will be found that both captains, masters and officers have pillage enough to bear each ship's charge, which, if it be, there is no reason the Queen should give them wages as well'. The search having been made, then Her Majesty's advisers were instructed to arrange to pay them or to 'take that which is so indirectly embezzled by them.' As for the seamen, Her Majesty had no wish to take 'such trash or petty matters as garments or other things fit for soldiers and mariners in like cases, but gross commodities, wares and other merchandise, of which money may be made towards the common charge.'[41]

Thus the hardship of this tight control of seized goods fell on the ordinary sailors and soldiers, most of who had been promised that their wages would be met from the sale of the booty. Now further payment was forbidden and Stallenge was ordered to 'see that the goods are well preserved, locked up, and inventoried.' The Council also instructed that 'payments are to be delayed to any who are found to have had large spoils, till further direction.'[42] Those with 'large spoils' were soon justifying, and downgrading, their haul. Sir Arthur Savage submitted that:

Having received small blows with stones, to which nothing had been applied, I was appointed the second night to lodge at a physician's house, which house fell to my lot, it being unworthy, and no one asking for it. I sold it just as it stood for £65 and six small pieces of plate. I also had a gold chain weighing 8ozs but sold it to Sir Henry Neville, and the stuff to Sir Richard Wayman, spending the money on wearing apparel. I got nothing more, except a gilt rapier and dagger, though my expenses were equal to the most, and beyond those that got 40,000 ducats.[43]

Sir Mathew Morgan, who had responsibility for the seizure of munitions, having explained why he had been unable to do a thorough job protested that:

I had a parcel of plate value £25, and by traffic, got some 20 pieces of tapestry; as my poverty and travail urged me to ask something for requital, their Lordships bestowed upon me the third part of the bells of Cadiz, which were given by warrant to Sir Wm Woodhouse, Mr Trever, and myself. I bought their parts, and also bought four chests of red caps of Captain Henry Carew, a chain of a soldier of Captain Charles Morgan's company for £4 10s, and a crystal bracelet set in gold of Lieutenant Baynard for £4 Captain William Morgan gave me an emerald worth £5; part of a chain worth 40 marks was given to my lieutenant for a prisoner. I had three butts of Spanish wine, a hogshead of vinegar, a butt of wheat, and other things outworth the valuing. By my asking, travails, and traffic, I hope I have made myself worth some £400 or £500.

However, while wholesale looting had taken place at Cadiz and on the return voyage, much wealth had, to Elizabeth's angry chagrin, been left behind or been burnt in the widespread conflagration of Spanish shipping. Such was the confusion that the accounts could never be complete, although the costs were well detailed. Thus income and expenditure were annotated side by side and submitted for a thorough examination by Cecil, who leaped on anomalies and queried any dubious claims. A sample of the paperwork shows that what had taken place at Cadiz, whatever the strategic justification, was a raid aimed at wealth creation; in short, a state-approved piratical assault.

Note of the money taken by the Earl of Essex and Lord Admiral, out of two Dutch ships, claimed by the States, and out of the moneys that were in the Castle of Cadiz, amounting to £12,700, of which £4,000 has been paid to Sir John Fortescue and the Lord Admiral for the Queen.

Report and valuation of goods captured at Cadiz, and found in ships since their arrival in the Thames; total, £2,959 8s 8d, out of which £1,299 18s worth was secreted by the masters and mariners of 15 English ships named; the rest from 13 other vessels remains in the custom house. With note by the officers of customs, that before these goods are delivered, the charges of those employed in the service should be defrayed there from.

Account sent to the Privy Council of the riches and merchandise, silver and gold, plate, tapestries, silks, &c, found in Cadiz, when the Queen's fleet arrived, none of which had been removed because the Spaniards did not fear, as the King's fleet was in the bay. The people bestowed their riches in the Castle, wherein were 40,000 ducats to pay the King's ships, and in numerous private houses, of which list is given; also list of Spanish merchants who pay ransom, and account of treasure found in churches.

Note of money delivered by Sir George Carew to Sir Gelly Merrick from the spoils of Cadiz; total, £1,723 10s.

Eleven interrogatories for the examination of Captain Parry, concerning the attempt to plunder the custom house, on the capture of Cadiz; relative to his own proceedings, those of Sir John Aldridge, Sir George Carew, and Sir Richard Wingfield; the care taken to preserve the place from spoil; what goods he saw there, as sugar, linen, cloths of gold and silver, &c, and what became of them. Also, eleven similar interrogatories to be delivered to Sir Anthony Savage, as to his appointment to take charge of the Castle, his mode of fulfilling it, the coming thither of Sir George Carew, his receiving messages from Topley, the delivery of money to him to be kept from spoil, its removal thence, and the proceedings thereon of Sir George Carew and Sir Gelly Merrick.[44]

From the above it is clear that the state wished to act as a highly professional raiding organisation, both by identifying and exploiting opportunities for plunder on station, and by using all the skills of inventory, examination and accounting to ensure that it maximised its returns from its speculative ventures. Both assaults on Cadiz were military successes, but there were other Spanish targets that might have been considered more strategically important. More emphasis, for example, might have been placed on seizing and holding a Spanish port, a century and a half before Gibraltar was taken. But that would have involved investment rather than income, a contrary approach to Elizabeth's belief in the efficacy of smash-and-grab. Such activities were no longer niceties—they had become necessities. In Handover's words, 'such prizes as the carrack were an essential item in the Exchequer revenues, an economic policy which made necessary the continuance of a state of war with Spain.'[45] The effect on the national mores is very clear from the printed evidence, let alone that which is unaccounted and unrecorded. It shows quite clearly that the consistent aim of every individual involved in pirateering was to benefit by more than that which was their due, by seizing that to which they were not entitled. Many would have considered themselves immune from prosecution or close enough to the Council to avoid questioning, but it was not always so.

As ever, when a prize dispute arose, the seamen who had risked most were rewarded least. In April 1602 Thomas Honiman, supervising the unloading of the prize *Saint Mark* on behalf of Cecil and Nottingham, wrote to the former:

Touching the havoc accustomed amongst mariners, I will be as circumspect to enquire as I have been forward to promise them good dealing, otherwise they would not have consented to the unlading without the proportion 'allotted' them aboard, for, to tell them no repartition could be made till a due trial and judgement whether it would be lawful prize, was in their opinion but words to deceive them. They have locks upon every cellar door, as we have, and take weight of everything with us. All being safe on land, they shall be called to account for matters embezzled. I send your Honour the names of the ships that claim part, most of which demands are frivolous.[46]

Later that year, Richard Leveson seized *Saint Valentine*, the last of the three great carracks that were taken in the war and escorted her back to Plymouth. Her arrival and audit was supervised by Fulke Greville and the local commissioners at Plymouth. Besides carrying out an audit, they also arranged for the cargo to be transferred to three of the queen's ships and three merchant ships. Yet, despite them taking every precaution, rumour was rife that a great deal of pillaging had taken place, equal to the quantity secured. This was an obvious nonsense for as the Lord Admiral explained:

> This is strange to me, how it should be carried away, for you see there is six great ships laden to bring this away. Now, if there were as much stolen as is left, where could it be put? I see no possibility in it; and yet no question a great deal is stolen.

The problem for Nottingham was not just the thievery, but that his son-in-law, Richard Leveson himself, was accused of being the major perpetrator. In a note to Cecil, Nottingham wriggled uncomfortably but not convincingly:

> I trust my son will answer it honestly for those things that were stayed in a town of my Lady of Warwick's in Gloucestershire. He wrote to me about it, and that he had sent to his wife to comfort her some things of no great value; and upon his letter I wrote to my Lady of Warwick to write to her officers to deal well with his men, which she very honourably did. The justices had written to her that if it were silver they carried, it was worth £4,000, and there were but three nags, as they did write. A good horse-load is but £500 in silver, so it could be but £1,500. But, sir, for myself directly or indirectly, if I have of the carrack the worth of a groat, I am a false villain to the Queen.[47]

Yet the accusation remained, and although Leveson continued to inspire and command, the case of the missing valuables remained open. It might have been closed at his death in 1605, had not a circumlocution-office-style feud erupted over his will, his lands and his rightful heirs. In 1607 Richard Leveson's former cabin-boy, Walter Grey, stated that his admiral had embezzled goods to the value of £40,000. This was a potentially disastrous suit for the family, whose possessions had already been put at risk by Richard's worthless father. The demand for restitution was pursued by the Lord Treasurer, Lord Buckhurst, by now the earl of Dorset, in an attempt, by fair means or foul, to obtain the Leveson lands. The case finally came before the Council in April 1608, before whom Dorset, while rummaging through his files for a document, 'suddenly fell down dead without

speaking a word': an event which that more superstitious age might have considered a form of judgement. The case was, however, resumed, but with Robert
Cecil, Richard Leveson's old friend, stepping in to the dead man's shoes. A
settlement of £5,000, plus £848 for stolen cloves, was agreed, for which favour, in
accordance with custom, Cecil and his son were paid by the Leveson family £45
12s and £59 10s 11d respectively. Cecil might have been a sea-green incorruptible,
but he knew how to benefit when in the company of those less particular.

CHAPTER 10

The Duke's Denial

The Duke cannot deny the course of law,
For the commodity that strangers have
With us . . . if it be denied
'Twill much impeach the justice of the state;
Since that the trade and profit of the city
Consisteth of all nations.

Shakespeare, *The Merchant of Venice*

With a philosophy that believed possession was a major part of the law, those in positions of authority took a dim view on being ordered to return stolen goods which they had bought. Thus Sir George Trenchard wrote, from Dorset, to Burghley in February 1591 stating that 'the reclaiming of the Venetian goods from those who purchased them in open market, after they had been sold by sentence of the Admiralty Court, has given more dissatisfaction than anything for many years.' He followed that moan with a note stating that he had 'carefully found out, on behalf of the Venetians and Florentines, such pepper, &c as was brought into Weymouth by Randalls Canther', and 'begged favour for the merchants and gentleman who have bought the pepper, as they did not buy till warranted by a commission from the Admiralty Court. They wish restoration of the goods, on security to answer the value, if the prize be not lawful.'[1]

The case put by Trenchard was part of a common failing that the authorities did little to amend. The audit, valuation and distribution of prize goods could take months or even years. Thus perishables were disposed of before judgement was made, but without the money raised being handed to the crew, who were often left penniless and destitute in port. Whatever the judgement, full restitution was seldom given, especially to foreigners, many of whom were denied the course of law even when their cargo offered salvation to starving Englishmen, as was the case during the famine years of Elizabeth's reign when the port authorities were licensed to stay any foreign vessels carrying grain and to purchase the shipment for an agreed and fair amount. Yet frequently the price offered was well below the market rate, but grudgingly accepted to secure the release of a ship and her crew.

For peculation in the management of piracy to percolate through every layer of Elizabethan society, it required to be drip-fed from the highest level. Many helped in the filtering of this unhealthy brew, but the interaction between the triumvirate of Lord Admiral Howard, Earl of Nottingham, the Secretary of State, Robert Cecil and the judge at the High Court of Admiralty, Julius Caesar, was essential to achieve saturation.

Lord Charles Howard of Effingham, Earl of Nottingham

Charles Howard was a man of two titles and two reputations. As Howard of Effingham he won renown as the commander-in-chief in both the Armada campaign and the assault on Cadiz in 1596. As the earl of Nottingham, a position to which he was elevated in 1597, he lost respect by presiding over a period of malfeasance that it would be hard to match in any other period of English naval history.[2]

The Lord Admiral was not only the ruler of the queen's navy but had authority over all who occupied themselves below the lowest bridging point of any river or the line of seaweed that marked mean high-water springs. There was no equivalent boundary to seaward. All ships that sailed, or were seized, sunk, salvaged, or wrecked in these waters were regarded as passing through his bailiwick, and thus their owners could be liable to pay some sort of due in cash or kind or bribe. The admiral even had his own court to which representation could be made, although the success of any supplication depended as much upon what judgement would benefit the admiral's purse as on the justification of the complainant. To administer this great watery empire, far larger and more profitable than Virginia, which had been gifted to Ralegh, the admiral appointed both a legal team and vice admirals in the maritime counties, who were expected to ensure that their superior's financial interests were pursued with vigour.[3]

And what interests they were. As well as his interests in all form of shipping, the admiral had rights regarding flotsam, jetsam, royal fish, mills, ballast, abandoned craft, dead men's valuables, fines for maritime offences, and many perquisites, all of which were jealously guarded, but the greatest earner of them all came from prizes, to which the Lord Admiral was entitled to a tenth share, although in 1560, during the French war, Elizabeth had raised this to one-third. Yet that was not the only way in which the Lord Admiral received a bounty from the work of others. Those requesting letters of reprisal had to pay a fee to the Admiralty Court for its issue. Once these were freely given, after 1585, the fee take shot up and, when it was linked to the requirement to post a bond for good behaviour, the admiral became richly rewarded even before the prizes, with his 'tenths' onboard, started being brought into English ports. Ironically, prizes taken during deployments commissioned by the queen were excluded from the Lord Admiral's share, and thus Howard had little return from the capture of the three great carracks.

The traditional reason for issuing letters of reprisal did continue in the early years of the undeclared war. In 1586 Judge Julius Caesar pronounced that Hugh

Lee and Thomas Alabaster and their associates, 'the lawful owners and proprietors', had certain goods 'unlawfully confiscated' by the 'authority' of the king of Spain, which they had been unable to recover by lawful means and lengthy appeal. They were thus authorised to seize goods in compensation to the value of £12,700. Yet in most instances, as neither proof of confiscation nor a value of goods taken was necessary, the issue of a letter of reprisal passed from being a judicial process to a justification for piracy. Their possession was further popularised when the English adopted the king of France's edict that enemies' goods in a friendly or neutral ship could be regarded as lawful prize. Such a ruling allowed all manner of mis-appropriation as luckless merchants failed to convince boarding parties that the wares in their hold were not destined for or owned by Iberians.

Soon the ports were receiving sufficient prizes to keep the Lord Admiral content. In December 1589 George Somers brought four vessels into Dartmouth from whose cargo of bullion, cochineal and hides the local admiralty officer, Francis Burnell, creamed off an admiral's tenth of £767 in money, 44lbs weight in bullion, 1lb of gold, 4lbs of musk, plus £1,650 from the sale of the cochineal, and £283 10s from the sale of the hides. Detailed research by K R Andrews, from admittedly incomplete records, indicated that licensed pirates landed in the three years 1589, 1590 and 1591 goods to a value of £420,000, which would have yielded the admiral an annual tenth of £14,000, a most considerable sum.[4] To increase this income stream, bonds for good behaviour were sometimes waived; disputed prizes were beneficially untangled; litigants were sent empty away and pirateering vessels could, and were, built, fitted out, victualled and manned at royal expense.[5]

Sir Julius Caesar

Watching and well aware of this malfeasance was the Admiralty judge, Julius Caesar, a man with unparalleled knowledge of the law as it applied to the maritime realm and an ability to apply it not to his own disadvantage. Caesar received fees from those who appeared before his court, but in 1589 he negotiated with Howard to be rewarded with one twentieth of Howard's tenth from prize goods, along with sundry other benefits from fines, penalties, forfeits and fees. This made him in turn a rich man and as he was also ambitious, he felt it desirable, within a limited elasticity of law, to make sure his boss would also be his benefactor. The simplest way to achieve this was to inform Howard that his judge would make the Lord Admiral the 'richest and greatest that ever was in England', provided that Caesar was given a free hand to administer justice and pursue perquisites to their mutual advantage. Caesar also prepared well for the bounty that war would bring his master, telling Walsingham in 1584 that it was of vital importance that all complaints of piracy should be handled exclusively by his court. In his document, 'Means to further the execution of Justice in England touching Admiral causes', Caesar sought total autonomy and increased influence through the creation of an Admiralty circuit to try cases along the coast. Sadly for Caesar, the one attempt to ride a circuit in 1591 was unsuccessful, and he also could see his ambition for promotion being dulled by his lack of earnings from his judicial position. In 1587 he wrote to Essex, seeking his support for his advancement and bemoaning the fact that his seven years in the Admiralty Court had cost him £1,200 more than he had received in income. A year later, almost to illustrate his investment ineptitude, he was complaining that Thomas Cavendish, newly returned from his highly profitable circumnavigation, was refusing to repay the £50 that Caesar had invested in the voyage by claiming the money was a gift not a loan.

Howard and Caesar were not averse to playing similar games to use as countermeasures against complainants. For example, in 1598, after the French ambassador had presented the Council with a list of grievances, Howard ordered Caesar to compile a collection 'of all complaints and grievances of any of our nation against the French for spoils done by them of late years', and to encourage the complainants to follow the ambassador, both night and day, to demand satisfaction and so to 'suffer him never to lie in quiet', although Caesar was told to ensure that the ambassador was never aware who was behind this sleep-depriving demonstration. [6]

A man, however incorruptible, desiring both preferment and pocket money, is likely to make decisions favourable to his patrons, and so it was with this ambitious Caesar. Yet, by and large, he was guilty of no grievous fault, even resisting the pressures brought to bear by such influential interests as that of Sir George Carey and Lord Thomas Howard.

In 1591 several ships owned by Sir George, Lord Thomas and John Watts, seeking prizes in the same waters, formed a loose confederacy on those occasions when it suited them so to do. Of the three groups, it was Watts's force that was the most successful, returning to England with some £40,000 worth of prizes, while Carey's fleet was severely mauled by a Spanish force under Diego de la Ribera, with *Bark Burr* blowing up and *Content* only managing to disengage after a day-long battle. Carey, weighing his losses against Watts's gains, felt that he was entitled to some of the merchant's money and that having Caesar on his side might help the balance in his favour. He thus wrote to Caesar, in October of that year that:

> I received from my servant Burley, a very kind and friendly message from you, in assurance of your unfeigned goodwill to me, and your desire to find return of the like. If you shall examine the course of my life and believe what you shall find most true, my deeds have ever accompanied my words, and my friendship was never professed, where not firmly performed, until cause was apparently given to the contrary; your goodwill towards me shall never die unrequited to the uttermost of my power but have usury paid in double measure. Now, sir, you shall further understand that I have a very poor prize come into Dartmouth, and Master Watts a very rich one, in which I assure myself, as in the rest of the prizes, I am to have by law an eighth part, therefore, in friendship, I beseech and in

justice desire you, to make no allowance of the sale to him of his prize . . . until he shall put in sufficient assurances . . . to answer me.

The case, prolonged by Lord Thomas Howard who had also demanded a share of Watt's winnings, seems to have been settled in the merchant's favour, but there is no reason to suppose that the friendly arrangements between Caesar and Carey recorded in the previous chapter did not continue outside the written record and that Carey was compensated in other, less obvious but most satisfactory, ways.

Yet Caesar seemed disinclined to indulge in major malfeasance; his main role in the rising tide of corruption was to allow his views to be ignored and never to protest too much should the Lord Admiral or his conferes require the law to be bent to their advantage. This was the case in November 1599 when the ships *Dragon*, *Concord* and *Amity* were seized as pirate ships. Caesar seemed inclined to dismiss the charges, but changed his mind on receipt of a note from Howard, praying and requiring him to 'go forward with the confiscation of those ships.' As this would mean that the vessels would become the property of the Lord Admiral, Howard had no compunction in stating that this was a matter that 'especially concerns my profit.' Caesar obeyed without query. On an occasion when he did question Howard's judgement, the latter replied with unrighteous indignation:

> how often have I charged you to do justice to all men . . . when did I either write or speak to you to do otherwise than right . . . I pray write to me in what thing I ever moved you either by word or deed or writing to hinder proceedings of justice.[7]

Occasionally, when the fine tightrope between applying the law and indulging his patron became so narrow as to cause Caesar to wobble, he caught a judicious flu, informing Howard in December 1597 that:

> I crave pardon for my long absence, and for not attending your lordship this day according to your appointment. I have an extreme cold that has possessed me full seven days in great extremity, and has broken out in my face in such sort, as that I neither dare venture out into the open air, nor am fit to present myself till I am in some sort amended. I have been examining the prisoners whom I have committed for the Florentine causes, and have, according to your direction, caused all such moneys and silks as are forthcoming, to be delivered into the hands of Sir John Hart, knight. I hope ere many days to bring together the moneys which have been distributed amongst many hands. I have already discovered about 5,000 pieces of eight, and 'cichinos' of gold which were missing, and have caused some part thereof which is extant to be delivered to Sir John Hart, to be kept with what he had before. For that which is missing, I keep them in prison who had it, till they restore it, or bring in other money in lieu thereof. I doubt not but that the Italians shall find cause to commend the speedy and careful carriage of this business.[8]

Caesar also used the same tactic in his dealings with Robert Cecil, the one man who could bring the whole peculative pack of cards crashing down, informing the Secretary in June 1601 that:

> I am in my body so ill-affected as that I do verily believe that age is crept upon me, for since my mischance on Thursday last, I have been made to keep my chamber and almost my bed till this morning . . . if it may please your Honour, I will attend you at the Savoy, and to-morrow where and at what time you shall assign me, albeit in body a cripple for the time.[9]

In fact, this seemingly delicate judge went on to became Chancellor of the Exchequer and Master of the Rolls, holding the latter post until his death at the age of seventy-nine in 1636.

Robert Cecil

In the sixteen years from his appointment as Secretary of State in 1596 to his death in 1612, Robert Cecil, the sharp-witted, workaholic son of Lord Burghley, turned a modest inheritance into a major fortune, this while receiving a limited income as Secretary of State, £366 a year as Lord Treasurer, and £1,600 per annum from his inherited estates. Of course, he had other legitimate sources of income, such as the £6,000 a year generated by his ownership of the silk farm part of customs and his wheeling and dealing as Master of the Court of Wards. Nevertheless, Cecil, like his fellow Council member, friend and adviser, Lord Admiral Howard, was not against using his official office for personal gain. As far as his dealings with Howard were concerned, these involved mainly the sharing out of prize money and, for a brief period, a joint pirateering venture paid for by the state.[10]

This enterprise began in 1595, just ahead of Cecil's much anticipated appointment as secretary, when the two men commissioned a ship, *Truelove*, to be built. Although incriminating evidence does not exist, it is reasonable to suppose that much of her cost of £800 was met through the use of naval materials and shipbuilders; indeed, the fact that the man who supplied the cordage was in the debtors' prison in 1603, still owed £95 by the partnership, indicates that *Truelove*'s construction was not well ordered.

Following service with the 1596 Cadiz expedition, *Truelove* was dispatched for a voyage to Barbary under the command of Captain Matthew Bradgate, whose order dated 25 February 1597 can be summarised as:

> 1. You shall take charge of my good ship the *Truelove*, laden as she is by the merchants, and shall have due care to preserve the merchandizes now on board and such goods as shall be laden into her from Barbary, as also the ship's own tackle, sea store, furniture, powder and munitions, from waste of the company or other disorderly usage.
>
> 2. You shall shape your course for Barbary and do there all manner of things that

in the said charter-party is expressed, so as the merchants may have no cause of grievance.

3. When you have unladen at Barbary and do seek adventures on the coast of Spain, you shall have care to keep out of the danger of the galleys which are wont ever at that time of the year to be stirring there.

4. If God bless you with any prize of good strength and able to go home, you shall put May into her, and shall send her for England if you can do it with safety; and if she be not worth the sending for England, you then may carry her for Barbary if her commodities be fit to be sold there.

5. The short ends of most value and such goods as shall not need to pester your ship with stowage, you shall, with the privity of your master and the sub-stantiallest of your company, take on board the *Truelove*, and shall make a just inventory thereof.

6. Lastly, because we must refer many things to your own discretion, we hope you will order all things with that due respect as may give us liking of your doings and cause to employ you in like sort hereafter.

Under Howard's signature, Robert Cecil added a note stating:

You shall suffer May, the servant of me the Secretary, to be acquainted with all such things as you shall take or do in your voyage. And if the winds will serve you shall bestow some time on the coast of Spain as you go out, both for intelligence and purchase.[11]

The voyage was expected to last for six months, during which time the ship was added to the payroll of the royal fleet. The latter was, however, only victualled for three months, an inconvenience which was solved with official contrivance by Marmaduke Darell, who informed Cecil from Her Majesty's store house at Tower Hill that:

As to the direction to be given to Mr Lake for adding *Truelove* to the rest of the ships in the great warrant, having perused the reckoning made of the victualling of *Truelove* I find her time to be for six months, whereas all the ships in the great warrant are to receive allowance thereby but for three months. Wherefore I think it fit, if it shall so please you, that her number of men to be set down in the warrant may be doubled and so made 120.[12]

Yet although Darell in London and William Stallenge in Plymouth made every effort to make Captain Bradgate's victualling a success, Bradgate informed Cecil, from Dover on 21 March, that Lord Buckhurst had ordered the ship to be searched off Gravesend for 'great sums of money secretly conveyed.'[13] Buckhurst, who in 1599 was to succeed the elder Cecil, Lord Burghley, as Lord Treasurer, had few reasons to be awkward to the younger man, but it will be recalled that he had asked for special favours ahead of the arrival of *Madre de Dios* at Dartmouth in 1592. The inspection of *Truelove* might just have signified the unrequited elder man's exercise of ire.

Joseph May, Robert Cecil's man on board *Truelove*, wrote first to inform his master about Spanish shipping movements and the dearth of prizes. The latter finally hove over the horizon and it is indicative of this pirateering age that one of the prizes seized on this voyage, commissioned jointly by the Lord Admiral and Secretary, guardians of the law of the sea, was a Dutch flyboat, *Black Eagle*, the taking of which flouted all of the rules. The merchants petitioned for the return of their goods, which had been offloaded at Dartmouth but, as a letter from Thomas Crompton to Cecil on Christmas Eve 1597 made apparent, if not abundantly clear, it was not going to be easy for them to be compensated in full:

> I have attended Mr Dr Caesar for the case against Captain Bredcake [*sic*], wherein your Honour is interested, and notwithstanding by the customs of Normandy and the Admiralty of England, the resistance and taking by force in this case, is cause of confiscation of the whole goods, yet, for that there is now made direct proof that the wines appertain to the demandants, and some better appearance for 17 chests and 8 half chests of sugar than at the first, I do not perceive, for that the Judge hath told me that your Honour is not disposed to stand upon advantages, but that he hath a purpose to take order for restitution of the goods aforesaid. There are 5 great vats of sugar, as I take it, without controversy due to your Honour, and, albeit it doth appear by the testimony of some of the *Truelove*, that divers sums of money have been disbursed on provisions for the ship taken, yet it appeareth that divers wines and sugars were taken out in Barbary, and since, to a great value (let Captain Bredcake answer it as he can), and it is thought hard to lay the burden of the charges on the merchants and leave them only their action against Bredcake. I have done my best to give the cause a more convenient end. May I advise that you should signify to the Judge that he proceed no further till you have conferred with Mr 'Carou' [Carew.] Upon speech with whom you may receive more content, and the merchants rest better satisfied.[14]

However, *Truelove* had also taken another undisputed prize worth £1,800, which put the partnership into profit as May reported:

> We took a Brazil man of 160 tons. Her sugars were white and others to the number of 250 chests; and as they were wet and ill-conditioned we carried them for Barbary, where we sold them . . . Since then the *Truelove* has taken another of 120, being a flyboat loaded with Canary sugars and Canary wine, but is Spaniards' goods, which by God's help we will bring for England. In the first prize there were negroes whom the captain sold for £60, and four bags of cotton wool which yielded £30.[15]

Although the voyage was successful, Cecil and Nottingham did not join forces again for the purposes of plunder until 1600 when they commissioned *Lioness*, a stout and well-armed merchant vessel to sail on a voyage to the Mediterranean. The Lord Admiral was very aware that such a venture ran contrary to his official duties, and he was keen to disguise the true nature of Captain Troughton's mission, as he explained to Cecil in November:

> I have signed both the commission and the articles, which are very well set down. It were not amiss if there were an article that if Captain Troughton should chance to meet in any place on the seas any of the ships belonging to the State of Venice, Genoa, or any of the subjects of the Duke of Florence, to give them notice to what end he is sent, for the taking of such fugitive pirates as frequent those seas, and trouble her Majesty's good friends' subjects; this will sound amongst them well and cut off slander if they hear of such a ship, a man-of-war, in those seas.[16]

They were certainly very dangerous waters as even English pirates were discovering. In the February before *Lioness* sailed, the pasha of Algiers wrote to Constantinople that he had arrested some Englishmen whose two ships had seized a Venetian trader and then burnt her in harbour when their right of ownership was disputed. The pasha was afeared that 'the English Ambassador in Constantinople may extract an order to the consul here to hand the goods over to the English.' However, by return the pasha was told to 'restore the merchandize to the Venetians, to give them one of the two English ships, and to punish the pirates. Even if the English should obtain an order for their release they are not to be released.'[17]

Lioness was also sailing with letters of reprisal into waters where few legitimate targets plied. Indeed, some English pirates, hoping for favours from the English ambassador in Constantinople, fled on discovering that he had orders from the queen to arrest them and send them to England. His Venetian counterpart, on challenging the ambassador, Henry Lello, to demonstrate his good faith, was told that:

> The Queen had no intention to molest Venetian shipping, and goods and persons on board should be secure as in a moveable fortress. She had accordingly given orders that privateers should only cruise outside Gibraltar and not in these waters. The Ambassador remained firm in his view that he could not surrender Spanish goods captured in Venetian bottoms as all that belonged to the Lord High Admiral.

Furthermore, the ambassador had ordered the dismissal and arrest of the English consul in Patras because he had taken a share in the booty captured by the pirates. In the absence of a consular official in Patras, a merchant, Matthew Stocker, had been ordered by the Privy Council 'to seize the captains, masters, and officers, as well as goods of all privateers that come into this harbour, because her Majesty is greatly annoyed at hearing that insults have been offered to her allies.' It was a task that Stocker felt he could not undertake as the Turkish cadi in residence was in cahoots with the pirates, and 'well prepared to release any that were captured on payment of the appropriate bribe.'[18]

It thus becomes apparent that either two of the queen's most senior ministers were acting contrary to her wishes or, knowing of their activities, she was still prepared to issue letters confounding those acts in which she knew they were involved. Either way, it indicates that pirateering now infected the very marrow of the state, the constant involvement by Lello in such matters being a clear indication as to how much piratical activity was taking place within the Mediterranean at the expense of Venice.[19]

The *Lioness* voyage brought Cecil a handsome profit of £6,000, although there is an indication that even this venture was open to scrutiny, for in April 1601 Nottingham, Thomas Howard and Lord Cobham, three of the four investors, issued a bond to indemnify Cecil, the fourth, for any portion of the goods which might be recovered from them.[20]

The successful foray into the Mediterranean encouraged Cecil and Nottingham to organise a further expedition to those waters, for which they deployed Nottingham's own 100-ton pinnace, *Lion's Whelp*, and the 300-ton *Marigold*, both of which appear to have been nominally hired, and thus fitted out, by the Crown. By October 1601 the voyage was underway, although Captain Charles Leigh was writing to his sponsors to complain of the delays caused by adverse weather in the Thames estuary. Leigh might also not have possessed a pirateering marrow for he went on to write that:

I have considered of his directions for the Straits, and I find that I must run four hundred leagues within the Straits' mouth unto the island of Gozo and to the South west end of Sicily, where, if we miss at Barcelona, we are to expect the hope of our voyage. Likewise, I am informed by my pilot that Sicily as well as Spain useth a great trade for Alexandria and other parts in the bottom of the Straits, carrying and returning rich commodities and in great vessels. Moreover, if I spend my time about that island and should want victuals, I must run to Zante or to Patras to seek relief, which is above 100 leagues further. Wherefore I beseech you that I may be supplied in Plymouth with six weeks' or two months' victuals more, which I shall need for the better performance of the voyage. Let me be thoroughly provided and then if I do not, with God's help, return home your charges to your desired profits, let me be accounted unworthy of the least part of your favour.[21]

It was to be mid January before Leigh reported taking his first and perhaps only prize, a flyboat of Hamburg, although he did report that he was setting off to Candy (Khania in Crete) in pursuit of an English pirate ship that had robbed a ship from Genoa of 4,500 pieces of eight.[22] It is obvious that Leigh and his fellow captain, Norris, had some doubts as to whether their solitary prize was legitimate, for they enclosed lengthy 'Reasons to prove the *Salvator*, of Hamburg, to be lawful prize.' These ranged from the fact that when 'she was summoned sundry times by all fair means to take in her flag and to strike her topsails to her Majesty's ship, and persuaded for the space of an hour together to submit unto her Majesty's forces, yet she did still in contempt wear her flag, keep up her topsails, and stand on her guard, and in the end made all the resistance by force of arms she could'. This was a most understandable reaction by any merchant ship in pirate-infested waters, but Leigh made an even lamer justification for his action, stating that the ship hailed from Hamburg, 'where many Spanish merchants are resident', a pretty poor excuse. After continuing in the same vein, the captains concluded that, whatever the strength of other justification, the goods 'ought to be confiscated, because the ship did not only deny to obey her Majesty's commission, but maintained fight against her ships and authority.'

Shortly afterwards, the two captains decided to disobey their own instructions to patrol the sea around Candy, and sailed for the Straits of Messina and a less risky life. Thus although dispatched 'for the apprehending of such English pirates as do impeach the quiet trade of her Majesty's friends in the Levant Seas', they stated that:

> to lie near Candy, as we are enjoined by our commission, would be most dangerous for us, by reason the state of Venice, pretending to be admiral of these seas, adherent to their own dominions which they account their chamber, have armed out two great galleasses and certain galleys to free the same coast from all men-of-war whatsoever, and especially from Maltezians and Spaniards and their neighbours and friends; who, lying to the eastward of Candy in course against the Turks, have offended the state of Venice by robbing some of their ships, so as for us to encounter with that Venetian armado can by no means be for the good of the journey.[23]

Such concerns well illustrate the ambiguity in their mission, for the Venetians were hardly likely to interfere with the ship of a friendly nation carrying out an anti-piracy patrol. The captains provided other reasons to head west, stating that if they remained on station 'we should not only incur extreme danger, but almost an impossibility of safety if the furious nor'west winds, which in these countries are called "mostrales", should take us and drive us upon that coast, where we have no harbour to friend but only Alexandria.' Finally, after complaining about the availability of victuals they concluded that 'the ship being unsheathed and the bottom of the Straits much subject to worms, it is to be doubted that the ship may be so spoiled with them, that she would not be able afterwards to carry us for England.'[24] Luckily for England she had many a mariner made of sterner stuff.

Cecil, however, had other maritime interests for, thanks to the good offices of William Stallenge, he stood to benefit from some pirateering voyages being undertaken by Sir John Gilbert, who retained the family tradition of sailing a little too close to the illegal wind. In 1597 he was asking for Cecil to intervene on his behalf over a problem with the legitimacy of a cargo that he had seized, claiming that:

> I have now sent unto the Lord Admiral the Spanish letters, with my reasons for thinking the Fleming to be a prize. These are, first, that the skipper has no

sufficient commission for his voyage, for in that which he has erased the name of the ship and the date; that he brought over a factor for some of Antwerp and promised to carry him and his lading back to Spain, saying that he would go only to Bayonne and that to escape the English fleet; that he had letters from Spaniards for Spain with intelligence of the return of our fleet shattered and their intention to go for the Islands; that he flung his letters overboard; that he forsook his company and ran aboard the coast of France to shun our ships; that he carried into Spain brass, lead, and other contraband of war; that the company admits most of the goods are Spanish; this are some of my reasons. My charge in this voyage has been nearly £100 and I shall think myself unhappy if so good a means to save myself be wrested from me.[25]

Gilbert, the possessor by his own admission of a 'choleric nature', caused his patrons endless problems, principally by an enduring feud with the mayor of Plymouth and a desire to make money on whatever venture he was entrusted to perform. Neither was he beyond trying the occasional knavish trick once ashore, as Stallenge informed Cecil:

There were certain parcels of goods brought home in his [Gilbert's] prize that, as he said, were claimed by the Flemings, which he promised should remain unseen until the rest were all divided. But in my absence he caused the said goods to be removed into another cellar, where, as he saith, there hath been stolen out more than £200 worth of silks and other things; but the general opinion is, himself, and others by his direction, have done it, and for my own part, I think no less, considering there was no cause to remove them from the cellars wherein they were first placed by themselves. It may be you shall understand thereof by other means, and therefore I have thought it my duty to write my opinion therein.[26]

Stallenge appears to have had the measure of Gilbert, writing to Cecil in October 1601, having just waved Leigh goodbye, that:

I have now ended viewing the goods of the carvel brought in by Sir John Gilbert's ship . . . We are now to view the fly boat, where I doubt there will be much goods found wanting, if the purser's book with such 'cargazo' and letters as are in the hands of Sir John Gilbert might be seen; for between her two decks where commonly the best things are laid, there was nothing left. Sir John Gilbert protesteth very deeply that himself nor any for him hath had to the value of £5 of the said prize goods, so that what is done must needs be by the captains and companies of the men-of-war. If your waiters at London do make good search, as well by sea as by land, there may be found such things as have escaped from these parts.[27]

Stallenge was, however, aware that his position required him to be seen to be an honest broker, even while acting to benefit the Lord Admiral and Cecil. He therefore wrote to them suggesting that to avoid disputed goods disappearing, 'It would be well if the chief officers of every port were ordered to detain doubtful prizes until due process can be made.'[28]

This was not going to be possible when the interests of his patrons ran contrary to those of natural justice, as a petition from the Merchant Strangers to the Privy Council in 1597 clearly showed. Their interest lay in the recovery of a cargo of sugar being carried by *Maria of Middleburgh* which had been:

> Lately taken at sea by Sir John Gilbert, knight, and a ship of Mr Richard Drake's, Esq, and others, and brought to Dartmouth. The said knight and Mr Drake, before petitioners had knowledge of the taking of the said ship and goods, have obtained a sentence in her Majesty's High Court of Admiralty and thereby gotten possession of the same into their own hands and dispose thereof at their pleasure, so that petitioners are void of remedy for seizing or arresting their own goods daily seen before their eyes to the value of £9,000.[29]

Others sought Cecil's support when their own ventures risked too close an investigation. In September 1601 Richard Gifford was writing to Cecil for support, seeing that:

> You have been informed that I committed great abuses at sea in taking certain ships of Marseilles laden with silks, nutmeg and indigo. I protest, what I did is as follows. I took a small bark of Olon under a castle by Malaga in Spain, being the enemy's and bound to Flanders. Secondly, I took a ship of Rusco, from which I had 9 packs of coarse linen cloth and boults of tuffed canvas, for I demanded to see their charter party, bills of lading and letters, and the answer was that they had neither, notwithstanding which I suffered the ship to depart with the rest of her lading. Thirdly, I took a ship of Majorca bound for Napoli laden with salt, oil and blankets. More, I met with a flyboat of Amsterdam before I came to the Straits, which lay adrift in the sea with only 6 men and 2 boys in her. I bought it of the shipper whom I left in my own ship. With this ship I then went to Algiers, and there did lade all my oils, which was done of purpose to come for England with them in company of the *Marigould*, but owing to extreme foul weather, I lost sight of her, and thought it best to go to Leghorn and put the goods in safety. The ship of Majorca I was constrained to leave at Algiers, in regard of trouble pretended against my goods and Captain Leigh's, who was then there, by reason of a ship taken by the *John and Francis* of London, wherein the king of Algiers and other Turks were interested. To avoid which trouble, I went in the night with my own ship and the flyboat out of command of the castle, whereupon they offered me all courteous usage. This is all I have done since being at sea, and if anything has been done by my ship since my departure from her, I know not thereof.[30]

Gifford also included a summary of his balance sheet which showed that he had made a loss on trade goods sold of £125 and paid his crew £550 while his profit was based on 'reprisals' worth £2,129 and a sale of salt worth £181, leaving him £2,620 the richer, not a negligible return, but one earned after a great deal of work at sea.[31] It was certainly not enough money to involve Cecil in any intervention on Gifford's behalf, so it must be suspected that there were some favours to be returned, possibly resulting from Gifford's meeting with Leigh in Algeria.

Back at Plymouth, Stallenge continued acting on Cecil's behalf, informing him that November that:

> In my last I certified what silks were found in the carvel, for the 20th part whereof I have taken 5 yards of velvet and 5 yards of satin, being so much in value as is due for the whole at an indifferent rate. On Saturday last were viewed 17 chests of the flyboat, and therein among other goods were found 29 pieces of tafty wrought and plain, 5 pieces of calikoo lawn, and some quantity of sewing and raw silk. I hope in the chests yet to open will be found more store of those commodities. In the meantime let me understand whether the 20th part thereof shall be sent up or sold here.[32]

Occasionally matters got out of hand and the commissioners appointed to survey the prizes were forced to protest to Cecil, as in November 1601 after they had:

> Sent for the masters of the supposed prizes. From one of them we have received certain boxes, bags, and small bundles of pearls and stones, besides by examination of three of the masters confession of great spoils and abuses offered, and to whose hands most of the spoils of money, pearls and stones came: We, missing one of the masters, demanded where he was. Sir Robert Mansell's man answered that Sir Robert had taken him from the rest, but where he was he knew not. A Dutchman, one Peter Michelson, standing by, said he knew where he was, at Westminster in the keeping of one of the yeomen of the guard; whereupon we sent the bearer with the Dutchman and a man of Mr Middelton's, with our warrant to bring them before us to be examined. But they were not only denied to have him but kept prisoners all night by the yeoman of the guard, the Dutchman beaten and not suffered to send anybody to Mr Secretary or to any other, our warrant made no account of, nor would look upon the warrant. If this be not remedied, but this disorder offered by her Majesty's servants against her commandments, in vain shall we be employed in this service. We therefore pray reformation hereof. Some of us are going on board the ships, the rest occupied in examining the rest of the masters, else had we waited on your Lordship.[33]

Even Stallenge found himself occasionally requiring an intervention from Cecil writing to his patron in 1601 that:

> I have received from your Honours a letter concerning one Abbycock Perrye, a mariner, who has complained that I did borrow of him in ready money, when I was in want, being the chiefest portion he hath to live on. I do remember such a

man, boatswain of the *Garland* in the Island journey, that had got by pillaging of a small Spanish frigate two pillow-beres full of 'Scottgineall,' which we sunk. He not daring to carry it ashore, made means it might be put into my trunk, and desired me to cause one of my men to sell it and keep the money for him. Accordingly, I had it sold to one Brown, a merchant, for £60, and because he said it was better worth, I gave him my bill for £80. Since which time he never asked me for any money, and hearing that he was condemned for felony and burned in the hand, I did not know whether it was fit for me without demand to pay the money to him, being a convicted man. But now I will be ready to do your pleasure herein, if I may hear of him.

Both Cecil's own papers and the State Papers for the last few years of Elizabeth's reign are full of such incidents. They provide an unmissable conclusion that every aspect of the prize war, from the issue of letters of reprisal to the actual capture of prizes and the disposal of goods, was exercised in favour of those wielding power and to the detriment of the many with legitimate grievances, but little authority. The fact that Spanish and Portuguese vessels, and the occasional French Catholic freight, were really the only legitimate prizes for the marauding English to take did not prevent even privy councillors from benefiting from the seizures of neutral shipping. When aggrieved merchants did protest, the lengthy, expensive and convoluted hearings to which they were subject at the Court of Admiralty make that august authority a worthy predecessor of Charles Dickens's High Court of Chancery.

Of all the neutral nations it was Venice that suffered the most and the longest, a fact of which Shakespeare must have been well aware when writing *The Merchant of Venice* in 1596. The deprivations by English pirates led to the state appointing Giovanni Carlo Scaramelli as secretary to Elizabeth's court where he arrived just in time to exchange pleasantries with the frail monarch before she expired. With James desiring both peace and an end to piracy, Scaramelli might well have considered his work to be done before he had begun, but it was not so.

For, with the outbreak of peace, the triumvirate continued to manipulate maritime law to their own advantage, which they needed to do if they were to maintain the comfortable standard of living to which their earnings had made them accustomed. And if they could not be further enriched by piracy, then corruption was necessary to take its place as a nice little earner.

This was the tragedy of the rule of the triumvirate, not that they succeeded in practising malfeasance, but that they allowed such malfeasance to become acceptable, to the detriment of naval administration and operations for generations to come. Even the wise and reforming James found his position weakened by their activities, but he had also the reputation of a much loved and missed queen against which to contend, and she had done much to encourage the irascible behaviour of her closest advisers.

CHAPTER 11

Disturbing the World

The English through their rapacity and cruelty have become odious to all nations. With Spain they are at open war and are already plundering her and upsetting the India trade; they are continually robbing with violence the French, whom they encounter on the long stretches of the open sea. They cannot sail at present to Poland and Prussia, because the Danish Straits are blocked against them. In Germany, at Hamburg, Lubeck, and other ports, for example, they are detested. . .The Venetians have suffered in the same way . . . inside the Straits of Gibraltar, . . . under the guise of merchants they plunder in the very vitals of foreign dominions all the shipping they find. Hence both those who command, and those who execute here in England, see quite clearly how great, how universal, and how just is the hatred which all nations, nay all peoples we might say, bear to the English, for they are the disturbers of the whole world.

Giovanni Carlo Scaramelli, Venetian Secretary in London,
to Doge and Senate, 20 March 1603

Throughout Elizabeth's reign, like a murder of magpies patrolling border hedgerows for fledglings, a plague of pirates persecuted any merchant vessels passing close to the English coast, regardless of their nationality. Yet another group migrated to warmer waters, where wealthier prey could be found, and returned richly laden, leaving a well-deserved national notoriety in their wake as the Venetian ambassador reported above.

Faced with these two very different forms of piracy, domestic and international, Elizabeth dealt with them in two very different ways, based upon how they affected her subjects and her exchequer. Most of the evidence from public records indicates that she was determined to use the full force of the law to eradicate the scourge of piracy from English waters and to summon those who were found to favour such activities to answer for their behaviour. She had little choice for, as the Venetian ambassador to France observed in 1563, 'in the seas of Flanders, France, and England, thousands of acts of piracy are committed; and trade there is quite interrupted.'[1]

So in 1565, after an extended session with her privy councillors, Elizabeth issued detailed instructions to all officials in coastal counties requiring them to act against 'divers evil disposed persons . . . [who] have of late in sundry vessels and ships frequented the seas upon the coast . . . robbing and spoiling honest quiet merchants, both our own subjects and of other princes being presently in league and amity with us.'[2] She also made it clear that she realised that such pirates could not be acting alone, but were being 'secretly refreshed' and supported to the 'manifest contempt of us and our laws . . . by many a dweller in the havens, creeks and landing places of this our realm.' To counter this infestation, Elizabeth named commissioners, who in turn were directed to appoint deputies, so that every possible landing place in the country came under their watchful gaze at least every month. Moreover, a survey, Domesday-like in its thoroughness, was ordered of all landing places and the habitations close by. The survey was also to include an inventory of the name, tonnage, trade, ownership and manning of every vessel working out of these ports. To discourage illegal trading, a list of prohibited exports, most especially grain in famine-frequent England, was produced, while all goods brought into the country had to be declared before sale. In addition, no unusual victualling activity could be arranged without the express permission of the commissioner or his deputies: most pertinently, no armament or munitions were to be provided to any ship, beyond that it was reasonable for her to carry for self-defence.

It was an impressive order, and if it had been executed with more than a little enthusiasm in the relevant counties, it would have had a most deleterious effect on the pirate community and its supporters. The trouble was, those supporters could earn themselves a more comfortable life aiding and abetting their local miscreants than they ever could by enforcing acts imposed from far away London. Faced with such widespread disregard of her orders, Elizabeth issued another series of instructions for the suppression of piracy during the late 1570s. The foremost of these was the appointment of new commissioners in September 1577, who were given detailed instructions as how to repress piracy. Each commissioner was required to survey the ports and creeks in his area, and also to appoint deputies so that the entire coast could come under surveillance and suspicious activities be investigated. In addition, an attempt was made to regulate outgoing shipping, so that only those involved in trade or fishing were licensed to depart.

Also in September 1577, a list was produced of the 'Names of certain persons in various ports who have been dealers with pirates; and upon whom warrants have been served for their appearance',[3] while in October the government issued a list of 'the Commissioners appointed in divers shires on the seacoasts to inquire of such as within five years past have set forth ships to the seas in warlike sort; and likewise to examine who have been favourers, abettors, and assisters of pirates.'[4]

The results, if the documentation is to be believed, were impressive – initially (Appendix 10) – but yet again, laudable ambition failed when faced with local, bribable interests. A report by a commissioner about the impediments around

Lulworth Cove in Dorset serves well to illustrate the problem. In it, Walsingham was informed that:

> such persons as we send for and would have them to be our deputies about Lulworth either they must be sick, either from home at London or Exeter, or taken some fall that they cannot, may not or dare not come before us to do their duty . . .[5]

Not all pirates were immune from prosecution: many were seized, tried and condemned. Some, such as Thomas Walton (aka Purser) and Clinton Atkinson, captured by William Borough, and hanged with seven others on 30 August 1583, arrived at the gallows in flamboyant finery and made defiant scaffold speeches. Others, such as John Callice, gained notoriety for flouting authority and flaunting his outlaw status, even highlighting the hypocrisy of local officials who condemned as criminals those whose ill-gotten gains decorated their dining halls. Indeed, Callice himself was pardoned on condition that he turned pirate-hunter, his acquired knowledge being considered to be worth several ships and an investment of over £20,000 by the queen. However, having accepted the pardon, Callice ignored the conditions and resumed his old career. Yet even Callice was, like most of his fellows, a piratical journeyman content to 'live and die a pirate-king'. Others saw that the opportunity for greater reward lay further offshore and in foreign hulls.

As far as the robbery from these vessels was concerned, it might be expected that the queen considered that her role was to placate, mollify, soothe, in a statesmanlike manner, and order release, restitution and recompense for wronged and innocent merchants, especially those with whose nation England was in amity. The evidence indicates otherwise, and as her reign grew longer, and the returns from overseas crime grew richer, so she gained the confidence to flout international sensitivities, a position abetted by her growing realisation as to how much she depended on foreign booty to keep her regime in business.

Fleecing her Foes

Elizabeth began her reign by taking placatory steps towards Spain. Between 1561 and 1564 she issued five proclamations against those attacking Spanish and Flemish shipping.[6] In 1564 another set of commissioners were appointed to hear and settle rapidly complaints from Philip's subjects. In addition, officials were directed to arrest anyone suspected of preying on Spanish or Flemish shipping. These initiatives did much to impress and placate the Spanish ambassador, Guzmán de Silva, who reported that the queen had 'issued very good regulations which were much needed and if they are carried out, as they appear likely to be, will be of great benefit.'[7]

De Silva, and his successor, Guerau de Spes, along with their fellow ambassador from Portugal, were soon disabused, for evidence that the queen might wield a big stick but fail to chastise became apparent, following Hawkins's voyage to the African coast in 1567 to seize slaves for onward passage to the Spanish Indies. As a result of his spoliations the Portuguese ambassador submitted claims for some 70,000 ducats in damages.

In response, Elizabeth exercised her growing skill at countering one claim with several of her own. In May 1568 she replied to the Portuguese demands, which included a desire to see English traders banned from Guinea, that not only did she deny the right of the king of Portugal to make laws binding on her subjects but that the ambassador's demand that John Hawkins should be tried *in absentia* was contrary to laws both divine and human. As for the compensation, ignoring the whole basis of which the international system of letters of reprisal was founded, she stated that it was unreasonable to hold her responsible for the faults of her subjects. As befitted her station she was, of course, diplomatic, stating in a note to King Sebastian of Portugal that she trusted 'that the ancient amity subsisting between their realms may not receive any injury', and promised redress by due course of justice to any of his subjects who suffered wrongs inflicted through any of hers.[8]

The queen's subtlety could be applied evenly.[9] Although she refused to grant Hawkins letters of reprisal to cover his exaggerated loss following his defeat at San Juan de Ulua in 1568, she was not prepared either to admit his guilt in disregarding treaties, seizing ships, plundering and burning towns, and slave-trading. Part of her reason was that she did not wish to harm further the strained Anglo–Portuguese friendship but, more importantly, she had more pressing reasons to sideline Hawkins.

For, while the claims and counter-claims were proceeding, Elizabeth was faced with both an opportunity and a dilemma, blown her way by the strong westerly winds of November 1568. In that foul weather a squadron of supply vessels heading from Spain for the Low Countries was forced to seek shelter from both the weather and Huguenot pirates in Plymouth and Southampton. De Spes stated that on finding that these ships were in danger, he called on the queen and, telling her that they contained the money needed to pay Alba's great army in the Netherlands, asked that the wages might be transported over land and under escort to Dover.[10] To this the queen agreed. Meanwhile, in Plymouth and Southampton the ships had been boarded and searched, and a great quantity of gold had been discovered which was taken ashore for safe keeping. This would not have been regarded as too cynical a ploy (William Wynter had already been forced to intervene to prevent the corsairs from boarding the sheltering ships, refusing their offer of a bribe of ten chests of money if he did but 'wink' at their approach), had not the authorities also removed all the sails and apparel as well.[11]

It was then discovered that the gold was not, technically, Philip's, but had been loaned to him by Italian merchants at a rate of 10 per cent, terms which Elizabeth felt sure she could better. The money, some £85,000 (£11.4m), was placed within the safety of the Tower, while negotiations got underway. De Spes sought an audience, but was now rebuffed, while the transports he had been promised failed to appear. Elizabeth was playing with the ambassador, knowing that he was in no position to reclaim the gold which was, morally, Spanish. All the frustrated Spanish ambassador could do was to rave impotently, while suggesting to his king, in March 1571, countermeasures for which:

> the road is now clear and open, we are prompted to take it by the wickedness, thefts and knavery of these pirates; all of whom were armed here, sell their booty here, draw their crews from here, and here obtain all they need for their evil deeds.[12]

Although the ambassador also forwarded that same month a document in which the queen had laid down five clauses, 'touching the irregularities on the Sea Coast', which proclaimed:

> 1. That no pirate of whatever nation shall enter any of her ports or the Downs, under penalty of losing the ship which he brings, and imprisonment for himself.
> 2. That no subject of the Queen, or other inhabitant of her realm, shall send or supply any victuals or stores of any sort to the said pirates, and shall not receive goods from them, or deal with them directly or indirectly.
> 3. That it is the Queen's will that these clauses shall be obeyed, and that any infraction of them shall be punished by the arrest of the offenders by the Governors of the ports, to be held until further orders from the Queen and Council.
> 4. That any person found culpable, after the publication of this, shall be punished as a disturber of the Queen's peace.
> 5. That any subject of the Queen who may have offended in this way, and will make confession of the same, and declare those whom he knows to be guilty, shall be himself pardoned.[13]

It was not long before De Spes was reporting how ineffectual or blatantly ignored were most of these articles. In the August following their issue, he was telling Philip that:

> The guns from the castle and ramparts of Dover had prevented the Flemish ships from taking the twenty-four pirate vessels which were there . . . The assertions made at Court that the pirates would be arrested is not true, and the reply which Lord Burghley gave to the Secretary, whom I had sent to complain to the Council of this insult, was that formerly Don Alvaro de Bazan had done the same thing in defending certain French vessels against the English.[14]

De Spes also implied that the queen would not return Alba's gold for at least another seven years. In response, the ambassador suggested that the Spanish seize eight ships that would be carrying 'great riches' to Hamburg.

The ambassador was justified in his anger. In a long letter to his king he reported that the pirates sheltering at Dover:

come on shore with impunity every day. They have enriched that place, the Isle of Wight, and nearly all the coast. The crews are, generally speaking, men of inferior class . . . not a ship sails that they do not know the hour of her leaving and her point of departure.

The ambassador also wrote of the supposed willingness of John Hawkins to abandon England to serve Spain, and that one of the tasks that he could be given would be to man ships 'with a very few men and filling them up with others chosen by your Majesty, and the least of these services will be to catch the pirates who infest the Channel which he considers very easy.'[15]

On 1 March 1572 Elizabeth, either to appease the Spanish or in an act of incredible prescience, or both, banned the Dutch pirates – 'the Sea Beggars' – from her realm. Departing Dover, they, under their leader La Marck, sailed to the small port of Brill in the Netherlands where they re-formed to continue their piratical anti-Spanish behaviour, repulsing every attempt by Spanish forces to capture this new stronghold.

At this time it would be wrong to accuse Elizabeth of complete disingenuous dissimulation, but only because she had yet to be made aware of what a valuable commodity she possessed in her own, still leashed, sea wolves. Incidents such as the seizure of Alba's gold were serendipitous, offering unforeseen opportunities to embarrass and benefit from Spanish discomfiture. Given such disorganised, sporadic behaviour, she was able to protest both her innocence and impotence when faced with the disgruntlements of mere merchants. Soon, her involvement would become more open and less defensible.

Elizabeth's fickle foreign policy frustrated friend and foe alike. In 1574 she, along with many of her merchants, wished to establish peaceful dealings with Spain. That August she ventured as far as Bristol to celebrate the signing there of a convention with Spain in which the English agreed to return Alba's gold and to no longer issue letters of reprisal to English seamen authorising the seizure of Spanish vessels. Amongst much joviality and present-giving to their courtly visitors, the city fathers made a strong case as to how much benefit peaceful trade brought to Bristol.[16]

On the practical side, as well as the return of the gold, both countries also agreed not to interfere with the rights of their visiting seamen and merchants, and to discourage piracy against each other's vessels. It was an agreement destined to be broken, rapidly, widely and completely and, if not blatantly, then by subtle interpretation, as a report of the commissioners appointed to enquire into the question of compensation to Spanish subjects made clear:

By Article 5 of the treaty of Bristol, the actions and rights of all ships' goods etc not specified in a schedule mentioned in that article are reserved to the subjects of the King of Spain against the subjects of her Majesty, by whom their goods are detained, or they are damnified. And by Article 7 it is agreed that justice shall be ministered summarily to the subjects of both princes, and those lawfully appointed by them to sue. It is requisite both by the said treaty, and by the order of the law, that such as make demands against her Majesty's subjects either in an ordinary court of law or before special commissioners shall exhibit sufficient procuration and authority from the proprietors interested in the thing reserved, to sue and recover the same; otherwise neither can the process be 'viable' in law, nor would her Majesty's subjects, if they should satisfy the ambassador or any other not so authorized, be discharged as against the true proprietors, but may be 'eftsoons' charged, either in this realm or in the King of Spain's dominions, for the same. And whereas above the value of £100,000 has been already restored or satisfied by way of compensation to the King's subjects, it is necessary that such as sue for the things reserved by the treaty shall specify the things for which they make suit and not intermix them with the things for which compensation has been made and a discharge given.[17]

The farce of flouted authority continued, while squabbling with Portugal and Spain over piracy became the weft and warp of Elizabethan maritime policy.

Two years later, in October 1576, the queen signed a treaty with Portugal whereby there would be:

[a] suspension of all arrests and letters of marque for the period of three years from 15 November 1576, and an agreement to the appointment of commissioners to determine all matters in controversy concerning the mutual traffic between the countries and dominions of the Queen of England and those of the King of Portugal, and also providing for the more effectual suppression of piracy.[18]

Instead of heralding a period of piratical suppression, it was only two years later that the Spanish ambassador reported that:

English pirates continue to capture the property of Spanish merchants every day, and the merchants send powers to their agents resident here to recover the goods. For this purpose and their own gain they come to terms with the pirates, the owners despairing of any other course. This is a direct incentive to the pirates, because when your Majesty's representatives request that the pirates should be punished, they are told there is no one to complain of them, as they have come to terms. It would be therefore advisable to order that no subject of yours should demand his property from the pirates, except through your representative, as otherwise it is certain that they will never cease their depredations, knowing that, happen what may, they will be left in possession of a great part of their booty.[19]

In December 1579 the latest Spanish ambassador, Bernardino de Mendoza, was reporting just how the English, claiming to follow the letter of the law, could still flout its purpose:

I handed your Majesty's letter of 11 April, about the seizures, to the Queen on the 10th of May, and she, in conformity there with and in fulfilment of the treaty of Bristol, ordered a commission to be issued, that your Majesty's subjects might claim their property, which by fraud and deceit had been concealed. The issue of this commission was delayed from day to day for two months, until the vacations, so that nothing could be done until the middle of October. I lodged a request with the commissioners that they should hear my claims, which they did, acknowledging your Majesty as Plaintiff, and I then demanded that the offenders should be brought up. They summoned them and gave them copies of my charges, which, in due course, were replied to, and the case proceeded with. When the decision was to be given, the commissioners informed my lawyers that they were not to present any more documents, since the property could not be claimed by your Majesty but only by the owners. I therefore addressed the Council, saying I was astonished, after they had seen your Majesty's letter, and the Queen had issued the commission and the commissioners had heard my claim, by virtue of such appointment, that when sentence had to be delivered this answer should be given. I desired to know if the agreement of Bristol was valid or not. They replied in general that they knew nothing of the commission, nor when it was issued, but they would make inquiries and give a reply. They did so a month afterwards, and, after recapitulating many of the pros and cons of the case, they said that the goods could not be demanded in your Majesty's name.

Mendoza, impotently, and in anticipation of the much heralded triumphant return of Drake from his circumnavigation, realised that:

The design of them all is to make profit in any possible way, and when they say they will do justice it is only with this object. I presented proofs that Knollys, a kinsman of the Queen, had taken a Spanish ship and put his plunder in one of the Queen's castles, where he sold it, and they told me that when this was established, they would have the property returned to the merchants; and yet afterwards they said it was necessary to prove the facts again, with the sole object of frightening away the witnesses, and making this an excuse for keeping the property. As the councillors themselves are the principal supporters of the pirates they have anticipated the arrival of Drake by appointing men in every port in England to assist him in concealing his booty, if he arrives safely with it.[20]

He did, and his reception was just as Mendoza had forecast. Just how much of a game-changer Drake's return from his circumnavigation with *Golden Hind* ballasted with bullion was can be best illustrated by comparing his reception with the one which John Wynter received when he returned prematurely from that same voyage a year earlier, having abandoned Drake in the Straits of Magellan and brought his command, *Elizabeth*, back to England in June 1579. Here he was faced with several dilemmas: first, he had to justify his decision to abandon his leader; secondly, he had to explain from whence came the low-valued prize cargo in the hold of *Elizabeth*, while, thirdly, ensuring he received no blame for its seizure from the Portuguese.

The expedition's sponsors were eager to sell Wynter's goods to recoup some of their investment. However, there was another claimant, the Portuguese ambassador, Don Antonio de Castillo, acting for the owners of the *Santa Maria*, one of the vessels that had been seized. The case was put before the Court of Admiralty where Wynter tried to put as much distance as it was possible for a captain to place between himself and the goods in his own ship's hold, stating in his evidence that:

> The taking of the ship . . . was utterly contrary to my good will which I could not let nor gainsay, for that I had no authority there, but such as pleased the said Drake . . . And now that I am come to a place of Justice I do here declare . . . that I did never give my consent or allowance anyway to the taking of any ship or goods unlawfully . . .[21]

Given Wynter's reluctance to soil his hands with the goods, and Don Antonio's desire to repossess them, along with the government's wish to remain on friendly terms with Portugal, Dr Lewes, the Admiralty judge, declared:

> that if John Wynter would pretend no interest or title to the same, the said ambassador might have the said goods upon caution to save her Majesty, the said Wynter, and other of her highness' subjects harmless against the King of Portugal . . .

Furthermore, Dr Lewes sought permission to instruct Thomas Parker of Bristol, 'in whose hands the said goods do remain to deliver the same . . .'[22]

Precious little of the original cargo remained accessible at this time but it is worth noting the items that Wynter recalled as being transferred to his own vessel, for they very much represented, along with the large quantity of wine kept by Drake, the sort of catch that many lesser pirates would consider most acceptable, consisting mainly of canvas, cloth, nets and knives, the intrinsic value of which was not great, but to a ship's company on a long voyage they were a godsend, as Wynter admitted:

> Because our sails through long being at sea, were almost utterly decayed we were constrained for saving of the ship, and our lives, to make with the said canvas a new main top sail, a drabler for the main course beside cross binding of all our old sails and parceling of the gunroom with other places of the ship.

He also used canvas to construct an awning to shade his deck for his crew, whose worn-out clothing he also replaced from captured cloth. He then used some more canvas to make sails for a pinnace, which had been assembled using the captured nails.

But it had not stopped there. With kindness and largesse, Wynter had handed out cloth to 'poor men', 'holy Fathers', and an Englishman dwelling at St Vincent. Finally, he stated, that further inspection had shown the remaining canvas had been 'spoiled with mice and rats'. Given his willingness to distribute that which was sound, his defence that he was the unwilling recipient of stolen goods must have looked a bit thin.

The Admiralty Court could afford to be even-handed with John Wynter's loot, for it was of little value when compared with keeping on friendly terms with Portugal, although this necessity disappeared once Philip had taken the Portuguese crown for his own in 1580. What is most significant is that John Wynter ended up in jail, while his one-time commander, and the master-thief, was lionised. This was not the end of the matter for the Wynter family. John's father, George, and uncle, the Clerk of Ships, William, had together bought the grand estate of Dyrham near Bath which was to be left to George's heirs.[23] With John in prison, there was every possibility that the family estate would be forfeited when John came into his inheritance. To guard against this, George's will, drawn up in 1581, left Dyrham to his wife and second son unless and until 'my eldest son shall be by order of law or otherwise thereby acquitted and discharged from all misdemeanors of piracy which is now supposed of him by the Portingales, that hath been committed in the time while he was upon the seas in company with Francis Drake.' A few months after George's death, John was cleared of his crimes and Dyrham became his.

Francis Drake should have endured a similar judicial inquiry by the Admiralty Court into his far richer haul. However, he had returned with so much booty that avarice overwhelmed justice, and the chances of the Spanish receiving any compensation were never likely. Instead, they had to endure a very public humiliation when, on 4 April 1581, following a fine lunch onboard *Golden Hind*, Elizabeth invited the ship's pirate captain to kneel before her and then, passing her sword to the French envoy, the Sieur de Marchaumont, invited him to knight 'the master thief of the unknown world'. With that act, to mix metaphors, she nailed her colours to the pirate mast and indicated her support for all who could deliver significant stolen goods to her treasury. From then on there could be no denying that England was ruled by a pirate queen. The policy of piracy was now in the open as Mendoza indicated, raging in March 1582, that not a day passed without Sir Francis stating that 'he will give the Queen eighty thousand ducats, if she will grant him leave to arm ships to attack your Majesty's convoys.'[24] That leave was not long in coming, although, at first it was concealed and caveated.

In 1585 Drake was permitted to sail on a joint-stock expedition primarily to secure the release of English ships stayed at Spanish ports, after which he was granted leave to go plundering and prize-taking across the Atlantic, provided he was content that his queen could 'disavow him'.

The queen's caution continued. Even after she had moved from being a receiver of stolen goods to an open investor in piratical enterprises, she was conscious of her reputation. So in 1587, when Drake was dispatched to raid those Spanish ports where the Armada was being fitted out, the Queen acted cannily in an attempt to avoid her fingerprints being found on the wrong-doing weapon. She contributed just three ships and two pinnaces to the force of twenty-three vessels, but could not disguise the fact that her arch-pirate was commanding the fleet from the deck of one of her ships, *Elizabeth Bonaventure*. Drake, well aware of what the much greater squadron of merchant ships expected him to deliver, had written that 'whatsoever commodity in goods, money, treasure, merchandise or other benefits shall be taken, by all or any of the aforesaid ships or their company either by land or sea, shall be equally proportioned . . . and will be divided as soon as wind and weather will permit.'[25]

Elizabeth, however, remained uneasy that a descent on a Spanish port led by her ships would, undoubtedly, lead to her being branded a pirate as well as a heretic. She, therefore, sent a note post-haste after Drake, ordering him to:

> Forbear to enter forcibly into any of [King Philip's] ports or havens or to offer violence to any of his towns or shipping within harbours or to do any act of hostility upon land. And yet . . . her pleasure is that you should do your best endeavour to get into your possession such shipping of the said king's . . . as you shall find at sea, either going from thence to the east or West Indies or returning from the said Indies to Spain and such as shall fall into your hands, to bring them into this realm.[26]

In other words, the queen preferred piracy on the high seas to the plunder of ports, although whether from the belief that the former posed less risk to her ships and her reputation, she did not state. Yet the lady protested too much, for the tardy dispatch of the letter ensured that it would not be delivered before Drake had sailed. Nonetheless, it was placed onboard a vessel departing late, but during its voyage south this pursuing pinnace diverted to capture its own prize, worth £5,000 back in Plymouth, after which success the crew might well have forgotten their original mission. Nevertheless, as a mission statement by the leader of a nation not at war, it is a clear indicator of piratical policy.

Frustrating the French

While relations with Spain dominated Elizabeth's foreign policy, her nation had a longer history of disputes with France. In the Channel, these quarrelsome neighbours continually seized each other's vessels, while all the time complaining of each others' piratical acts. In December 1576 the French ambassador wrote to the Privy Council that:

> The Queen promised to him at her last audience that certain ships laden with wines for Picardy and Normandy, which had touched at Rye, should be released. Nevertheless the matters have turned out otherwise, and the merchants have had taken from them 80 tuns of wine.[27]

The following year Roger Poittou, a Norman merchant, complained to the Privy Council that his ship *Pelican*, returning from Newfoundland with fish and oil, had 'been taken and plundered by John Granger, of Plymouth, and three of the mariners killed.' In response to attacks such as this, the queen ordered the barks *Achates* and *Merlin* 'to be set to the seas in warlike manner, for apprehending pirates in the mouth of the river Thames.'[28]

Little else was organised. This lack of a positive response led to the French king himself writing to Elizabeth in January 1578 that:

> Though we make no doubt that the commissioners deputed by you to enquire into the depredations committed by your subjects on ours, yet we would draw your attention to the fact that Guillaume Lefer and his partners, of St Malo, have been long seeking redress for the capture of their vessel *le Saulveur* by the English ship *Castle of Comfort* in May 1575; neither our letters in their behalf nor their own suit having so far profited them.[29]

Given the proximity of their long coastlines and their seamen's shared proclivity towards piracy, it is not surprising how many accusations and counter-charges of maritime misdemeanours were ferried across the Channel, only to be ignored or disdained. Even official, or semi-official, envoys, felt unsafe in these waters. In December 1584 Segur-Pardeilhan, the king of Navarre's envoy, informed Walsingham from Southampton that his return home was delayed because:

> I cannot find a single armed vessel, only passage boats from the islands and some poor little ships. I have been warned from a good source that notice of my going has been given to the pirates, of which there are many near here, and they have been led to believe that I had a great quantity of money and of rings with me, in order to increase their zeal in taking me. That, and the contrary wind, keeps me here and I must tell you frankly that I think I ought to be given the means to cross safely to France.[30]

Afraid of pirates the beached legate might have been, but he was not afeard of giving Walsingham advice, telling the Secretary, shortly before he dashed down to Plymouth to make his crossing, that:

> The mouth of this harbour is so well guarded by the pirates that yesterday a Jersey passage boat, wishing to put to sea, was attacked and obliged to come back into the river. I could not have chosen a worse place to embark, for most of the pirates of this country are between the Isle of Wight and Poole. If there were some ships of her Majesty at Portsmouth, they would free all this coast from these brigands, who are not content to rob only those who are at sea, but come into the harbours and pillage the merchants even at this place, which is ten or twelve miles inland; yet the vessels here are not safe without very good guard.

Protest as they might at the highest level, the seizures of French ships continued with no intermission. In May 1586 the French ambassador, Chateauneuf, wrote to Walsingham:

earnestly Praying (from my desire to maintain amity between the King and the Queen) that, together with the lords of the Council, you will take some order for these French merchants who are spoiled, especially for those of St Jehan de Luz and of Toulouse, seeing that your English ships have been stayed there; and I wish to send so good an answer to the King that the matter may go no further, but that they may all be set free. I send you a memorial of the depredations of which complaints have come to me within this fortnight, and three or four of which call for speedy remedy, that the goods may not be sold.

In an annex the ambassador listed a number of depredations committed by the English upon French ships between 1584 and February 1586, including one in which *Urrugne* of Bayonne 'was attacked by five English ships, who forced her to surrender, after killing the Master', and then sailed her to Purbeck where the ship was 'discharged, the goods sold, and the mariners sent back to their country without a farthing.'

It is not surprising that the miscreants listed by the ambassador included Sir John Gilbert and Walter Ralegh, who attempted to avoid the full cost of restitution by proposing that the merchants pay for the salvage costs of their now unseaworthy ship. After several pages of complaints, the ambassador ended his letter with the plea that 'the Lords of the Council take order in conformity with the treaties between their Majesties, that justice may be done and restitution made.'[31]

The ambassador's submission was submitted to the Lord Treasurer, the Lord Admiral and Walsingham, in other words a sub group of the Privy Council, at which meeting Julius Caesar was also present to put the Admiralty case. The response was to make counter-claims with a list of English vessels seized by the French. This failed to bring closure and more disgruntled French government views were passed back to Walsingham by Edward Stafford, the English ambassador in Paris. On one occasion, following an earlier unresolved complaint about the seizing of a French ship in Portland, Stafford forwarded a message from the king asking that 'justice may be done', while, for his part, Stafford had told the king that if one of the queen's ships had been involved, restitution would soon follow but 'if it were (as I was informed by others) a pirate, then likewise they should have all redress possible in such case, they knowing themselves that in no place in the world was more severe justice done upon pirates than in England.'[32]

The evidence suggests otherwise, for the English government's inaction was the cause of many rulers of divers nations being 'compelled to hear so many complaints from their seamen and merchants that they are nowhere more miserably infested by pirates (and those English) than around the coasts of England.'[33]

The hopelessness of the French search for justice can be illustrated by the fact that in October 1585 the English pirate about whom they were complaining was none other than the queen's favourite, Francis Drake, whom the French king, in a letter to Elizabeth, alleged had seized a French vessel laden with salt from Portugal and taken her along with 'her artillery, equipage and merchandise, saying that he had need of her for her Majesty's service, the whole being valued at 2,800 crowns.' The king concluded with the usual remarks about 'peace and amity between them', and that 'her general ought not to touch what belongs to his subjects', but it is unlikely that he believed that she would adhere to his request to 'give him orders to make no further such seizures, and to recompense the said merchant.'[34]

The official French protests while Henry III was on the throne were somewhat blunted by the fact that the English favoured a Protestant claim for that crown and were willing to bend the rules in support of that group. In 1586 five French ships were carried off to the Protestant stronghold of La Rochelle, by a squadron escorting the prince of Condé. On arrival at La Rochelle, the prince had sold their cargo of woad to some English merchants. Shortly afterwards, a Scots ship had also been relieved of its cargo of French woad by Englishmen holding letters of marque issued by Condé and the king of Navarre. In forlorn hope, Henry wrote to Elizabeth asking 'her Majesty to do prompt justice to the said merchants, as is fitting by the treaty of alliance between their crowns.'[35] The English response was their traditional one – they presented the French ambassador with a long list of counter-claims by English merchants relating to piracy against their ships by the French.

Irritating Allies

A state of war, or undeclared war, even a state of mutual maritime mugging, might have justified some of the acts of piracy committed by the English, but it is much harder to justify the behaviour of Elizabeth's seamen when the opportunity arose to seize the ships of the nation's allies, which with England's isolation mainly meant the Dutch.

In October 1576 the prince of Orange was instructing his ambassador to complain to the queen that, inter alia, 'since the beginning of these troubles the English merchants under colour of traffic have greatly assisted their enemies with victuals and munitions, and likewise by false charter parties, attestations, and other deceits enabled them to get what they wanted to the ruin of the common cause. To stop these frauds the goods of the said merchants were seized and adjudged lawful prize by the Admiralty of Zealand, whereupon they have had recourse to calumniations, and by means of false representation have obtained letters of marque and reprisals.'[36]

The queen took few measures to placate the Dutch, whose merchants were not exempted from running the gauntlet of the Narrow Seas. The result was not an occasional complaint but a lengthy litany of almost daily losses, which included violations by ships owned by the queen's favourites Ralegh, Grenville and Cumberland (Appendix 11), estimated to amount to a staggering £200,000 between 1585 and 1589, for which recompense, although requested, had not been granted.[37]

The summary concluded that 'several other inhabitants of the United Provinces trading to Spain have touched at or been driven by weather into English ports', where instead of receiving help they:

> are daily in divers ports of this kingdom spoiled and abused as open enemies, under colour of frivolous objections that they be laden with Spaniards' goods. So that everybody almost is and will be his own judge, misusing and tormenting the poor men in sundry sorts according to their own will and pleasure; keeping them whole months together imprisoned at shipboard, not suffering them to come a-land to make their complaints where it belongeth until they have enforced them to give a general acquittance. And though good and sufficient sureties be offered, yet can the same not serve for their release, but the poor men are driven, to their singular grief and undoing, to see their goods robbed and embezzled by night and undue times.

Even when reasonable appeals were presented to the court, the outcome was often in doubt and redress was not forthcoming. The Dutch remedy was simple, logical and fair. They asked that any 'ships and goods arrested anywhere in England, may upon proof of title be restored, according to the statutes of this realm and the articles of the Intercourse.' They also asked that:

> for the avoiding of the like inconveniences hereafter, their honours consider the following articles:

1. That letters of reprisal be granted only to merchants who have sustained losses, and who give surety for their good behaviour at sea.
2. That, knights and merchants who let out their letters of reprisal to untrustworthy third parties be nevertheless held answerable for the conduct of their ships.
3. That the proclamation of March, 1585, forbidding, under pain of being punished as pirates, any attacks under colour of letters of reprisal upon other ships than those of the King of Spain and the kingdom of Portugal, may be reissued and enforced.
4. That no prizes be taken into ports where the officers and magistrates participate and make large profits outside the process of the Lord Admiral's court.
5. That no prize taken at the sea is accounted lawful or sold until a proper judicial procedure had been followed and judgment made.
6. That when goods or ships of the United Provinces are seized by any English men of war that the recognized laws be applied concerning their handling.
7. That buyers of goods taken by pirates be compelled to restore them upon sufficient proof of title, 'without any shifting of the matter by prohibition at the Common Law.'
8. That their honours would set down their opinion touching the staying of ships of the United Provinces engaged under the colours of other nations in the long established trade with France, Spain, Portugal, and the Islands, which is so

essential to them: will carry no victuals, munitions, or materials for rigging ships, to the Spaniard.[38]

In reciprocity, the Dutch envoy, Ortell, suggested that the United Provinces would 'by public act forbid upon pain of death any of their inhabitants to convey any Spaniard's or enemy goods or to allow the conveyance of any victuals, munitions, or materials serving for rigging of ships', a measure that should have enabled the English to allow Dutch vessels to 'pass through the Channel unmolested', if carrying goods 'not harmful to Her Majesty.' To secure this arrangement the Dutch were prepared to pay £200,000 a year for a licence, while to avoid the frequent frustration through the prevarications of the Admiralty Court, Ortell also proposed that no goods should be removed from seized ships until a judgement had been made by the Privy Council. This sensible suggestion foundered on the Privy Council's suspicion that the Dutch were somehow trying it on, and would receive benefits far greater than the cost of the licence would indicate.[39] The council also thought that any agreement should wait 'until the result of Sir John Norreys and Sir Francis Drake's enterprise is seen. Trade would hardly be safe while so many men-of-war be upon the coast of Spain.'[40]

By 1594 the United Provinces claimed to have lost over £200,000 with little redress, although both the Admiralty Court and the Privy Council indicated that they had ordered restoration to be made.

Even Scottish shipping was not exempt from the attentions of English pirates. In this instance, however, the English were prepared to apologise, as Walsingham did in July 1577 telling the Scottish Regent that:

> Touching the disorder committed by the Fenwicks and Shaftons, her Majesty will see that they are punished according to their deserts, if they may be apprehended. For the matter of piracies there needs only effectual execution of the order which is taken, which is as good as could be desired, her Majesty having sent three of her ships to scour the seas; and hath given most strict commission for the examination of all such as victual them or give them any means of support, minding that the fines which shall be levied upon them shall be employed to the answering of the losses which the subjects of that realm have sustained by her Majesty's subjects being pirates.[41]

Scottish rovers behaved as badly, they just happened to be not so good at it. Between 1564 and 1586 the English were reputed to have seized goods to the value of £20,717 from Scottish ships, while only losing £9,286 themselves.[42]

Annoying Neutrals

If Elizabeth could treat a nation as strong as Spain with foul scorn, she had no reason not to be similarly inclined towards the lesser powers whose shipping had to pass through the Channel. A glance at just a few months in 1586 gives a clear indication as to the extent of their deprivation.

In March, Frederick, king of Denmark, wrote to Elizabeth, on behalf of a number of his merchants, whom the Diggory Piper gang had relieved of their goods, that he was:

> much amazed that such things should be done by her subjects, although no interdict of navigation has been made, nor any admonition given beforehand; and especially, he can hardly be induced to believe that the pirates who did these things are seen going about openly in London without constraint; which things being unjust in themselves and contrary to all law, he cannot but take very amiss, and craves that she will severely punish those wicked men who have violated the rights of his people and made attack upon their lives and goods. For otherwise, they will not cease to complain to him touching their wrongs, and to demand that English ships shall be stayed in his realm, in which he could not be wanting to his subjects, although otherwise ready to show all fraternal affection to her Majesty. And since they have sent one Thomas Fennker to plead their cause, he prays her in friendly and brotherly manner, that they may in justice and equity receive what is fair and right, according to treaties and to humanity.[43]

In May, the Senate of Hamburg wrote to the queen, forwarding a petition for restitution written by John Heins and his partners, that stated that an English ship laden with their goods had been viciously attacked by an English pirate, named Damithus [sic], 'who shot iron balls at her so that her sides were split, ship and goods were sunk, and of the nineteen men in her, all but five were drowned.'[44]

A month later it was the turn of George Frederick, duke of Prussia, to draw to the queen's attention the inappropriate behaviour of her trading subjects, who had been caught trying to evade customs duties at Konigsberg by lying about their cargo manifest.[45] Although this was not a piratical act, it indicated the fast and loose way English traders behaved in regard to both their own laws and those of other nations. Before being described as a nation of shopkeepers by Napoleon, the England of Elizabeth was a nation of shiplifters.

Then, in October, Prince Charles of Sweden thought it advisable to write to Elizabeth that he was despatching a ship with corn to Italy and asking that 'he may be allowed freedom from port dues, taxes and all other burdens; and that they will not in any way hinder, hurt or molest him, but rather treat him with all kindness, and so much as in them lies, forward and care for him.'[46] A little while later the king wrote again to request that 'his subject, Olaf Werne, sent with his ship, the *Angel*, into Spain, may pass through her maritime possessions without let or hindrance.'

The hindrance continued. In August 1587 Frederick of Denmark wrote again to Elizabeth, this time on behalf of certain merchants from Bergen, whose well-laden ship had been seized and carried off to London, where it had 'been fitted out for the practice of piracy and adorned with her Majesty's insignia' by a well-known pirate. The king kindly requested 'her Majesty's royal favour, and that the matter may be duly investigated and decided by proper judges delegate, and not only restitution made or equitable compensation awarded, but also that there may be allowed just costs and damages.' But the king had little hope of a just resolution complaining that:

> Her highness knows how often he has gently brought to her notice complaints on behalf of his subjects; but though she has often led him to hope that she would proceed against the delinquents with due severity, yet he rarely finds the procedure against them, when caught, to be so exemplary as to deter others who meditate such offences. The consequence of which is, that where there is no fear, there is likewise no end of depredations, no end of complaints to be hoped for.[47]

Some actions were taken, but as one of the vessels that had preyed on the Danes had been sent forth by Walter Leveson, Richard's crooked father and the deputy vice admiral of north Wales, due severity was not in evidence, while when the less influential Diggory Piper was brought to court he was twice acquitted by juries of his peers.

Thus, while the Privy Council blew a great wind, in safe havens around the coast, under the benign eye of the authorities, the sails of the pirates scarcely flapped, although some arrests were made. When, for example, it was brought to the queen's attention that certain of her subjects had raided Galicia, seized some cattle and sacked a hermitage, she did not hesitate to order their arrest and assure the ambassador that they would be justly punished.[48] These were the small-time gamblers; the serious poker players were left to play their game unmolested.

The piracy continued. In April 1589 the magistrates of Augsburg wrote to the queen asking for her to intervene in the case of George Sulzer whose goods, including 'Hungarian copper ingots, linen, cotton, silk, gold and silver thread, wine and twelve gilded hides', all marked with the merchant's mark, were seized and carried into England. The magistrates thus asked the queen that 'as the goods are his and he has had nothing to do with the Spanish war, her Majesty will restore them.'[49]

Violating Venice

Many of the attacks on foreign shipping were carried out on trade passing through the Channel. Many more were justified by reference to letters of reprisal and the continuous game of tit-for-tat that was played at sea. Yet there was one nation whose ships generally sailed well away from England's shores, and against whom no letters of reprisal were issued. Even so, Venetian merchants became a major target of English pirates who, eventually, pursued this wealthy source of income right into the eastern Mediterranean. Venetian galleys had made annual visits to England, even after having been twice commandeered by Henry VII and Henry VIII for their own use. However, in 1570 two Venetian ships were seized in the Solent by vessels acting under letters of marque issued by the queen of Navarre, but quite evidently supported by the English local authorities.[50] In response, such trading voyages virtually ceased.

It was in England's interests to have good relations with Venice. Elizabeth even suggested to the newly arrived Venetian secretary, Giovanni Carlo Scaramelli, that she 'suffered deeply because she could never find a safe and suitable occasion to propose to the Republic means for reducing the King of Spain.'[51] Yet, at the same time as soliciting their support, Elizabeth dissembled and cloaked her subjects' faults, informing the Doge in 1602:

> Concerning the ships you now write of, the *Cornelio* and *St Marke*, we have given special commandment to our judges that with all speed they despatch the same. That said our judges have humbly declared unto us that in the examining of like causes they find great injury daily offered unto our men-of-war by such as profess friendship with us: some of them confidently interposing themselves to assure and colour our enemies' goods that happen to be taken from them by the law of war, and others lightly using our enemies' bottoms for transporting their goods, whereas by the express laws of our kingdom and of other nations. Whatsoever goods found in enemies' bottoms are esteemed to be of like condition with the bottoms themselves: for that such free confusion of other men's goods in enemies' ships may otherwise yield means and occasion of much danger and prejudice to the contrary party. The which their information, as we think, in your own judgment maketh it manifest that some time will be necessary for the examining of the truth, and that it appertaineth to our dignity duly to pursue what the law of war urgeth us unto and in like cases hath ever been usual amongst all other princes – yet at your intercession we have given our order that all convenient speed be used in examining both the said causes, and, for the better performing of justice, that the goods in question be kept in sequester till the issue, then to be delivered to whom they shall justly appertain.[52]

Eventually, the Venetian senate voted to send one of their secretaries to 'England at the sole charges of the interested parties; and to furnish him with letters and instructions.'[53] It was a much-needed mission, for about the time that it was being organised, reports were arriving in Venice of:

> the miserable misfortune which befell the illustrious Signor Zuanne da Mosto when, returning from his consulate in Cairo, he was plundered by English buccaneers. If the pirates are, as is reported, at Modon disposing of their booty, I will do all I can to attempt its recovery. It will be difficult to root out the English from Zante, for there are seven English bertoni [ships] lying in the port, and though they are said to be merchantmen, more than one of them would not shrink from piratage.[54]

The senate thus wrote, diplomatically, to Elizabeth that:

Great damage is being done and large booty made by the English who infest these seas. The English ill treat and plunder all alike. More especially, a short time ago near the isle of Zante, the galleon *Veniera* was seized by a ship under the command of William Piers, of Plymouth. The *Veniera*'s cargo was entirely the property of Venetians, and was destined for this city, and on board her was a Venetian nobleman, a public servant, on his way back from his consulate in Alexandria.

This and the other acts of piracy committed on the high seas, tend to destroy the ancient trade between our respective countries. To meet this mischief it is necessary that both parties should concur, your Majesty with prudence and justice, ourselves by a similar response, for the common good.

For this purpose we have expressly charged Secretary Scaramelli to negotiate with you for compensation for the losses suffered; and we beg you to yield to our Secretary the same credence as you would give to ourselves; and we pray God to preserve your Majesty in wealth and all happiness.[55]

That note was enclosed in a letter to Scaramelli ordering him:

in suitable and weighty words to draw attention to this grave excess, to our just resentment and the need for punishing in every way these villains, who are unworthy to live under the glorious standard of her Majesty. The suitable means for such punishment would be not only to publish a severe sentence against, them and to confiscate all their property in England, but to give express orders to the Captains of all vessels that if they fall in with William Piers, of Plymouth, or others who commit such villainous deeds, they are to punish them.

In Venice itself the senate summoned the chief English merchants to appear before them, so that they could 'point out that the news of these excesses has caused extreme displeasure; for while the English are so well treated in every part of our dominions we receive such a poor return.'[56]

If the senate thought that their petition would be welcomed, they were soon disabused by Elizabeth, who resorted to her usual strategy of counter-attack, as Scaramelli reported back:

After presenting my credentials, I briefly recalled the excellent treatment which her Majesty's subjects enjoyed in the States of your Serenity, and on the other hand, the gravity of the excesses committed by the English corsairs, and the serious nature of the damage inflicted on Venetian subjects for some years past; also how much your Serenity had it at heart that her Majesty should speedily cause the restoration of the booty, and finally touching on the reciprocal importance that the world should see the result of the mission of one of your Serenity's Secretaries to this kingdom for so just a request.

The Queen, who held your Serenity's letter in her hand, passed it to the Secretary who opened it and gave it back to her, her Majesty took it, sat down, and read it all through. Then rising to her feet again, she handed it back to the

Secretary; her countenance, which had hitherto been placid and almost smiling, assumed a graver aspect, and she said 'I cannot help feeling that the Republic of Venice, during the forty-four years of my reign, has never made herself heard by me except to ask for something, nor for the rest, prosperous or adverse as my affairs may have been, never has she given a sign of holding me or my kingdom in that esteem which other princes and other potentates have not refused. Nor am I aware that my sex has brought me this demerit, for my sex cannot diminish my prestige nor offend those who treat me as other Princes are treated, to whom the Signory of Venice sends its Ambassadors. But I am well aware, and so far I excuse the Republic, that in the many discussions on this subject she has not been able to obtain leave from certain Sovereigns. But for all this I would not be discourteous to her, though I would have you know that this kingdom is not so short of men that some bad ruffians may not be found among them. As the question touches my subjects, however, I will appoint Commissioners who shall confer with you and report to me, and I will do all that in me lies to give satisfaction to the Serene Republic, for I would not be discourteous.'[57]

The next day Scaramelli was sent for by the queen to be told that she 'had named the Lord High Admiral, the Secretary of State, and the Privy Councillor, Edward Wotton, to hear my requests and to report them to her', thus including in the negotiating team two men who had dispatched their own pirate vessel to the Mediterranean the previous year. Elizabeth also made an initial grant in restitution of 50,000 ducats, provided that this was seen as a gesture of goodwill rather than an admission of guilt. Even this gesture was grudgingly given, the amount being almost immediately reduced to 10,000 ducats.[58]

However, others found that Elizabeth would respond to pressure. In March 1603 Scaramelli was writing about the seizure by the English of a very rich cargo belonging to a Spaniard naturalised in Morocco. There, the king, rather than 'making any remonstrance or complaint to the Queen of England, without more ado seized all the goods belonging to English subjects in the kingdom of Morocco, which amounts to a very large sum, and adjudicated it all to himself after deducting the indemnification to the Spaniard, his intimate.' As soon as this became known in England, and the queen was petitioned by her own 'tearful' merchants, she had all the stolen goods collected and sent back to Morocco at her own expense. Scaramelli also quoted a similar action by the king of Denmark, which had a less beneficial outcome for his subjects. In this case, English pirates had seized a large quantity of hemp and cordage bound for Spain, but when Denmark demanded restitution or purchase by England, with the tempting codicil that they would sell all the next year's crop to England, to prevent it being purchased by Spain, the queen refused to negotiate. The Danish monarch therefore ordered an embargo on all shipping trading between England and the Baltic, which route carried much of England's maritime necessities. This resulted in an inconclusive ambassadorial conference, in commentating about which

Scaramelli penned the damning opinion about England's piratical behaviour with which this chapter begins. Scaramelli did, however, note a method in the queen's mischief stating that:

> whereas the Kings of England, down to Henry VII and Henry VIII, were wont to keep up a fleet of one hundred ships in full pay as a defence, now the Queen's ships do not amount to more than fifteen or sixteen, as her revenue cannot support a greater charge; and so the whole of the strength and repute of the nation rests on the vast number of small privateers [sic], which are supported and increase to that dangerous extent which everyone recognizes; and to ensure this support, the privateers make the ministers partners in the profits, without the risk of a penny in the fitting out, but only a share in the prizes, which are adjudged by judges placed there by the ministers themselves.

History, at least English history, has been kinder to the queen, indeed, and for many a good reason Elizabeth is generally considered to be the nation's favourite and most glorious monarch. Yet without her pirates her reign might not have lasted as long. When Drake presented himself to the Queen in 1580, he was the only one of her adventurers who had returned with anything to show for his efforts and her faith. Frobisher had imported ballast; Gilbert had not even made it to the shore beyond which Her Majesty had been generous to grant him overlordship. Drake alone had proved that he could make voyaging pay. Had Frobisher found a route to Cathay or a mine of great worth, had Gilbert returned with tales of a brave new world, then Drake might well have been disowned as an embarrassment to a queen wishing not to go to war with Spain. Their failure, shortly to be joined by the flop of Ralegh's Roanoke expedition, encouraged Elizabeth to put her trust in pirates. But she went beyond this. She was content for her Lord Admiral to issue letters of reprisal to whoever requested one and permitted him to maintain a conflict of interest between the perks and prosecution of piracy; she wrote commissions to her piratocrats, releasing them to sail on roving voyages; she rewarded and knighted those pirates whose success she approved; she dismissed the justifiable complaints of ambassadors from countries with whom she was allied.

As an exercise in positive propaganda her policy worked well and lasted long. Her favourite pirates became known affectionately as 'sea dogs', while even her lesser local malefactors were mustered together under the much loved 'Jolly Roger'. To avoid over-criticism of her piracy policy, much has been written about the forays to seize the Spanish *flotas* and Portuguese carracks, which belonged to nations with whom Elizabeth was at war, albeit for much of the time an undeclared one. Yet her great pirate, Francis Drake, captured his two richest prizes before a state of war was deemed to exist. Even Walsingham was proposing, in March 1585, to seize Spanish shipping off Newfoundland, listing the benefits of such a move to 'annoy the King of Spain.'[59] Much less mention is made of the seizure of the ships and goods belonging to allied or neutral nations. For instance, two recent books on the subject

The Cattewater off Plymouth provided a sheltered, but often extremely crowded anchorage for many of John Hawkins's and Drake's pirate ships. But, as Richard Hawkins discovered, when the wind blew from the wrong direction ships could soon be driven onto the all-too-close rocks. (British Library)

Dartmouth, because it was a quiet backwater, was a favoured harbour for the pirateering Gilbert clan and it was into this haven that the prize *Madre de Dios* was brought, and much of her cargo illegally landed before Cecil and Ralegh arrived to restore order. (British Library)

ABOVE: This painting of Henry VIII's fleet at Dover clearly shows how, with friendly forces manning the fortifications, a pirate fleet could lie safe from attack by vengeful vessels. (Author collection)

LEFT: Elizabeth's own propaganda depicted her as the glorious sovereign who defeated the might of Spain. In truth, there were many smaller nations whose merchants were preyed upon by the queen's privateers and to whose protests the queen turned a deaf ear. (Author collection)

Elizabeth believed that the 1596 raid on Cadiz would yield a rich reward. She was furious that opportunities for prize-taking were ignored, and that many of her senior officers filled their own pockets rather than hers. Once again Cecil was called upon to uncover the illegal bounty. (© National Maritime Museum, Greenwich, London)

Drake's death in 1596, depicted on his monument in Tavistock, opened the last act of the pirateering play. With Elizabeth's death in 1601, the curtain fell: nevermore would the state openly support such an illegal practice, relying on the quasi-legal fiction of privateering to justify its future involvement. (Buzzy Howatt)

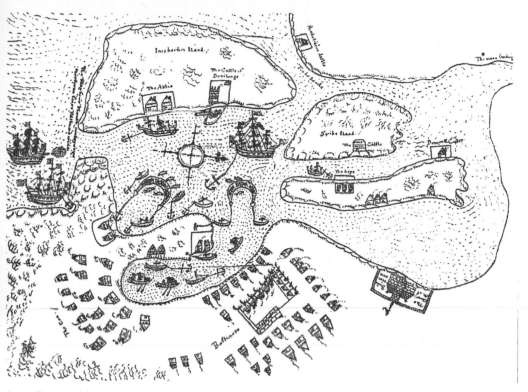

James I's opposition to piracy forced the pirates to operate from out of the way ports such as Baltimore in southern Ireland where, by 1607, most of the population made their living by servicing pirate ships and their crews. (Author collection)

The charts drawn by John White during the first settlement of the proposed pirate base at Roanoke marked the beginning of England's interest in overseas hydrography. (Author collection)

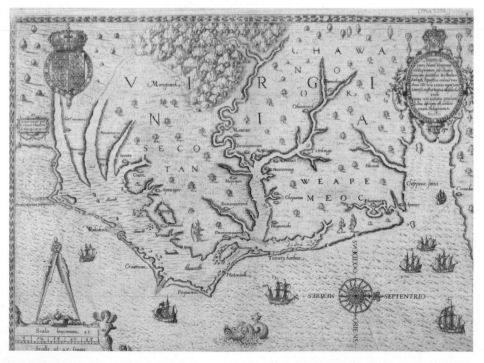

ABOVE: English pirateers sailing into the Mediterranean to prey on the Venetians were themselves at risk from the Barbary pirates, like those attacking this French vessel, which seems to be giving a good account of herself.
(© National Maritime Museum, Greenwich, London)

LEFT: Elizabeth's reliance on pirateers to fill command posts in her navy deprived the Stuarts, for several reigns, of a cadre of competent naval officers, a shortfall highlighted by numerous failures. (© National Maritime Museum, Greenwich, London)

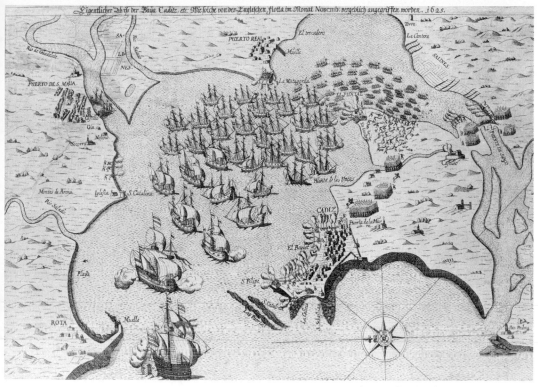

ABOVE: A print showing the
disastrous expedition to Cadiz in
1625 which was led by the
inexperienced and cautious Edward
Cecil, who lacked Drake's skill,
Ralegh's charisma and Essex's
daring. (© National Maritime
Museum, Greenwich, London)

LEFT: This globe, dating from 1590,
is the earliest known to have been
made in England. Based on the work
of Mercator it would have been
modified by the reports of Drake and
the other ocean navigators.
(© National Maritime Museum,
Greenwich, London)

LEFT: This exquisite, multi-functional astronomical compendium was made in England in about 1569 and, allegedly, owned by Drake who would have understood its workings far better than Frobisher who never seemed to master ocean navigation. (© National Maritime Museum, Greenwich, London)

BELOW: The backstaff, which allowed the altitude of the sun to be measured without looking directly at its glare, was invented by the explorer and pirateer John Davis, who sailed with both Cavendish, Ralegh and Michaelbourne, before joining the East India Company in whose service he died, in a fight with pirates. (© National Maritime Museum, Greenwich, London)

of Elizabeth and her pirates fail to mention the smaller nations which her rovers repeatedly ravished.[60]

The evidence clearly indicates that Elizabeth had little interest in responding to the legitimate complaints laid before her by foreign ambassadors. In 1586 one shrewd observer of the international scene wrote that 'when ambassadors began to deal in such matters [reprisals and restitution] all find it to be dreams and fables.' The writer went on to say that the only way forward was for the debate to:

> be so treated that no question be made who began it; for those who invent such things, understand very ill the sweetness of the war to them that have no experience of it, and that the profits of it go to the pirates and the losses to the princes and the people. The treasures slowly gathered waste and consume, and at length the victory.[61]

It was to ensure that the profits did not go solely to the pirates that Elizabeth and her council insisted on the rules regarding breaking of bulk be observed and that, by right of commissioning voyages, they had prior claim on the seized cargo. However, if she was to be the major claimant, she had to keep her piratocrats eager to serve her, and not frustrated by her own greed. If this meant being both blind to their faults and deaf to the pleas of the ravished innocent, then so be it.

For, however legitimate the protests were, Elizabeth could not afford, even without her parsimonious inclinations, to spend vast sums on a protective navy. By 1564 she had reduced its 'ordinary' budget from '£13,000 to £6000, in spite of the effects of rapid price-inflation', only to see her annual average naval costs of £25,000, for the peacetime years of 1566–85, leap to £87,000 for the war years of 1585–1603. The Armada campaign cost her some £100,000, while the 1596 expedition to Cadiz cost another £172,260.[62] Her only way of managing such enormous increases in expenditure in a state whose GDP was not growing was to hire merchants or deploy pirates to augment her own naval forces in their pursuit of plunder.

So, to label Elizabeth a 'pirate queen' is not to condemn outright her policies, statecraft or avarice. She had ascended to the throne of a religiously divided, bankrupt and sparsely inhabited offshore island, whose very independence was threatened by a host far greater and richer than that which she could deploy in her defence. She left the nation united, uninvaded, solvent and Protestant, while also securing an unchallenged heir. Her pirates contributed much cash, courage and competence to achieve this, while also keeping the seas around her coast secure as they did so. Yet they caused, and she condoned, much collateral damage to innocent merchant shipping. In so doing she created a culture of greed and corruption that her successor could deprecate, but not destroy. It would be no idle summary of her behaviour to state that she did the wrong thing for the right reason, but even this handy excuse does not justify her dismissal of the complaints made by foreign ambassadors and her disinterest in the wrongful treatment of their merchants.

The last decades of Elizabeth's reign was an age of giants, both at sea and on the stage. To claim that Shakespeare's plays were written by Bacon rather than the bard does not diminish the stature of those works: to state that Drake and his colleagues were pirates, rather than privateers, does not lessen the successes, failures or legacy of those extraordinary fellows. To consider Elizabeth to have been his approving partner probably enhances rather than diminishes her status as Gloriana. These were desperate times for their tiny nation and whatever means were utilised to keep England afloat in the tumultuous years which brought the sixteenth century to a close can, understandably, be cherished and admired by all who are heirs of those who chartered her passage to global greatness, and have since enjoyed the benefits of those endeavours.

CHAPTER 12

Low Water

But nothing is thought to have enriched the English more or done so
much to allow many individuals to amass the wealth they are known to
possess as the wars with the Spaniards in the time of Queen Elizabeth.
All were permitted to go privateering and they plundered not only the
Spaniards but all others indifferently, so that they enriched themselves
by this constant stream of booty. Accordingly, nothing was more
unpopular with the English than the peace with the Catholic king, and
they desire nothing better than a return to war so that they may enjoy
the liberty from which they profited so much before.[1]

Piero Contarini, Venetian ambassador to England,
to Doge and Senate, December 1618

In sombre line ahead, as Elizabeth's reign drew to a close, her piratocracy escorted
her outbound across the waters of Lethe. Grenville took the van, fighting his fierce
lonely ship action against overwhelming odds off Flores in 1591. Frobisher followed
when, leading a charge on 7 November 1594 against a Spanish fort constructed to
keep the French fleet bottled up in Brest, he received a wound that, turning
gangrenous, claimed his life three weeks later. One year on, it was the turn of Drake
and Hawkins to succumb to disease during their poorly planned and badly executed
final voyage to the Indies: Hawkins off Puerto Rico on 11 November 1595, and
Drake off Porto Bello on 28 January following. While their expedition was at sea,
Dom Antonio, whose dreams of seizing the throne of Portugal, or at the least the
Azores, had been the catalyst for several memorable voyages, died in 'great poverty'.
Then, in 1600 impetuous Essex departed, ahead of any assigned station, executed
through his own grievous fault.

In close company with Elizabeth, who died in March 1603, went George Carey,
Baron Hunsdon, poisoned by mercury being ingested as a false cure for venereal
disease, an itch he shared with many of his seamen. By this time Cumberland had
already retired from active sea service, writing to Cecil on May 1600 that he was
declining the offer of a sea appointment because 'my thoughts must turn from
intercepting carracks, to sowing of corn, from rigging ships to breeding sheep, and
from honour to clownish cogitation.' He departed, disillusioned, feeling that he

had 'built an anchor to save others only to be drowned himself.' He had not long to put his neglected estates in order, for he died in October 1605 aged just forty-seven. Neither did Leveson linger long, dying that same year, having been hastened to slip anchor early at the age of thirty-five by those who accused him of taking too much from the carrack he had captured at Cezembra.

Only Ralegh, of all Elizabeth's favoured seagoers, missed that tide and, unable to cross the bar, was left stranded in the Stuart shallows, under lingering sentence of death following a travesty of a trial in 1603 on charges of treason brought in by a jealous James I. He was encouraged by the courtier's one-time colleagues, but cruellest of counsels, Cecil and Nottingham, who, turning from pirates to piranhas, stripped their colleague of his assets, with Cecil seizing Ralegh's London property portfolio and Nottingham his farm of wine imports. After a more decent interval, in 1607 the king joined in, evicting Bess Ralegh from the family estate of Sherborne, to hand it to his boyfriend Robert Carr. Ten years later he released his prisoner from the Tower on licence to find gold in Guinea, only to deprive him of his life when he failed to do so but succeeded in infuriating Spain in the process. James had little option, given the stance he had taken against piracy and for peace on his succession.[2]

The piratocrats produced just three male heirs: the dull Bernard Grenville; the like-father, John Grenville, who sailed with Frobisher to Spain, thus missing out on a share from the capture of the *Madre de Dios*, and then died at sea while taking part in Ralegh's 1595 expedition to Guiana; and Richard Hawkins, who continued behaving as if nothing had changed. Appointed vice admiral of Devon, he had ambitions to make money ashore from the same business which had paid him so little afloat.

In 1608 a French merchant named Buillon, sailing in a 50-ton vessel called *Le François*, was attacked and robbed by a pirate named Thomas Pinn, whose own ship had been armed and victualled by Hawkins. To him Buillon hastened to demand the restitution of his goods, valued at £8,280. Hawkins handed over £2,000, but kept the rest, earning for himself the following pithy and precise critique by Buillon that for

> pure thefts and piracies too odious to justice, specially in the person of him who is the judge thereof, who instead of bringing to it moderation and temperance according to the ordnances, makes himself an accomplice of these evil designs which he has caused to succeed to the disadvantage and ruin of petitioner.

Sixteen months later Buillon had to admit defeat after the Admiralty judge had first required him to purchase a bond for £1,000 to have Pinn prosecuted and then, precipitately, ordered the offender to be executed which meant that, by law, all his possessions were confiscated, so that the unfortunate Frenchman saw his own goods:

> placed in the hands of the Mayor of Plymouth; which they have converted to their own use, even (which is much the most extraordinary thing) having

compounded with those who had bought and concealed the said merchandise. And not content with having reduced this poor merchant to extremity and almost to despair, upon the complaints he made to the said Judge of the Admiralty of this execution, and instead of restoring his merchandise or the price thereof as he had promised, he rifled with his officers all the goods of the executed pirate, parted and wasted all that petitioner had been able to recover of his merchandise. The said Judge instead of pity and compassion, had so turned his face from justice, that upon petitioner's saying he should complain to his Majesty he caused him to be made prisoner, where he would have remained a long time but for the succour of the Sieur de Beaumont [the French ambassador] who caused him to come out of the said prison afterwards.[3]

Despite such examples of maltreatment the tide had turned, even in Plymouth. No longer was behaviour by corrupt servants such as Richard Hawkins to be cynically tolerated and, shortly after the Bouillon incident, a piracy commission had Hawkins removed, albeit temporarily, from his post.

The wise decision of James I to declare peace on Spain and war on piracy when he came to the throne in 1603 had other unforeseen, and in some cases undesirable, consequences. That he held true to his aim is supported by the fact that more pirates were captured and convicted in his reign than in the previous hundred years.[4] Yet James's actions did little to cure the disease. The war had swelled England's maritime population from some 16,000 in 1582 to about 50,000 in 1603. Many of these men had turned to the sea because the land, with its frequent crop failures, offered them even less reward. As ships paid off, the ports filled with drunk, disorderly and disgruntled seamen, ready recruits for those offering them a share of piratical loot. Most sobered up and, realising that they would no longer have either the neck-saving safeguard of a letter of reprisal or the guarantee of a friendly welcome from a corrupt official on the quayside, opted to retire. Just a few thousand returned to their old ways but they were responsible for a twenty-year whirlwind.

Some joined the Dutch, who were still at war with Spain. Some, remembering the joys of life in the Caribbean, returned there to begin a century-long period of buccaneering. As early as 1606, the Venetian ambassador in London, Zorzi Giustinian, having informed the doge of the capture by the Dutch of six rich carracks in the Indies, went on to say that:

Certain English gentlemen, who have been used to the hardships of war and of privateering, being now deprived of their profession by the peace, propose to fit out a number of ships and to sail for the discovery of unknown country in the West Indies, where, they say, there are indications of rich gold fields and other precious material. Spain will oppose the scheme and the Council will support it, and this will furnish a fresh cause for friction.[5]

Prescient though Giustinian was, he could not have foretold that the fresh cause of friction would be furnished by the arrival in the Indies in 1617 of Walter Ralegh, searching unsuccessfully for those non-existent gold fields and the fact that several of his captains abandoned him to go pirating.

No longer able to bring prizes openly into English ports, most pirate commanders took their business elsewhere. The southern Irish towns at Baltimore and Crookhaven experienced a boom from this trade, helped in no small part by the fact that the Lord Admiral exercised control over them as vice admiral of Munster. Other rovers sailed for the Barbary Coast where they established an expat pirate haven at Mamora in Morocco, from where they operated in harmony with the Arab corsairs in the Mediterranean.[6]

These developments brought with them a coarser lifestyle and a cruelty towards captives, for whom no ransom was now payable, that had little resemblance to the behaviour of Drake and his contemporaries, who had disarmed their captors with their gallantry, and cared for their needs whilst they held them in custody. The new lot were as likely to cast their captives overboard, for now that all ship seizures were regarded as illegal, it was dangerous to release witnesses to their crimes, besides which, a ship that disappeared at sea might be regarded as lost due to bad weather and no search be made for her crew or cargo. In one particularly horrific example, John Jennings, a long-time pirate, seized a French ship in the Channel and killed her entire crew. He then fled to Morocco, but later surrendered in expectation of mercy, only to be tried and hung at Wapping on 29 December 1609.[7]

Venice continued to bear the brunt of the assault. In November 1603 one of their vessels was assaulted on a moonlight night by a 300-ton, twenty-six gun, English ship which, as the supercargo reported:

> opened fire from her harquebusses and artillery, and her crew cried, 'down with your sails.' We had to obey, for we were not strong enough to fight. They came on board us, and thrashed us all for not taking in sail fast enough. About thirty of them swarmed on board, using great violence and foul language to us. They took all our artillery; sent us all below and fastened down the hatches. They then proceeded to help themselves to everything, including thirty casks of wine. With great cruelty they kept us under hatches for four days and four nights, and sailed our vessel along with theirs up and down, looking for more prey; but finding none they let us go . . . The Captain is a fair-bearded, red-faced little man, thin, dressed in purple satin and English breeches; about thirty years old. We were all in terror of death, for they bullied us, and went so far as to put the noose round our necks every day.[8]

The noose trick was in the tradition of Drake, but by the following October things had turned nastier as the governor of Zante described, while giving a pen-portrait of the typical ruffian pirates that would flourish in the new century and would become the villains, and heroes, of book and film hundreds of years later. He wrote bemoaning the fact that his galleon *Spelegato* was:

Boarded and captured by an Englishman. Our mizzen mast and sails were set on fire. Thirteen people were killed between crew and passengers, and five taken prisoners. Our crew numbered thirty-one, and there were about fifteen passengers; the berton [British boat] was of about two hundred tons burden, and had one hundred and twenty people on board. He cannot give her name; but it was said that two Knights and two Captains were on board, and one of these was called Formin, a man of about forty years of age, black beard, medium stature, well built; the other squinted, but deponent remembereth not with which eye, thinketh it is the right; well built; about forty; thick brown beard, ordinary moustaches. Of the Knights one was thickset, pale, black beard, about thirty; has a mark on one lip; short; fat; called Saint Andrew. The other is short; thin; blond; deponent does not know his name. The ship had a variety of flags, and used them as suited her.[9]

Even before the above incidents, Scaramelli had realised that with James would not come justice when Cecil, to whom he voiced his first request concerning the restitution of pirated goods, 'sent to beg me to abstain from presenting any petition until I had received my new credentials from Venice, the ones addressed to the late Queen being of no further value; moreover these were letters of limited credence, referring to a single subject.'[10]

Thus did the tricks learned under one sovereign prove to be adaptable and useful when her successor came to the throne. Scaramelli was, however, optimistic, for the new king informed him that 'the affairs which you could not discuss with the Queen I am ready to conclude with you.'[11] The need for such a dialogue was not long in coming.

Shortly after James's succession, William Piers docked at Plymouth with his prize *Veniera*. In an indication of a change of wind direction he was captured and sentenced to hang, only to be released after naming his associates and paying a bribe, for, as Scaramelli wrote in frustration, 'he is not without a golden key to open the doors of the great, especially of the High Admiral, who has charge of this business.'[12]

A few tides later Scaramelli sought an audience with James, to raise the matter of Captain Tomkins, who had captured a Venetian vessel, *Balbiana*, and offloaded her cargo in the Isle of Wight, securing his immunity from prosecution by bribing both the island's infamous governor, George Carey, now Lord Hunsdon, and the Lord Admiral. Seeking restitution was not easy for, as Scaramelli informed the doge:

I would have gone myself in person to the King, but for the next twenty days he will be without his council, away upon a hunting party, and everything is at a standstill . . . [The pirates] are growing all the bolder because the King, in spite of all the heroic virtues ascribed to him when he left Scotland and inculcated by him in his books, seems to have sunk into a lethargy of pleasures, and will not take any heed of matters of state . . . had the King or the Council sent a single ship inside the Straits [of Gibraltar] to arrest and proclaim these pirates, as his Majesty, out of his own mouth, promised me, we would not have to fear any serious damage for the ensuing winter.[13]

Nothing seemed at this moment to have changed. Scaramelli reported, despairingly, that Tomkins was of 'noble birth', with all the protection that went with such a position. Thus the pursuit of justice followed traditional lines for, having dispatched the sequestration order against Tomkins, Scaramelli discovered that the pirate had been warned, and disappeared although six of his crew were captured and hanged at Southampton.

The dogged secretary next sought an audience with the Lord Admiral, who freely admitted to receiving six sacks of silver from Tomkins, as his legal 'tenth' from what he had been told was a Spanish ship, but was prepared to return it should the prize be proved to be Venetian. What is more, Howard explained, Tomkins had sailed without a letter of reprisal and thus the ship itself was forfeit to the admiral, who would, of course, release it if it turned out to be Venetian. Yet Howard was still wheeling and dealing in a way that he felt would not be approved by his new sovereign, for he informed Scaramelli that the latter could leave the business entirely in his hands and need not trouble the king. His assurances did not convince, for shortly after they were given, Scaramelli was informing the doge that 'I have little faith in his promises, and far less in my own, by which I hold out hopes of reward at so much per cent, on the value of the goods at stake.' Yet on 5 October, when Scaramelli eventually saw the king, he:

> listened to me with extreme impatience, twisting his body, striking his hands together, and tapping with his feet. He took the memorandum I handed to him, and said in a loud voice, 'By God I'll hang the pirates with my own hands and my Lord Admiral as well.'

However, a moment later Cecil, realising things were not going the way that he would wish, intervened, lecturing Scaramelli that he had no right to refer such matters to the king because they fell fully under the jurisdiction of the Lord Admiral. What was more, he went on to say, the pirates about whom the Venetian complained had sailed while Elizabeth was on the throne, and not a single one had sailed since the new king had ascended to the throne. Wearily, Scaramelli pointed out that it would be difficult seeking justice from Nottingham, who had admitted receiving part of the plunder. Unexpectedly, the king joined in to state that 'If the Admiral has Venetian goods in his possession he must give them back.' Reluctantly and sulkily, Nottingham restored 13,000 ducats and one hundred and fifty lengths of cloth to Scaramelli, but retained all the gold coins, disingenuously declaring that as they were Spanish he could not restore them to the Venetians. He did not, however, have any qualms in approving the sacrifice of the bit players in this sordid tale, for five of Tomkins's crew were arrested and condemned to death, only to be saved by Caesar, who stated that he could get none of them to confess to the crime. Clemency was also extended to William Piers, who was kept in jail but no longer faced execution, as he had been part of the general amnesty issued by the king on his ascent to the throne. However, although such pardons were established by ancient law, James was even prepared to ask his judges to review the issue and also to insist that Piers be not released until he had paid his debts or agreed terms. But the counterstroke was now gathering momentum, with Caesar explaining that, on examination, he found that the booty seized by Tomkins was not as great as had been claimed because 'it was proved that some of the ship's own crew fled on shore at Cyprus with two barrels of gold.'[14]

James's determination to 'do something' was further demonstrated when, on 25 October, a delighted Scaramelli was able to forward to the doge a copy of James's commission against piracy which stated that the king, being:

Informed, through the manifold and daily complaints made by his own subjects and by others, of continual piracies and depredations, committed on the seas by certain lewd and ill-disposed persons against whom the ordinary proceedings have proved ineffectual to stop the mischief has now made the following orders:

That not only Captain and mariners, but for owners and victuallers of any man-of-war which shall commit piracy, depredation, or murder at the sea upon any of his Majesties friends shall suffer pain of death.

That anyone who seizes any goods belonging to subjects of allies shall suffer pain of death.

That all fresh 'Admiral causes' are to be summarily tried by Admiralty Judge with no appeal against sentence.

That a record of the restitutions to strangers to be kept.

That all Vice-Admirals were to inform the Court of Admiralty every quarter of all men-of war put to sea, or returned home with goods taken at sea, or the produce thereof and to be fined forty pounds for each breach of this order.

That the King's subjects shall forbear from aiding or receiving any pirate or sea-rover and likewise from all traffic with them.

That the Vice-Admirals, 'Customers,' and other officers shall not allow any ship to go to sea without first searching her; to see whether she is furnished for the wars and not for fishing or trade. In any case of suspicion, good surety shall be exacted before they let the ship sail. The officers shall answer for such piracies as may be committed by those who have sailed with their licence.

That Captain Thomas Tomkins and his crew who had returned from the Mediterranean with goods and money which they had, scattered, sold, and disposed of most lewdly and prodigally, to the exceeding prejudice of his Majesties good friends, the Venetians, were to be arrested.

The king went on to assure Scaramelli that few pardons would be issued and that perpetrators would be punished in person as well as having to forfeit the stolen goods. [15]

Cecil, however, dismissed the Venetian idea that any bonds forfeited should reflect the losses incurred, by stating that with the peace the issue of letters of reprisal had ceased and 'so all caution money ceases to be due.' This did not satisfy the king, who insisted that they all meet again the following day at which time it was 'decided that Piers' pardon was of no value, and the Judge of the Admiralty was instructed to condemn him to death, and the accomplices and guarantors to their just deserts.'

Further embarrassment soon followed, for Scaramelli had to report that pirates had seized the goods of the incoming Venetian ambassador, Nicolo Molin, who arrived in England at the beginning of November. This drew a response from James which differed from that which his predecessor might have made, for the 'accident' was 'deeply regretted by the King and Court', while orders were sent to 'to every port to use all diligence to arrive at the truth.'

It seems that this king meant what he said, for early in the New Year ambassador Molin was informed by Caesar that:

> his Majesty sent for him a few days ago and told him that he was to use all diligence for the summary despatch of the piracy cases before him, exhorting him to administer justice, so that none should have cause for complaint, otherwise he would have him hung; he is ordered not merely to restore the stolen property, but to punish the culprits. [16]

Yet Cecil, Caesar and Howard had further wiles to deploy. Molin was informed that the prisoners were all willing to offer several thousand crowns to purchase their liberty, as well as providing information that would lead to the capture of their colleagues. Resorting to moral blackmail, Molin was informed that the decision to hang or release was his to make while the Council also urged upon him 'thousand other considerations besides.' [17]

The bullying continued along with the blackmail. When Molin raised new concerns with the king, Cecil told him that:

> I believe your Lordship is aware that in all well constituted states there are various tribunals and judges for hearing and deciding all cases; they are various in kind, to meet the convenience of suitors, and because the nature of the cases is various; one set of tribunals taking civil, another criminal cases; for the King and his ministers are reserved the most important cases only, those which affect the State; I, therefore, think your Lordship might have refrained from troubling the King and myself upon a matter which belongs to the Admiralty Courts. I am sure had you applied to the judge of that court you would have received all fitting satisfaction, but had it not been so then you would have had a legitimate reason for approaching the King.

Then when the ambassador stated that he would rather see the return of his goods than have the men arrested for that theft hanged, Caesar told him that 'Your Lordship knows that the two in prison are miserable devils, without any possessions save their life, and with their life they must pay their debts.'[18]

This manipulation of the law and the king's changeable mind continued, although James retained his desire to eradicate piracy, informing the Venetians several years into his reign that:

He would extirpate [the pirates] with the fleet which he was preparing. He said that this accursed plague introduced by Queen Elizabeth by permitting piracy to her subjects, is even now too deeply rooted among this people, and almost all his subjects who went to serve other princes, and especially the Grand Duke, have become pirates. His concession [pardon] to Sir [Henry] Mainwaring was upon the condition aforesaid, and also because he had committed no great wrong, but he recognized afterwards that even this had produced a bad effect through the bad example, so that it had not only induced many others to take to buccaneering, but divers of those who returned with him had gone back to that infamous profession.[19]

The king was over-optimistic for two reasons, succinctly indicated in a letter to the doge from the Venetian ambassador who wrote that His Majesty's:

perpetual occupation with country pursuits, though possibly not distasteful to those who hold the reins of government, is extremely annoying to those who don't. The discontent has reached such a pitch that the other day there was affixed to the door of the Privy Chamber a general complaint of the King, alleging that his excessive kindness leaves his subjects a prey to the cupidity of his Ministers [20]

One result was that, with his income from piracy and letters of reprisal reduced, Nottingham felt entitled and at liberty to augment his legitimate earnings with perquisites of office and patronage, and plain peculation. In this he was assisted by yet another relative, Sir Robert Mansell, whose career, reaching a high with his part in the defeat of Spinola's galleys off Calais in 1603, plummeted into an ooze of greed, as he made full use of the enriching opportunities available to him after he became Treasurer of the Navy. Thus began a rapid reversal in the nation's maritime status and moral stature, its shameful nature nowhere better described than in the three chapters that deal with the early Stuart Navy in Rodger's seminal work, *The Safeguard of the Sea*. During this time Nottingham and his corrupt cronies made gain their guiding principle, not caring in the least how they came by their profit, so that ships and men suffered greatly from neglect. Much of the rampant peculation was well-known, but so well-established was the elderly earl that, even when investigations exposing the corruption over which he presided were presented to the council, he remained in post.

Nottingham survived two such investigations, instigated by his relative and enemy, Northampton, but was forced to retire in 1618, being replaced by the king's new favourite, Buckingham, whose shapely ankles the king preferred to the old earl's avarice. The new broom proved just as capable of brushing badly.

Buckingham began well by launching an attack on the coastal pirates. During Nottingham's tenure, ports that complained about the deprivations of pirates were granted commissions to set forth their own ships to capture the predators. Over thirty-two such commissions were issued between 1609 and 1618; thirty-two instances of the state derogating its responsibilities to those to whom it should have provided protection. Under Buckingham such commissions were seldom granted, and the navy was sent to sea to provide protection both off the coast and in more distant waters such as Newfoundland.

There was some logic in Nottingham's reluctance to pursue the coastal pirates. During the war with Spain the navy had concentrated on building galleons, deep-draughted enough to weather the Atlantic, and sturdy enough to exchange batteries with any foe. Such ships could neither outsail, outmanoeuvre, or pursue into shallow ports the vessels most favoured by the pirates, which tended to be of less than 150 tons. Yet faced with a thousand enervating bites from these maritime mosquitoes, the Navy Board not only let its unsuitable warships rot, but did not build more pinnaces and cutter-like craft to patrol the seas: in the sixty-mile reach of the Thames, from London Bridge to the open sea, just one ketch was available to police this notoriously lawless stretch of water.

It was not lack of vessels only that reduced the competence of the navy. Unloved, untended, undermanned and poorly-led, the navy's fortune slumped, reaching a nadir in 1625 with a deployment which Trevelyan summed up in this telling and pithy paragraph:

> An expedition which was sent to capture Cadiz, the emporium of Spain and America, would, if successful, have gratified the desires of England, but not have affected the relief of the Palatinate. The city had thirty years before been carried at a rush by the sea-dogs who sailed with Raleigh into its harbour, and the hardened veterans who followed Essex and Vere over its walls. But on this occasion it was perfectly safe when assailed by crews prostrated by sickness and starvation, mismanaging rotten ships under the orders of captains ignorant of the sea, and by ploughmen and footpads suddenly collected according to the principles of Sir John Falstaff to do duty as English soldiers. The expedition was perhaps the lowest point ever reached by our warfare on sea or land.[21]

The finger of failure pointed at the leadership. In 1587 Francis Drake himself had led the fleet into Cadiz; in 1596 it was Ralegh and Essex who had vied for glory. By 1625, no seaman of any worth was available to command this major return match. Instead, the appointment went to Edward Cecil, great Burghley's lesser grandson. This Cecil had seen active service in the Netherlands between 1596 and 1610, but none afterwards, before his recall to lead the military expedition to Spain in October 1625. His mismanagement and cautious approach to his deployment, which included failing to seize the Spanish treasure fleet, his major objective, did his career no harm. He returned to be created Viscount Wimbledon and to be sent to command English troops in the Netherlands until 1629, before ending his career as governor of Portsmouth, enabling him to watch in comfort the fleet he had not commanded with courage.

It is unlikely that the alternatives to Cecil would have fared much better. The obvious choice would have been Sir John Penington, whose long naval career included service with both Ralegh and Mansell, and a difficult deployment in 1625 when ordered to support the French against his fellow Protestants besieged in La Rochelle. On that occasion mutiny was only avoided when diplomacy saved its two faces with a compromise agreement, by which the French took control of the ships but without their crews.

In 1626 Penington was ordered to sea to provoke the French into war by sinking several of their ships in Le Havre but he returned, unamused, to write to Buckingham that he had sailed, 'at the bad time of the year, with only three weeks' provisions on board, his ships in bad order, badly supplied and badly manned, so that if we come to any service, it is almost impossible we can come off with honour or safety.'[22]

Disgruntled, he sailed again, but this time under orders to cruise the Channel to seize some valuable cargoes, which he did, returning with £50,000 worth of prizes. A little while later Lord Willoughby entered harbour with more prizes. The result was that the French sallied forth and captured the whole of the English wine convoy, some two hundred vessels, a grand reprisal for Penington and Willoughby's piratical action against a nation with whom England was, at the time, at peace.

Buckingham too had his share of ignominy In 1627 he lost half of his expeditionary force for La Rochelle when the French crossed over to the Ile de Ré and fell upon the re-embarking, mutinous, troops. One year later the English naval force watched La Rochelle surrender, while they lay off the mole refusing to go into action. In two years, English maritime forces had been dismissed contemptuously, not only by the two European powers it held in scorn during Elizabeth's reign, but by its old ally and new enemy, the Netherlands.

The glory, and the gratification, had even gone from pirateering. Buckingham issued letters of reprisal as freely as had Howard, with the result that almost one thousand prizes were taken between 1626 and 1630. Yet instead of gold, silver and spices, these ships unloaded cod, cordage and corn, the staples of pre-1570 ship seizures.

The underlying reason for the navy's fall from grace is twofold and Elizabethan in origin. First, her policy of minimising costs and employing, where possible, the piratocrats to pursue her maritime policy meant that the opportunity to create a cadre of war-trained and experienced naval officers was thrown away. The departure of these pirateers left the nation with no seaman competent to command a large naval force and this absence of talent soon showed. Secondly, all her naval commanders assumed that their deployments would provide them with a generous return. Once piracy was prohibited and naval operations reduced, there was little incentive to remain behind, serving a laid-up peacetime navy. What remained was the desire for enrichment and if this could no longer be had through the taking of prizes, then it had to be obtained from corruption: it seemed to matter not whether one robbed from one's friends or one's foes, so long as one made money. Hawkins may have provided the nation with a solid fighting fleet, but Howard, and Elizabeth, failed to man it with naval men inculcated with the desire to serve selflessly and thus establish the essential creed of naval professionals.

Were the ignominy isolated, then it would be possible to refute the view that the ways of the Elizabethan navy were directly responsible for the woes of the Stuart navy. But it is not so. From the accession of James in 1603 to the appointment of military men to command the fleet against the rampant Dutch, during the interregnum, the nation's navy was ill-led by lesser men, while several of those who would have been fit for high command chose to earn their living as pirates. Among those who went 'on the account', a synonym for piracy, but had the skills necessary to make good naval officers was Peter Easton who, offered a 'gracious' pardon by James I in 1612, declined it with the remark that 'I am in a way a king myself.' Another was Henry Mainwaring, whose naval career was delayed while he practised piracy between 1613 and 1615. The skills that he learned while so doing served him well, for he rose to the rank of admiral, and became both a knight and an MP. He also became the government adviser on matters of piracy and, as befitted a scholar of Brasenose, wrote a most readable account of life at sea, as did that other reformed pirate Monson, whose gossipy and sometime inaccurate tracts throw a bright and erratic light on life at sea during his time.[23] In 1617 Mainwaring published, as a guide to his new employers, *Of the Beginnings, Practices and Suppression of Pirates*, a work deserving of greater recognition, although its practical advice was ignored to the extent that by the 1620s there were probably ten times as many pirates active in the waters around England, and in the West Indies, than had been the case in Elizabeth's time.

The fighting skills of the pirates might no longer be required by a navy at peace, but those attributes would not be forgotten entirely, and the lessons that had been learned would one day be revived in similar circumstances, when the sight of a sail banished months of boredom in a trice, and there was a need to lie fearlessly alongside what was often a larger and more heavily armed and manned foe. This was to be the way the English navy fought. In this its professional seamen were different. Spanish and Portuguese escort commanders judged their success by the number of hulls saved; English captains, by the number seized. That success had also to include the ability to salvage a sinking hull, their own as well as the target, for a ship beaten but sunk was a defeat not a victory, as in the case of *Cinco Chagas*, which Cumberland's pirates turned into a most valuable bonfire. Killing the crew and saving the ship was a tactic that held true even unto the battle of Trafalgar in 1805.

Apart from retiring, relocating abroad or joining the navy, there was a fourth route for redundant pirates to chart, and it was along this track that they made their major and most enduring contribution to the re-emergence of Britain as a great maritime power. Low water might have exposed mudflats of corruption, neglect, poor leadership and purposelessness, but a new fresh tide was washing in from far distant shores. Hawkins and Drake, and those who followed their lead, whatever their immediate desire for gain, had created a generation of English mariners to whom being out of sight of land for days, even months, was no feared challenge. To intercept a gold-filled galleon required much patience, as well as the seamanship and navigational skills necessary to make ocean passages, accurate landfalls and a far-distant rendezvous.

If such successes were to be repeated, then an accurate record needed to be kept of tides, currents, landfalls, watering spots and sheltered coves. Drake and his nephew, John, presented the meticulous observations of their circumnavigation to Elizabeth, who managed to lose them. The value of such detailed records is nowhere better shown than in the desperate return voyage of *Desire* through the Straits of Magellan in 1591 when it was recorded that:

> The Straits being full of turning reaches we were constrained by discretion of the captain and master in their accounts to guide the ship in the hell-dark night, when we could not see any shore, the channel being in some places scarce three miles broad. But our captain, as we first passed through the Straits drew such an exquisite plot of the same that it cannot be bettered; which plot he and the master so often perused and so carefully regarded, as that in memory they had every turning and creek, and in the deep dark night without any doubting they conveyed the ship through that crooked channel.[24]

Anyone seeking to discover the origins of Britain's renowned Hydrography Service might look no further than that dark passage of 1591 in waters later charted by one of the most famous of that persuasion, Captain Fitzroy in *Beagle* in 1829.

It was not only from their personal observations and tutelage that the piratocrats' successors benefited. For his voyage of 1589, Cumberland persuaded the Cambridge academic, Edward Wright, to join him. From his experience, Wright made significant and practical improvements both to Mercator's projections of charts and to those used for spherical navigation. His *Certain Errors in Navigation*, published in 1599, and dedicated to the earl, was a seamark in the understanding of the science of ocean travel. Back at Durham House in London, Ralegh hosted and encouraged similar contributions to that science by such academics as John Dee and Thomas Herriot. Neither is it a coincidence that the inventor of the backstaff, which allowed sun sights to be taken without looking directly at that heavenly body, was John Davis, the explorer and navigator, who learned his trade while sailing with Cavendish and Ralegh.

Apart from competent navigation, any ship deployed on these long ocean voyages needed to be strong enough to withstand enemy guns and Atlantic gales. Along with this came the requirement to victual well and to replenish in a timely manner both with food and water. Above all, crews had to be well-managed, so that they too endured deprivation and did not mutiny nor demand to return home. This was the training that was to produce both a worldwide merchant marine and a navy that could remain for months on station, ill-fed but well-disciplined. It was thus no accident that it was the piratocrat, Walter Ralegh, who initiated the first English settlement in Virginia in 1585, principally as a pirate base, with his settlers being conveyed to their destination in a fleet commanded by another pirate, Richard Grenville. Nor was it other than a logical decision that led to the East India Company's first voyage to the East Indies being commanded by the ex-pirate, James Lancaster, sailing in Cumberland's ex-flagship, *Scourge of Malice*, renamed *Red Dragon*.

With Ralegh's Virginia settlers disappearing without trace and with piracy forbidden, another ex-pirate, the one-armed Christopher Newport, who had been present at the taking of *Madre de Dios*, led three small ships, *Susan Constant*, *Godspeed* and *Discovery* up the James River in Virginia, where in May 1607 he helped establish the first permanent English settlement in America.[25] Among the eight 'suitors' who were sponsoring this voyage were Ralegh Gilbert, George Popham, William Parker and Sir George Somers MP, all members of the piratocracy, as were at least six of the fourteen members of the council for Virginia. Newport and Somers, the latter as admiral, the former as captain, were onboard the Virginia resupply ship *Sea Venture* when she grounded in a hurricane on the Bermudas in 1609, miraculously without loss of life, in circumstances that gave Shakespeare his opening dramatic scene in *The Tempest*. The two men then worked together to build ships from the wreckage to enable them to continue their voyage to save the starving Jamestown colony, from where the gallant, elderly and ill Somers set sail almost immediately to obtain essential supplies in the Bermudas (aka, appropriately, Somers Isles), only to die on the voyage and to be carried home to Lyme Regis for burial.

The involvement of the ex-pirates in both England's eastern and western trade and settlement ventures show that the skills of both seamanship and command did not die with the arrival of James and peace with Spain. Rather, they lived on in the emerging oceangoing merchant fleet, which has attracted far less attention from naval historians than the rump royal navy that ill served the Stuarts. So it was with compass rather than cannon, with log and line rather than linstock, with shooting the sun rather than the Spaniards, that the legacy of the Elizabethan pirates lived on. It was the pirates who turned to trade that helped make Britain a major mercantile maritime nation and a colonial power which would, before long, need a new professional navy to guard the seas over which they sailed. Piracy had not taught the English how to fight naval battles, but it did teach them how to navigate safely far from shore and how to endure any great voyage. This was their contribution, worth far more than the richest cargo of any captured carrack, for it was to be on this navy that the future wealth and prosperity of the nation would chiefly depend.

Appendix 1

Letters of Reprisal and Bonds for Good Behaviour

A

Letter of reprisal authorised by Lord Admiral Howard in favour
Lord Thomas Howard

Master Caesar, whereas a ship appertaining to my good Lord the Lord Thomas
Howard named *Flighte* of the burden of sixty tonnes, coming from the West Indies
in Anno 1593, was stayed by *Lieutenant*, of the Isle of Rhe, near Rochelle, upon an
arrest made by a Frenchman of Olderney de Barges, named Viodett and since he
could never have restitution of his said ship, whereof this is to pray and require you
to grant our commission unto his Lordship or his assignees to stay any such ship
or goods of the said island or of Olderney aforesaid as his Lordship or his assignees
shall at any time hereafter find within any of her majesty's dominions to the value
of one thousand pounds for to that sum did his Lordship losses extend.

And for the same let this be your warrant from the court at Greenwich the 8th
June 1595

Your loving friend
C Howard

Source: High Court of Admiralty, 14/32 No 155.

B

Warrant for the grant of letters of reprisal for Golden Dragon, Prudence
and Virgin

Master Caesar, I am content you make out a commission of reprisal unto John
Moore of London, merchant, and William Jones, master of *Trinity*, whose to set out
and furnish to the seas the good ships called *Golden Dragon* of London of the
burden ninety tonnes or thereabouts and *Prudence* of London of the burden of
sixty tonnes or thereabouts with their pinnace, *Virgin* of London of the burden of

233

twenty tonnes, in warlike manner against the King of Spain and his subjects and his or their goods under such articles and conditions as are agreed on betwixt the Lords of the Council and merchants on that behalf. And let this be your warrant for the same.

From the Court at Whitehall, 26 December 1591

Your loving friend, C Howard

To my loving friend, master doctor, Caesar Judge of the high court of Admiralty

Source: High Court of Admiralty, 25/3 (9) 26 December 1591.

C

Bond for the good behaviour of pirateers

Christopher Newport and Robert Keeble, captain and master respectively of *Golden Dragon* of London, of one hundred tonnes burden, which is to be set forth with letters of reprisal by Henry Clitheroe and John Moore of London, merchants, and William Bygate, Edward Wilkinson and Edmund Burton, mariners bind themselves to pay to the Lord Admiral £3,000. This bond to be of no effect provided that the ship engages in no piratical activities, returns its prizes to port for the payment of customs duties and tenths.

Dated 19 January 1591

Hugh Merrick and John Paul, captain and master respectively of *Prudence* of London, of one seventy tonnes burden, which is to be set forth with letters of reprisal by Henry Clitheroe and John Moore, Robert Cobb, John Newton and William Jones, bind themselves to pay to the Lord Admiral £3,000. This bond to be of no effect provided that the ship engages in no piratical activities, returns its prizes to port for the payment of customs duties and tenths.

Henry Kedgell and Cuthbert Grippe, captain and master respectively of *Virgin* of London, of forty tonnes burden, which is to be set forth with letters of reprisal by Robert Cobb, John Moore, George Southwick and Thomas Gardener, bind themselves to pay to the Lord Admiral £3,000. This bond to be of no effect provided that the ship engages in no piratical activities, returns its prizes to port for the payment of customs duties and tenths.

Robert Thread and James Bragge, captain and master respectively of *Margaret* of London, of fifty tonnes burden, which is to be set forth with letters of reprisal by Robert Cobb, John Moore, George Southwick and Thomas Gardener, bind themselves to pay to the Lord Admiral £3,000. This bond to be of no effect provided that the ship engages in no piratical activities, returns its prizes to port for the payment of customs duties and tenths.

Dated 22 January 1591/2

Source: High Court of Admiralty, 25/3 (9).

Appendix 2

Commission issued by Queen Elizabeth to the Earl of Cumberland, 28 March 1595

The Queen to George, Earl of Cumberland. Considering the many hostile attempts against the realm and our person, without any just cause, we are moved to consider means to prevent all occasions of hazard and danger, and disable and weaken the forces, strength, and wealth of all persons so maliciously affected against our dominion and subjects; knowing your approved fidelity and valour, we hereby commission you to chose and constitute captains and other deputies, to levy, assemble, arm, and victual so many of our subjects as are willing to serve, and are fit and apt for war, by land and sea, as you shall think fit, and transport the same to invade and destroy the power, forces, &c., of the King of Spain, his subjects or adherents, and those of any Prince not in league and amity with us.

For the better strengthening you in this service, you are to victual and arm for sea the *Malico Scourge*, and such other ships and pinnaces as shall be appointed by you, not exceeding six. All prizes that shall be taken by you, or by any person or persons appointed by you, are to be brought into the most convenient haven, without breaking bulk or making any distribution of shares, until our further pleasure is known. The persons whom you shall send with such ships are to have the same authority to execute anything for this service as you might have done if you had been personally there. We charge all those who shall serve in any of the ships to yield duty and obedience to you, or to such as you shall appoint, and to avoid all causes of disorder to the hindrance thereof; also all others to be aiding and assisting therein.

Source: Calendar of State Papers Domestic: Elizabeth, 1595–97 (1869), pp14–25.

Appendix 3

'The Storm' and 'The Calm' by John Donne, written after the Island
Voyage, 1597

'The Storm' (*extract*)
Then like two mighty Kings, which dwelling farre
Asunder, meet against a third to warre,
The South and West winds joyn'd, and, as they blew,
Waves like a rolling trench before them threw.
Sooner than you read this line, did the gale,
Like shot, not fear'd, till felt, our sails assaile;
And what at first was call'd a gust, the same
Hath now a stormes, anon a tempests name.
Jonas, I pitty thee, and curse those men
Who, when the storm rage'd most, did wake thee then.
Sleepe is paines easiest salve, and doth fulfill
All offices of death, except to kill.
But when I wakt, I saw, that I saw not.
I, and the Sunne, which should teach mee'had forgot
East, West, day, night, and I could onely say,
If'the world had lasted, now it had been day.
Thousands our noyses were, yet wee 'mongst all
Could none by his right name, but thunder, call:
Lightning was all our light, and it rain'd more
Than if the Sunne had drunke the sea before;
Some coffin'd in their cabins lye, equally
Griev'd that they are not dead, and yet must die.
And as sin-burd'ned soules from grave will creepe,
At the last day, some forth their cabins peepe:
And tremblingly 'aske what newes, and doe heare so,
Like jealous husbands, what they would not know.

Some sitting on the hatches, would seeme there,
With hideous gazing to feare away feare.
Then note they the ship's sicknesses, the Mast
Shak'd with an ague, and the Hold and Wast
With a salt dropsie clog'd, and all our tacklings
Snapping, like too-high-stretched treble strings.
And from our totterd sailes, ragges drop downe so,
As from one hang'd in chaines a year agoe.
Even our Ordnance plac'd for our defence,
Strive to breake loose, and scape away from thence.
Pumping hath tir'd our men, and what's the gaine?
Seas into seas throwne, we suck in againe;
Hearing hath deaf'd our saylers: and if they
Knew how to heare, there's none knowes what to say.
Compar'd to these stormes, death is but a qualme.

To Mr Christopher Brooke: 'The Calm'
Our storm is past, and that storm's tyrannous rage,
A stupid calm, but nothing it, doth 'suage.
The fable is inverted, and far more
A block afflicts, now, than a stork before.
Storms chafe, and soon wear out themselves, or us;
In calms, Heaven laughs to see us languish thus.
As steady as I can wish that my thoughts were,
Smooth as thy mistress' glass, or what shines there,
The sea is now; and, as the isles which we
Seek, when we can move, our ships rooted be.
As water did in storms, now pitch runs out;
As lead, when a fir'd church becomes one spout.
And all our beauty, and our trim, decays,
Like courts removing, or like ended plays.
The fighting-place now seamen's rags supply;
And all the tackling is a frippery
No use of lanthorns; and in one place lay
Feathers and dust, to-day and yesterday.
Earth's hollownesses, which the world's lungs are,
Have no more wind than the upper vault of air.
We can nor lost friends nor sought foes recover,
But meteor-like, save that we move not, hover.
Only the calenture together draws
Dear friends, which meet dead in great fishes' jaws;
And on the hatches, as on altars, lies

Each one, his own priest, and own sacrifice.
Who live, that miracle do multiply,
Where walkers in hot ovens do not die.
If in despite of these we swim, that hath
No more refreshing than our brimstone bath;
But from the sea into the ship we turn,
Like parboil'd wretches, on the coals to burn.
Like Bajazet encag'd, the shepherds' scoff,
Or like slack-sinew'd Samson, his hair off,
Languish our ships. Now as a myriad
Of ants durst th' emperor's lov'd snake invade,
The crawling gallies, sea-gaols, finny chips,
Might brave our pinnaces, now bed-rid ships.
Whether a rotten state, and hope of gain,
Or to disuse me from the queasy pain
Of being belov'd and loving, or the thirst
Of honour, or fair death, out-push'd me first,
I lose my end; for here, as well as I,
A desperate may live, and a coward die.
Stag, dog, and all which from or towards flies,
Is paid with life or prey, or doing dies.
Fate grudges us all, and doth subtly lay
A scourge, 'gainst which we all forget to pray.
He that at sea prays for more wind, as well
Under the poles may beg cold, heat in hell.
What are we then? How little more, alas,
Is man now, than before he was? He was
Nothing; for us, we are for nothing fit;
Chance, or ourselves, still disproportion it.
We have no power, no will, no sense; I lie,
I should not then thus feel this misery.

Appendix 4

Inventory of *Malice Scourge*, on her transfer to the East India Company, October 1600

A fore course, [sail] bonnet and drabler, little used
A main course bonnet and drabler little used
A main topsail little used
A mizzen and mizzen bonnet little used
A new spirit sail little used
An old main course bonnet and drabler
An old fore course
A top gallant sail
A spirit sail topsail
10 iron stanchions
2 iron chains 4 nettings
3 cables by which ship rides – broken
2 anchors of 30 cwt. Or thereabouts a piece
1 anchor of 16 cwt.
1 anchor of 12 cwt.
3 old muckes
A whole suite of rigging as the ship came from Chatham saving that the most
part of the small running ropes is spent and hath been otherwise used.
A suite of winding tackle blocks with 4 sheeves of brass
Brass sheeves more 50
10 iron pump staves
3 iron pump brakes
3 crows of iron
2 pair cannon hooks
1 pair bellows
5 eyes of main chains of iron
3 dead men's eyes with chains of iron
6 tackle hooks

5 port hinges
4 boat hooks
2 fidd hammers
2 fidds
4 capsquares for carriages
A loose hooke
2 dipsy leads
1 harpoon iron
1 fisgig
I hawser of 7 inches
2 hawsers one of 7 1/2 inches the other of 7 inches
40 gunners' tackles
120 role of matches – decayed
4 dozen of plate cartridges which are in 2 chests
14 exceltries
17 plates of lead to lay over the pieces
5 great brass balls
3 old brass ladles
36 sprigs and runners
4 ladles
2 wadhooks
3 cwt. Square shot
16 breechings
1 table in great cabin with 4 stools and 1 chair
2 earthen pots for water
1 pumphook
A bell of brass
A longboat lying in Plymouth very little used
2 furnaces in the cook room with iron works to bind the cook room
The top masts and yard – serviceable
Demi cannon shot 49
Culverin shot 162
Demi culverin cross bar 49
Demi culverin round 34
Saker cross bar 14
Saker round 12
Demi Cannons   2 of 60 cwt. Apiece, total weight 6 tons
Culverins   16, of which 8 of 42 cwt. apiece, 8 of 36 cwt 2 qtrs. apiece, total
                weight 31 tons 8 cwt.
Demi culverins 12, of which 2 0f 29 cwt. 2 qtrs, 10 of 29 cwt, total weight 17
                tons 8 cwt.
Sum total of the tons of ordnance, 62 tons 27 cwt.

Source: Stevens, *Court Records*.

Appendix 5

Estimated cost of equipping a pirate vessel for six months (in £ sterling)

Ship's burden	Crew	Value of ship	Value of guns	Value of powder, shot, etc	Victuals	Other provisions	Repairs	Total cost of fitting out	Total invest- ment
350	175	1750	387	398	683	32	175	1288	3425
200	100	800	252	249	390	18	80	737	1789
100	50	300	79	80	195	9	30	314	693
50	30	150	36	37	117	5	15	174	360
30	20	90	20	21	78	4	9	112	222

Source: K R Andrews, *Elizabethan Privateering.*

Appendix 6

Authorisation to Equip a Vessel of War under the Admiralty of Zealand

We, William Prince of Orange, Count of Nassau, on behalf of the King's Majesty, as Lieutenant and Captain-General of Holland, Zealand, Friesland and Utrecht, have appointed as our Lieutenant at sea, and admiral, William of Blois and Treslong, who will have command over all ships of war, both those in the service of the country, and those seeking adventures at sea. The admiral or our vice-admiral will take the oath required from all captains fighting under our commission, on the following points, before putting to sea. All prizes acquired by the adventurers shall be brought to the same port from which they started, saving the fortunes and perils of the sea, without calling elsewhere. Nor shall they proceed to break bulk until a proper disposition has been made by the Admiralty, that the general cause be not injured. Nor may they sell, ransom, or otherwise alienate any prize or booty acquired at sea; nor any persons. Any captain or other who may be guilty of doing so shall be punished by attachment of their persons, ships, and goods. No ship is to go to sea insufficiently found in admonition and victuals according to the requirements of the voyage it is proposed to make.

Every man shall hand over to the admiral-general all booty, concealing nothing great or small, on pain of physical punishment. He is to keep a full register. If any ship, friends or enemies, is met with and taken, no one shall open any boxes or examine any secret letters, but place them in the hands of the admiral-general, on pain of the gibbet. If any prisoners are taken, they shall not be concealed or kept in secret, but brought before the admiral-general without delay to be examined. Captains and sailors shall ask no questions and make no complaints of each other during the present fitting-out of ships of war, under such penalties as the law may direct and the captain-general appoint. No one during this outfitting shall sue afresh for any debts or damages, nor mention them; except in the case of misdeeds, of which the captain-general shall take notice. If anyone is sent ashore by his superior officer, he must not stay longer than he is ordered, without notable and legitimate excuse, on pain of forfeiting a month's pay, besides being 'arbitrarily' corrected. If any man is not at his post, he shall be punished at the direction of the admiral and the other captains. Anyone who wastefully spills his beer, or throws victuals overboard, or takes them ashore and sells them, or anything of the sort, shall be corporally punished, and may be hanged. Whoever does not wake at the sound of the whistle, shall the first time be punished at the captain's discretion, on the second occasion be thrashed by all the crew, and the third time keel-hauled. If anyone having taken the oath or received pay departs without written permission from his captain, he shall be corporally punished, and proscribed as a rogue. If anyone wounds another in the hand, he shall lose his hand at once. If anyone kills another with blow or thrust, the dead and the living shall be tied back to back, and thrown overboard. If anyone on board goes on fighting after hostilities have ceased, he shall lose the hand with which he broke the peace. If anyone signs on in two or more ships, he shall be incontinently hanged. No one shall handle fire, candles, or anything of that sort, save those appointed thereto by the captains. No one shall receive or send any letter save in the presence of the captain, who shall first examine them, and be bound to declare them to the admiral-general, on pain of corporal punishment. No one shall venture, after beating to quarters, to speak in a foreign language, or give the signal for fire, or make any noise or alarm, unless he actually sees the enemy about to attack, on pain of personal arrest. No one in any vessel, merchantman or other, shall venture to speak with the shore save by express order of the captain, nor commit any violence in such vessels by beating, wounding, or otherwise maltreating, under pain of such punishment as the offence demands. No officer, gunner, seaman, or other, shall hide, sell, or take ashore any casks, clothing, or horns; nor any powder, balls, ammunitions; under pain of being punished for a thief by the gibbet. No person whatever shall hide, sell, or make away with any implements or materials belonging to the gunners or the carpenters, under pain of being punished without favour, as right demands. Gunners and seamen shall be bound to keep their watch, to lookout, to go to the boat, and take charge of, and manage the small boat, under pain of arbitrary correction. No one shall move from the mess assigned to him to go and eat in another mess, nor hide or sell victuals, under pain of correction at his captain's direction. No one shall give food or drink to prisoners in confinement, under pain of losing a month's pay, and being under arrest for eight days on bread and water. No one shall remain standing still after beating to quarters, but shall at once go to his appointed place, under a penalty of two sous gross, half to go to the poor, and half to the provost. When it is anyone's place or turn to stand by the boat, when the quartermaster calls to go to the boat any defaulter shall be liable to the last-named penalty. When the whistle goes for morning or evening prayers, any defaulter shall be placed before the mast, and thrashed by his watch; and also pay a fine as above. All these articles the King's Majesty and the Prince of Orange, his lieutenant-general for Holland, Zealand, Friesland, Utrecht, etc. order to be observed under pain of the penalties therein contained, by all captains, officers and seamen, and all persons great and small; who shall take the proper oath to the admiral-general, or person by him appointed.

Source: Calendar of State Papers Foreign, Elizabeth, vol 15: 1581–1582 (1907), pp459–78, January 1582, 21–31.

Appendix 7

The Little *Revenge*, A Ballad of the Fleet
At Flores in the Azores Sir Richard Grenville lay,
And a pinnace, like a fluttered bird, came flying from far away:
'Spanish ships of war at sea! We have sighted fifty-three!'
Then sware Lord Thomas Howard: 'Fore God I am no coward;
But I cannot meet them here, for my ships are out of gear,
And the half my men are sick. I must fly, but follow quick.
We are six ships of the line; can we fight with fifty-three?'

Then spake Sir Richard Grenville: 'I know you are no coward;
You fly them for a moment to fight with them again.
But I've ninety men and more that are lying sick ashore.
I should count myself the coward if I left them, my Lord Howard,
To these Inquisition dogs and the devildoms of Spain.'

So Lord Howard passed away with five ships of war that day,
Till he melted like a cloud in the silent summer heaven;
But Sir Richard bore in hand all his sick men from the land
Very carefully and slow,
Men of Bideford in Devon,
And we laid them on the ballast down below;
For we brought them all aboard,
And they blest him in their pain, that they were not left to Spain,
To the thumbscrew and the stake, for the glory of the Lord.

He had only a hundred seamen to work the ship and to fight,
And he sailed away from Flores till the Spaniard came in sight,
With his huge sea-castles heaving upon the weather bow.
'Shall we fight or shall we fly?
Good Sir Richard, tell us now,

For to fight is but to die!
There'll be little of us left by the time this sun be set.'
And Sir Richard said again: 'We be all good English men.
Let us bang these dogs of Seville, the children of the devil,
For I never turned my back upon Don or devil yet.'

Sir Richard spoke and he laughed, and we roared a hurrah, and so
The little *Revenge* ran on sheer into the heart of the foe,
With her hundred fighters on deck, and her ninety sick below;
For half of their fleet to the right and half to the left were seen,
And the little *Revenge* ran on through the long sea-lane between.

Thousands of their soldiers looked down from their decks and laughed,
Thousands of their seamen made mock at the mad little craft
Running on and on, till delayed
By their mountain-like San Philip that, of fifteen hundred tons,
And up-shadowing high above us with her yawning tiers of guns,
Took the breath from our sails, and we stayed.

And while now the great San Philip hung above us like a cloud
Whence the thunderbolt will fall
Long and loud,
Four galleons drew away
From the Spanish fleet that day,
And two upon the larboard and two upon the starboard lay,
And the battle-thunder broke from them all.

But anon the great San Philip, she bethought herself and went
Having that within her womb that had left her ill content;
And the rest they came aboard us, and they fought us hand to hand,
For a dozen times they came with their pikes and musqueteers,
And a dozen times we shook 'em off as a dog that shakes his ears
When he leaps from the water to the land.

And the sun went down, and the stars came out far over the summer sea,
But never a moment ceased the fight of the one and the fifty-three.
Ship after ship, the whole night long, their high-built galleons came,
Ship after ship, the whole night long, with her battle-thunder and flame;
Ship after ship, the whole night long, drew back with her dead and her shame.
For some were sunk and many were shattered, and so could fight us no more –
God of battles, was ever a battle like this in the world before?

For he said 'Fight on! fight on!'
Though his vessel was all but a wreck;
And it chanced that, when half of the short summer night was gone,
With a grisly wound to be dressed he had left the deck,
But a bullet struck him that was dressing it suddenly dead,
And himself he was wounded again in the side and the head,
And he said 'Fight on! fight on!'

And the night went down, and the sun smiled out far over the summer sea,
And the Spanish fleet with broken sides lay round us all in a ring;
But they dared not touch us again, for they feared that we still could sting,
So they watched what the end would be.
And we had not fought them in vain,
But in perilous plight were we,
Seeing forty of our poor hundred were slain,
And half of the rest of us maimed for life
In the crash of the cannonades and the desperate strife;
And the sick men down in the hold were most of them stark and cold,
And the pikes were all broken or bent, and the powder was all of it spent;
And the masts and the rigging were lying over the side;
But Sir Richard cried in his English pride,
'We have fought such a fight for a day and a night
As may never be fought again!
We have won great glory, my men!
And a day less or more
At sea or ashore,
We die – does it matter when?
Sink me the ship, Master Gunner – sink her, split her in twain!
Fall into the hands of God, not into the hands of Spain!'

And the gunner said 'Ay, ay,' but the seamen made reply:
'We have children, we have wives,
And the Lord hath spared our lives.
We will make the Spaniard promise, if we yield, to let us go;
We shall live to fight again and to strike another blow.'
And the lion there lay dying, and they yielded to the foe.

And the stately Spanish men to their flagship bore him then,
Where they laid him by the mast, old Sir Richard caught at last,
And they praised him to his face with their courtly foreign grace;
But he rose upon their decks, and he cried:
'I have fought for Queen and Faith like a valiant man and true;

I have only done my duty as a man is bound to do:
With a joyful spirit I Sir Richard Grenville die!'
And he fell upon their decks, and he died.

And they stared at the dead that had been so valiant and true,
And had holden the power and glory of Spain so cheap
That he dared her with one little ship and his English few;
Was he devil or man? He was devil for aught they knew,
But they sank his body with honour down into the deep,
And they manned the *Revenge* with a swarthier alien crew,
And away she sailed with her loss and longed for her own;
When a wind from the lands they had ruined awoke from sleep,
And the water began to heave and the weather to moan,
And or ever that evening ended a great gale blew,
And a wave like the wave that is raised by an earthquake grew,
Till it smote on their hulls and their sails and their masts and their flags,
And the whole sea plunged and fell on the shot-shattered navy of Spain,
And the little *Revenge* herself went down by the island crags
To be lost evermore in the main.

Alfred, Lord Tennyson

Appendix 8

Cargo Unloaded from Treasure Fleet at Seville, August 1593

Francesco Vendramin, Venetian Ambassador in Spain, to the Doge and Senate.

Enclosed is the invoice of the precious cargo just arrived from the West Indies, and now unlading at Seville.

Madrid, 28th August 1593.

[*Italian.*]

List of the cargo of the Western fleet, consisting of gold coin and jewels:—

	Ducats	Reals	Maravedis
From the mainland, for His Majesty, Castilian ducats of eleven reals each	1,806,442	8	18
For the crusade	43,550	6	6
For the salaries of the Council	12,752	10	20
	1,862,746	3	1/10

Deduct ducats 198,292, reals 10, maravedis 15, detained by the Generals Luis Alfonso Florez, Don Francesco de Leyva, Martin Perez de Olacabal and Don Francesco della Colonna, for the cost of the fleets; and by the Lieutenant-Governor Antonio de Puebla for the garrison of the Azores, so that there remains net for his Majesty, the crusade and the salaries

	Ducats	Reals	Maravedis
	1,664,453	3	19

In addition; for his Majesty, four chests of pearls of different kinds; 2,595 pesos of emerald, and one loose

emerald. Two chests of bar silver and bezoar stone sent
by the Vice-Roy of Peru. Fifteen pesos of unsmelted silver.

For private merchants and mortgages	3,696,015	1	1
From New Spain			
For the King	297,018	2	16
For the crusade	102,867	5	5
From the sale of offices	75,416	2	32
Total	475,301	10	19
Deduct ducats 37,467, reals 9, maravedis 1, which the Generals Martin Perez de Olacabal, and Luis Alfonso Florez detained for payment of their fleet, and Antonio de Puebla, for the garrison of the Azores; leaving net for his Majesty	437,834	1	18
For private merchants and mortgages	1,445,861	10	29
Grand Totals			
For the King	2,102,287	5	3
For private individuals	5,141,877	30	0

The amount of jewels for private individuals, the grain,
the skins and other merchandize not known.

Source: Calendar of State Papers Relating to English Affairs in the Archives of Venice,
vol 9, August 1593.

Appendix 9

The Appraisement of Prizes

*Letter to the right worshipful Doctor Caesar Judge of the Admiralty,
13 October 1591*

The apparaiment and valuation of a small bark called *Equina* laden with sugars, hides and
other things late taken at sea by a bark called *Margaret* of London, Captain Christopher
Newport, made by us Nicholas Barnsley, Thomas Pigott grocers, Richard Mooorecocke,
salter, John Cave, clothworker, Robert Bragg and John Severn, haberdasher, the 27th of
August 1591

Imprimis we the said Appraisers diligently viewing
and perusing the said sugars being 28 chests of St Domingo
sugars in powder weighing net 6 cwt one with another we esteem at
28s the cwt. Which amounteth to   £235 4s 0d

Item, 400 dry and merchantable hides we esteem at 6s the hide
with another which amounteth to   £ 120 0s 0d

Item, 353 wet hides and rotten withal we esteem at 2s 6d the
hide amounteth to   £044 02 0d

Item, 11 cwt cashew nuts (Cashia Fistula) being wet having
Taken salt water we esteem at 10s the cwt which amounteth to   £005 10s 0d

Item, four thousand one hundred three score pieces of silver
plate of 8 rials Spanish the piece we estimate at 4s sterling
which amounteth to   £832 00 0d

Item, forty pound weight of silver being in platters,
Saucers and salvers, we esteem at 4s 8d the ounce
which amounteth to   £112 00 0d

Item, we esteem the hull of the said ship called *Equina*
being of the burthen of 30 tons being old & rotten at   £006 13 4d

Somme Tottalls amounteth to   £1355 9 10d

In witness whereof we the said appraisers have hereunto set our hands

Source: HCA, 24/60 no 160.

Summary of prizes brought into Portsmouth by the Earl of Cumberland's ships, May – June 1594

By *Hope Bonaventure*
Two Brazil prizes carrying:
    465 chests white Brazil sugar
    25 chests of Muscavado
    16 chests of unpurified sugar (panele)
    10 tons 19 cwt of brazil wood
Of which the Lord Admirals tenth:
    $46^{1/2}$ chest white sugar, $2^{1/2}$ muscavado, $1^{1/2}$ pannelus, valued at £7 10s per chest
    21 cwt 3 qtrs 6 lb brazil wood, valued at £40 per ton
    Total £418
One small leaguer carrying:
    788 casks of oil
Of which the Lord Admirals tenth:
    79 casks at 6s. 8d. each
    Total £26 6s. 8d.
Customs on these prizes being paid by the Earl of Nottingham
By *Pilgrim*
One small West Indian Spanish frigate carrying:
    821 raw hides
    115 tanned hides
    3 tons of blockwood
Of which the Lord Admirals tenth:
    82 raw hides, 12 tanned hides valued at 9s. 6d. per hide, 6 cwt. Blockwood,
    Total £57 6s. 4d.
Out of *Pilgrim*
    4 chests Domingo sugar
    7 lbs weight of pearls
    1 ingot of gold
    9 buttons of gold with emeralds
Of which the Lord Admirals tenth:
    The pearls delivered to the Lord Admiral by the Earl of Cumberland
By *Anthony*
One West Indiaman, carrying:
    4,333 hides, raw and tanned
    57 chests of indigo
    64 bags of the same
    $6^{1/2}$ tons of blockwood
    6 chests Domingo sugar
    23 lbs 7 oz of pearls
Of which the Lord Admirals tenth:
    433 hides, 11 kintails $33^{1/2}$ lbs indigo, 13 cwt blockwood, one chest Domingo sugar
Total   £534 1s
The whole sum of the Lord Admiral's tenths amounting to £1,035 14s.

Source: British Library, *Harleian*, MS 598, folios 28–29.

Appendix 10

Notes from the State Papers on Issues Concerning Piracy During a Few Weeks in 1578

January 31.
Commissioners for Piracy in the Cinque Ports to the Council. Insufficiency of the powers given to them by their commission for examining suspected persons on oath. Inclosing,

Feb. 2. Yarmouth.	29. Bailiffs of Yarmouth (Norf.) to Sir Fr. Walsyngham. Have apprehended the pirate named Tho. Hitchcok; and Scarborough the other pirate has been taken by Lord Clynton, in Lincolnshire.
Feb. 3.	30. Examination of John Penrose, of Bethick, in Cornwall, for matters of piracy, on board Hicks's ship.
Feb. 4. Exeter.	32. Earl of Bedford, and others, Commissioners for Piracy, to same. Their proceedings in matters of piracy, wherein they find no great matter of importance. Complaints against Gilbert Peppit, servant of the Lord High Admiral. *Inclosing,*
	32. I. *Examinations relating to pirates, taken at Exeter on the 4th of January.*
Feb. 8. Greenway.	35. Sir John Gilberte to the Earl of Bedford. Report of the attack and capture of a French ship by one Clarke, a pirate, in Dartmouth harbour; and plunder committed by other pirates.
Feb. 11. Aukland.	37. Richard Barnes Bishop of Durham to the Council. That as he had not been appointed a commissioner in matters of piracy, he had forwarded their Lordships' letters to Sir George Bowes.

Feb. 18.   42. Articles for the examination of the pirate Hitchcok, of Great Yarmouth.

Feb. 18.   43. Bailiffs of Yarmouth to Sir Fr. Walsyngham. Have examined the pirate
Yarmouth.   Hitchcok on the interrogatories sent by Mr. [Adam] Fullerton. *Inclosing,*

Feb. 20.   48. Griffith Rise and William Davids, Commissioners of Piracy for
Carmarthen.   Carmarthenshire, to same. Stating the cause of their not proceeding in the
                 commission.

Feb. 21.   49. Commissioners for Piracy in Cornwall to same. Reasons offered in
                 excuse for not having before certified their doings. The imperfection of the
                 presentments from their deputies prevented them from making any earlier
                 return. *Inclosing,*

                 49. i. *Copy of the letter given by them to Sir John Killigrew, to be presented to
                 their Lordships, dated Truro, Jan.* 10.

Feb. 21.   52. Declaration of the quantity of gold and silver contained in two proofs of
                 the ore brought by Captain Furbisher, according to Dr. Burchard's process.

Feb. 21.   53. Dr. Burchard Raurych to Sir Fr. Walsyngham. Sends the gold and silver
                 obtained by him from 1 lb. and 1 cwt. of ore, and promises that from every
                 ton he will obtain twenty times the amount.

Feb. 24.   57. Estimate of the charges for victualling and transporting seven of the
                 Queen's ships from Chatham to Portsmouth, by John Hawkyns and Edw.
                 Baeshe.

Feb. 26.   58. Dr. Lewes to Sir Fr. Walsyngham. Has examined Gilbert Peppit, servant
London.   of the Lord Admiral, relative to pirates, according to the order prescribed.
                 Is of opinion that Peppit was free from all suspicion of being an aider of
                 pirates.

                 58. i. *Articles for examination of Gilbert Peppit, as to his dealings with pirates
                 and pirates' goods.*

                 58. ii. *Answer of Gilbert Peppit, Serjeant of the Admiralty in Devon, to the
                 articles of the presentments against him, touching his dealings with pirates.*

Feb. 26. Norwich.	59. Commissioners for Piracy in the County of Norfolk to the Council. Have prosecuted with diligence their inquiries about pirates. Interpose in favour of Eustace Rolf, who had offended by compulsion.
	59. i. *Certificate of the true and just value of the lands and goods of certain persons detected in dealing with pirates.*
Feb. 26. Winchester.	60. Commissioners for Piracy in Hampshire to same. Excuse the delay, and certify their proceedings in the matters of piracy.
Feb. 27.	61. Dr. Burchard Raurych (Dr. Burcott) to Walsyngham. Justifies the proof of the ore already made. Is indignant at the charge of incompetency raised against him by Jonas. Proposes to try on 2 cwt. more of the ore, and that two honest men should be appointed to see that it was roasted fairly.
Feb.	62. Details of the proceedings of Jonas Shutz and Dr. Burchard in the trial of the gold ore brought by Mr. Furbisher. Jonas accuses Burchard of evil manners and ignorance, and would have no dealings with him.

April

Commissioners for Piracy for the Town of Ipswich to same. Return the certificate of persons presented to be traffickers with pirates, with remarks thereon; particularly in the cases of Mr. Poolyeand the widow Alice Hugget.

Commissioners for Piracy in the County of Kent to the Council. Certify that they had taken care to make diligent inquiry, and could hear of no pirates, or dealers with pirates, except John Turnor of Whitstable. That the most part of the harbours and ports were within the liberties of the Cinque Ports.

Commissioners for Piracy in the West part of Sussex to same. The jury have acquitted all persons charged with dealing with pirates in those parts except Francis Cradle, who confesses receiving certain salt and fish.

Inventory of goods taken from pirates by Captain Luke Warde, and landed at Southampton.

[Walsyngham?] to Lord Chandos. The Council are disappointed in not having received certificates of the aiders of pirates in the County of Gloucester. Desires him to forward them without delay.

Depositions of Hugh Randall respecting the piracy committed within the Straits of Malega by Philip Boyt, of late executed for the said piracy.

Note of the charges wherewith certain persons in Cornwall are charged as aiders and abettors of pirates.

Note of matters wherewith the persons of Cardiff are to be charged for piracy.

Certificate from Adrian Gilberte, Deputy of the Port of Dartmouth, for matters of piracy.

Charges against persons presented for dealings with pirates, particularly Robt. Plomley, Mayor of Dartmouth, with their answers to the same.

Note of the persons in Kent discovered by Jasper Swift to have bought goods of Captain Goore the pirate.

Names of the chief dealers with pirates in Dorsetshire.

Note of persons in Lincoln, with sums set against their names, probably fines for dealing with pirates.

44. Order by the Queen for the remedy of spoils and depredations committed by English pirates on the subjects of foreign princes in amity.

Appendix 11

The Complaints of the Dutch Concerning Piracy, March 1589

The inhabitants of the United Provinces have lost over £200,000 sterling during the last five years. Desires that some absolute and final order be taken by the Privy Council 'for the present spoils and injuries late done, and [goods] yet in part extant.'

Complaint of Albert Reynerson. His ship, *Waterhound*, of the Briell, taken by Rawlegh's ship in 1585. Rawlegh's ship, *Roebuck*, in January last took the *Angel Gabriel*. Petitions that the *Angel Gabriel* and such goods as remain be restored to the owners, both they and Rawlegh giving sufficient sureties.

Walter Artson. *Roebuck* took, last January, from a ship of Holland bound for London, 4 butts of sack consigned to a subject of the United Provinces resident there: also took his servant and factor. Petitions for restoration, upon sureties if thought necessary.

Walter Artson. *Roebuck* about the same time took goods belonging to merchants of the United Provinces from a Hamborough ship (Henry Croeger, master). 'The English soldiers at the sea' broke up the packs of goods and made themselves apparel of some part thereof. Petition for restitution of remaining goods and satisfaction for what spoiled.

Michael Leman. Last August *Roebuck* took mace and sugar from the Post Horse of Amsterdam. Petition as above.

John Jacobson Decker, John Dowson, and others. 3 fishing boats and another, spoiled in August and November, 1586, by Sir Walter Leveson's ship. Petition that Leveson may give satisfaction, as he did to the Dane.

Adam and Everard Hulcher. Restitution of 242 chests of sugar, worth £3,800, was ordered by the Admiralty Court after 15 month' suit against Robert Flicke: but Thomas Cordall and others, agents for Flicke, broke into the cellars and warehouses where the goods were and carried them away to private houses, so that no satisfaction yet obtained. Petition that the Council (as the Judge of the Admiralty will deal no further herein, Flicke having appealed to her Majesty) will restore the goods upon sureties, despite Flicke's appeal, according to the practice of other countries and to 'the Civil Law in force in this realm in a cause of this nature.'

Nicholas Henrickson. Master and owner of a ship of Home, taken on return from Brazil in October, 1587, by *Centurion* of London, Nicholas Brokebancke, master; goods worth £1,500 unladed and sold at Plymouth. Proof thereof made in Admiralty Court, but no redress. Petitions for speedy judgement, for restitution of ship and goods, and for damages for the interruption of his trade.

Adam Hulcher of Middelborough, merchant. 130 chests of sugar consigned to him in Henrickson's ship. Had safe-conduct from the Lord High Admiral of England, and has proved his claim in the Admiral Court, yet the Judge adjudged them away from him. Petitions that the case be reviewed by 3 or 4 indifferent persons, rather than according to the ordinary 'tedious course of appeal.'

Durtes, Roelland, and others. *White Falcon*, of Amsterdam, with sugar, cinnamon, mace, and other spices, and also 12 bags of rialls of 8 (landed it is said by their honours' order), a packet of 500 ducats, and 4 packets of precious stones; *Rose*, of Amsterdam, Berrent Jasperson, master, with salt and also 291 rialls of 8 belonging to Peter Linters and others of Amsterdam; a third ship, Lawrence Swart, [master]. All brought into Plymouth lately by William Hawkins, Thomas Drake, and Edmund Clifford. Petition for restitution of ships and goods, proof of ownership being made, and sureties given: and that the said 'English rovers' may hand up the bills of lading, etc, and give sureties to make satisfaction if the goods are proved to be the petitioners'.

Salvator de la Parma. In January last, Capt Baker with a ship of Sir Richard Grenvile took from *Sampson* of Flushing, oils and figs worth 1,000l. sterling belonging to Parma of Middelborough. Petition for restitution, if title proved.

Martin France. Master of a ship of Flushing from which £1,000 sterling in coin, belonging to himself and others of Middelborough, was taken by Benett Wilson serving under William Walton alias Snowe of Bristow. Petitions for restitution, damages, and interest, if title proved.

Capt Miller of Weymouth, serving under the mayor there, took from *St Peter* of Amsterdam 57 chests of sugar, 10 pipes of wine, 52 arrobas and 24 barrels of conserves, belonging to Lyntors and other merchants of Amsterdam, as was proved in the Admiralty where restitution was ordered. Petitions for execution of the order.

Peter Lyntors. The said *St Peter* taken in April last by Capt Fullsid and John Flemynge, and the goods sold. Petitions that those who bought the goods from the pirates make restitution or satisfaction.

Peter Lyntors. *L'Esperance* of Rosco, with 1,000 'pieces of raisins' and 10 pipes of tinto belonging to Lyntors and others of Amsterdam and Middelborough, taken in February last by the warship *Saucy Jack* of Hampton, owned by Thomas Eaton, customer of Hampton. Petitions for sequestration of ship and goods and for restitution upon proof of title.

Jacob Fresse, of Home. A chest with goods worth £100 taken from a ship of Amsterdam by Francis Brooke, serving in one of the Earl of Cumberland's ships.

Giles van Houtehuse, master of a galley of Flushing. Robbed, last November, by Frauncis, captain of *Grace of God* of Hampton, set forth by William Walker of Taunton.

Anthony Williamson Belleman, master of a flyboat of Rotherdam: ship and goods taken in July last by Gilbert Leae.

Desires that these, and any other, ships and goods arrested anywhere in England, may upon proof of title be restored, according to the statutes of this realm and the articles of the Intercourse.

Source: Calendar of State Papers Foreign, Elizabeth, vol 23: January–July 1589 (1950), pp158–69.

References and Bibliography

Most of the original documentation referred to in this book has been drawn from three sources. First, the very accessible records at the visitor-friendly National Archives in Kew; secondly, their online presentation at British History Online, which is a magnificent source for anyone not close to Kew; and thirdly, the wonderful publications of the Hakluyt Society, in which original manuscripts are presented and commented on with scholarship, erudition and an infectious enthusiasm which makes them a joy to read.

National Archive Records as listed by British History online

APC	Acts of the Privy Council, ed J R Dasent.
CSPH	Calendar of State Papers – Domestic, Henry VIII.
CSPE	Calendar of State Papers – Domestic, Elizabeth, ed R Lemon.
CSPJ	Calendar of State Papers – Domestic, James I, ed M A E Green.
CSPI	Calendar of State Papers – Domestic, Interregnum, ed M A E Green.
CSPFE	Calendar of State Papers – Foreign, Elizabeth, ed J Stevenson.
CSPV	Calendar of State Papers – Foreign, Venetian, ed A B Hinds.
CSPS (Simancas)	Calendar of State Papers – Foreign, Spain at Simancas, ed M A S Hume.
CCPH	Calendar of Cecil Papers at Hatfield House.

Additional abbreviations

CUP	Cambridge University Press
HT	*History Today*
MM	*Mariners' Mirror*

Hakluyt Society

First Series, Part I, nos 1–50 (1847–1873)

1. *The Observations of Sir Richard Hawkins, Knt, in his Voyage into the South Sea in the Year 1593*, ed C R Drinkwater Bethune, 1847.

3. *The Discovery of the Large, Rich, and Beautiful Empire of Guiana*, by Sir W Ralegh, ed R H Schomburgk, 1849.

4.   *Sir Francis Drake his Voyage, 1595*, by Thomas Maynarde, ed
            W D Cooley, 1849.
5.   *Narratives of Voyages towards the North-West, in Search of a
            Passage to Cathay and India. 1496 to 1631*, ed Thomas
            Rundall, 1849.
7.   *Divers Voyages touching the Discovery of America and the
            Islands adjacent*, collected and published by Richard Hakluyt,
            1582, ed J W Jones.
16.   *The World Encompassed by Sir Francis Drake*, ed W S Wright
            Vaux, 1854.
38.   *The Three Voyages of Martin Frobisher, in search of a Passage to
            Cathay*, ed R Collinson.

First Series, Part II
57.   *The Hawkins' Voyages*, ed C R Markham, 1878.

Second Series, Part I
2/71.   *Documents concerning English Voyages to the Spanish
            Main/1569–1580*, I A Wright, 1932.
2/83 & 2/84. *The Voyages and Colonising Enterprises of Sir Humphrey
            Gilbert*, ed D B Quinn.

Second Series, Part II
2/93.   *Richard Hakluyt & his Successors*, ed E Lynam, 1945.
2/99.   *Further English Voyages to Spanish America/1583–1594*, ed I A
            Wright, 1951.
2/104 & 2/105. *The Roanoke Voyages/1584–1590*, ed D B Quinn, 1954, 1955.
2/111.   *English Privateering Voyages to the West Indies/1588–1595*, ed
            K R Andrews.
2/113.   *The Troublesome Voyage of Captain Edward Fenton/1582–158*,
            ed E G R Taylor.
2/121.   *A Regiment for the Sea and other Writings on Navigation by
            William Bourne*, ed E G R Taylor, 1963.
2/142.   *The Last Voyage of Drake & Hawkins*, ed K R Andrews, 1972.
2/148.   *Sir Francis Drake's West Indies Voyage*, ed M F Keeler, 1981.
2/161.   *The English New England Voyages/1602–1608*, ed D B & A M
            Quinn, 1983.

Third Series
6.   *The Third Voyage of Martin Frobisher to Baffin Island, 1578*,
            ed J McDermott, 2001.
15.   *Sir Walter Ralegh's Discovery of Guiana*, ed J Lorimer, 2006.

Extra Series

Extra [1–12]   *The Principal / Navigations Voyages / Traffiques &* *Discoveries / of the English Nation / Made by Sea or Over-land to* *the Remote and Farthest Distant Quarters of the Earth at any* *Time within the Compasse of these 1600 Yeeres*, by Richard Hakluyt, 12 vols, 1903–1907, pub by MacLehose, Glasgow.

Extra [14–33]   *Hakluytus Posthumus / or / Purchas His Pilgrimes / Contayning a* *History of the World in Sea Voyages and Lande Travells by* *Englishmen and others*, by Samuel Purchas, 20 vols, 1905– 1907.

Extra 45   *A Particuler Discourse Concerning the Greate Necessitie and* *Manifolde Commodyties that are like to Growe to this Realm of* *Englande by the Westerne Discoueries lately Attempted, Written* *in the Yere 1584.* By Richarde Hakluyt of Oxford, known as, *Discourse of Western Planting*, ed D B & A M Quinn, 1993.

Occasional Booklets

James McDermott, *The Navigation of the Frobisher Voyages*, 1998.

Felipe Fernández-Armesto, *Philip II's Empire: A Decade at the Edge*, 1999.

Sarah Tyacke, *Before Empire: The English Cartographic View of the World in the Sixteenth and Seventeenth Centuries*, 2001.

Naval Records Society

The Life and Works of Sir Henry Mainwaring, ed G E Mainwaring & W G Perrin, NRS vols 54 & 56, 1920–2.

The Naval Tracts of Sir William Monson, ed M Oppenheim, NRS 22, 23, 45, 47, 1902–1914.

Boteler's Dialogues, ed W G Perrin, 65, 1929.

Papers relating to the Spanish war 1585–87, ed J S Fisher, 11, 1898.

Fighting Instructions, 1530–1816, ed J S Fisher, 29, 1905.

State Papers relating to the Defeat of the Spanish Armada, ed Laughton, 1 & 2, 1894.

Documents relating to the Law and Custom of the Sea, ed R G Marsden, 49, 50, 1915–16.

The Expedition of Sir John Norris and Sir Francis Drake 1589, ed K Andrews.

Other Publications

Andrews, K R, *Drake's Voyages*, Weidenfeld & Nicholson, 1967.

———, *Elizabethan Privateering*, CUP, 1964.

———, *Trade, Plunder & Settlement, 1480–1630*, CUP, 1984.

Appleby, J C, *Under the Bloody Flag*, History Press, 2009.

Bicheno, H, *Elizabeth's Sea Dogs*, Conway, 2012.

Butler, N, *Boteler's Dialogues, 1630*, ed W G Perrin, NRS, 1929.

Cecil, A, *The Life of Robert Cecil*, John Murray, 1915.

Childs, D, *The Warship Mary Rose*, Chatham, 2007.

———, *Tudor Sea Power*, Seaforth, 2009.

Corbett, J S, *The Successors to Drake*, Longmans, 1916.

———, *Drake and the Tudor Navy*, 2 vols, Longmans, 1917.

Dale, R, *Who Killed Sir Walter Ralegh*, The History Press, 2011.

Dee, John, *The Perfect Arte of Navigation*, 1577.

Earle, P, *The Pirate Wars*, Methuen, 2004.

Edwards, E, *The Life of Sir Walter Ralegh*, Macmillan, 1868.

Fury, C A, *Tides in the Affairs of Men*, Greenwood, Connecticut, 1966.

Gorski, R, ed, *Roles of the Sea*, Boydell, 2012.

Gosse, P, *The History of Piracy*, New York, 1932.

Handover, P M, *The Second Cecil*, Eyre & Spottiswoode, 1959.

Hill, L M, *Bench and Bureaucracy*, James Clarke & Co, 1988.

Hughes, P F & Larkin J L, eds, *Tudor Royal Proclamations*, Yale, 1964, 1969.

———, *Stuart Royal Proclamations*, Oxford, 1973, 1983.

Hutchinson, R, *House of Treason*, Weidenfeld & Nicolson, 2009.

Hutchinson, R, *The Spanish Armada*, Weidenfeld & Nicolson, 2013.

Jowitt, C, ed, *Pirates? The Politics of Plunder, 1550–1650*, Macmillan, 2007.

Kenny, R W, *Elizabeth's Admiral, The Political Career of Charles Howard. . .*, John Hopkins, 1970.

Kelsey, H, *Sir Francis Drake*, Yale University Press, 1998.

———, *Sir John Hawkins*, Yale University Press, 2003.

Loades, D, *The Tudor Navy*, Scolar, 1992.

———, *The Making of the Elizabethan Navy, 1540–1590*, Boydell Press, 2009.

———, *The Cecils*, National Archives, 2007.

Lacey, R, *Sir Walter Ralegh*, Weidenfeld & Nicholson, 1973.

McDermott, J, *Martin Frobisher*, Yale UP, 2001.

McGhee, R, *The Arctic Voyages of Martin Frobisher*, British Museum Press, 2002.

McKee, A, *The Queen's Corsair*, Souvenir, 1978.

MacMillan, K, *Sovereignty and Possession in the English New World*, Cambridge University Press, 2006.

Meide, C, *The Development of Bronze Ordnance*, College of William and Mary, 2002.

Nelson, A, *The Tudor Navy*, Conway, 2001.

Nicholls, M, & Williams, P, *Sir Walter Ralegh*, Continuum, 2011.

Quinn, D B, *England and the Discovery of America, 1481–1620*, London, 1974.

———, *European Approaches to North America, 1450–1640*, Aldershot, 1998.

———, *England and the Discovery of America*, Allen & Unwin, 1974.

———, *Ralegh and the British Empire*, Pelican, 1973.

Rodger, N A M, *The Safeguard of the Sea*, Harper Collins, 1997.

Ronald, S, *The Pirate Queen*, Sutton, 2007.

Rowse, A L, *Sir Richard Grenville*, Jonathan Cape, 1937.

Senior, C, *A Nation of Pirates*, David & Charles, 1976.

Smith, John, *The Complete Works*, ed P L Barbour, University North Carolina, 1986.

Spence, R T, *The Privateering Earl*, Stroud, 1995.

Stone, L, 'The Fruits of Office: The Case of Robert Cecil', in *Essays in the Economic & Social History of Tudor & Stuart England*, CUP, 1961.

Sugden, J, *Sir Francis Drake*, Pimlico 2006.

Taylor, E G R, *Tudor Geography 1485–1583*, London, 1930.

———, *The Haven Finding Art*, London, 1967.

Tinniswood, A, *Pirates of Barbary*, Vintage, 2011.

Unwin, R, *The Defeat of John Hawkins*, Allen & Unwin, 1961.

———, *A Winter Away From Home*, Seafarer, 1995.

Waters, D W, *The Art of Navigation in England in Elizabethan and Early Stuart Times*, Hollis and Carter, 1958.

Wheeler, J S, *The Making of a World Power*, Sutton, 1999.

Williams, N, *The Sea Dogs*, Weidenfeld and Nicolson, 1975.

Wilson, D, *The World Encompassed*, Hamish Hamilton, 1977.

Articles

Baker, R, 'A Manuscript of Shipbuilding, circa 1600', *MM*.

Mekens A, 'Michael Coignet's, Nautical Instructions', *MM*, 78, 1992.

Ransome, D R, 'An Instrument of Early Stuart Sea Power: The Armed Merchantman, Abigail, 1615–1639', *MM*, 1999.

Solver, C V, & G F Marcus, 'Dead Reckoning and the Ocean Voyages of the Past', *MM*, 44, 1958.

Notes

Chapter 1

1 *CCP*, vol 4: 1590–1594, pp70–6.
2 The Lord Admiral's authority, an area in which robbery could be defined as piracy, included not only the high seas, but all coastal waters and inlets up to the high water mark and all rivers and streams as far inland as the lowest bridging point.
3 See J C Appleby, *Under the Bloody Flag.*
4 *CSPH*, XXI, I, 1879.
5 *CSPH*, XX, I, 1004.
6 The property tax of a one-tenth rate for towns and a one-fifteenth rate for counties was, in the parliament of 1589, increased to two subsidies instead of just one of four-fifteenths and tenths. This raised some £280,000, a high point in parliamentary grants which came with the caveat that the money was to be spent only on the fight against Spain.
7 See D Loades, *The Tudor Navy.*
8 *CSPFE*, Jul 1588, vol 22, pp363–72.
9 *The Safeguard of the Sea,* op cit.
10 *CSPE,* 25 June, vol 179, pp244–9.
11 *CSPF,* Elizabeth, 8, 1566–1568, 580–92.
12 K R Andrews, *Elizabethan Privateering.*
13 *CSPE,* vol 251, April 1595, pp25–34.
14 *CSPE,* Jan 1593, vol 244, pp303–312.
15 *A Voyage to the South Seas.*
16 N Williams, *The Sea Dogs.*
17 See A L Rowse, *Sir Richard Grenville.*
18 As summarised by P M Handover, *The Second Cecil.*
19 *Drake's Voyages.*
20 *Sir Francis Drake.*
21 See A Tinniswood, *Pirates of Barbary.*

Chapter 2

1 PRO SP/70/32, 72.
2 An excellent account of sea apprenticeships can be found in C A Fury, *Tide in the Affairs of Men.*
3 *CSPE,* vol 9, 24 Feb 1570.
4 A document of 156*8**.
5 *CSPE,* vol 35.
6 See H Kelsey, *Sir John Hawkins.*
7 R Unwin, *The Defeat of John Hawkins.*
8 Quoted in J Sugden, *Sir Francis Drake.*
9 R G Marsden, *Select Pleas in the Court of Admiralty.*
10 For the fitting-out of *Sampson* see T Spence, *The Privateering Earl.*

Chapter 3

1 *The Observations of Sir Richard Hawkins Kt in his Voyage into the South Sea in the Year 1593.*
2 R Hakluyt, *The Principal Navigations, Voyages, Traffiques and Discoveries of the English Nation.*

3 Z Nuttall, *New Light on Drake.*
4 R C Anderson, The *Golden Hind* at Deptford, *MM*, 27, 1941.
5 Ibid, Declaration of John Drake.
6 Hakluyt, *Voyages.*
7 Ibid.
8 Ibid.
9 *Purchas his Pilgrimage.*
10 Ibid.
11 Purchas, *His Pilgrims.*
12 Hakluyt, *Voyages.*
13 See D J Childs, *Invading America.*

Chapter 4

1 For a description of these weapons see Childs, *Tudor Sea Power.*
2 See www.alderneywreck.com for an excellent description of these weapons.
3 See C Meide, *The Development of Bronze Ordnance.*
4 *Observations*, op cit.
5 Hakluyt, *Voyages.*
6 Such a cannon was raised from *Mary Rose*, whose team proved the truth of Norton's warning through casting and firing such pieces. See A Hildred, *Weapons of Warre*, which although reflecting on an earlier age (*Mary Rose* sank in 1545) is by far the most thorough work on the subject available.
7 *Observations*, op cit.
8 Oppenheim, *Instructions.*
9 See McDermott, *Martin Frobisher.*
10 *APC*, vol 8, 1571–75.
11 See I Friel, 'Guns, Gales and God', *History Today*, vol 60-1, Jan 2010.
12 Ibid.
13 *The Art of Shooting in Great Ordnance.*
14 *A Sea Grammar*, op cit.
15 *CSPE*, Aug 4 1588, vol 214, pp520–24.
16 *The Art of Shooting.*
17 *Observations.*
18 See Corbett, *Drake and the Tudor Navy.*
19 *Monson's Tracts*, III, 43–4.
20 Hakluyt, *Voyages*, vol 5.
21 Ibid.
22 See Nuttall, *New Light on Drake.*
23 *CSPV*, vol 9, 1592–1603, pp141–2.
24 Drake claimed he had been following some suspicious sails overnight, but his failure to inform Howard makes this story less than credible.
25 Hakluyt, *Voyages.*

Chapter 5

1 *CSPE* 95, 63–4
2 *CSPS* (Simancas), vol 2: 1568–1579, pp478–82.
3 *CSPE*, vol 99, pp488–469.
4 Ibid.
5 *CSPF*, vol 11: 1575–1577 (1880), pp206–24.
6 See Z Nuttall, *New Light on Drake.*
7 E G R Taylor, 'More light on Drake', *MM*, XVI.
8 Z Nuttall, *New Light on Drake.*
9 Ibid.
10 *CSPS* (Simancas), vol 3: 1580–1586, pp238–54.
11 *CSPE*, vol 235, Addenda.
12 See Z Nuttall, *New Light on Drake.*
13 Ibid.
14 Ibid.
15 Ibid.
16 Ibid, pp71–82.
17 See E G R Taylor, *The Troublesome Voyage of Captain Edward Fenton.*

18 See Hakluyt, *Voyages*.
19 Ibid.
20 C R Drinkwater, ed, Hakluyt Society pub.
21 *CSPE*, vol 245, 1591–94, pp375–81.
22 See the petition by the ship's company of *Delight of Bristol*, written while trapped in the Straits of Magellan, February 1589, Hakluyt, *Voyages*, op cit.

Chapter 6

1 See K MacMillan, *Sovereignty and Possession in the English New World*.
2 See Quinn, *The Discovery of North America*.
3 *CSPE*, 1547–80, pp587–9.
4 Ibid, vol 123.
5 *CSPS* (Simancas), vol 2: 1568–1579, pp606–609.
6 APC, 1579, pp109.
7 *Diverse Voyages touching the Discoveries of America*.
8 BM Cotton Mss XIII.
9 A replica of *Elizabeth* is berthed at Roanoke.
10 Hakluyt, *Voyages*.
11 Grenville's boat of chests was not the only occasion when such an almost nonsense-rhyme craft was used. In 1590 *Delight*, on a voyage that belied her name, became separated from her consorts, *The Wild Man* and *The White Lion*, and entered the Straits of Magellan on her own. A disastrous few days ensued. First of all they lost their boat with fifteen men onboard in a storm in which the ship also lost two of her anchors. So, needing to seek for sustenance in the ominously named Port Famine, they built a boat from seamen's chests and had it paddled ashore by seven armed men. Yet despite being armed the five crew who landed were slain by the 'wilde people'. The boat, however, proved sturdy enough to make the return journey. In so doing it showed the same characteristics of the ship which weathered six weeks of 'the furie of the elements' in the Straits, losing three anchors and thirty-eight men in those unwelcoming waters.
12 Quoted in R Hutchinson, *House of Treason*.
13 These are dangerous waters which recently claimed the life of a modern sailing ship, the replica HMS *Bounty* caught by a similar hurricane.
14 See R Lacy, *Sir Walter Ralegh*.
15 Best accessed through www.gutenberg.org.
16 For a more detailed account see D Childs, *Invading America*.

Chapter 7

1 Hakluyt, *Voyages*.
2 *CSPS* (Simancas) vol 3: 1580–1586, 28 Nov 1580.
3 Ibid, 4 July 1581.
4 Ibid.
5 Ibid, 14 July.
6 Ibid, 2 June 1581.
7 Ibid, June 1581.
8 Ibid, 24 June 1581.
9 *CSPS* (Simancas), vol 3: 1580–1586, pp152–64.
10 Ibid, pp152–64.
11 Ibid, pp238–54.
12 Ibid, pp632–44.
13 *CSPS* (Simancas), vol 4: 1587–1603, pp118–31.
14 Ibid.
15 *CSPE*, 1581–90, pp418–21.
16 Ibid.
17 J Sugden, *Sir Francis Drake*.
18 *BL Harleian*, MS 6994.
19 *CSPE*, vol 206, p61.
20 *CSPE*, vol 225, July 1589.
21 Monson, *Tracts*.
22 Quoted in G C Williamson, *George, Third Earl of Cumberland*.
23 A L Rowse, *Sir Richard Grenville of the Revenge*.
24 *CSPV*, vol 9:1592–1603, pp46–47.

25 Hakluyt, *Voyages.*
26 *CSPV*, vol 9, August 1593.
27 Ibid, May 1595, pp159–61.
28 Quoted in E Edwards, *The Life of Sir Walter Ralegh.*
29 Williamson, op cit.
30 *CSPE*, 1601–3, pp126–37.
31 *CCPH*, Apr 1602, vol 12, pp109–36.
32 CCP, June 1602, 1–30, vol 12, 1602–03, pp180–208.

Chapter 8

1 *CSPV*, vol 8, 1581–91, pp363–72.
2 *CSPE*, vol 215, 1581–90, pp299–304.
3 *CSPS* (Simancas), vol 4: 1587–1603, pp92–101.
4 Letter written by Francisco de Valverde and Pedro de Santa Cruz, prisoners of war in England, to Bernardino De Mendoza. Ibid, pp207–25.
5 Ibid.
6 *APC*, 1588.
7 Ibid.
8 Corbett, *Drake and the Tudor Navy,* vol 1.
9 *CSPE*, 1581–90, pp508–20, July 22.
10 Hawkins, *Observations.*
11 See Nelson, *The Tudor Navy.*
12 Hakluyt, *Principal Navigations.*
13 Quoted in Laughton, *The Defeat of the Spanish Armada.*
14 *CSPE*, vol 7, pp143–5.
15 *CSPE*, vol 193, Sept 1586, pp349–58.
16 Ibid, vol 209, pp466–72.
17 Ibid, vol 200, pp401–409.
18 Ibid, pp472–81.
19 *Sir Francis Drake*, op cit.
20 *Drake and the Tudor Navy.*
21 *Sir Francis Drake*, op cit.
22 *CSPE*, 1581–90, pp520–9.
23 D Hart-Davis, *Armada*, and others.
24 *The Development of Broadside Gunnery.*
25 It is also considered by Martin and Parker that the fine armament viewed onboard the captured *Rosario* made the English wary of coming too close to her colleagues.
26 *CSPS* (Simancas), vol 4: 1587–1603, pp299–306.
27 *CSPE*, vol 215, pp529–41.
28 *CSPDI*, vol 33, 1652–53, pp137–93.
29 *CSPV*, vol 8, Oct 1588, 788.
30 *Drake's Voyages*, op cit.

Chapter 9

1 *CSPFM*, 1553–1558, pp227–31.
2 *APC* 1554–56, 52.
3 *CSPM*, Aug 1556, vol 9, pp85–6.
4 H Mantel, *Bring up the Bodies.*
5 *CSPE*, Addenda, vol 14, 1566–79, pp50–2.
6 *CSPEF*, vol 9: 1569–1571, pp40–56.
7 *APC*, 1576.
8 *CSPE*, vol 225: July 1589, pp607–12.
9 *APC*, 27, 31.
10 *CSPFE*, vol 20, pp416–32.
11 Ibid, pp582–92.
12 Ibid, vol 20, pp672–701.
13 See K R Andrews, *Elizabethan Privateering.*
14 *CSPEF*, vol 21, Part 1: 1586–1588, pp89–104.
15 F E Dyer, 'Reprisals in the Sixteenth Century', *MM*, 21, 1935.
16 *CSPEF*, vol 21, pp104–23.

17 Ibid.
18 Ibid, pp123–46.
19 Ibid, pp199–217.
20 Ibid, pp297–310.
21 Ibid, pp320–8.
22 *CSPE*, vol 204: October 1587, pp428–34.
23 Ibid, 22 Oct.
24 *APC*, vol 22, 37.
25 Ibid, 44.
26 Proclamation 302.
27 *CSPE*, vol 243, Sept 1592, pp266–77.
28 Ibid.
29 *CCP*, vol 4: 1590–1594, pp232–42.
30 Ibid.
31 Ibid, pp226–32.
32 Ibid, pp232–42.
33 Ibid.
34 Ibid, pp249–77.
35 Ibid, pp242–9.
36 Ibid.
37 Ibid.
38 *CSPC*, vol 4: 1590–1594, pp521–42.
39 Proclamation 326.
40 *CSPE*, Aug 1596, vol 259, pp264.
41 *CCPH*, Aug 1596, vol 6: 1596, pp309–38.
42 *CSPE*, 1595–97, pp264–75.
43 Ibid.
44 Ibid.
45 P M Handover, *The Second Cecil*.
46 *CCPH*, vol 12, pp109–36.
47 *CSPC*, August 1602, vol 12: 1602–1603, pp276–91.

Chapter 10

1 *CSPE*, vol 238: February 1591, pp8–15.
2 See N A M Rodger, *The Safeguard of the Sea*, Chap 24, 25.
3 See R W Kenny, *Elizabeth's Admiral*.
4 *English Privateering Voyages*.
5 For a summary see R W Kenny, *Elizabeth's Admiral*.
6 Ibid.
7 *Additional MSS*, 15, 208.
8 *CCPH*, vol 7: 1597, pp518–47.
9 Ibid, vol 11: 1601, pp214–33.
10 L Stone, 'The Fruits of Office', in F Fisher (ed), *Essays in the Economic History of Tudor & Stuart England*.
11 *CCPH*, vol 7, 1597, pp63–87
12 Ibid, pp139–59.
13 Ibid, pp121–39.
14 Ibid, pp518–47.
15 Ibid, pp261–84.
16 Ibid, vol 10, pp384–401.
17 *CSPV*, vol 9: 1592–1603, pp449–57.
18 *CSPV*, vol 9: 1592–1603, pp457–62.
19 See *CSPV*, vol 9, 1600.
20 *CCPH*, vol 11: pp165–88.
21 Ibid, pp401–20.
22 Ibid, vol 12: 1602–1603, pp22–43.
23 Ibid.
24 Ibid, pp528–81.
25 *CCPH*, vol 7: 1597, pp386–410.
26 Ibid, pp527–31.

27 *CCSH,* vol 11: 1601, pp440–65.
28 *CCPH,* vol 7: 1597, pp433–59.
29 Ibid, Dec 1597, vol 7, pp518–47.
30 *CCPH,* Sep 1601, vol 11, pp374–401.
31 *CSPC,* vol 11: 1601, pp374–401.
32 Ibid, pp465–491.
33 Ibid.

Chapter 11

1   *CSPV,* vol 7: 1558–1580, pp369–71.
2   *APC,* 1565, pp278.
3   *CSPE,* vol 116: Oct 1577, pp557–9.
4   Ibid.
5   *CSPE,* vol 12, 1577–78, p122.
6   Hughes and Larkin, *Tudor Royal Proclamations,* vol 2, nos 482, 499, 513, 519, 523.
7   *CSPS,* 158–67, p496.
8   *CSPF,* vol 9, pp1–13.
9   *CSPE,* May 1568, vol 8: 1566–1568, pp457–72.
10 *CSPS,* 10 Jan 1568.
11 *CSPF,* vol 8, pp576–81.
12 *CSPS* (Simancas), March 1571, vol 2: 1568–1579, pp294–302.
13 Ibid, pp294–302.
14 Ibid, pp325–34.
15 *CSPS* (Simancas), Aug 1571, vol 2: 1568–1579, pp325–34.
16 Franky Wardell, Smugglers' City Special Field Project, 2009/10.
17 *CSPF,* vol 14: 1579–1580, pp102–7.
18 *CSPF,* vol 11: 1575–1577 (1880), pp402–10.
19 *CSPS* (Simancas), Aug 1579, vol 2: 1568–1579, pp683–94.
20 Ibid, pp706–11.
21 Quoted in Wilson, *The World Encompassed.*
22 For a full account of the return of the *Santa Maria*'s goods see Nuttall, *New Light on Drake.*
23 Now owned by the National Trust. George's grand tomb can be seen in Dyrham church.
24 *CSPS* (Simancas), vol 3, 1580–1586, pp299–317.
25 BL Lansdowne, 56, f.175.
26 Quoted in Hutchinson, *The Spanish Armada.*
27 Ibid, pp435–44.
28 *CSPE,* 1547–80, pp553–4.
29 Ibid, vol 12: 1577–78, pp464–82.
30 Ibid, Dec 1584, vol 19: August 1584–August 1585, pp186–97.
31 *CSPFE,* vol 20: September 1585–May 1586, pp582–94.
32 Ibid, pp228–34.
33 Ibid, Addenda: Miscellaneous 1585, pp693–9.
34   *CSPFE,* vol 20: September 1585–May 1586, pp79–88.
35 Ibid, pp416–432.
36 *CSPF,* vol 11, Oct. 1576, pp387–403.
37 *CSPFE,* vol 23, January–July 1589, pp140–58.
38 Ibid, pp158–69.
39 See Introduction, *CSPFE,* vol 23: January–July 1589, ppV–LXII.
40 *CSPFE,* vol 23, pp140–58.
41 Ibid, vol 12: 1577–78 (1901), pp34–53.
42 D Loades, *The Tudor Navy.*
43 *CSPFE,* March 1586, vol 20: September 1585–May 1586, pp491–510.
44 *CSPFE,* May 1586, vol 20: pp672–701.
45 Ibid, pp123–46.
46 *CSPF,* vol 21, Part 1: 1586–1588, pp104–23.
47 *CSPF,* Aug 1587, vol 21, Part 1: 1586–1588, pp355–67.
48 *CSPS* (Simancas), Sep 1579, vol 2: 1568–1579, pp694–701.
49 Ibid, 23: pp211–24.
50 *CSPV,* vol 7: 1558–1580, pp434–53.
51 *CSPV,* vol 10: 1603–1607, pp16–28.

52 *CCP*, December 1602, 26–31, vol 12: 1602–1603, pp528–81.
53 *CSPV,* vol 9: 1592–1603, pp510–13.
54 Ibid.
55 Ibid.
56 Ibid, 526–31.
57 Ibid, 531–48.
58 Ibid.
59 *CSPE*, vol 177:1581–90, pp229–35.
60 S Roland, *The Pirate Queen*; H Bicheno, *Elizabeth's Sea Dogs.*
61 Ibid, pp466–91.
62 J S Wheeler, *The Making of a World Power.*

Chapter 12

1 *CSPV*, Dec 1618, vol 15: 1617–1619, pp405–22.
2 See R Dale, *Who Killed Sir Walter Ralegh.*
3 *CCPH*, Jan 1608, 1–15, vol 20: 1608, pp1–20.
4 P Earle, *The Pirate Wars.*
5 *CSPV*, April 1606, vol 10, 1603–1607, pp329–41.
6 *CSPV*, vol 10.
7 A Tinswood, 'Captain Jennings Causes Chaos', *HT*, May 2010.
8 *CSPV*, vol 10,1603–1607, pp109–15.
9 Ibid, pp184–9.
10 *CSPV*, vol 10, pp42–57.
11 Ibid, pp28–42.
12 *CSPV*, vol 10: 1603–1607, pp58–72.
13 Ibid, pp99–109.
14 Ibid.
15 Ibid, pp116–26.
16 Ibid, pp126–30.
17 Ibid, pp130–4.
18 Ibid, pp154–64
19 Ibid, vol 16: 1619–1621, pp342–60.
20 Ibid, May 1606, vol 10, pp341–54.
21 G M Trevelyan, *England under the Stuarts*, Penguin, 1960.
22 http://en.wikipedia.org/wiki/John_Penington.
23 *The Naval Tracts of Sir William Monson.*
24 Hakluyt, *Voyages.*
25 See D J Childs, *Invading America.*

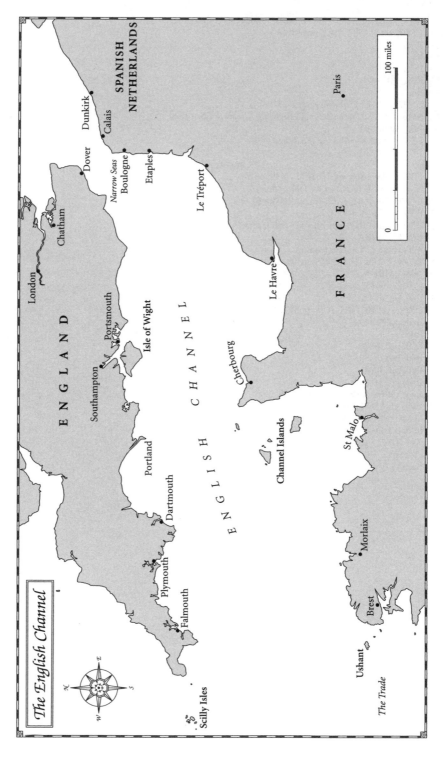

The English Channel

ENGLAND

SPANISH NETHERLANDS

FRANCE

ENGLISH CHANNEL

London

Chatham

Dover

Narrow Seas

Dunkirk

Calais

Boulogne

Etaples

Le Tréport

Le Havre

Paris

Southampton

Portsmouth

Isle of Wight

Cherbourg

Portland

Channel Islands

St Malo

Dartmouth

Plymouth

Falmouth

Morlaix

Brest

Ushant

The Trade

Scilly Isles

100 miles

0

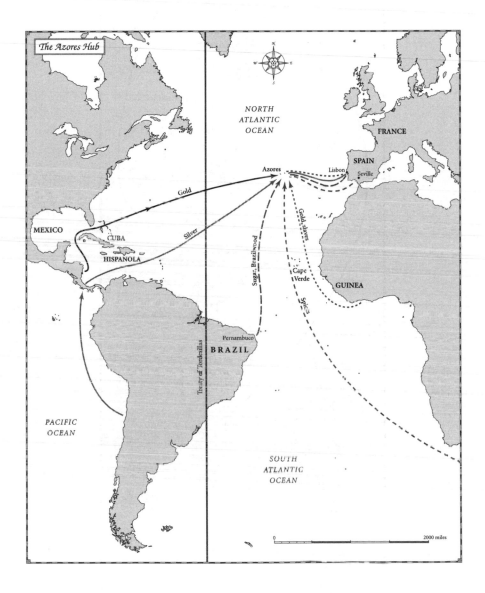

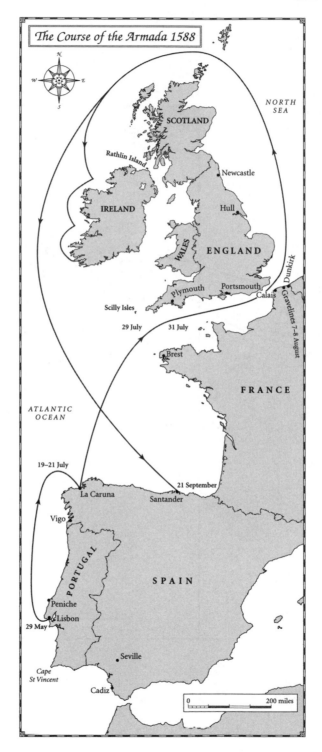

The Course of the Armada 1588

NORTH SEA

SCOTLAND

Rathlin Island

Newcastle

IRELAND

Hull

WALES

ENGLAND

Dunkirk

Plymouth

Portsmouth

Calais

Scilly Isles

Gravelines 7–8 August

29 July

31 July

Brest

FRANCE

ATLANTIC OCEAN

19–21 July

21 September

La Caruna

Santander

Vigo

PORTUGAL

SPAIN

Peniche

Lisbon

29 May

Seville

Cape St Vincent

Cadiz

0   200 miles

Index